Power Points in Time
and how time passes

Ancient Festivals, Lunar Phases,
Planetary Line-ups and Historic Moments

Palden Jenkins

With illustrations by Jan Billings
and charts and diagrams by the author

Completely revised edition of *Living in Time*
first published in 1987 by Gateway Books

Penwith Press

First published in 2014 by:
Penwith Press
Cornwall
United Kingdom

www.penwithpress.co.uk

ISBN: 978-0-9533316-7-3

Cover:
Eclipsing fullmoon over Bethlehem, Palestine, June 2011.
Merry Maidens stone circle, West Penwith, Cornwall, 2009.
Sunset over the Mediterranean, Kantouni, Kalymnos, Greece, 2014.
Photos by Palden Jenkins.

Illustrations by Jan Billings
www.facetsofavalon.com

Charts and diagrams by Palden Jenkins
palden.co.uk/time
this might interest you too:
palden.co.uk/historical-ephemeris.html

Typesetting, design and layout:
Jonathan How
www.coherentvisions.com

Contents

Part One: The Basics

Part Two: The Nub of the Matter

Part Three: Want More?

Appendices

More notes and appendices are available at palden.co.uk/time.html

Before We Start

This book is about developing a sense of *timing* and coming to understand the deeper aspect of time. This involves cultivating a receptivity to what's in the wind, what's going on within us and what appears to be the underlying meaning of situations in our lives and in the world around us. Never fixed, our experiences and perceptions cause us to view life from so many different angles, and this is one of the evolutionary purposes of life on Earth.

Time is what stops everything happening all at once. Time is a gift, since we encounter such a wide variety of learning experiences over the course of our lives, and also it's a challenge because we don't usually get what we want when we want it. But things do come to us when we're truly ready. That's life on planet Earth – the world doesn't obey orders.

There are many paths to awareness and each of us must follow our heart in pursuing paths appropriate to us. Astrology adds to your path – it doesn't replace it. In this book we are using the language and symbology of astrology by which to identify the ever-varying facets of time and our position in it. By this means we can become more aware of what's *really* going on, of the underlying threads and undercurrents behind life's situations.

Astrology is precise and well developed, ages old, and over time it has gone through a number of revolutions too, in the way it thinks. It uses precise degrees of space and exact angles, pleasing to brainy people, yet it's delightfully circular, fluid and organic too, and pleasing to people who follow their feelings and intuitions. It's a bag of tools, not really a subject in itself, and it's always attached to something else, such as psychology, horticulture, economics, history or medicine, with a dose of good old commonsense and life-observation too. Being a deeper and more dimensional language than our customarily spoken languages, in generations to come it will eventually move into centre-stream as a language for understanding time and change. If it doesn't, this means the world will not have achieved the kind of deep sustainability it needs for the successful furtherance of human life.

Even if you are not particularly interested in immersing yourself in astrology – it takes a few years – it is undoubtedly worth picking up the basics, in ways that are useful for you. If you're reading this book simply to broaden your general knowledge, then Parts One and Two are for you. If you're interested in more than that, then read Part Three also. The key chapters are chapters 10 and 11, about *power points in time*. If you're already conversant with astrology, these two chapters sum it all up, but you won't understand them if you aren't. So the preceding chapters give an all-round introduction to the astrology of time and timing. So please derive from this book whatever you need. Some chapters are dense, more for reference – particularly those bits that are typeset in a sans font. Some are more for easier reading, to give you some interesting ideas. Chapter one is optional.

Some astrologers will enjoy this book because it isn't about birth charts at all. It offers a different angle on astrological concepts since, instead of studying people, we're studying time itself. The people who most appreciated the 1987 edition of this book were people who love ancient sites and the deeper dimension of nature, not necessarily astrologers. But many astrologers loved it too, especially 'cottage astrologers', and it became a minor classic. Still receiving e-mails about it 25 years later, and slightly amazed that, to my knowledge, the book has not been bettered or replaced, I decided to rewrite it.

Sense of Timing

In this book we're talking about subjectively-experienced time, with little to do with clocks and calendars. It is an elastic, ticktock-free stream of feeling-tones, head-spaces, moods, angles on life, insights, phases and chapters, experienced both individually and collectively. It concerns not just a personal human experience but also nature, the weather, the vibe, people's car-driving patterns, birdcalls, the growth of plants, the behaviour of worms, the tendency of traffic lights to turn red or green when you approach them, the way fires burn and babies sleep, and the periodic habit of the internet to go faster or slower for reasons that even web-techies don't understand. These are all symptoms and indicators of 'the nature of the times'.

It also concerns waves of spam, the arising and spread of infectious diseases, the fluctuations of interest rates, the outbreak and resolution of conflicts, news themes in the public domain, spiders' activities, the taste of food, aircraft bookings, patterns of rainfall, quirks of government policy and a host of 'chance occurrences'. It concerns *everything*, and the way that everything multi-facetedly comprises a unity, which sometimes we see or sense, and sometimes we don't. Ancient and first-nation peoples might say "the Earth is crying", "the weather is angry" or "the flowers are smiling", and this isn't just superstitious twaddle – it says something about a deeper and wider sensitivity and perception of reality than we currently exercise.

When we talk about 'time' we usually refer to clocks and calendars: "I'll meet you at the station at 2.30 on Wednesday 26th April". This is a socially-agreed mode of measuring duration for the coordination of our activities in a complex, urbanised, hurried world. It is based on the diurnal cycle of the day and the annual cycle of the year – though the Western calendar is unnatural and abstract, wobbling, creeping and needing periodic adjustments. Our calendar has uneven months and it isn't even anchored in the natural turning points of the year such as the solstices and equinoxes. It looks on time as a rather abstract statistic.

The kind of time we are looking at here is *qualitative*, as in Bob Dylan's song… *the times, they are a-changing*. With this usage of the word 'time' we allude to the essential temperamental character of the times we live in – a subjective assessment but nonetheless real. This kind of time stretches and compresses, rises and falls, with all sorts of flavours, atmospheres, connotations and subtleties to it. Annoyingly, it seems to go faster when you're happy, dragging out when you're unhappy.

It's very useful to tune in to this kind of time because it makes our lives easier, rather like watching where you're walking so that you place your feet in the right places. With this sense of time we can understand the immediate moment in terms of context and wider scenarios, giving us a sense of direction and purpose amidst life's otherwise confusing whirlpools and eddies. We become aware of life as a *process* with meaning and purpose to it.

This matters a lot during 'bad' times, because when things are hard it can feel as if it is going to go on like that forever and our difficulties will burden us indefinitely. It matters during 'good' times too because it helps us remember that (apparently) good times, like (apparently) bad times, don't actually go on for ever. This scraping and friction of our anticipations, extrapolations and judgements up against the transitoriness of ever-changing reality is the stuff of life.

I met a young German in Egypt, in the midst of the Sinai Desert, who taught me a useful aphorism. *Everything is okay in the end. If it's not okay, it's not the end.* We're perpetually travelling a road with beginnings, good times, bad times, crisis points, still points, times of relief and times of tumult, always trying to 'get there', to wrap things up once and for all. We never do finally wrap things up – even death is just a milestone on a path leading somewhere further. It's the journey that matters, not the perceived destination, and the destination, once you get there, simply reveals another one further along the road. Life is a pilgrimage through time.

Sooner or later we realise that we are here *to learn*. If we dedicate ourselves to learning from life, *everything* becomes a success, whatever life throws at us. Wealth or poverty, success or failure – it's a learning experience and you've gained something from it. Don't worry. I have difficulty remembering this truth too! Forgetting why we truly are here is perhaps one of the great unidentified big issues of today – we all do it. It's an institution.

When things are all 'wrong', learning from life makes them good, investing them with meaning and purpose. Today, the notion of redemption is too often forgotten: yes, we're here to learn from life and get things better next time around. There are two key elements to grapple with here: *what's happening*, and *how we choose to experience and deal with it*. Customarily we focus on the former, forgetting that our true realm of power lies with the latter. We can't always affect what happens, but we have a lot of choice about how to experience and deal with things, and herein lies our free will. There are some things we can change and some we can't, and 'Lord, give me the wisdom to know the difference'.

About Astrology

Astrology helps us work with time-energy and make magic with it. Magic involves engaging with available subtle energies to effect outcomes that weren't understood to be likely or possible beforehand. If we can recognise what Mars energy is like compared with Jupiter energy, or distinguish what it's like when these two energies work with each other, then it is possible to work with them more clearly when they are around. Or, at least, we can reduce some of the scraping, jarring and conflict that they might otherwise bring when we are blissfully unaware of them.

Moving into phase with time or even adding to its qualities by doing the right thing at the right time, we conjoin with the *energy weather* of the times. We start creating future history rather than having it just come at us. Time is both cyclic and evolutionary, circular and spiral, and astrology allows us to identify different qualitative cycles and interrelationships characterising any given moment. It gives an ability to see the length and context of those cycles. This gives us more tidal lift when we're on-beam and, when we're not, it helps us get back on-beam.

Astrology is but a language of symbols. These contain no judgements of right or wrong, good or bad: such judgements are created by our cultural values, memories, prejudices, fears, superstitions and neurotic anticipations – and unfortunately by some astrologers and astrology books. They're transient social judgements, memes and tropes, changing in response to differing circumstances. Astrological symbols define forms of energy, simply and directly, like wind and rain. Our own responses to these energies and their patterns are what make the times feel either welcome or adverse.

The best source for learning astrology is your own life. Astrology books and experts provide insights but their words and ideas do not replace observations you derive from your own experience. A real living *feel* for astrology and time is what's most useful in making astrology work for us in our lives, and making our lives work.

So what we're doing in this book is looking into cycles of time, what they do, how long they last, how they interrelate, and how we can see them at work in our own lives and in the world around us.

It's all about getting a living feel of what fullmoons are about, or what goes on when Mercury opposes Pluto. This book will help you get 'in the zone'. I'm sharing with you what I understand of astrology and life, and if this is useful and stimulating then we have lift-off. If it isn't, then having something to disagree with also helps!

In the end, the honest aim of all astrologers is to become redundant. Astrology is a *tool*. Similarly, dowsing rods are a tool for detecting subtle earth energies, but it isn't the rods themselves doing this but *you* – the rods help distinguish details and confirm your feelings but their movements reflect your own inner knowings. Yet it's also possible to 'finger dowse' without rods. Similarly with astrology. Quite often I'll have a sense that something might be happening – perhaps Mercury turning retrograde or the Moon going void. I'll look it up in the ephemeris and, lo behold, indeed it is happening! Or perhaps I get it half-right, thinking that the Sun might be aspecting Neptune when, actually, the Moon just went into Pisces.

It is possible to develop an intuitive sense of timing without using astrology, but this would be more indistinct and unverified. Any receptive person can sense the right time to move forward or when it is best to hold back – and we learn from previous experience how to be more attentive next time round. People who are less well educated tend to have a better sense of timing than educated people – they'll sniff the wind and bother less about fitting things in with their plans and with the thoughts rattling around in their heads. Astrology gives a remarkably accurate means by which to do this, and every aware person would do well to understand the basics: lunar cycles, annual cycles, power points and a sense of time. There will come a time when such people as astrologers will no longer be needed. But that might take quite a while – in our day, the world needs more, not fewer astrologers.

Learning Astrology

Absorb astrology at your own speed, in your own way. You don't need to struggle through vast tomes explaining astrological concepts one by one and systematically: learn whatever matters to you in the present time – things you can watch, smell and experience, getting a feel for them and identifying their flavour. After a while, your attention will move onto other things as they become relevant. Eventually, something will click together and you'll come to understand all twelve signs of the zodiac (for example). But start with three or four signs that you can resonate with right now and work on from there.

Astrology bridges our thinking mind, our feelings and deeper self, our left and right brains, our feminine and masculine sides, our psyche and world, our personal dualisms. Many of the best astrological insights come when you're sitting on the bus or on the toilet or lying in the sun by a waterfall – the conscious mind relaxes, allowing deeper knowledge to filter through. "Aha! Yes, of course! That's it!"

Deeper consciousness doesn't think in thoughts: it sees things in bundles and wholes, grasping things in visions, flashes and moments of connectedness. Perhaps you've just had a tiff with a loved one, you're feeling a bit shocked and you suddenly realise, *ah yes, Venus is squaring Mars and I've just acted it out without knowing it*! This kind of realisation helps greatly in learning astrology, as well as handling life and its rigours. Also, when you can chuckle over life's experiences, you're beginning really to understand them. Learning astrology and learning about life walk hand in hand.

The unconscious works by associations, images, urges, flavours, meanings, knowings, sensings, dream-stuff and internal horror-movies, and it is well for us to allow it to talk in its own language and to understand it on its own terms. Astrology gives a framework for this. Our unconscious is a resource for living rather than an impediment to our ego and the conduct of our turgidly normal routines.

Astrology is a multilevel language far outstripping many other languages in its expressiveness and dimensionality. When learning a new language, we enter first into a phase of translating back to our mother tongue. With practice, one day we suddenly find ourselves thinking and speaking in the new language, without need for translation. After a while we grasp its subtle nuances, inflections and wordplays too. It all falls into place piece by piece. It might become a second language which stays with you throughout your life.

Cycles of Time

Astrology didn't begin with birth charts: these became significant in the last two millennia only. Astrology was studied at least 40,000 years ago when people carved notches on bones and stones to count lunar cycles. Since around 5-6,000 years ago, incrementally we have been individualising, seeing ourselves as independent personages distinct from the world around us and from each other. We have evolved birth charts to reflect that self-preoccupation.

Birth charts were devised by advisers to chiefs and monarchs, since chiefs and monarchs were seen to embody the tribe, nation or people, and their fortunes were seen as the fortunes of the people. Nowadays we think of ourselves as terribly isolated as individuals, on our own and up against a challenging world. We're fascinated therefore with birth charts and personal issues. Yet astrology began long before birth charts, developing as a way of understanding the nature of time and the pattern of change in all things. It's a form of pattern-recognition, a key facet of learning.

The ancients watched life's cyclic seasons. If they caught the right time for migrating, planting crops, culling, getting pregnant, lying low or doing great deeds, things worked better. Why go against the intelligence of nature? They were connected with their world to the extent that if they did not *ask* the seasons to roll on, the seasons might cease doing so. This might seem silly or superstitious to us, but the ancients had a lot more sense than we give them credit for, feeling they were both recipients of the bounty of life and also proactive ingredients in it. They came to understand the right times for certain activities and observances, and they sensed the optimum times for planting and harvesting, taking initiatives or having a celebration.

I do not seek to follow in the footsteps of the people of old – I seek what they sought. My friend Sig Lonegren taught me this, and he learned it from his teacher, a native American grandmother called Twylah Nitsch. The ancients timed and located their sacred ceremonies carefully, building medicine wheels, stone circles and landscape temples to enhance energy flows in the world and the cosmos in order to balance energy interactions between earth and sky and to participate fully in the passage of time. This made life simpler yet mightier, happier and deeper in significance. We don't need to copy them nostalgically, but we do need to incorporate their knowledge into our lives today, and find out more.

The ancients observed and mapped out the cycles of time by observing the motions of Sun, Moon and planets and their interrelations, and also the daily rotational antics of Mother Earth. They watched the rising and setting points of the Sun,

Moon and planets on the horizon because these were a good way of measuring their cyclic periods and positions. Hence that stone circles and other ancient temples were astronomically aligned to such rising and setting points – it wasn't just to do with understanding the Sun, Moon and stars, but also with actively 'turning the wheel of time'.

Nowadays we have a crazy notion that the planets up there, zillions of miles away, beam down rays which somehow affect us down here, as if we're puppets on etheric strings, having our freedom interfered with by the cosmos. Sad to say, this narrow, mechanistic way of looking at things doesn't credit us moderns with much intelligence or insight.

A wholeness, a system, is a unity in which its parts move in harmony with and in response to its overall movement and flow. Each planet is a pulsing, breathing, resonating energy mass with its own patterns and frequencies. The Earth is like this too – it thrums at an approximate rate of eight cycles per second (Hertz), alternating slightly higher and lower over time. Other planets thrum at their own rates and frequencies. These thrums co-vibrate at times in forms of dissonance, at other times they resonate, and most times they are somewhere in between, modulating through all sorts of changes. Kepler and Newton saw this as 'the music of the spheres'.

The energy we ascribe to the planets is actually *here on Earth* and *in* the Earth. This is important. Earth is the resonator that affects us most, and we live totally enveloped within its energy-field. The Earth's resonances, thrums, hums, clangs, rumbles, silences, chords and discords are affected by the other planets in our solar system and their own modulating frequencies. Earth also affects them. They are all interrelated, one integral system in perpetual motion.

Thus, by tracking the motions and interrelations of the planets, we can distinguish the resonance-fields and rhythms of nature here on Earth. What's happening *up there* with the Sun, Moon and 'wandering stars' gives indicators about what's happening *down here*. That's why astrologers study and track heavenly motions. Forget the puppet-strings bit – that's the prejudice of reductionist scientists who see things simplistically in terms of cause-and-effect, with a rather insecure need to have us believe that their own worldview is the only valid one.

As you might have noticed, life on Earth is rather complex. So using the motions of the planets as indicators of the nature of time and change on Earth is rather useful – it helps us identify life's patterns. The proof is in the pudding: use astrology and you will find it works, serving you in creating a more coherent and meaningful life.

Sceptics might belittle, question and complain, but just leave them to stew in their own juice since, if truth be known, they're missing something.

We are only victims of fate, time or anything else if we use the planets, God, governments, football teams, neighbours, the cat or the weather as scapegoats for our hangups, omissions and weaknesses. When things go well, *I did it*, and when things go badly, *they did it*. But no. We have the power to be creators by owning our actions of thought, word and deed and taking responsibility for our causative involvement in what happens to us. If it is raining and we are attached to the idea that it should be sunny, then we'll have a hard time. If we accept the rain and make of our lives the best that we can with that day, miraculous things take place. Making good use of *what is*, this is freedom. It makes life easier.

Acceptance is a different thing to victimhood: it involves a fundamental decision to live *with* the world as it stands and presents itself – it is sustainable, resilient behaviour. This approach ceases imposing wishes, intentions, illusions and prejudices on life. It allows us to get our fingers into the dynamics of life, co-creating with the universe. The situations, spaces and outcomes of life are in phase with universal need. We are living *in time*. In the Middle East, when they say anything about the future, such as "Meet you tomorrow", they tack on the word *inshallah* at the end of a sentence – literally meaning 'if it is the will of God' but equally meaning 'if it fits'. We need to think a bit bigger, *inshallah*.

Serving Time

We are at a critical point in history and you don't have to be an astrologer or to have a doctorate to know this. Nowadays, it's necessary to do a thorough ostrich job to avoid seeing what's going on and, unfortunately, ostrich behaviour is the case for too many people.

We humans can bring about world change either by using our wisdom and foresight, or by being forced to do it. We seem to have habituated ourselves to the latter option, and nowadays we are being shocked into change – just listen to the news and it's a nightmare. Every single department and detail of life is in for a very fundamental work-over. No stone can be left unturned and no person is exempt.

There have been many crises throughout history – Mongol invasions, infectious diseases, white men with big guns, the falls of empires or the crashes of financial markets, with earthquakes and storms thrown in for good measure. But today's world crisis has a new dimension to it: *everyone and everything* is now involved, globally, the stakes are high and there is a cast of billions in the drama. We possibly have more choice available to us now, as a planetary race, than we have ever had. We have little choice but to use that choice.

To survive and thrive, we need to become more sensitive to our environment, and in terms of subtle energy too. We need to work *with* the tides of energy and appropriateness, to operate *in time*, not despite it. Doing this would give us more time. This involves an enormous cultural, psychological and spiritual change from rat-racing and competing with life to going with the flow. The moaning and groaning of global catharsis is all around us, eating away at our hearts. What will finally resolve the situation in today's world is anybody's guess. We can make this a creative or destructive catharsis. What matters is that we make a quantum jump in the deepest place in our beings, using our circumstances to learn and change.

The seed for this book came from a bunch of Glastonbury women back in the early 1980s who were doing protest and consciousness-raising work at Greenham Common, near Newbury, England. They were campaigning against the siting of American cruise missiles there in the days of the Cold War. These women twigged that lunar cycles were important: some of them asked me, as an astrologer, to fill them in on all that I knew about such things. Astrologers, meanwhile, were not really addressing themselves to these questions.

So I focused on this, taught them all I knew, and along came the first edition of this book, published in 1987. Now comes the second edition, and I dedicate it to all of you who know in your hearts what needs to be done. If my reality-bubble is useful to you inside your own reality-bubble, then the purpose of these pages, and of the trees sacrificing themselves in the process, and of the people who have played a part of the weaving of these words, is fulfilled.

One person worth mentioning is Alick Bartholomew of Gateway Books, who first suggested I write the book in 1985 and published it in 1987. Thank you, Alick. Also Jan Billings, who in the 1980s went to great trouble to specially design the illustrations of the planets, signs and other astrological images for the first edition of this book, reproduced here, and Faith Warn, for her suggestions and feedback. Finally, thanks to Jill Moss at Penwith Press, right honourable publisher of this second edition, and to Jonathan How, valiant book designer extraordinaire.

In the first chapter we're going to look into the way our solar system works and the way it affects us here on this pulsing, resonating, breathing, singing planet we call Earth. The good news is, if you find it heavy going, you can scan through it and come back to it later. Okay, let's go: let's stop the clocks and do some real time.

Astrological Symbols

The Zodiac Signs

♑	Capricorn	♈	Aries	♋	Cancer	♎	Libra
♒	Aquarius	♉	Taurus	♌	Leo	♏	Scorpio
♓	Pisces	♊	Gemini	♍	Virgo	♐	Sagittarius

The Planets

	Planet	Period	Home	Detriment	Exaltation	Fall	Orb
☉	Sun	1 year	Leo	Aquarius	Aries	Libra	5-10°
☽	Moon	27d 8h	Cancer	Capricorn	Taurus	Scorpio	5-10°
☿	Mercury	± 1 year	Gemini Virgo	Sagittarius Pisces	Aquarius	Leo	3-5°
♀	Venus	± 1 year	Taurus Libra	Scorpio Aries	Pisces	Virgo	3-5°
♂	Mars	2 years	Aries Scorpio	Libra Taurus	Capricorn	Cancer	3-5°
♃	Jupiter	12 years	Sagittarius Pisces	Gemini Virgo	Cancer	Capricorn	2-4°
♄	Saturn	29 years	Capricorn Aquarius	Cancer Leo	Libra	Aries	2-4°
⚷	Chiron	51 years	Undecided, possibly not relevant				2-3°
♅	Uranus	84 years	Aquarius	Leo			·2-3°
♆	Neptune	165 years	Pisces	Virgo			2-3°
♇	Pluto	248 years	Scorpio	Taurus			2-3°

The Aspects

	Aspect	Angle	Signs apart	Division	Orbs
☌	Conjunction	0°	0	1	6-12°
⊻	Semisextile	30°	1	1/12	2-3°
∠	Semisquare	45°	1.5	1/8	2-4°
✳	Sextile	60°	2	1/6	3-6°
□	Square	90°	3	1/4	5-8°
△	Trine	120°	4	1/3	4-7°
⚼	Sesquiquadrate	135°	4.5	3/8	2-4°
⚻	Quincunx	150°	5	5/12	2-3°
☍	Opposition	180°	6	1/2	6-12°

1

The Astronomy of Astrology

This chapter exists to help you understand how things work in our solar system and how they affect life on Earth. Grasping all the details in this chapter is not essential to understanding the rest of this book. It's unusual to say this with the first chapter of a book, but you can skip through it and read it later if you wish.

Apologies to readers in Chile, Argentina, Southern Africa, Australia and New Zealand: this book is northern-hemisphere chauvinistic. Use a little deduction and imagination and this 'northernist' book will still prove useful to you.

Planet Earth

We live on a smallish but colourful planet, third child of the Sun, our local star. The Sun is eight light-minutes away from us (93 million miles, 150 million km). The nearest *major* neighbouring star, Sirius, a sister to our Sun, is eight light-years away (525,600 times the Earth-Sun distance). The physical distances involved are enormous. It makes our little lives on Earth seem puny. Nevertheless, to us, life on Earth is a Big Thing. This is problematic and a root cause of today's parlous world situation: we think we're big but actually we're really small.

Our solar system represents a macrocosmic analogy of an individual human. A human is made up of a collection of different psychological components we can call *sub-personalities,* and the orbit of these sub-personalities around the core of our being is analogous to the orbit of the planets around the Sun.

The planets move variously in their orbits over time. Thus they are indicators of things that change through time. The *stars*, however, have not moved appreciably in relation to each other during the entire course of human history, and thus they cannot be used if we are studying time and change. When the popular media talk about 'what's in the stars', they are incorrect – it's what's in the planets that matters to us.

Earth is a living being, with its energy-centres, meridians and acupuncture points spread across the Earth's surface and originating from the Earth's core and connected both with outer space and inner space, a bit like plug-sockets or antennae. Earth has a spirit, psyche and physical body, and taking care of her on all levels is one of the main issues of our time. She rotates on her polar axis like a spinning top. This gives us here on Earth the impression that the Sun, planets and stars rotate around us each day, as if they were decorating the inside of a vast heavenly sphere, half of which is sky-blue, and half of which is dark, bejewelled with stars.

Using Earth as our frame of reference, the cosmos rotates around us, but looking at Earth from an outer-space viewpoint, Earth is rotating on her axis on a daily basis. This is another psychological analogy: we as individuals tend to believe that the world rotates around us, when in fact the world is fine as it is, and we are the ones who are spinning.

Sun and the Solar System

Sun is a being too, a parent to Earth, far bigger, made up of a hot gaseous/plasmic thermonuclear body. It is one of billions of suns in our galaxy, and not a very big or remarkable one at that. Our home galaxy takes a lenticular, spiral shape, with a vast centre, dense with suns and all sorts of activity. We live 15,000 light years from the centre of the galaxy (one light year is 60 trillion miles).

Though this sounds like a ridiculously long distance, it is significant only within the context of our own galaxy. Ours is one of a cluster of galaxies, of which there are, in turn, many more, and no one really knows how much these clusters of galaxies actually form parts of larger clusters and systems.

The distances and time-scales involved are so immense that to us they might as well

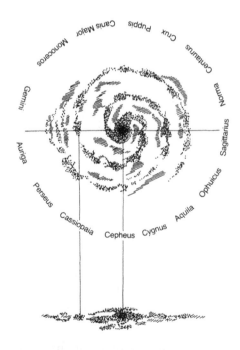

The Sun's position in our galaxy. The constellations on the plane of the galaxy, as seen from Earth, are named around the edge. A side view of the galaxy is on the left.

be infinite: living on a densely-physical planet like ours involves squeezing ourselves into a timescale and space-localisation which is infinitesimally small if looked at from a 'God's-eye view'. The history of human life on Earth is like the life of a grain of sand on a beach, and the personal history of each of us in terms of the whole of human history is like an atom in that grain of sand. You and I are very small indeed!

Let's now look at the distances of the planets from the Sun. The two most eccentrically-moving planets, Chiron and Pluto, vary greatly in their orbital distances from the Sun – they have egg-shaped, elliptical orbits, moving closer and further away over time. Other planets have only small variations, their orbits being near-circular. Distances in the diagram here are expressed in Astronomical Units (AU), where the distance between Sun and Earth is 1AU.

The planets are lit up by the Sun. They are a very different thing to the stars or the Sun – they exist on a much smaller scale to suns, being children of them. They orbit around our Sun at varying distances – Earth is quite close – on a more or less flat plane. This gives the impression, as seen from Earth, that Sun and planets move along a narrow belt of the sky, called the *ecliptic*.

Mild exceptions to this are the planets Mercury, Chiron and Pluto with their eccentric and elliptical orbits, inclined somewhat to the ecliptic, giving the impression that, in the course of their orbital cycles, they move above and below it. Earth's Moon also moves above and below the ecliptic by a small amount: the difference between the ecliptic, Earth's plane of orbit around the Sun, and the Moon's plane of orbit around Earth is about 5°. In chapter 2 we'll meet up with lunar maxima and minima, which highlight this.

All the planets orbit in the same direction. When looking at them in Earth's sky, they move from west to east along the ecliptic. Don't confuse this with the Earth's daily rotation on its axis, which causes the Sun, Moon and planets to appear to move together, much faster as one lot, from east to west. The west-to-east movement is more gradual, each planet being on its own cycle – while the east-to-west movement is daily or diurnal.

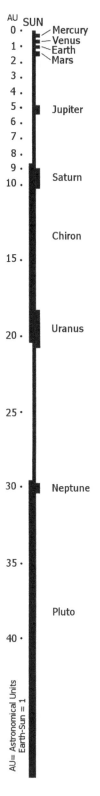

This is perhaps a bit confusing, but the best way to figure it out is to spend time outdoors observing the skies and the way the heavens move. Find a place free of light-pollution, take something to sit on, perhaps a flask of tea, and go there regularly during the course of at least one lunation cycle, and again at least once or twice a month for a whole year. It's a gift to give yourself – rather like visiting a volcano, seeing humpback whales or watching the northern lights.

Zodiacal Oscillations

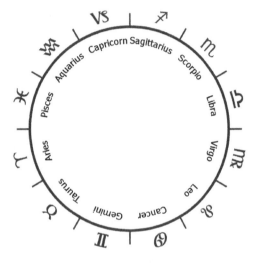

The ecliptic is divided into twelve equal segments or *zodiac signs,* each of which is subdivided, for measurement purposes, into 30 *degrees.* Thus 12 × 30° = 360°, a full circle. We can state the position of a planet at any moment by giving its degree and sign – for example, Mars at 12° Taurus or Jupiter at 27° Libra, which in astrologese is written ♂12♉, or ♃27♎. We can be more exact by giving minutes ('), of which there are 60 to a degree, or even seconds ("), to which there are 60 in a minute – though such extreme accuracy isn't needed in astrology. Thus we can write ♂12♉42. There are 60 minutes to a degree, and 360 degrees to a full circle.

The signs are *not* stellar constellations, even though the constellations along the ecliptic confusingly share the same names. Over history, the signs and the constellations slowly shift in relation to one another – known as the *precession of the equinoxes.* They move at a rate of 1° every 72 years (actually 71.6 years), or one sign every 2,148 years, or the whole zodiac in 25,772 years, thanks to the wobble created on the spinning motion of Earth by the combined effect of Sun and Moon. It's like a spinning top rotating rapidly on its own axis, tilting and moving around in a slower movement generated by the spinning.

When the constellations and zodiac signs picked up the names they possess today, in later classical Greek times, though later Latinised, they were one and the same in position, but this precession has now moved the constellations nearly one sign apart. Conventional wisdom has it that the Greek philosopher Hipparchus discovered precession in 129 BCE but it is built into the mathematics of some stone circles dating from at least 2,500 years earlier, and some ancient sites in the Middle East demonstrate it was known even earlier than that. It was also known that the Earth orbits around the Sun, but modern astronomers don't like to acknowledge that ancient peoples had such advanced astronomical knowledge.

The zodiac signs are rooted in our earthly experience, in terms of earthly time-coordinates: they are temporally anchored in the *solstices* and *equinoxes*, the axes of the four seasons – and the seasons matter a lot as far as earthly life is concerned. The seasons are brought into being because Earth, with her poles leaning 23.5° from perpendicular to the ecliptic, exposes her north pole to the Sun for half of the year, and her south pole for the other half, as she orbits annually around the Sun.

Looking at the horizon from any point in the northern hemisphere, the Sun rises north of east in summer and south of east in winter, and this becomes more emphasised, the further one moves from the equator. This changing orientation of the rising and setting points of the Sun was the means by which ancient peoples set and checked their calendars. Even later churches were usually oriented to the rising points of the Sun on the saint's day to which each church was dedicated.

In temperate climes, the Sun moves higher and lower in the sky, seasonally – and again, the further from the equator that one moves, the more emphasised this is.

The cycles of the Earth's orbit around the Sun and its polar leaning are slightly out of sync by around one minute of time each year, and this is what creates precession: as history moves on, spring equinox takes place at the same point in the Earth's seasons, while the backdrop of stars slowly changes.

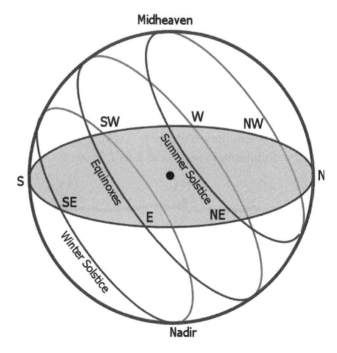

The quarter-points and seasons.

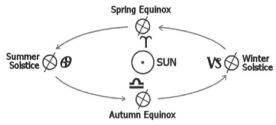

The inclination of the Earth's poles to the ecliptic and to the Sun brings about Earth's seasons, as it orbits around the Sun.

The main point of all this is that the zodiac signs are not the same as the constellations. We use the *zodiac signs* in astrology, for they are related to Earth experience and the seasonal modulation of its energy field, and this is the real stuff of life as far as we're concerned.

In the northern hemisphere, the summer-solsticial signs, Gemini and Cancer, ride high in the sky (regardless of whether or not the Sun is there) and the winter-solsticial signs, Sagittarius and Capricorn, ride low – and each increasingly so the further north we move on Earth. This means that if the Moon or any other planet is in a summer-solsticial sign (Gemini or Cancer) it will ride high in the sky, and if in a winter-solsticial sign (Sagittarius-Capricorn), it will ride low.

Thus, if Sun, Moon or a planet is in a winter sign it will rise in the SE and set in the SW, and if it is in a summer sign, it will rise in the NE and set in the NW. If it is in one of the equinoctial signs (Pisces-Aries or Virgo-Libra) it will rise eastwards and set westwards. This oscillation of rising and setting points on the horizon increases the further north we go, such that north of 66.5° north latitude on Earth (the Polar Circle), Sun, Moon or planets do not set when they are in summer solsticial signs, and they don't rise when they are in winter solsticial signs. This is remarkable to witness.

Consider fullmoons. In summer, when the Sun is high in the sky, fullmoons will be low, since the fullmoon will be in a winter sign – Sun and Moon are opposite each other at fullmoon, as seen from Earth. In winter, when the Sun is low, fullmoons

Eastern Horizon

will be high, being in the summer signs. So, fullmoons are most prominent in our sky in winter.

Rising points of the Sun at different times of the year in upper-middle latitudes such as Britain, looking eastwards, as if from a stone circle. The ecliptic oscillates daily back and forth as successive signs rise – regardless of where the Sun is located in the zodiac at the time. At summer solstice the Sun rises in the NE, at the equinoxes due E, and at winter solstice it rises in the SE. This variation in rising points increases as one draws closer to the Earth's poles, until it goes bananas at the polar circle at 66.5°N or S.

The ancients made their zodiacal and calendrical measurements by keeping track of the rising and setting points of Sun and Moon on the horizon, as seen from carefully-located and designed places such as stone circles, standing stones or mounds, often aligned with sight-lines to the rising and setting points at critical or chosen times of year.

Some of these sight-lines are quite dramatic. From Trencrom Hill, a 3,500 year old ancient hilltop settlement in West Cornwall, near where I live, the summer solstice sun rises straight over a hill twenty miles away northeast called St Agnes Beacon (Agnes being the goddess of fire). At winter solstice it rises between two conspicuous hills, Tregonning Hill and Godolphin Hill south-eastwards. Then,

to crown it all, the summer solstice sun sets behind a neighbouring hill north-westwards, with a slice of the sun following the slope of the hill for some distance until it disappears in a nick between the hill and a neighbouring hill. These are all natural hills – not placed stones. However, I have not found a landmark south-westwards to mark the winter solstice setting sun. Trencrom must have been a wonderful hill to live on 3,500 years ago, probably in summertime – in those days looking over a landscape of endless forest. Forest claustrophobia was one of the reasons people chose to live on hilltops in ancient times, especially in summer.

Cycles

Astrology is all about cycles of time and solar, lunar and planetary motion. These cycles take on different durations and patterns.

The Diurnal Cycle

The fastest cycle in astrology is the cycle of daily rotation of the Earth on her own axis. In a birth chart, the four angles (the Ascendant-Descendant and the Nadir-Midheaven) together with the twelve houses show the relationship at any given time between Earth and the zodiac. This cycle of relationship lasts 24 hours.

Wherever we are on Earth, half of the heavens are above us and visible, and half of the heavens are below the ground we stand on, obscured by it. This changes rapidly, on average by the width of one zodiac sign crossing the Ascendant or eastern horizon every two hours. Hence the importance of the exact time and place of a person's birth or of an event in question, in the calculation of an astrological birth chart.

The sign on the *ascendant* (eastwards, where Sun, Moon and planets rise) changes every 1-3 hours, depending on which sign it is, and how far from the equator the birth takes place. The springtime signs rise fast and the autumntime signs rise slowly.

Having said all this, we won't be covering the diurnal cycle in this book since it is rather too fast for our purposes. The main power points in the diurnal cycle are sunrise and sunset – you just need to witness them to know why. Though transitional times, they have a certain timelessness to them. Some astrological programs quite usefully show the rising and setting of Sun, Moon and planets and the current movements of the planets in relation to each other.

The Lunar Cycle

The second fastest cycle we observe in astrology is the cycle of the Moon. Earth and Moon are a twin planet, co-orbiting around each other. The barycentre, or centre of gravity of both together, is not at the centre of the Earth, though it still lies inside it, about 1,060 miles or 1,700km below the surface, and 2,940 miles, 4,700km from Earth's centre.

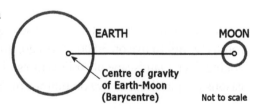

The Earth and Moon co-orbit around a common barycentre which, while it lies inside Earth, is not at the Earth's centre.

So the Earth wobbles slightly, pulled around on a lunar-monthly basis by the gravitational pull of the Moon. Moon moves around the zodiac in 27 days 8 hours on average. She is by far the fastest-moving heavenly body in our sky. She moves through a zodiac sign roughly every 2⅓ days, depending on her speed at the time. Her speed is dependent on her closeness to or distance from Earth – another cyclic motion, lasting 27 days 12 hours. When the Moon is close to Earth it is in *perigee*, and when furthest it is in *apogee*. These cycles coincide once every 14 lunations or cycles of phases of the Moon, once every 13½ months. For some reason we tend not to pay much attention in astrology to this cycle of lunar distance. Perhaps we should.

The Lunation Cycle

The light of the Moon is reflected sunlight. Since the Moon moves around the Earth, its light and dark sides show themselves to us in ever-changing ways, and this is the cycle of phases of the Moon or the lunation cycle.

This cycle of phases is longer than the cycle of motion of the Moon around the zodiac

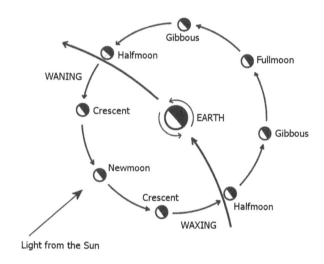

because, in the course of 28 days, the Sun moves through almost one sign of the zodiac, so the Moon must move further to catch up with it.

This is like the hands of a clock, where the minute hand has to move through about 1hr 5mins of movement to catch up with the hour hand. Thus the lunation cycle lasts 29 days 12 hours, over two days longer than the average cycle of lunar motion through the zodiac (27 days 8 hours). The Sun has moved one sign, and the Moon needs two days to move through that extra sign to catch up with the Sun. So every time it conjuncts the Sun at newmoon, it has moved through roughly thirteen signs.

The Annual Solar Cycle

The next-longest cycle we use is the cycle of the year. Sun moves through the zodiac in 365 days and 6 hours, and it is directly related to the Earth's seasons. A year is subdivided into twelve astrological months (zodiac signs) of thirty-odd days. The Sun moves into each sign on 20th-23rd of any calendar month – our calendar is not accurately astronomically-based and it has odd month-lengths, so these dates vary. While the cycle of seasons is obvious to all of us, the underlying energy-currents hidden within it are not so obvious, since we are trained to ignore or overlook such energies and subtle tides. Re-attuning ourselves to the solar year is very necessary – and this is what chapters 4 and 5 are about.

Planetary Cycles

Then we come to the planets, which have various lengths of cycle, ranging from one year to 250 years.

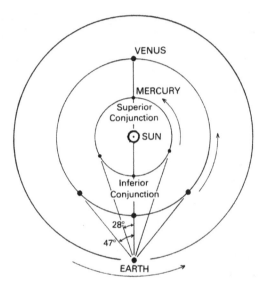

Mercury (☿) and **Venus** (♀) both orbit the Sun *inside* Earth's orbit, appearing from Earth's viewpoint always to hover around the Sun like yoyos as it moves through the zodiac. Sometimes they conjunct the Sun, passing in front of or behind it – called inferior and superior conjunctions, respectively. It's the Sun, not Mercury, that is considered superior when Mercury passes behind it. At other times Mercury can move up to 28° and Venus up to 47° ahead of or behind the Sun in the zodiac.

When Mercury or Venus are ahead of the Sun in the zodiac, they are visible in the evening westwards after the Sun has set – because, in the northern hemisphere, when a planet is *ahead* in the zodiac it is *leftwards* in our sky. When they are behind in the zodiac, they are visible in the morning, eastwards before sunrise.

Mercury is not so easily seen because it is quite close to the Sun and its light is usually overpowered by the light of dawn or dusk. But Venus can at times be very bright, sparkly and prominent, as a morning or evening 'star'. Sometimes each of them moves faster than the Sun through the zodiac, sometimes slower than the

Sun and also at times appearing to move backwards or *retrograde.* This backwards motion is an illusion deriving from the fact that we stand on a moving observation platform. Imagine someone walking around you, swinging a ball on a string around their head – from your perspective the ball would move forwards and backwards, while the net motion would be forwards.

It's different for the planets outside Earth's orbit. They don't follow the Sun around the zodiac like Mercury and Venus – they each have their own cycles with different durations, and they can go through a complete cycle of aspects to the Sun.

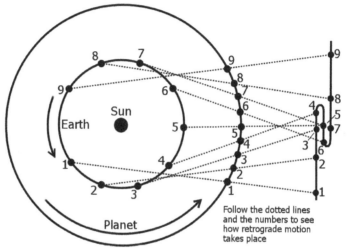

Earth, being closer to the Sun, moves on its orbit around the Sun quicker than the planets outside its orbit. (Actually, they're not necessarily moving slower, but they have further to travel, being further out than we.) This means that, when we're coming between them and the Sun we seem to overtake them and they seem to go backwards, and always around the time when they are in opposition to the Sun as seen from Earth. They don't actually go backwards – it's rather like being in a fast train overtaking a slower train. The planet is moving forwards, but the Earth is overtaking on the inside.

Follow the dotted lines and the numbers to see how retrograde motion takes place

The planets outside Earth's orbit move around the zodiac each in their own wise.

Mars ♂ is reddish in light and quite bright when around opposition to the Sun, when it is prominent in our night sky and closest to Earth. This is the case with all of the planets orbiting outside Earth. Mars takes 1 year and 10 months, or 687 days to move round the zodiac.

Jupiter ♃ is very bright, blue-white and sometimes twinkly when prominent. Apart from Venus when bright, Jupiter can be the brightest body in the sky when at opposition to the Sun. This sparkly and tinted quality is due to light-effects in the Earth's atmosphere, created by the extra amount of light coming from Jupiter diffracting as it passes through the atmosphere. Its cycle is nearly 12 years in length.

Saturn ♄ is a dull, tarnishy yellow, not so bright but still noticeable when it is prominent, and it takes 29ish years to orbit the Sun. Until recent centuries, this was the furthest known planet, and it is the most distant naked-eye visible planet.

Chiron ⚷ is a newly-discovered planetoid, invisible to the naked eye (as are all those which follow). It takes 51 years to orbit the Sun. It has a very eccentric orbit, moving closer in toward the Sun and faster when it's in the sign Libra, then further out and slower when in Aries.

Uranus ♅ takes 84 years, spending seven years in each sign. It's very big, as also are Jupiter, Saturn and Neptune. It is invisible to the naked eye, and it's on a regular orbit.

Neptune ♆ takes 165 years, spending 13 years in each sign, and it's on a regular and circular orbit.

Pluto ♇ takes 248 years and it is on an eccentric orbit. When closer to the Sun and moving fast, in Scorpio, it takes 12 years to move through that sign – the last time was between 1984 and 1996. It actually comes slightly inside the orbit of Neptune and, when it does so it moves slightly faster than Neptune, just for five years or so. But in Taurus it is way out, very far away, and it takes 36 years to move through that sign. It's a small and dense planet with a large moon, arguably a double planet, slightly confusingly called Charon.

Mars is retrograde for 60-80 days every two years. All the other outer planets are retrograde for 4-5 months per year. The naked-eye visible planets amongst these, Mars, Jupiter and Saturn, are at their most prominent in our skies each year around the time of their opposition to the Sun – they are both closest to us (on the same side of the Sun as we) and highlighted in the dark midnight skies. When they are passing round the other side of the Sun, near conjunction to it, they move forwards (direct), but they are invisible, distant and outshone by the Sun in the daytime sky.

Cosmic Clocks

All this means that astrology is using a kind of clock with eleven hands. Telling the time by this clock is not as easy as with a normal analogue clock, since there are so many more permutations when eleven hands are involved. The language of astrology has developed to help us in this. The basic language involves planets, signs, aspects (angles between the planets at any time) and houses (which are related to earth's orientation to the planets and signs), and there is a family of astrological shorthand symbols too.

The interrelations between the various planetary cycles thus start becoming very interesting. These interrelations are especially noted by examining the zodiacal angles (aspects) between any pair or number of planets. Then the aspects, planets and signs are all taken into account and brought into a big picture, to understand the nature of the 'energy-weather' at any moment.

A *note*: for simplicity, in astrologese, Sun and Moon are often called 'planets', even though they are of a completely different order to the planets. What is meant here is 'heavenly bodies' but, for shorthand astrologers lump Sun, Moon and planets together as 'planets'. This is not done out of ignorance!

Birth Charts

An astrological chart is a slice out of time, as if someone said "Cut!", and drew up a map to show how Earth, Sun, Moon and planets stood at the exact moment chosen for that map, as seen from the position on Earth of the observer. The place on Earth is important, in that two people born exactly simultaneously on opposite sides of the globe (for example in Britain and New Zealand or California and Afghanistan) will have exactly the same planetary positions and interrelations in their birth charts, but completely different house-orientations of those positions. One will have the Sun perhaps rising, the other will have it setting – and they were both born at the same moment (though in different time zones).

A four-minute difference in time, or a one-degree difference in longitude (east-west measurement of position on Earth) will make for a one degree difference in the orientation of the zodiac to the Earth. This can make a critical difference if, say, the signs on the ascendant are on the point of changing from one sign into another. In this book, however, we are not looking at time-slices, or birth charts – we're looking into the overall flow of time, at time-cycles. Plenty of other books cover birth charts.

The most important planet in a birth chart is the Earth, as shown in the houses in a chart. This is because the Earth is an energy-resonator within the energy-field of which we live, and this energy-field cross-resonates with those of the other planets of the Sun's system. This is how the planets affect us – through the Earth. The Earth gives us our physical body, and our body and its senses give us a vehicle through which to experience life on Earth.

Describing the Nature of Time

A useful term we shall use here is *energy-weather*. Just as the weather is made up of a combination of factors interrelated to one another (warmth, wind, humidity, pressure, and so on), so also is the case with energy-weather. Many interrelating factors meet to make up an atmosphere, a nuance of time or a vibrational situation.

In astrology, we give names to these factors, giving them symbols, and we play around with different ways of relating them to each other and deriving meaning therefrom. Any one moment and its energy-weather is characterised by a complete pattern involving Earth, Sun, Moon and all the planets. The major contributing factors can be disentangled into several main components:

- **the relationship between the zodiac and the particular place on Earth we are looking from.** This concerns the rotation of Earth and the orientation of the sky to us at any particular moment. The sign that is rising in the east is prominent in characterising the moment, and it changes every 1-3 hours. The orientation of the zodiac as a whole is significant in a very short-term sense – if it's a question of leaving on a journey now or in a few hours' time, this would be relevant. At any time the Sun is at some point in the zodiac and, to us, of course it makes a big difference when the Sun is above or below the horizon, and what time of day it is;

- **the positions of Sun, Moon and planets in the zodiac signs** – for example, Sun in Aries or Mars in Leo – more about this in chapter 5. They can be spread out in different ways, conglomerating for a time in certain signs, sometimes concentrated, sometimes widely spread, and always in motion;

- **planetary positions in relation to each other**, which are measured by the aspects (angles) between them – for example, Venus trine Saturn (120°) or Mars sextile Pluto (60°). More about aspects in chapter 7. These spark off transient circuits of relationship between Sun, Moon and planets, making things happen and stirring the nature of the times.

Confused or overloaded? It will come clear, and these things will be explained again.

Throwing together all of these factors and sorting them into a synthesised whole, partially logically, partially intuitively, a skilled astrologer can 'tell the time' in terms of 'energy weather'. If it concerns the time of birth of a person, then that astrologer can say things about the energy-potentials inherent in that person's life, by looking at the energy-weather that person chose to be born into and to take on. This is based on the notion that the beginning of a cycle (in this case, a person's birth into life) has within it the seed-potential and patterning of the whole cycle.

When you look at a seed, you can visualise the possible end-product, the plant or tree, might look like. The eventual form that tree takes depends on its own inbuilt growth-programs, on environmental factors and on weather and events during

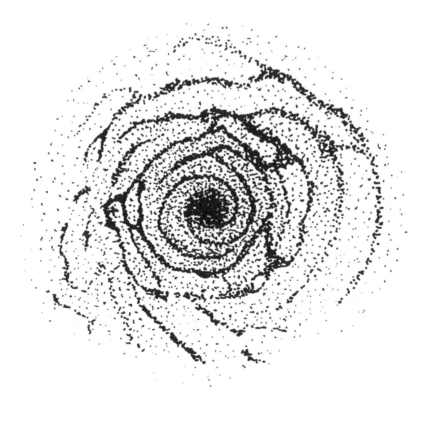

its life. Similarly a person's seed-potential is understood by looking at a birth chart, though a good astrologer also factors in the inherent soul of the person, their upbringing and social patterns and the life experiences they have had. And when looking at the nature of time, as well as astrological variables we need to factor in the situation we're located in, the company we might have, our mood and perception, what has just passed and what is anticipated.

If all this has thoroughly lost you, don't worry. A vision of the motions of all these rotations and orbits comes of its own accord, as your understanding of the parts of the ever-moving astrological jigsaw grows.

It can help to spend some time wrapped up in a blanket, lying on the ground at night, observing the planets and stars every week or two over the course of a year, to help that vision come. Camping out works wonders. You don't *have* to do this, but it helps, and it can give quite a lift. Astrologers nowadays use a book of computer-calculated tables, called an *ephemeris,* which shows the exact positions of the planets for each day, and such a vision can come to the inner eye through working this way. YouTube has plenty of movies of the solar system too.

The main point to note is that *all things move perpetually, and they move in cycles.* And it's amazing, when you keep track of them. These cycles never repeat exactly: time is forever unique. This is the basis of astrology.

Now let's look at the cycles of the Moon. Did you realise that we live on a double planet, Earth-Moon?

2

Cycles of the Moon

The Moon is an excellent starting point for learning the astrology of timing because it moves quite quickly – but it's still slow enough that it doesn't make you observationally dizzy. It provides us with a stream of noticeable situations and atmospheres to experience and observe. It's a good initiator into the secrets of time because of its short 28-29 day cycle. It therefore helps us train our sensitivities and sense of time.

In this and the next chapter, astrological terms (such as the stages of the cycle of aspects) will be introduced to familiarise you with them, but they will be explained more fully later on. This is an introduction to the pattern and flow of time-cycles as well as a study of the Moon. In chapter 3 we'll go through a complete cycle of lunar phases.

Lunar Sidereal Cycles

The Moon's cycle of motion around the zodiac is one thing, and that of its phases is another. The first is the *sidereal cycle* of the Moon (*sidus* is the Latin for 'star'). Using a clock as an analogy, this is the cycle of movement of a hand of the clock from a particular point on the clock and back to the same point.

The second cycle concerns the Moon's motions in relation to the Sun, a body that is itself in motion in our sky, though it moves more slowly. This is the *lunation* or *synodic cycle* of the Moon (from the Greek *sunodikos*, meaning 'meeting'). An analogy is the cycle of two hands on the clock in relation to each other. Starting at 12 o'clock, they will subsequently meet, or conjunct, around 1.05, 2.10, 3.15 and so on, since the slow hand moves forward an hour and the fast hand must catch up with it by doing a whole round of a clock plus an extra bit.

So the sidereal cycle is shorter than the synodic. The sidereal cycle is around 27 days and 8 hours and the synodic cycle is around 29 days and 12 hours.

It is well worth keeping track of Moon's zodiacal motion for you will soon come to recognise a spectrum and sequence of lunar tones and flavours. Take note particularly of the times when the Moon changes sign, since a distinct change of atmosphere can take place, literally within the space of thirty minutes. A change of sign is called an *ingress*. You don't have to wait long for successive sign-changes of the Moon – 2⅓ days, roughly. Their timings can be found in an ephemeris.

When the Moon is in Libra it's timely to hang out with others, negotiate, make up if necessary and enjoy people's company, yet when the Moon moves into Scorpio it is time to face up to imperatives, have a serious discussion about trickier issues and get to grips with raw facts. Moon in Sagittarius can bring out the fun and gregariousness in us, bring people together and extend our horizons, while Moon in Capricorn asks us to get on with what we ought to be doing, commitments and responsibilities, focusing on practicalities and making things work. So on it goes: if you observe lunar movements through the signs for a few lunar cycles, you will quite quickly start getting the feel of it and how to respond to it.

So when the Moon passes through the signs, it's a bit like one of those old theatre spotlights with a revolving wheel in front of it by which the colour of the light is changed. Same light, different colour filters. When the Moon moves through the twelve signs it passes through a cycle of filters or energy-qualities in a sequence of changing stages.

As mentioned above, the lunar zodiacal or sidereal cycle lasts on average 27 days and 8 hours. Because the Moon swings slightly closer to and further from Earth during its cycle too, it sometimes moves marginally faster, sometimes slightly slower, through the signs. For this reason, a fullmoon can sometimes look larger, being nearer the Earth, sometimes smaller, being further away.

Just try to visualise these things in an organic way, and you will gradually get a sense of the elegance and beauty of all this.

Security

Moon plays a key part in affecting our daily-life responses to things as they arise – our moods, transient frames of mind, underlying urges and our responses to the collective atmosphere around us. Our mood and feelings change several times each day, and this is related to the Moon and its movements. Its influences and events last a few hours or up to a day before they change into something else.

In astrology we measure the positions of heavenly bodies using a 360° zodiac. There are twelve signs, each of 30°. So when we talk about the Moon's position at a particular time, we might say '12 Taurus' or '25 Sagittarius' – in astro-shorthand, that's ☽12♉ and ☽25♐. The Moon moves 12-15° every day – therefore it crosses a sign of 30° in just over two days. It's moving roughly a degree every two hours. It is about ½° wide – so while you read this chapter, it might move up to a Moon-width.

As the hours pass by it might form aspects (angles) to other planets, and it will be rising, culminating and setting in our sky too – so there's quite a bit of motion going on. Other bodies are slower – Pluto, for example, takes 250 years to move round the zodiac, so you'll need to live three long lifetimes to see a whole cycle of Pluto.

A sign-change of the Moon infects us with swells, standpoints, humours, modes and vagaries of being which can pass relatively quickly. Yet, at the time we experience them, they can feel total and pervasive, as if we always had them and always will, as if they are *really important*. In a way they are so, in a way not, though critical, defining events can be rapid but they can also take a long time to build up. The Berlin Wall started coming down in hours, during a moment of high drama, but the buildup to those events took months and years, and its final removal from sight took years after that – and now it is but a memory. So the Moon plays a critical and precise role in triggering events which are playing out in a longer-term context.

All this involves subjective feelings that are often unclear and non-specific but they particularly affect our basic feelings of alrightness or discomfort with life, on a momentary yet deep-seated basis. Our moods and viewpoints change several times each day between waking and going to sleep, and these 'humours' immensely affect our way of seeing and dealing with life – at times crucially. A burst of happiness, anger, sure-footedness or confusion might have its deeper, longer-term origins, but it can be triggered in specific short and intense situations that highlight the issues fermenting underneath. Our sleep and dreams are affected too – some people have difficulty sleeping on the fullmoon, but sleep is affected in more subtle and less noticeable ways too.

The Moon doesn't directly *steer* these moods: our feelings of okayness or agitation, centredness or scattering are our own. They are very much affected by our conditioning patterns, going right back to birth, even to conception. The Moon is associated with our subjective feeling-responses to otherwise impartial situations and atmospheres. It might be raining or shining, yet our responses to these conditions vary over time, and they vary between different people. The Moon's energy is like the surface of water, sometimes still, sometimes ripply, sometimes choppy and occasionally fierce – how we swim in it is our own concern.

There are psycho-emotional decisions involved – such as the decision to make a big deal of what's happening or to let it be as it is and stay calm. If the Moon is in Gemini there might be a buzzy, chatty, frenetic or contradictory atmosphere or situation, but what we do with this is our creation and choice. This is true even when we feel the situation is others' fault, or a result of circumstances beyond our control.

We can go *with* the energy of the time, or we can be hoodwinked by it, responding to life situations on auto-drive, without insight or awareness of the consequences we might create through our responses. We can use every time-frame we live through to solve or to create problems – and, as Gemini is quick to point out, this has a lot to do with mental attitude, though underneath this emotional issues are the true driver. Are we fully and awarely present in the driver's seat of our life? Answer: in many cases, *no*, or not completely.

People who are most critical of astrology, believing that it implies a loss of free-will and self-determination, are therefore unaware or in denial of the way that energy-weather changes and affects them. Paradoxically this makes them greater victims of forces beyond their control, in comparison to those people they accuse of possessing flaky, hocus-pocus and superstitious beliefs in astrology.

The most crucial steps each and all of us take in the carving of our life-story are often focused in periods of minutes and hours. Tuning into lunar motions and changes can help us grasp the deeper, overall significance of these short moments and the way they contribute to the total play of life. It's a question of mindfulness, allowing the watcher within us to observe and take note.

Lunar Synodic Cycles

Now we're going to look at lunar phases – its synodic or lunation cycle. These phases are not the Moon's business alone: they derive from the interrelationship of Moon, Sun and Earth – Earth being our moving observation platform. Earth orbits around the Sun, and the Moon orbits around the Earth. More correctly, Earth and Moon are a twin planet co-orbiting the Sun together. But from Earth, where we live, it looks as if the Sun and Moon orbit around the Earth and, in our daily reality they do. Not only this but, amazingly (and no one has satisfactorily explained it) Sun and Moon look the same size as seen from Earth. Can this be ascribed to some sort of fortuitous astronomical accident, or is this a sign of something more intelligent or intentional to the universe than we moderns like to believe?

The Sun provides the light that the Moon changingly reflects, and the Moon's position relative to the Sun and Earth dictates the phase the Moon shows us at any time. Viewed from our earthly viewing-platform, Moon and Sun behave similarly to the minute and hour hands of a clock, both of them being in motion but at different speeds. In this sense, energy-wise, Moon mediates between Sun and Earth, filling in extra details in the Earth-Sun energy-relationship.

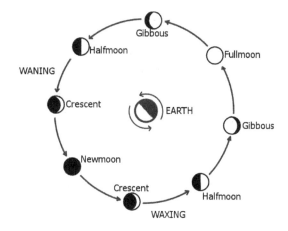

In northern climes, at spring equinox in late March the Sun climbs higher in the sky and the season changes, generally getting warmer. Often the actual critical shifts in the emergence of springtime happen around fullmoons and newmoons near the equinox – this shift often happens on one specific day, or over just a few days. Suddenly the flowers come out, the weather changes, migrating birds arrive and, if the weather is nice, you strip off a layer with a sigh of relief. That's an example of the way the Moon triggers trends that otherwise were developing more slowly and gradually.

The Sun is the giver of life on Earth, through its warmth and energy. Astrologically, it represents our essential being-nature, the selfhood that we are and its mode of expression through us. If I tell you "I'm a Virgo" – the Sun was in Virgo when I was born – then my soul will manifest in my being in a Virgo kind of way. As you will see in this book, I'm a sucker for details, but it all eventually adds up to become a whole. That's a classic Virgoid trait. Us lot, we sort the world out and we're pretty helpful types, though we complain lucidly if you mistreat us. Also my Moon is in Gemini, so I might rattle on at length, hopping all over the place, but I hope you find it interesting!

Earth symbolises the physical body we live in as well as the planet we live on, and it also concerns our body's experience-gathering senses, the interface through which worldly experience comes to our awareness. Through our responses to this experience we act upon the objective situationality of our life and its circumstances. Lunar energy affects the states and moods influencing the relationship between these, and the way that we interact with, interpret and respond to situations as they arise, on an hourly and daily basis.

Just as the sun in the sky can be obscured by clouds, so the enactment of our life path can be obscured by the succession of intervening details and pressures we encounter daily – obstructions, chores, kids, money, ingrained habits, lunch-breaks, thoughts and flaps, obsessions, hiccups and all manner of diversions. Life becomes an interplay between getting our way (Sun), and accepting and handling (Moon) all that is straight in front of us (Earth). Our capacity to deal with these elastic interrelations greatly affects the success we make of our lives and the degree of happiness we derive from them.

Life is an interplay of creativity and receptivity, of solar and lunar power. Our challenge is to become clearer in working our way through this process. Easier said than done. Interestingly, since Sun and Moon appear to be the same size in our sky, so too, the little things of life, like feeling tired or hungry or needing a pee, sometimes look as big as life's greatest questions. If you really need a pee, it becomes top priority. But seen more objectively, from a distance, such little things aren't top priority. Try telling yourself that when you're desperate for a pee, though. Similarly, seen objectively from off-Earth, the Sun and Moon are definitely not the same size. But in our Earth's sky, they are the same.

The lunation cycle is thus an interactive cycle in which intentions and purposes, conscious and unconscious, meet up with evolving realities, particularly through the agency of our habitual and learned responses to life. When driving from A to B (pursuing an intent), you meet a herd of cows blocking the road (an objective fact), and your reactions to this situation might vary and also present choices to you. It could be treated as a comical quirk of fate and a minor annoyance, as a good opportunity to pause and relax or as a boring experience, an outrageous imposition, or even cause for a heart attack. Take your pick! The cows were simply *there*, and our power to handle that fact presents us with choices.

These reactions will, more often than not, be influenced by past experiences, memory of which is prompted by specific circumstances arising in life. Our deep memory stores these impressions, tapes and programs, serving them up in spoonfuls during the day and bringing with them associations and feelings that might actually have little or no direct relation to the situation at hand. Our responses and the 'stuff' they bring up present us with choice, whether or not we exercise such choice. This is free-will: it's not so much a *wanting* thing as a matter of *response* and staying tuned to our purpose in life, as it manifests that day.

Cycle Riding – *le Tour de Chance*

The lunation cycle (the cycle of phases) lasts 29 days and around 12 hours. Each cycle begins at newmoon when the Moon is invisible, in the same place as the Sun in the sky. Its sunlit side is facing away from us and also, being up in the sky in daytime, it's invisible. (Theoretically we could see some reflected Earth-light, from the light emitted by Earth's clouds, but daylight prevents this). Occasionally, the Moon's and Sun's positions are so accurately aligned that the Moon passes in front of the Sun, causing a solar eclipse.

The lunation cycle reaches a climax at fullmoon, half-way through the cycle, when the Moon has moved to the opposite side of the Earth from the Sun. At this time, when the Sun sets, the Moon will rise – but only at fullmoon. If the alignment of Sun, Earth and Moon is exact, we see an eclipse of the Moon in which the Earth's shadow passes over the Moon.

Each lunation cycle, of which there are 12-13 in a year and about 125 in a decade, has its own story to tell, its own issues that are featured and explored. If a year is a chapter of life, then the lunations in a year mark the subheadings and sections of the chapter.

Each lunation is flavoured according to the sign in which the opening newmoon takes place. When the newmoon is in Capricorn, the whole lunation will be involved with Capricornian kinds of issues, even if the Sun moves into Aquarius part way through the cycle. Such a lunation starting in Capricorn will underlyingly concern issues of realism, organisation, tradition, social roles, obligations, routines and practicalities.

This will shift at the next newmoon, in Aquarius (when the Chinese have their New Year – quite a good time for it). During this Aquarian lunation the issues concern making circumstances different and trying to shake them around, while still feeling embedded in them. The emphasis is on the future and how to loosen up old routines or resolve unchanging situations. Sometimes things do need changing and at other times we need simply to consider change, even if we realise that things are alright as they are.

It is valuable to clue into the under-the-surface themes in each cycle. Retrospectively seen, these are usually quite simple and straightforward, taking us through learning processes or developments while revealing to us different facets of the same question. But at the time the lesson can be more tricky to discern. If the cycle is, for example, about working hard, then sometimes the experience will be joyous, sometimes productive, and at other times a bane and a labour, all in the same cycle, revealing to us facets of that aspect of life called 'work'.

During each cycle of lunar phases, all sorts of ins and outs are there to be investigated – they constitute oscillations and wobbles around an emergent life-question. It is as if we were circumambulating the question at hand, seeing it from differing viewpoints, problematic one day, pleasant and hopeful the next, as a future potential and then as an established past fact, dull then colourful, rough and then smooth.

If you observe how your standpoints change during the course of a lunation, you'll see more clearly what the underlying, abiding question is about. For life is not only about what is happening to us – it also concerns how we internally experience and respond to it. Our initial instinctive or conditioned responses might be different from our later considered responses: the salient question is whether we acknowledge and take charge of our patterns, or whether we blame life, others, God or, guiltily, ourselves, for what's going on.

The four quarter phases of the Moon (newmoon, halfmoons and fullmoon) particularly test our fundamental sense of okayness with life-as-it-is: they are crisis points, marked in most diaries, and they are worth watching. Watching them, we can observe ourselves and gain insights into how to reduce all this rather exhausting internal rhetoric, chatter and turbulence that we plague ourselves with on a daily basis.

Hemicycles

A lunation has two main halves or *hemicycles*. In the first or *waxing* hemicycle, when the Moon moves from new and dark toward full and bright, the future is being opened up and potentials are being explored – something new is growing. In the *waning* hemicycle after fullmoon, where the Moon grows thinner and eventually disappears, the consequences are being worked on and we consolidate and integrate the outcomes of whatever was achieved, or not achieved, around fullmoon. As the cycle closes, the seeds of the next cycle lie under the surface waiting or germinating, hatching at the newmoon or after it.

When the Moon waxes, new possibilities, scenarios, life-tracks and situations emerge. When it wanes, already-established forms and arrangements have to be lived with, utilised, made to work and consigned to posterity.

The Moon waxes after the newmoon and up to the fullmoon, moving ahead of the Sun in the sky – that is, to the left of the Sun when seen in the northern hemisphere, looking south. It starts as a crescent, growing to a halfmoon, then to a gibbous (fat) moon and finally becoming full, moving further away from the Sun each day. Since the Moon is about ½° wide, it moves about 25ish Moon-widths leftwards each day. This leads to a star-gazer's trick: look at the Moon and stick up your finger to compare their widths, and then you can roughly measure the positions of other planets or stars in the sky, using your finger.

When the Moon is full it is opposite the Sun. Therefore, on the Cancer newmoon both Sun and Moon are in Cancer, but at the following fullmoon the Sun will be in Cancer while the Moon will have moved forward to Capricorn, the opposite sign. Though sometimes, if the Sun has moved into Leo, the fullmoon will be in Aquarius.

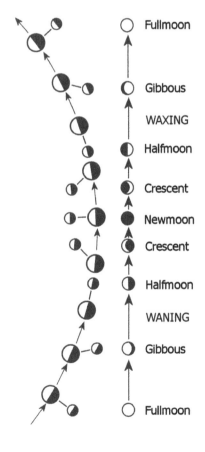

At fullmoon the Moon fully reflects the Sun's light. Its influence involves subtle energy as well as visible moonlight. You can *feel* this on fullmoons, particularly on the one-to-two days before exact fullmoon, especially when it is rising. The atmosphere is different on successive fullmoons, but there is an intensity and poignancy to fullmoons that is easy for anyone to perceive.

Moon wanes after fullmoon, rising later each night, gradually catching up with the Sun by the time of newmoon. In the meantime, while the Moon has moved all the way round the zodiac, the Sun will have moved through nearly one sign. The Moon moves approximately thirteen signs to catch the Sun.

The Sun has an annual cycle with twelve main shades to it, shown by its movement through the signs, each lasting roughly 30 days. Moon has its own zodiac cycle of 27⅓ days. Moon acts as an independent-but-related factor in bringing these two cycles together in the cycle of phases. Each successive time the Moon moves through

Taurus, or any other sign, it will be in a different lunar phase, owing to the Sun's own motion.

Similarly, newmoons and fullmoons wander in sequence from sign to sign, usually having one of each during the Sun's sojourn in each sign, but occasionally having either two newmoons or two fullmoons at the beginning and end of the same sign. Successive newmoons in the same sign (roughly a year apart) wander gradually backwards through the zodiac. This is a very organic cycle to visualise.

Lunar Energy

Tuning in to the Moon and its phases has great implications. It is not only a way to familiarise ourselves with lunations, cycles and the astrological language, but it can also facilitate significant changes in the way we handle life and feel about it. Lunar phases time and trigger the daily-life unfoldment of larger, longer changes. Things that last centuries still take place in events, decisions and situations that take place at particular moments. The fall of Rome in 410 had many and long causes, but there was a specific moment on a particular day when everyone there knew and had to accept that it was actually happening.

Consciously living in tune with lunar energy opens cracks between the worlds and new pathways through life's jungle. When it is time to act, act, and when it is time to lie low, lie low – this is the simple order of life, which hasn't changed since people like Lao Tzu wrote such advice 2,500 years ago. There's a certain energy-efficiency to it – we don't pit ourselves so much *against* the tidal flow of life, so more can be achieved.

In ancient times the Moon's light, nowadays outshone by street lights, played a big role in people's lives. It was easier to do things at night outdoors under a fullmoon, so people's activity-patterns would change with the Moon. In fact, many indigenous peoples don't think so much in terms of the waxing and waning Moon, but more in terms of the Bright Moon and the Dark Moon, between the halfmoons. It's not just an environmental influence the Moon exerts, in terms of light: it's an energy influence too, and you can feel it when out under the Moon. Moonlight affects hormonal and psycho-emotional issues to a much greater extent than modern society and its purveyors of official wisdom would accept. The Bright Moon was a time for activity and productivity and the Dark Moon was a time for cogitation and introspection – and it still is. It has simply become less conscious.

For women, awareness of lunations is important. There is a theory that, once upon a time, menstrual and lunation cycles were synchronised – women ovulated at fullmoons and menstruated at newmoons, and they were in more active, naturalesque connection than now with a deep feminine power. Whether or not this was true or generally the case, it's certainly true that, when women live closely together over time, their menstrual cycles tend to harmonise.

This lunar periodicity reflected a power amongst women to attune to their bodies, their hormones and psyches in a wavelike way which men do not experience in the same way. A Czech psychiatrist in the 1950s, Dr Eugen Jonas, studying fertility and contraception, defined a time he called the 'cosmic fertility period' when a woman had optimum reproductive potential if it coincided with her ovulatory time. This was an energy condition in a woman that gave her a certain subtle-electrical and hormonal receptivity that worked in a deeper way than physical ovulation-menstruation.

The cosmic fertility period was the time of the lunar month when the Moon was in the same phase as it was when a woman was born – so if you were born on the waning halfmoon, that's your cosmic fertility time, and when your ovulation coincides with it, make use of it or avoid it, depending on your preference. Using this method in combination with the customary rhythm method, his clinic achieved a 98.5% success rate in either preventing or producing conception amongst its clients. One of the reasons you probably haven't heard of this is that little money can be made out of it – drugs and IVF interventions are far more profitable, and medical intervention has achieved cult-like status.

Women were in bygone days more in tune with the natural, instinctual secret of their beings than many women are today, also asserting a stronger influence in the life of the human family and tribe. We will see a major world transformation when womankind regains this harmony – including hormonally – within herself and in society. It will involve social and cultural changes that have already started, though it's early days and historic in scope. It's not just about women getting jobs, gaining power and equality: it concerns the sensitisation and rebalancing of society in all its aspects. Becoming more aware of lunar energy and its modulations is one way this process will be helped. But that won't be very good for profit-making either.

Tracking lunations helps men to tune into their deeper sensitivities and their a-rational side, their innocence, humanness, naturalness and *anima*. A man in touch with his femininity expresses his manhood without feeling the need to be macho: his strength lies in his sensitivities and vulnerabilities, which attune him more clearly to his strength and courage, helping him lose his fear of weakness or personal insignificance. Macho men might feel they are strong and significant but actually they are trying to measure up to a conception of what they feel they ought to be – and at heart they aren't that. It's all a big cover-up and shut-off, a desperate attempt to prove that one isn't what one fears oneself to be. Without opening to the feminine, whether as a woman or a man, we do not properly receive what we need in life. We don't feel nourished, supported, at home, alright, a full member of humanity, here in the world. If one thing causes cancer, it's this.

Eclipses

When poring over an ephemeris (a book of astrological tables), keep your eyes peeled for eclipses. Only sometimes is an eclipse visible in the sky because it might be taking place under the Earth, or because it is not exact enough to be visible as an eclipse, or because the weather doesn't oblige. In a longish lifetime you might see but 3-5 total eclipses of the Sun and perhaps twentyish total eclipses of the Moon, though you'll see many more partial eclipses. That is, if you look.

Even if you don't see them you can *sense* them – there's a powerful stillness, sometimes eerie and rather magical, to an eclipse. Time warps and funny thoughts or situations can arise – sometimes rather oracular and significant. It's a time to treat specially, to pause for. Yes, go on, stop what you're doing, go out under the Moon, open your arms to it and let it clean your heart of worries and woes. And observe your thoughts and feelings and what comes up inside you – they mean something.

The Moon is eclipsed only at fullmoons (when Earth's shadow falls on the Moon, lasting up to 1 hour and 20 minutes). The Sun is eclipsed only at newmoon (when the Moon passes in front of the Sun, lasting up to 8 minutes, and throwing a dark shadow on certain parts of the Earth but not all of it).

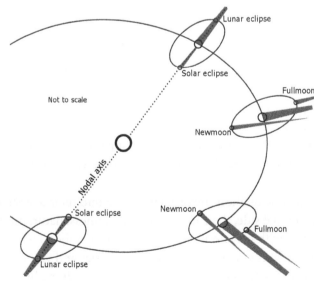

Lunar eclipse

Solar eclipse

Fullmoon

Not to scale

Newmoon

Nodal axis

Solar eclipse

Newmoon

Fullmoon

Lunar eclipse

A solar eclipse is a rarer occurrence than a lunar eclipse because, to be total or even noticeable, the positioning of Sun, Moon and Earth need to be more exact than is the case with a lunar eclipse. The shadow of the Earth on the Moon, which causes a lunar eclipse, is wider than the diameter of the Moon. Not least because Earth, casting its shadow, is bigger than the Moon.

When you're watching a total lunar eclipse, you're watching the progression of a complete cycle of lunar phases in just over one hour, starting and ending at fullmoon. That is, a bite is taken out of the fullmoon which eventually covers it and makes it go dark. Eventually a crescent appears, turning gradually to full again. It's very moving to watch *and feel*. It takes only a short time but often it feels far longer. It's a moment when time expands, and whatever thoughts or experiences you have at that time can be significant and oracular, suggesting the way things truly are, or how they could be.

Only sometimes are eclipses exact or 'total' – and it also depends on where on Earth you're standing, whether it's total where you are. This matters particularly with solar eclipses. If they are 'partial' or less exact, you might see a bite taken out of the Sun on a solar eclipse or out of the Moon on a lunar eclipse, but it doesn't go completely dark. With some partial eclipses of the Moon, the Moon just reddens or dims without going dark, because only the Earth's penumbra, or side-shadow, is covering it because the alignment is not quite exact. Then there are 'annular' eclipses, where the Moon is far from the Earth (at apogee) and thus smaller than the Sun, never fully covering it in a solar eclipse.

Eclipses are extraordinary newmoons or fullmoons that can prove to be major turning-points. Around the time of an eclipse, a pensive, lurking, becalmed quality pervades the airwaves, as if everything is waiting for something. Birds return to their nests. Water surfaces or ocean waves can go still – or if they don't, an uncanny timelessness can still make it very atmospheric. An eerie quietness pervades, even amidst chaos or activity. There's a kind of empty feeling, or one of noticeable peace. It's not exactly the Moon or Sun doing this directly: it's the way they affect the resonance-field of the Earth, within which we live and have our being.

Eclipses take place when the Moon and Sun conjunct or oppose one another close to what are called the *Moon's Nodes*. These are theoretical points out in space where the Moon's plane of orbit around the Earth intersects the Earth's plane of orbit around the Sun – these planes are 5° different in inclination, intersecting at the axis of the nodes. The nodes are a nexus-point connecting the Sun and Moon. At one end of the nodal axis is the north node, where the Moon's plane of motion is moving north across the ecliptic, and at the other end is the south node where it is moving south – and the two nodes are exactly opposite one another. They are traditionally known as the Dragon's Head (north node) or the Dragon's Tail (south node).

The nodes move slowly backwards (retrograde) through the zodiac, making a complete cycle every 18.6 years. This is called a *draconic cycle* which the ancients regarded as very significant, to the extent that they built stone circles and other edifices to calculate, mark and predict them, or to emulate them. Many stone circles in Britain have 19 stones, reflecting this. The draconic or nodal cycle was a time-period spanning one human generation, in a time when mothers frequently gave birth in their mid-to-late teenage years. People who felt that the souls of the ancestors lived on through the living, and who had a strong sense of longterm timing spanning generations or incarnations, counted the draconic cycle carefully.

In August 1999 I participated in an outdoor camp under an exact solar eclipse in Cornwall, UK. There were various earth-energy dowsers present and they conducted an experiment, mapping out the energy lines in the vicinity before the eclipse. Then when it happened – it was surprising how quickly the light went down as the Moon's shadow fell over us – they found that these lines literally rolled up and disappeared temporarily, restoring themselves when the light came back. It was as if the earth-energy system of the Earth in that locality was re-booting itself. It's possible that this happens to an extent globally, though perhaps less than in the locality where the eclipse exactly falls. We could not track that, of course.

Eclipses take place at two opposite periods of the year when newmoons or fullmoons are near the nodes, wherever the nodes are at the time. Most of these eclipses are partial and inexact, but some are total, and usually there will be a newmoon solar and a fullmoon lunar eclipse – though on some occasions there might be three, the middle one being total or close to it. The position of eclipses moves slowly backwards with the nodal axis on its 18.6 year cycle.

When an eclipse occurs within a degree or two of one of the two nodes, it will be a total or near-total eclipse, somewhere in the world. Most eclipses are partial or annular eclipses, some of them hardly visible and inexact – they occur several degrees away from the nodal axis. If the node is at 15° Aquarius and a newmoon is at 2° Aquarius, it will be a hardly-visible partial eclipse. If the node is at 15° and the newmoon at 14° it's pretty exact and total or almost so – it might have a narrow, bright band of sunlight at one side rather than going total. And it depends on where in the world you're observing it from.

There is also an eclipse *period*, between these eclipses, two weeks apart. This can lead to a period of two weeks or, occasionally, one lunar month, where things go critical and funny things can happen – it's a rather weird period when life's roulette-wheel spins a bit crazily. It can be visible in world events, or in our personal lives or those of people around us. It can be a slightly creepy, unusual and pattern-setting, rather decisive period.

Different zodiac signs get singled out and featured by an eclipse – in the case of lunar eclipses, two opposite signs are featured but in solar eclipses it is one. Opposite signs work with the same basic question from two different sides of the same coin. Lunar eclipses bring out the contradictions and contrasts in opposite signs. If, for example, the Sun is in Aries and the Moon in Libra, there is a tension between self-interest and mutual benefit, between 'my way' and 'our shared interests'. On a spiritual-psychological level, eclipses require resolution of conflicts into harmony, or they can bring a big contextual shift where everything suddenly looks different even if little has changed.

Try to observe the energy-weather at eclipses. They are awe-inspiring times when it can be auspicious to get clear on intents, perspectives and deep choices. It can be timely to cross watersheds or make a significant shift. It's a propitious and ominous time. These are excellent times for ceremonies and meditations, or for pausing and dwelling on matters that lie outside time and circumstance.

Lunar Maxima and Minima

Returning to the draconic or nodal cycle, we come to the major and minor standstills of the Moon, or the lunar maxima and minima. These are important in stone circles and ancient sites: many alignments of stones point to the rising or setting points of the Moon at its major or minor standstill. The major standstill or lunar maximum takes place when the north node is at the spring equinox point or 0° Aries, and the minor standstill or lunar minimum takes place nine years later when the north node is at the autumn equinox point, or 0° Libra. This is a little complex, and you don't have to remember it! Current lunar maxima are in June 2006, January 2025 and August 2043, and minima are in November 2015, June 2034 and December 2052.

The significance of this is that, at the major standstill, when the Moon is around the summer solstice point in the zodiac, at 0° Cancer, it is 5° higher in the sky than the highest point that the Sun reaches in the sky at summer solstice. When at 0° Capricorn, on the other side of the zodiac, it is 5° lower than the Sun at its lowest point in the sky at winter solstice. At the minor standstill this emphasis and variation of height in the sky is minimal. At times of the major standstill the Moon's influences are more extreme than at the minor standstill, and the ancients considered this to be significant.

So much so that there are two major stone circles in Scotland, one at Callanish on the Hebridean Isle of Lewis, and the other at the Ring of Brogar in the Orkney Isles. What's special here? Well, when the Moon is at its major standstill – highest in the sky – it is seen to skim the northern horizon without setting. This is a sea horizon, so it's impressive. It's rather like the midnight sun further north, except that this pertains to the Moon. The midnight sun happens at latitudes over 66°N, but at lunar maximum the non-setting Moon can be seen from 60°N, the latitude of Callanish and Brogar. This is particularly marked when the fullmoon is at the end of Gemini or in early Cancer, around winter solstice at the time of the lunar maximum. This makes for super-solstices where you get a solstice close to a fullmoon at lunar maximum – and they can be quite momentous. In ancient times that called for a major gathering of the clans.

To add an extra twist to the saga of the Moon, whenever the Moon (or Sun) is on the horizon, a quirk of refraction or bending of light across the surface of the Earth makes them look larger than they actually are – they're magnified as they rise or set. This will be emphasised even more when the Moon is in perigee, larger and closer than usual. There's another twist too: the bending of the light means that, when the Sun or Moon have their lower side touching the horizon, they are actually already just below the horizon, because of the bending of light. So at the specific time of the lunar maximum and fullmoon at winter solstice, the Moon is large when on the horizon, and it skims the northern horizon at these two stone circles, showing itself at super-large size – and this happens only once every 18.6 years. Neat, huh?

Void Moons

One more detail: void-of-course moons. These are a little obscure and arcane, but well worth being aware of. A void-of-course moon is a short period of minutes or hours, though occasionally a day or more, when things can go rather odd, sometimes disjunctive or rather flat. This is not necessarily bad unless you make it so.

The Moon is void during the short period between its last major aspect (or angle formed) to another planet, and its crossing into a new sign (an ingress). Since the

Moon changes sign every 2⅓ days, voids happen regularly, often passing quickly in minutes or an hour or two but sometimes they're longer. In some ephemerides there are special tables showing the times of last aspects and subsequent ingresses, and on some computer programs void Moon periods are shown.

What's special about void Moons? Well, things don't go according to plan, so the pursuit of plans or the starting of something new is likely to go awry somehow. There can be a strange atmosphere of pointlessness, vacuity, directionlessness, lack of connection and things simply going amiss and astray. What to do about it? Let things be and allow things to take their course. Stay in the moment and do whatever you feel like at the time. Or don't do anything. Take this approach and things are fine, sometimes interesting, and magic can happen. Or you just get a short break from normality.

A void is a minor incursion of the unknown. If you try to make things happen in the normal way, they generally won't work, or work as planned, so there's little point trying. You'll just get a puncture, find yourself stuck in a traffic jam, the person won't be there, you lose your shopping list, or misunderstandings might arise. Things go wobbly or flat and there's little you can do except relax and go with it. A time will come when things start up again when the ingress of the Moon into a new sign takes place, often after just a few hours. However, although void moons are inauspicious times for starting new things, if you've already started things they might well continue well enough as long as you don't try to push the river. Just let things unfold as they will.

Void moons can be a gift in disguise. Sometimes it's not best for things to go according to plan because plans can exclude chunks of reality that are very important, or your plans might be inappropriate. Sometimes the Unknown interjects possibilities or solutions we didn't know we needed or we didn't know could happen. Perhaps you had an appointment and you were late, so you struggled to get there on time, and then you find that the person you were going to meet is not there either. So you wasted your time, possibly getting frustrated in the process. The other person might have done so too! If the Moon is void, it's also void for others. So relax, it's okay, something will work out. To end this story, you went to a cafe after the missed appointment and came upon another person instead, who later on offered you a new job, out of the blue. So if the mishap hadn't happened, that opportunity wouldn't have arisen. Magic! The lesson: in life, be prepared to bend or suspend your plans.

It's worth noting void moons, especially when they are longer in duration. How can you tell whether they'll be longer? Well, sometimes all of the other planets are located early on in their respective signs, which means that the last aspect formed can take place when the Moon is only at, say, 12° or 15° of a sign. This means that it could take a whole day for the Moon to travel the remaining 15-18° before it changes sign. This is a long void. Most times, voids aren't so long in duration – often they're just a couple of hours long. But even though a void might be short, it's worth noting because, if you have a journey to make or an activity to start, waiting an hour or two until the void moon is over might actually make it quicker and easier. The bus might well have been late anyway.

So...

Studying the Moon and its motions is very valuable. That's how I first learned astrology, as a young man on a quest in the early 1970s: I had a copy of *Raphael's Ephemeris* and consulted it regularly, noticing times when planets changed signs, when aspects were formed and how patterns emerged. This coincided with a time of self-examination and pondering the secrets of life, after having gone through an intense period of momentous events (flower power in Liverpool and London, and the LSE student 'troubles').

Interestingly, my learning of astrology took place in a rainy mountain area in Wales where the heavens were only occasionally visible and long rainy days were spent indoors, studying. This attuned me to the interiority of the energies of the Sun, Moon and planets, the inner feeling of them, based on inner observation and mindfulness rather than book definitions or courses.

Thanks to the speed and regularity of the Moon's antics it is particularly useful to work with. It's a matter of bringing instinctive lunar knowings, often exhibited through our unconscious behaviour, into consciousness. Unconscious behaviours are very much tied up with the Moon. Moving into phase with the Moon is all about timing our actions and following our feelings more awarely than we normally do.

In the next chapter we shall go through a complete cycle of the Moon.

3

Lunations

Here we shall look at the way the lunation cycle works by tracking a complete cycle of the Moon's phases. In doing so, you'll also be introduced to the sequence and structure of astrological cycles in general. This is covered later in the book too because it's really important to an understanding of living in time.

Keeping Track

Soli-lunar panegyrations are best followed by using the astrologers' holy book, an *ephemeris* or book of tables of planetary motions. There are also computer programs and phone apps that show moonphases, while others give the astrological chart and positions for the current moment. Although such software exists, it's still worth having a book, for easy reference. Look in the Appendix for a lowdown on ephemerides and software usage.

Spending time outdoors, keeping an eye on the heavens, observing the rising and setting of the Sun and Moon and noting the changing moonphases is the way that most people in history have learned about the Moon. Ancients and medieval astronomers kept careful tallies of time to keep track, but now we have books and digital gizmos available, giving exact readings. Something has been lost and something gained.

To start with, watch what goes on in your life around the new and full moons. Since there's a lot to absorb in astrology, the best way to deal with it is to be selective about what you focus on, and stick to the basics first. Diaries often give the dates of newmoons and fullmoons but ephemerides are better, giving a more exact time and the zodiacal positions too. Observe what goes on within you and around you. Seek not to form judgements or conclusions: simply *watch*, take note and pick up experience. Notice how, around these times, the atmosphere changes and things move on from where they were before.

We need to open up a gut-level instinctual *feel* for life, in a part of us where thoughts and learned information play little part. Animals have it and so do we, but it gets socialised and educated out of us. Sleep with your curtains open if you can, to let the Moon shine in. If you live in a place flooded with street lights, give some consideration to what you might do about that in the longterm, if you can. Getting closer to nature isn't just a romantic ideal: it is central to life and to getting things in the right proportions.

While observing what happens around newmoons and fullmoons, watch your reactions to life situations around those times – resistance, acceptance, control agendas and relaxation of them, efforts, ideas, hopes, fears and inspirations. Watch your physical energy-levels. It might be worth keeping notes on your observations: if you get snuffles, an uncomfortable stomach, a tic or an ache, note it down – and also note when such things disappear.

Note the ever-changing paradox between what you seek to create and what actually happens. Note the ways you deal with this at different times and the choices you make. Take a look at nature, especially at everything related to water – clouds, rain, water flows, groundwater levels, tides, plant growth and water within your own body. Observe changes in weather-patterns, the activities of animals, the feeling in the air.

The Sun brings warmth and the fluxing of the seasons but the Moon regulates the medium of water and the way it affects temperature, humidity, weather, growth and decay. Water is a carrier of memory, a conductor and a transmitter of subtle energy, and its tides and changes are meaningful.

The Moon times the development of seasonal changes induced by the Sun – just watch the blooming of flowers, the falling of leaves or other natural signs and omens and you will notice it. Watch road traffic, listen to ambient noise levels, watch the behaviour of crowds and of children, observe the people on the bus, the spiders in your house, the house-plants, the football on TV, your patterns of sleep, patterns of thought and the phases in your relationships with others.

When you have had a taste of what fullmoons and newmoons are about, look into the two halfmoons and, after that, expand your observations to the whole lunation cycle. Give it a year – it's worth it. This should be a standard part of life-training for 15 year olds in school, to help us become more of a fully-fledged human. Since the Moon moves quite fast, you don't have to wait long to experience a whole cycle and its sequence of stages. In one year of observation you'll have tracked thirteen lunar cycles. As time goes on you'll find that something in your body-consciousness starts moving into greater harmony, giving you more reliable messages – messages your brains wouldn't see.

The lunation cycle is a goodly potted cycle to observe, for it is rapid and repeating, thus illustrating how other astrological cycles work. It will also attune you to other planets, since a Moon conjunct Venus is quite different in feeling to a Moon conjunct Saturn. While no two lunations are the same, there is an underlying pattern to all lunations and all cycles, and there is also a pattern of responses within you to them and to their unfoldment.

The Lunation Cycle in detail

Now we shall trace the lunation cycle sequentially. Try to observe these stages at work on a daily basis, using your life and your surroundings as the material with which to learn how to move more in tune with lunations.

NEWMOON (☽☌☉). When the Sun and Moon conjunct, an old cycle ends and a new one begins. The Moon is invisible at this time, being in the sky with Sun at daytime and under the horizon at night, with its dark side facing us (the Sun's light is on the other side because the Moon is sitting between Sun and Earth). The new time-cycle starts with a feeling of possibility, openness, expectancy or perhaps just quietness, depending on what's been happening thus far: here we stand, just *being*, and little can be done to change the past yet the future is not started either. A page is turning and there is no writing visible yet – unless perhaps it's a summary of the former chapter or a set of ideas and intents for the next one. In this sense of beingness lie the seeds of the new.

Starting or planning new activities is auspicious, now or soon. If there's no plan, then it helps to be receptive to possibilities. Or perhaps it's good to review your parameters, what's acceptable and what's not. Having a plan isn't essential but, whatever is going on for you, it's worth understanding that you're entering a four-week cycle of unfoldment. Rumination, resting before activity, starting over, preparation of the ground or catering for eventualities are the keynote here. Or it might be time simply just to *be*, reclaiming ourselves, releasing our addictive attachment to finding reasons, making plans and lists and to compulsive activity. Energy can sometimes be low at newmoon or occasionally zippy and charged with potency: after observing a few newmoons you will notice their characteristic flavour. As with turnings of the tide, nothing much necessarily happens, but it's nevertheless an important time.

The sign in which the newmoon takes place is worth looking at, for both Moon and Sun are at that moment illuminating this sign. Sometimes we can feel void and vulnerable, sometimes we are raring to go, and sometimes it's simply time to get on with what's in front of us: either way, what starts now reaches a climax in two weeks' time at fullmoon. What begins as a potential seeks to become actual.

What comes from me-in-here must connect with that-out-there during the waxing hemicycle over the next fortnight. The newmoon period lasts two days either side of the exact newmoon conjunction, and although there is a shift from the past to the present or the future around the precise newmoon, the whole period is one of being with what's here, with what we have. It's a time of transition into a new storyline or a new quirk or twist in an existing story.

WAXING CRESCENT MOON (☽⊻☉). Two days after the exact newmoon, the crescent Moon becomes visible westwards around sundown – it is 30° or semisextile to the Sun. Possibilities are beginning to take shape and the way becomes a little clearer. Details emerge to give shape to the future. The theme here is the fleshing-out of potential and the emergence of threads of possibility. A roadmap emerges or possibilities present themselves – some of them will work out, some will work out differently and others will fall by the wayside, yet things are beginning to move.

On the third day after exact newmoon, when the Moon forms a 45° or semisquare angle to the Sun (☽∠☉) and it's a fatter crescent, some choices need to be made. Potentiality is moving into activity and things must be sorted out, narrowed down, decided and committed to. This can arise from a sense of urgency or imperative within or it can be prompted by events, or both. Developing avenues of possibility might be attractive or something to fight against, or somewhere in between, but an affirmation of intent must now be made in order to set some definite tracks for the future.

Wilder, vaguer or unrealisable possibilities need to be weeded out, plans need modifying and things need clarifying with the further future in mind. Get clear, for decisions are needed if things are to take off. Or perhaps circumstances are steering things in what seems like the wrong direction and you need to react to that. Devise a plan or make necessary adjustments right now, to match current emergent facts with your longterm aim, or to amend your thoughts to reflect the way that things seem to be going.

Four days after newmoon, when the Moon is 60°, or sextile from the Sun (☽✶☉), things are by now moving, developing and gathering momentum. We're either getting closer to where we need to go or developments are happening to which we must respond – depending on how much we are the active or the passive ingredient in life at this time. New factors enter the calculus that weren't there before. Things develop and flourish, or the pace accelerates, sometimes flowingly, sometimes too much. This phase, when the Moon sets later and later after the Sun, is fruitful, even frenetically productive, and much is afoot. Possibilities widen or become more tangible, and the enjoyment of progress can make this time rewarding. Or perhaps it's just really busy. But there's still some way to go. The story is developing – carry on, just do it.

WAXING HALFMOON. Seven or so days after the exact newmoon, the Moon forms a 90° angle to Sun, called a square (☽□☉). Now she sails high in the sky as the Sun sets, rising around noon and setting around midnight. At halfmoon we must really do something to make things work. We must apply ourselves, make choices and face facts. Either this, or we must accept that some things aren't working and should be changed or discarded in favour of what does work – otherwise life's evolving circumstances and other people will make the decisions for us. Decisive, pattern-setting events can impact on us here. Or we cross a big hump. Or it's simply a matter of facing obstacles, problems and challenges – getting the difficult stuff over with, since now is the time.

We don't have far-sighted vision at this stage – the time for this has passed – and we must simply get on with what's straight in front of us, yelling for attention. We must do what we know we must do, dealing with the facts or acting to save the day. Everything has been set up and we just have to do it, moving into a new stage and making a further commitment of energy, resources, promises or time. We have to sign on the dotted line, place our cards on the table. Things have taken shape, the down-payment is paid, there are no refunds and there's no turning back. New elements or old problems can surface, requiring attention. Stuff must be done, or sometimes it's just a matter of making the best out of a tricky situation.

Imperatives and realities drive things here. It's time for work or taking steps, overcoming blockages, making things move and squaring up. Here arises a big question: are we doing life or is life doing us? The halfmoon period lasts one day either side of the exact 90° aspect, and much can be achieved at this time. It's just a matter of digging that hole, clearing the rubbish, sorting out the papers and paying the bills, in order for the next stages to be enabled. A transition is happening between a subjective, what-I-want-out-of-life viewpoint, and an objective, what-life-will-actually-accommodate reality. We must board the train, fix the car, have that difficult conversation, climb the hill, face the music and do the business.

WAXING GIBBOUS MOON. If the halfmoon slammed us when we weren't looking, then during the next few days we get over it and deal with the consequences. If on the other hand we used the halfmoon to jump through the hoops, then the momentum gathered is running in our favour now. Two days after halfmoon, the Moon and Sun form a 120° or trine angle (☽△☉), and things progress well, running along lines that by now have been established. It's not necessary to push things, since momentum has been achieved – it's more a matter of going along with what's unfolding. This can be creative and industrious, or it can be like a day off, a relaxation, or it can be a simple continuation of developments, which we just need to keep going with.

This is a space for creative input, reflection or simply allowing things to unfold as they will. The possibilities and implications are widening. Life is lighter if we grappled well with our issues at halfmoon. If we didn't, the trine can take on something of a void or sluggish, droopy flavour, though not necessarily a crisis. Wider perspectives can regain ground and fun is possible, or time drags and it's a waiting game. If action is what you seek now, this is not a time for changing course: it's for carrying on with what has been established and letting it flesh itself out. Things connect and progress here if we *allow* them to move forward, helping them on their way, but they don't necessarily work if we try to push and mould them. It's a time of progress, with a fair wind in our sails and an even pathway to follow. Or it's a time to let things unfold and develop of their own accord.

The Moon is now growing larger. When it is 135° (or sesquiquadrate) from the Sun (☽⚼☉), 10-11 days after newmoon and three days before fullmoon, a realignment and re-prioritisation is needed, with the longterm in mind. It's not just the next horizon that is important, but the one after that and the overall direction of travel. We need to consider the patterns being set here. A sharp-edged, busy, compelling situation can oblige us to square the current facts with our overall aims and to adjust either. Unworkable intentions should be honed or dropped, and doable developments should be fine-tuned, worked on or supported. Here our personal dreams and schemes meet the world *as is*, and a reality-jousting occurs. This is a good time for letting go of preconceptions, re-positioning ourselves and making ready for further developments. The gears are grinding, the stuff is happening, and we must carry through our foregoing commitments to make sure the sought-after results happen as well as they can. The fullmoon period is building up, and an energetic tension is growing.

FULLMOON. The fullmoon period lasts four days, two days before and two days after the time of the exact opposition of the Moon to the Sun (☽☍☉, 180°). In this case, the Earth stands between the Moon and the Sun, so the light side of the Moon is fully visible to us. The fullmoon period starts when Moon and Sun are at quincunx or 150° from each other (☽⚻☉), when the Moon is almost full but not quite, rising before sundown.

Here at the quincunx we get a crisis of perspective. Things take on a different light and context. After all that has happened thus far, it can feel as if we no longer know what we are doing and why – we're just carrying on with what we started. Or perhaps we do know what we're doing but everything looks and feels rather different to what we thought it would. So the job interview was good, but now you must wait for the results and think through what might actually happen if you get it, or if you don't. At this stage we must stand by what we have created and do the business as well as possible, for the stage is set, the lights are up and everything hangs on what happens next. Whatever we feel about things, it's too late to change anything much.

If we are unsure what we are doing or why, we might feel rather empty, lost or disoriented. If we are hanging on to fixed ideas they can come into question or be overwhelmed by developments. If we play things by ear, staying clear about our priorities and intent, things can come to a head and the next few days are crucial. The pre-fullmoon period can be a time of intense suspended animation or of frantic activity, sometimes with tension. The world can quiver and zizzle as the energy-cycle climaxes. It is a time for letting go, suspending judgements and dropping stances. It's necessary to accept emergent facts and do our best with them. The truth will out, and the issue here is to face the reality that has emerged, as it is presenting itself at fullmoon.

The fullmoon itself can sometimes be electric, zingly. At times it can be riddled with contradiction and paradox, at times highly-strung and complex, and at times calmly, quietly potent, pregnantly still. Things *happen* at fullmoon, bubbling over. Or they collapse. Or they shift into something else. At the exact fullmoon there is an energy-change and perspective-flip which can create a remarkably different situation – although the difference is often in our feelings and perceptions. Sometimes things turn inside-out, sometimes they break through and sometimes they grind to a halt and we're left standing, wondering what's next.

At fullmoon the Moon rises as the Sun sets, and moonrises at this time can sometimes be edgy, intense or headachey until it swings above the horizon. Sometimes the wind switches direction or the weather can change, or animals pursue strange antics, or things go very quiet. This is often a busy time for ambulance drivers and crisis counsellors. After fullmoon, what was high energy can fall flat, or subdued energy can erupt or explode. New elements can suddenly appear. Sometimes a sense of clarity can lapse into dreaminess or emptiness, or sometimes confusion and nonplussment can move into profound understanding.

Tradition has it that the Buddha attained enlightenment on the fullmoon. The story goes that he did it by breaking his ascetic religious rules, accepting some milk to drink from a passing maiden whom he first thought was there to lead him off track – but the milk gave him new strength to make the final step.

Fullmoon is a prime time for inner breakthrough and growth, facing what's in existence and what's for real, letting go of old hangups, accepting life and generally sorting out our relationship with others and the world around. It is a time of revelation and truth. Be aware of your reactions and reactivity around fullmoons, and ask yourself whether they are truly appropriate or helpful.

This is the climax of the lunation cycle. It starts a new hemicycle in which contexts, outcomes, results and effects matter. We move from a future orientation to a position where we're sorting out the outcomes of what has happened. At fullmoon, Sun and Moon are in opposite signs, and they contrapose the messages of those two signs in a dynamic paradox: the question is, how do we get the contrasting elements of these signs to work together?

The waxing hemicycle was dedicated to exploration, opening channels, manifesting intents and establishing a new position. The waning moon now asks us to complete the course, making things more sound and useful in a larger context. In the waning hemicycle we're giving what we have done to the world, to posterity. We are asked to make things last, to finish what has been started, to derive the benefits we deserve or contribute what we now must. If we have omitted or failed to develop a situation, a contribution, a statement, or if we have not taken responsibility for what has been unfolding, then the waning Moon can be a period when things go rather slack, or the ways of the world take us over, and we must to some extent follow along and learn from the outcomes we have created. If we have in some way succeeded during the waxing moon, it's a matter of making these outcomes really work and serve their larger purpose.

The fullmoon period lasts until Moon and Sun are again 150° apart two days later, in a waning quincunx aspect (☽⚻☉). But now the Moon is on the home stretch. Its light is beginning to wane and it rises later after sunset each evening. During the two post-fullmoon days before the waning quincunx we digest the impact of the fullmoon and prepare to move on with the outcomes we have created. The deed is done, and now for the next bit.

This is a time of new understanding and perspective, of lessons learned and new orientations. It's a bit like a period of post-coital bliss or regret, a glow or a shadow, setting the tracks for the coming hemicycle. At the end of this period, it's often quite clear what we next must do. Alternatively, we might feel lost and dissipated, awaiting our fate. It all depends on how we have created our realities and how things actually went. But at this phase, it's the world's response to our waxing-moon initiatives and imperatives which is most critical. So you might have built a house, painted a picture or achieved a goal, but what are you going to do with it now, and how will the world respond?

WANING GIBBOUS MOON, otherwise known as the Disseminating Moon. When the Moon is 135° away from Sun (☽⚹☉), three days after exact fullmoon, the world wants something of us or offers something to us, and it's time to get into gear, get down on it and follow through on what has been set up. Winning or losing battles is one thing, and what happens after that is another. Life is something of an ongoing pyrrhic victory – a success with a price attached. We must live with what's happened and make the best of it, fixing up what needs to be done next because the world is waiting for it and the consequences we've created need dealing with.

Here the social contract is signed and we become engaged with wider obligations and things we hadn't thought of or seen before. If we cannot carry things through, or if we don't like what's on offer, we might feel adrift, excluded from life, off-beam, or perhaps we feel like victims of others' demands. If we thought ahead during the waxing hemicycle and are ready for the next bit, it's now time to act on it. We are all a part of each other and everything is interdependent: we are needed. To some extent we're chess-pieces in a larger game, the overall meaning of which we gain only glimpses of.

On the fourth/fifth day after fullmoon, when the Moon moves into a waning 120° angle to the Sun (☽△☉), things move into an easier, more relaxed mood, or they might be moving quite fast as if carried along by a current. Space opens out to allow new meaning, new contacts and new creativity, adding to what's already there. It's all happening, and what became a reality at fullmoon is now unfolding, developing, propagating and becoming something much more. It has a life of its own. It's a matter of making use of the situation or helping it along. There's a breeze in our sails and distance can be covered. This can be a fulfilling time when the fruits of our efforts are showing themselves and having an effect. Either that, or if we missed the bus, things can be pretty flat and we just have to serve time until the next bus comes.

During the waning hemicycle the world affects us and our relations with the wider world take on new significance – we belong or we don't, and at this stage this is largely others' choice. What we have brought into being is now part of the world. It's time to catch up on things that have fallen behind or to follow along with whatever is happening. Having painted your painting, this is the time when a buyer comes along to view it. Having moved into your new house and finished the decorating, it's time to live the life the house was built for – with all that that entails. We're dealing here with the fruits of all that has developed – they're ripening and things are looking good. Either that, or we're stuck with the consequences of what we've created and we just have to live with them, this time around.

WANING HALFMOON. The halfmoon period (☽□☉) lasts one day either side of the exact halfmoon, and the Moon rises around midnight. This is a time to stand by our agreements, square with the world, do our duty and fulfil our promises whether we like it or not, carrying out our side of the bargain in hope, trust or knowledge that others will do their side. It's all about contractual obligations: by this time, we might or might not feel like doing what we signed up for, but we must do it anyway. Everyone is waiting for it and there's a deadline, with specifications to fulfil. Halfmoon brings a need to focus energy on the task at hand or, if we avoid or miss this, it brings a crunch where life sooner or later confronts us with our true assets and failings.

This can mean things going 'right' and progress being made, or it can mean things going 'wrong', where obstacles create problems, things become turgid or an uphill grind, or they fail to work out, or they turn out differently to what we expected. We finally make the sale or complete the project, or not, as the case may be, and now it's a matter of seeing what results from it all. We're faced with the truth of how we fit with the world and we're shown the outcomes of our actions, sometimes rewardingly, sometimes harshly or burdensomely.

The roulette wheel is spinning – we've had our chance and the world is giving its judgement. Does your painting get sold or not, and will the cheque they paid actually clear? What is done has been done, and the matter is sealed. At the waning halfmoon, the past is beginning to end and a glimmer of the future is latently beginning to brew: in the involvements of the moment, with their lessons and outcomes, new potential emerges for future attention. It's time to start thinking about painting another painting.

Having created a context for our lives and a role in which we are accepted or ignored by the world, a question pops up: what have I derived from all this and where does it really lead me? What has truly been achieved? Whatever is the answer, from now on nothing much can be done to change it, unless perhaps to work to make good what has been lost or fouled up. What once was the future has now become the past. What's done is done.

WANING CRESCENT MOON. At this phase the Moon rises before dawn, thinning as the days pass. When the Moon is 60° from the Sun (☽✶☉), about 9-10 days after fullmoon, we move into a productive time where payoffs, fruits and consequences are uppermost, for better or for worse and usually a mixture of both. Things move along habituated lines and grooves, or perhaps things at last finally slot into place. We're all in this together – this can be disjunctive and grating or rewarding and happy. Life is continuing and things are running as normal, as established. We're here because we're here and this is where life has led us.

Underneath, new possibilities or concerns, perhaps previously unseen, emerge out of the existing flow of events and situations. Perspectives and understandings arise about the past and its effects on the present. This is a time of completing, a time for adding finishing touches, tying up loose ends, dealing with rough edges, cleaning up the mess and putting things away for another day. Momentum is strong, moving along lines already created and agreed. It's rather like retirement after a long life of work – though new possibilities we've hoped and waited for can come to pass as a result. Here we can compensate for previous deficiencies or excesses, or we can catch up on what was cast aside in the rush.

This can be rewarding or leave us feeling rather empty or stuck, depending on how we're feeling, though it can also generate a longer-term urge to create changes in a future time. Even if our past actions seem to have failed, positive outcomes can nevertheless emerge from all this – it's all a matter of how we see things and what we do to make things good.

When Moon moves to 45° or a semisquare from the Sun (☽∠☉), the waning crescent moon, it's clean-up and let-go time, time for resolving past arguments, dropping old grudges, clearing up your piles, wiping up the mess and auditing the situation. We're called upon to release the past and commit it to posterity, yet this becomes a foundation for the future too. Things are perhaps not exciting or promising but they can nevertheless be rewarding. Using the analogy of retirement, it's now time to make a life of it. We must complete things, tie things up and give them away.

What we once identified as our own now belongs to the world and to memory, like a book that has been published or a child that has grown up and gone away. The sharp edge of releasing the past can give a clarity of longterm purpose, or a sense of perspective over the overall drift of our lives, or a feeling of release, or a lifting of a burden. Or perhaps we get the feeling that things just didn't work, we didn't achieve our objectives, and that's that – too late now, and there's always another day. But usually it's somewhere in between, since life is always a mixed bag, and everything has its compensations.

Still, however, there are two to three days before newmoon – this is the old-moon phase. At the waning semisextile (☽⚻☉, 30°), the thinning lunar crescent, rising before the Sun at dawn, many are the issues to contemplate, and the distant as well as the recent past loom large, even acting as a drag factor. Yet new hopes and possibilities emerge from the dust of the old. Either that, or we simply have a past with little sense of future.

Side-issues need sorting out, things need cleaning, polishing, mending, fixing, and our resource-base demands attention – perhaps we need some new kit for the next journey. Habit prevails and we're waiting for the old to end. Old moon is sometimes a low-energy time, thoughtful, a carrying-on phase for accepting the past and letting bygones be bygones. It might be a busy time if things need finishing or if preparations for the future need doing. The old moon, while past-dominated, hatches within it new potentials.

NEWMOON (☽☌☉). After all this cyclical hyperactivity, it is well to spend some time just living with what's here and with what we have. This is a transition time and things cannot be hurried. Seeds are lying dormant, not yet germinating, taking no distinct form. It's time to dig over the soil in which we're going to plant new crops, or clear the ground on which we hope to build a new edifice. Or perhaps we need to make a journey to a new place where the next cycle will unfold. Or perhaps nothing much is happening. Yet the qualities of our thoughts and feelings, the setting of our intents and the omens presented by events can have great relevance here.

If things are lined up to be carried out, it is well to begin them at newmoon, or to prepare to begin them – though wait until newmoon actually comes, if possible. If things in the past have been busy and if the future is as yet unclear, it is well to take advantage of the hiatus to create space for new possibilities to emerge. A new cycle is coming and a change of perspective is taking place, setting off a new tone and a new set of themes for the future. The past is gone and the future not yet here. At this stage an overview of life is available, as if we're temporarily outside the process, looking in. And then the next cycle starts.

Successive lunations might or might not have a sequential connection, in terms of storyline. Sometimes the underlying theme of a lunation can come from further back or concern something further forward. It's difficult and unwise to try to describe things too closely because different cycles can be so very different. Yet the overall pattern described above is the classic pattern of a cycle of change. This is the pattern of things in a world characterised by perpetual change, wrung out of the stuff of time. Yet these patterns, while perennial, are rather like the seasons of the year, predictable in overall pattern, while variable in the way they manifest this time round.

If you do conscious work with yourself, meditation or ceremony, or if you simply take a magical approach to life, then it's the newmoon and fullmoon you need to focus on. The newmoon concerns clarifying your goals and intents, releasing the past and readying yourself for the future. Try to sort out inside yourself what your objectives are and where the parameters lie – what's acceptable in the coming cycle and what's not. It's a good time to go to a healing well or a woodland, or to sit by the fire and watch the flames, to sit watching the waves or to listen to the birdsong. It's a quiet time, a time of reorientation.

The fullmoon is a bit like the calm at the centre of the hurricane – though hopefully not quite so dramatic. It's a chance to step out of time, shift a level up, and get used to the way that things actually are. This reality-check approach gives a basis for re-entering the fray from a new viewpoint. Calm down, it's alright! There are bigger meanings to life, and here's a chance to see them, amidst the activity.

And everything always works out in the end. Next, we're going to look at the solstices and equinoxes.

4

Ancient Festivals and the Four Seasons

This is about the high-points of the cycle of the year, the solstices, equinoxes and cross-quarters. The year is not just a calendrical and climatic affair: it is a cycle of growth, consolidation and decay on a subtle-energy level that is fundamental to our existence. Neither is it just a matter of changes in the availability of heat and light: it's a multi-level energy cycle affecting the basis of events and trends in our lives and across the world. Observing and synchronising ourselves with the ancient festivals is one way of participating more actively in this pulsation and even adding to it. It's a matter of playing a proactive part in its evolutionary unfoldment, as gardeners and custodians of the planet.

Years Roll On

We tend to take the cycle of the year for granted, viewing it in a rather reductionist, calendrical and mechanical manner. This is partially because the Western calendar has no natural basis, so we tend to think of a calendar as a matter of dating with no further significance. For a solar-based calendar it would make better sense to anchor it in the solstices and equinoxes, allowing us to move more in harmony with the seasonal undertow of life and nature and with overall energy-conditions.

The seasons are brought about by Earth's orbital relationship with the Sun, in which she exposes each of her poles to the Sun for half of the year as she orbits around it. Each pole is maximally exposed to the Sun around the time of summer solstice, experiencing the midnight sun, while the other pole is in perpetual darkness during its winter solstice.

Outwardly, the Sun gives Earth light and heat, and inwardly there is a deeper *energy-weather* cycle activating and modulating life-force on Earth, connected with the solstices. Life-force courses through the subtle meridians of the Earth and the energy-systems and patternings of all living things. In terms of our daily lives, a year takes a while, but for the Earth it is just a short inbreath and outbreath in the long course of geological time.

The ancients took it upon themselves to invoke favourable seasonal change, in the knowledge that change is the essence of earthly life and rhythm is the breathing of life-force. They knew also that subtle energy patternings are the energy-framework upon which physically manifest things are draped.

Psycho-spiritually, the Sun within us resides at the centre of our being, around which all of the constituent parts of our psyche orbit. The Sun represents our fundamental *raison d'être*, our will-to-live and our source of aliveness. It gets us up in the morning to meet a new day. You could say it channels the soul through into our personalities and earthly natures. It's a vibrant, shining place within us which seeks to make something good out of life and to evolve through life's experiences. Through the Sun in our birth charts, we seek to become something more than we now are, to evolve and serve our purpose, to be part of the life-process and to contribute to it.

This inner Sun goes through its own cycle of the year. We each relate differently to it, depending on the position of the Sun in our birth charts, but we have a common cycle too – the Earth's cycle. It's about the fluxings of energy in life and nature and the thrumming of the resonant sphere of the Earth – we're bathed in it, even when we live in big cities, even on the 25th floor. The Sun moves around the zodiac in the course of a year, exposing us to different shades and tonalities of life-experience as it moves through the signs. An Aquarian day can feel quite different from a similar Piscean day, and what we make of each is up to us.

There are twelve signs of the zodiac, and the zodiac is anchored in the four *quarter-points* of the year – the two *solstices* and two *equinoxes*. The solstices represent turning points and the equinoxes represent tipping points in the four seasons. There's a three-sign sequence in each season. The zodiac has little to do with the stars and everything to do with the solstices, equinoxes and seasonal alternation, outlining the qualitative and archetypal undertow of the four seasons.

An archetype is an image or root-model of fundamental patterning behind and within all happenings and situations. If I say 'oak tree' then you will immediately form an image of an idealised oak tree, even though oak trees vary in shape, size and detail. So an archetype represents a basic patterning or template by which living beings and things shape themselves, even though the precise manner of their shaping varies enormously in real life. And yes, trees have thoughts and feelings.

There's something interesting here. In Britain, NW Europe and other temperate climes (between about 40° and 60° from the Earth's equator), nature manifests its actual physical changes in an eightfold, not really a twelvefold pattern. This eightfold pattern is marked out by the four quarter points and also by the mid-points (or *cross-quarters*) between these. These are important in temperate higher latitudes because the alternation of light and dark, day-length and temperature are more emphasised there. This also happens on a subtle-energy level, and it is these changes which pull us around and squeeze us through certain kinds of experiences at certain times of year.

In latitudes closer to the equator, other factors are emphasised by local circum-stances or traditions, such as prevailing winds, rainy seasons, river floods, the rising points of stars such as Sirius or the orbital cycles of Venus. Localised cultures saw things in the light of what was visibly important in their own localities. In Europe, the great ocean is westwards, yet in China it is eastwards, and in Brazil the rainy season determined the way indigenous peoples structured their beliefs, while in Europe or Canada spring and autumn do so.

An eightfold calendar is more natural in NW Europe than a twelvefold one, which originated in Mesopotamia – though they interlock. The Sami (Lappish) people of far-northern Europe have an eightfold year, five seasons being different kinds of what most of us would call winter. The ancient megalith builders of Atlantic Europe 4-5,000 years ago, stretched between Portugal and the Baltic, embodied eightfold mathematics into the alignments and placing of the standing stones and stone circles they built. But both eightfold and twelvefold calendars are anchored similarly in the solstices and equinoxes. So they are related.

The *energy principles* behind each year are represented by the twelve zodiac signs, and *manifest seasonal changes* are represented by an eightfold subdivision of the year. This interlocking of principles and practicalities has meaning to it. Here we'll look at the eight annual subdivisions, and in the next chapter we'll examine the twelve, the zodiac. The eight, the *quarters* and *cross-quarters*, were marked in ancient times by festivals when fires, beacons and lights were lit, representing and re-invoking the life-force.

The Four and the Eight

The Solstices

The solstices are the two exact points in the year when the days are longest and shortest – that is, when the poles of Earth are maximally inclined toward the Sun, or when Sun is directly above the Tropics of Cancer and Capricorn. Strictly speaking, the solstices are a six-day period (three days each side of the exact solstice), during which time the Sun does not change its height in the sky or its rising point on the horizon.

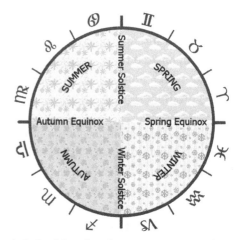

These rising points were marked by the megalith-builders by aligning stones to the rising and setting points of the Sun at the solstices. Stone alignments have been found to be aligned very slightly off exact, to the point four days before and after solstice when the Sun can first be seen to have moved very slightly each day when rising or setting. This allowed more accurate calendrical counting. It also marked out a six-day solstice period, celebrated by gatherings, ceremonies and feasts.

Energywise, the solstices are times of pause or *stasis* in which the movement of change from one light/energy condition to the other – long days or long nights – stops and reverses. It is like the turning of the tides in the sea, during which nothing much visibly happens, though it can be sensed, and it's important. There's a pregnant potency to it.

These processes of light/energy change can nevertheless be felt underground in caves, fogous and catacombs where light and the seasons are not physically seen or felt. This is one reason why ancient people and trainee lamas and shamans often closed themselves away for retreats in such places, to attune to subtle energies by depriving themselves of light and sensory input, thus becoming more sensitive to subtle energies. Once they had mastered this they could emerge into daylight again.

Some people went underground to die consciously too, since this would attune them to the subtle landscape of the afterlife, away from the relative jangle and fuss of the living world – but this was but one part of an ongoing spiritual process throughout life, for those who chose it. One mistake archaeologists make is that they frequently interpret 'chambered tombs' to be tombs, when they were primarily not so – just as churches with graveyards were not built solely for burying the dead. Chambered mounds were built for initiatory and spiritual purposes, to help trainees attune to the subtle timeless energy behind and within all manifest forms.

Following winter solstice, initially the constraining effects of the natural environment is strongly felt in temperate climes – it's cold, the nights are long and growth in nature is dormant and held back. An evolutionary process of growth, development and variegation gathers steam by spring equinox, encouraged by the increasingly favourable conditions of spring – though often a newmoon or fullmoon triggers the manifest change. Plants, animals and people grow, extending into their available space, establishing and expressing their individual potential.

When the light decreases between summer and winter solstice, it's time to give something back in the way of seeds, fruits and compost, shelter, participation and integration. This process accelerates as summer bears its harvest and fruit. After autumn equinox, as winter approaches, there's a die-back in nature and, for humans, a sense of reintegration with society and the greater wholeness. Animals flock together to migrate or bed down in their wintertime hideaways.

You can observe this annual process: it's about stepping out and rising up in summer and returning home and hunkering down in winter, both in terms of life-activities and the inner life. By incorporating the energy-year into our plans and actions, we move more in tune with the planet's energy-fields. Things work better. Winter solstice is a good time for thinking things through, spring equinox is a good time for executing them, summer solstice is a great time for realising projects, and autumn equinox is a good time for reaping the benefits.

The solstices are characterised by a feeling of stillness, a timely contrast to the rushing changes happening around the equinoxes preceding them three months earlier. The solstices give us a chance to stop and take stock, to assimilate all that has happened and just *be* with that. The equinoxes represent a state of *becoming*, moving toward something else, while the solstices represent a state of *being*, of existentiality. The solstices are gateways or turning-points in the cycle of the year while the equinoxes are milestones or transition-points in the middle of change.

At summer solstice, all beings experience the fullness of life, rising to whatever is their potential this time around, while at winter solstice they experience their involvement, belongingness and interrelatedness to each other and the whole. Summer solstice is about potentiality and winter solstice is about background and roots. There is always something of the opposite within each of these states, since opposites in a polarity always exist in contrast to each other.

As a gateway of consciousness, winter solstice represents a pause to perceive the inherent seeds of future growth hiding within latency and death, to gather intent and a sense of possibility and to make goals or resolutions for the future. New Year's resolutions are a modern leftover of this. At the other end of the year, summer solstice marks a pause in the midst of the vivid life-process, a break for re-gathering and reassessing where we've got to, having reached this far. It's an intermission between springtime and harvest activities.

Since winter solstice is relatively lifeless in the northern hemisphere, it symbolises all that is relatively changeless, formless, concealed, and lying between completed and impending. In northern climes, candle and fire rituals (such as yule logs and the lighting of Advent candles) represent the quiet survival of the light in the midst of darkness and cold.

Since summer solstice buzzes with life and activity, it symbolises all that is living, transient, productive, actual and vibrant. Light within in winter and light without in summer: these two contrasting aspects of the annual cycle of life-force are vital to an understanding of natural faiths and the movement of life. At these points we come to accept *what is*, and we live with it, as it stands.

If you seek to move into inner harmony with the underlying motion of energy within the year, observe the solstices, marking them with a tone of respect and perception, and you will find yourself opening up more consciously to a fundamental energy-undertow that lies within the pattern of the year.

The Equinoxes

The equinoxes are midpoints between the solstices, when the length of the days and nights is changing fastest and yet they are equal in length. The further you move from the equator, the more that day-length changes each day around equinox. Equinoxes are times of becoming and transition where change properly gets into gear. At spring equinox the restraining influences of winter give way and plants, animals and people go forward pursuing their goals, mutating and growing each as best they can, staking out their space and making the best of circumstances while there is opportunity.

While the solstices mark pauses, the equinoxes mark midpoints in the process of becoming something else – they're transitional highpoints in the progression of change, mid-course realignments where a shift occurs from buildup to breakthrough, following paths already chosen. It's time for releasing past ways to make space for what is to come.

Things can be busy at the equinoxes, making the folk gatherings seen at the solstices not so easy at equinox. Hence that, in many traditions, there are often bigger festivals around the solstices. Yet all of the quarterpoints are magical times well worth noting: look at what goes on for you at these times, and 'listen more closely to things than to people'. The most potent time for observance of the atmosphere and character of these festivals is the two or so days *before* their exact timing. The exact timing can be found in an ephemeris.

In recent decades many people have begun instinctively to observe these festivals again. A surge of interest took place when the planet Neptune hovered around the winter solstice point in 1984, and then in 1988 Uranus did the same – these planets drew attention to the solstice points at the time by upstepping their potency. Around this time the celebration of the quarter and cross-quarter points in modern times really lifted off, and it has grown ever since.

The Fire Festivals or Cross-Quarters

It takes time for solar energy to filter through into nature and actuality. The quarter points mark the inception of each of the seasons, but mainly *in principle*. As with everything, there's a difference between setting out to do something and actually seeing it happen. In nature there is a 45ish-day time-lag between the quarter days and the cross-quarters, when the season in question is really in full swing, in visible, manifest terms.

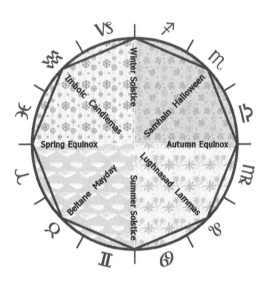

Thus, the hottest part of summer is not necessarily at summer solstice but later, around the beginning of August at Lammas or Lughnasa, when the heat has gathered momentum. Likewise, the coldest, crispest part of winter can be in early-to-mid February, about six weeks after winter solstice at Candlemas or Imbolc. Autumn really does its business in early November and spring really blossoms in early May – give or take the vagaries of weather and climate, which can vary annually and from place to place.

This is where the *cross-quarters* or fire festivals come in: as the midpoints between the quarter-points, they mark the times when nature and actuality respond concretely to the energy-changes initiated at the quarter points.

The zodiac is measured in terms of 360 degrees (°). The Sun moves more or less 1° per day. The quarter points are 90° from each other, and the cross-quarter points are 45° from the quarter-points (and also 90° from each other). The ancients, at least in Europe, where the seasonal changes of light and dark matter a lot, marked these cross-quarters as important festivals, celebrating and participating in the power of nature and her manifest expressions.

Historical quirks have shifted these festivals away from their original auspicious times (just as Yule has been shifted to Christmas, 3-4 days after winter solstice). The cross-quarters occur when the Sun reaches 15° (the middle) of one of the four so-called *fixed signs* – Aquarius, Taurus, Leo and Scorpio. The astrologically-true cross-quarter points thus take place around 2nd-7th May, August, November and February.

Tradition places these festivals a few days earlier – such as Beltane or Workers' Day on 1st May, Candlemas or Imbolc on 2nd February, Lammas or Lughnasa at the beginning of August and All Souls or Hallowe'en at the very end of October (or Samhain on 1st November). This said, the ancients were not as calendrically-fixated as we, and they often shifted the festivals around a little each year to coincide with a new or full moon, or any other energy-blip that was hovering around at the time, on that year. A remnant of this remains at Easter, which occurs on the fullmoon following spring equinox (nowadays on the Sunday following that fullmoon). Only later on, with the coming of the institutional church and calendrical dating systems, were such dates nailed down at regular, fixed dates.

Outwardly, there are visible seasonal changes at the four cross-quarters, and inwardly there is a quality of very real engagement in the life-process, a feeling of breakthrough in relation to the theme being explored underlyingly in each season.

The cross-quarters used to be known as Witches' Sabbaths, when the inner intents (or spells) of witches would work through and become reality. A 'witch' is a person with natural, herbal, oracular and magical knowledge and training, often practising midwifery, healing, rites of passage and death rites, who acted as an adviser and spiritual friend to the people around them. By the 1500s across Europe they were often misunderstood, demonised and accused of heinous crimes, particularly by the church. The sabbaths are times of coming-to-pass, stages of manifestation and transition. The times for clarifying intent are the solstices, and those for adjusting or reaffirming intent are the equinoxes. At the cross-quarters, it is necessary to actualise those intents, or stages of them, and give thanks too. Things actually *happen* at the cross-quarters.

Conscious energy-working is a process of bringing things from the stage of visualisation into manifest reality, intertwining our attention, intelligence, will and activity with the natural flow of subtle energy. This is the true meaning of the Sanskrit word *tantra*, or interweaving (of self with universe), which is the essence of magical-spiritual work. In so doing, we engage with and enhance the natural energy-flows of the world and are supported by them. We harmonise our lives with the energy-weather, with the deeper realms and with the karmic threads interlacing all events and developments. Nowadays, this isn't witchcraft so much as a sense of 'deep ecology', the spiritual aspect of respect for nature, or perhaps even 'magical politics', a deeper aspect of working for social change and justice.

In ancient times, people would gather together at the quarters and cross-quarters to celebrate life and focus their collective spirit, keeping the human family moving in tune with the times – especially since, with sparse populations, people, families and clans didn't actually cross paths with each other very much. They'd have meetings, markets, negotiations, flirting, marriages and rites of passage too. Today, people are doing this again – not for the romantic purpose of fantasising about the ancients (though this happens) but because they sense that it is auspicious and necessary in our time. It's a form of para-politics, voting with our feet, spiritually, and communicating with the subtle worlds to say that at least some of us do care.

Tuning into these eight points of the year, the quarters and cross-quarters, we move into greater harmony with the energy-cycle of the solar year. It puts us into gear with natural cycles. Thereby are our lives enriched. Try it. It sheds new light on the seasons and the underlying learning process within them.

To repeat, there is a distinction between the quarters and the cross-quarters. The quarters represent change-points in *energy-patterning*, in terms of light. The cross-quarters represent change-points in *manifest energy*, in terms of visible seasonal changes. The peaks of the four seasons show themselves at the cross-quarters.

The Four Seasons

In temperate latitudes we have four distinct seasons, and each of these seasons has its hidden flavour. Living as most of us do in heated and lit-up buildings, in towns and with modern lives, the seasons have been somewhat neutralised and homogenised. We don't notice life's atmospheres, variations, periodicities and subtle promptings as much as we might, since modern life demands a certain distracted insensitivity and wilful blindness. But not giving attention to the more elusive messages life gives us doesn't mean they're not there – instead they work through our unconscious psyche and its behaviour.

Since the year is a cycle, there is strictly speaking no beginning or end to it. Concepts such as 'new year', different in different calendrical systems, are human inventions. So, in looking at the cycle of the seasons, let's start randomly with autumn. Here I am describing the seasons as experienced in northwest Europe and similar temperate climes.

Autumntime

At autumn (fall) equinox, relationships, togetherness and belonging become important. Summer has ended and nature is beginning to close down for winter. Increasing darkness and cold encroach on nature and people – we are *affected*, whether we like it or not. People, animals and plants must adapt if they are to survive the winter. We're given notice about this at autumn equinox and it gets serious at the cross-quarter day, 45ish days later.

The need to really engage with what envelops and surrounds us arises at the autumn cross-quarter. In Britain and Ireland this is called Hallowe'en or Samhain. Strictly speaking, this cross-quarter occurs when Sun is at 15° Scorpio, around 5th-7th November. In Britain 5th November is Guy Fawkes Night, celebrating a terrorist attack and attempted *coup d'etat* in 1605, but the tradition of bonfires, burning a 'guy' or straw-man and setting off fireworks is really a leftover of a much older fire festival. At this time the dark and cold is definitely coming down: leaves fall off the trees, migrating birds have gone, frosts and icy blasts impinge on us and animals go into hibernation – except climate change is nowadays changing that. In the agricultural cycle it's time for the annual slaughter, and all the firewood must be ready and stocks laid in for winter.

Humans, animals and plants must accept that winter is intruding: together we stand, divided we fall. In the plant world a composting process ensues, to feed the ground and cover the seeds, spores and rhizomes for winter. The relative freedom and bounty of summer is gone. It's fact-facing time, concerning me-as-part-of-something-larger. Our urges to belong to a family, to groups, society, tradition and social mores grow stronger – it's more about a sense of heritage than a sense of future at this time of year.

The ancients held a fire ceremony at Samhain to recognise that, while the solar light is dying, the light within must be cherished, to be reborn later. This is a time of the death of the old, and within it is the eventual promise of rebirth of the new, but that's some time ahead at Imbolc or Candlemas. Another aspect is 'All Souls' and 'Hallowe'en' – a recognition of souls and beings beyond this life and beyond visible reality, of ancestors and things that go bump in the night. It's a time of forced adjustment – like death, it's something we must accept when it comes, powerless as we are to do anything much about it except to work with it. Once these impinging realities are taken on board, new hitherto concealed possibilities are revealed – the power to survive and make something good of challenging circumstances. It's a time to get out your knitting, do some woodwork or wade through thick astrology tomes!

From Samhain to the winter solstice, a dark time, we start with winter's hard, sometimes harsh facts and end with a celebration of our social togetherness around a warming fire. At solstice comes Yule and the assembling of the clans. Yet in early winter there can be a stark beauty too: wintry gifts, with crisp air, frosts and the first snows, and warm fires to come home to. In northern Europe there were candle-lighting traditions: the christianised Santa Lucia in Scandinavia, honoured in December, is a blond maiden dressed in white and wearing a crown lit up with candles.

Winter

To deal with winter we must consolidate, come together and work at it. This shift happens fully at winter solstice, when the darkness is maximal and everything stands still. It's a time for celebration around the fire, eating and making merry – or perhaps sorting out some of the family stresses that no one had time to work through before! We have made it through the changes and challenges of life and we find ourselves still here, together once again as a kinship group of blood, soul or commonality – and it's a time for grandparents, for harking back and reflecting on a sense of posterity.

This is our family. Ultimately our family is humanity, but our emotional security needs require something more local and personal, made up of people whose names we know, with whom we have common history and/or genetics. We are capable of feeling a personal connection with and looking into the eyes of perhaps 50-80 people at any time – beyond this things get impersonal, no matter how friendly we might be. This is the basis of extended families, whether genetic or of the soul.

The fruits of the past year are shared and eaten, even to excess, after a solsticial pause for awareness or prayer, or for moments of wonder and goodwill. The seeds of the coming year are laid here in the relative quietness of this time of contemplation and rest. In former days when resources were meagre, the Yule feast represented a necessary stocking up of fat and nutrition to help everyone survive the winter. Modern affluence has turned this into an orgy of consumerist excess, sozzled stupor and TV overdoses, but it wasn't always so.

To get through winter we must engage in regularised routines, fulfil our social obligations, act sensibly, pace ourselves and stay within the bounds of socially-acceptable behaviour. It's time to be low-key, sleeping and recharging our batteries at the opposite end of the year to frenetic summertime, with its work and activity. Summer gives meaning to winter and vice versa. While autumn was a time of *becoming*, winter is a time for living with what we have and what we are. That's what you get, and that's that. If last year's harvest was insufficient, you go hungry and hide in bed, lying low until a better time.

Forty-five days after winter solstice the ascending light is clearly evident. It's still cold, perhaps even colder, but a change is apparent. This is the winter cross-quarter, Candlemas or Imbolc, when the Sun is around 15° Aquarius. By this time winter has been with us long enough to become tiresome, and something in us starts looking forward to a change. We relish the growing light. The first signs of growth will come in the weeks that follow – in Britain, that's snowdrops followed by daffodils. In colder climes this is a snow-covered period of light and crispness, good for getting out the skis or skates, bringing in the felled logs on sledges from the forest, or breaking holes in the ice to drop a line through for fishing.

Acceptance of winter realities gives way to an urge for something different, a hankering for springtime. Yet the winter quarter is not done – not yet. The coming change is so great that we must be held awhile in arrested progress to help us put things on the right footing. Gardeners must dig the earth, spread compost and prepare seed-beds. Tools need fixing, houses need cleaning, things need sorting out – it's a necessary time of preparation.

The back end of winter, leading up to spring equinox, is spent fulfilling our obligations to the situation we're in, accepting that everything has its time. Something is stirring deep down – the hope, the aspiration, the necessary understanding that will act as a foundation for what is to come. By now we're tired enough of winter to generate the will to wrench ourselves free of winter habits and move forward. A time of reality-adjustment is here, starting after Candlemas and peaking just before spring equinox.

Springtime

Up to spring equinox we must accept the restraints, obligations and routines of winter. Social change often arises from individual impulse and social mores and institutions have a way of constraining freedom, so we need to be ready to branch out on our own if necessary, to create our own path through life's jungle. At spring equinox, life-force rises from slumber and seeds germinate, fertilised by water released in the thaw and triggered by rising light and warmth. We feel empowered or driven to strike out on our own, to take risks and get on with it, motivated by an urge to *make something happen*.

In ancient times many people lived transhumant lives – they had different winter and summer residences, or they moved round several places during the year – and around spring equinoxes they'd set out for their hilltop settlements, to get above the trees, away from the mud and flies, to a place where the animals and kids could roam and the shadowy life of the forest was left behind for the summer.

This push gathers momentum over the ensuing weeks but it is not until the spring cross-quarter, Mayday or Beltane, that things are really moving and the last frosts and cold spells have gone. In May the flowers bloom, birds sing, bees are buzzing and nature is alive with bounteous fertility. It's a bundle of joy. In ancient days Beltane was a fire festival when folk celebrated the greening of their world, the eruption of blossom and the rising of the sap. There's a primal urge to play, frolic and do naughty things in the woods. The Beltane tradition of jumping over the fire or driving the cattle between two fires was a symbolic purification, a spring-clean and shaking off of cobwebs, a statement of emergence into the future. In ancient times it was a form of flirtation.

People invoked fertility in all its forms and practised it too. With human procreation in northern climes, the ideal time for conception lies between Beltane and summer solstice, leading to birth at or just before spring equinox, giving a baby spring and summer for its first few months of life. Beltane also marked male-female gender distinction, a separateness which, in mating, perpetuates the race and creates the greatest of pleasure. And no, I didn't say gender inequality, I said *distinction*.

Heaven warms and Earth blooms. From Beltane (early May, 15° Taurus) until summer solstice, everything is pell-mell and full-on, and every animal and plant, every person, is growing and moving, feeling free. Well, at first. By solstice, bigger plants crowd out smaller ones, and a gardener has a lot of weeding to do to favour chosen species.

This seeming separation of once-united people has its twinge of pain too – everyone is off on their own trajectory, groups break up for summer, people are busy, things are moving on and there's much to do. It's relentless, yet variety is the spice of life, and life is a game for the playing thereof. On the approach to summer solstice, the lightest time, everything is colourful, lively and frenetic, people are heading off everywhichway, and it's a time for festivals, pilgrimages and get-togethers – or nowadays agricultural shows, sports and other events.

Summer

Rampant growth, flowering and buzzing can make for a beauteous cacophony – and flowers and crops also get hopelessly mixed up with weeds. Yet just after summer solstice, with its light and warmth there's also already a detectable hint of reversal. People may pause for a celebration of life in the solstitial gap between spring and harvest, staying up through the short night and dallying with each other, yet a deep urge sets in amidst all this to settle into some kind of habit and coherence, to go back home.

It's great to be out and about but it's nice to enjoy home at the best time of the year. If every plant, animal and human is to realise its full potential and bear fruit, some stability and focus is needed so that we can make hay while the sun shines. Calves grow up and the chickens are laying. Crops must be watched and cheese made. Fruit is appearing and nuts forming. Bees swarm in the heat and it's a time of fermentation. Though it's busy, it's a time of relative stability, of doing what's in front of you, and tomorrow is another day.

The heat grows as the summer cross-quarter approaches. This is Lammas or Lughnasa, around 15° Leo in early August. Nature ripens, young animals grow to full size, the corn is nearly ready and what once were possibilities are now actualities – they have by now developed to the full extent that they can this time around. Green grains move to gold and summer matures. Summer, like winter, is a time of *beingness*, of living in a state that is already established. It's all about each of us, or our families, our own people, doing our thing. In modern times it's holiday-time, our ration of freedom from the treadmill. In former times it was a time of fun, fresh nutritional food, travel, visitors and relative plenty. Yet as individuals we collide and interfere with each other in our apparent liberty and, at Lammas, underneath all this, lies a lurking concern that things have gone far enough and it's beginning to end. At harvest everyone's going to have to work their socks off together to bring it all in.

After Lammas follows the harvest – grains, then vegetables and fruits, then mushrooms and nuts, finally the meat slaughter – when the results of growth must be processed and stored up for the winter. We have potential hard times ahead if we fail to lay in what we need. Evolution has reached its culmination and things will soon change. Days are getting shorter and mornings cooler and dewier.

We start looking forward to winter or at least accepting that it can't be stopped. We begin again to explore relationship and the benefits of cooperation – not least through bringing in the harvest and preparing the woodpiles. Late summer becomes lank and less lively, with a golden grace of its own, yet the urge for change is brewing. The sun's light, at the blue end of the light-spectrum in spring, is now at the red end. It's time to migrate back to the winter residence, fix the roof, lay in winter stocks and enjoy the late summer evenings.

Much has happened. A pause to assimilate it all, like the reality-adjustment period just before spring equinox, takes place on the approach to autumn equinox. It's time to rein ourselves in and get down to thinking, studying, craftwork and working together. The change sets in at autumn equinox. People start coming back together, getting involved and sorting out their relationships. By Hallowe'en, the full implications of membership in society will come to the surface and a change ensues.

Transformations

Transformation has two faces: death at Samhain in autumn and growth at Beltane in spring. Beingness takes on two faces too: consolidation at Candlemas in winter and creative self-expression at Lammas in summer. The solstices and equinoxes mark points in time when things are started, the cross-quarters mark points where they are fulfilled, and in the period preceding the next solstice or equinox is a time of assimilation.

Candlemas is a time for gently cultivating light and energy, transitioning from stability toward change, invoking the life-force and a rebirth of its potency. *Beltane* is a time for bringing forth life and breaking free, onward-bound in a fulsome burst of growth, extension, variation and expansion. *Lammas* is a time of climax, peaking growth, ripening and the beginning of collecting and harvesting. *Samhain* is a time of in-drawing, uncovering the inner secrets of life as its outer forms die off.

Fires were lit at these times to represent different facets of the life-force and its capacity to transform and enliven at different times of year. Thus the symbolism of the seasons was played out in a naturally spiritual, ritualised form. People who nowadays seek to return to the roots of faith feel drawn to mark the quarters and cross-quarters, as if Mother Earth is calling her children back after their long sojourn amongst the complexities of modern life and its spiritually-obscuring effects. Civilisation, bringing many worthy achievements, has also brought with it war, alienation, burdens and restrictions, wherein spirit has separated and lost. We suffer separation syndrome.

You don't have to adopt a pagan or druidic path to observe and mark these points in time – I am neither of these, yet I still love nature, auspicious moments and magical experiences. The fire festivals are natural and connected to the seasons, so anyone who lives, works or spends time outdoors will be aware of them. Those of us who spend so much of our lives indoors need to get out, feel the ground under our feet and the stars that we have for a roof.

At one of the quarter or cross-quarter days, visit a special place – an ancient site, a hilltop, a woody glade or a favourite natural spot – and lend your spirit to the time and to the land and trees, or whatever is there. You will find a peaceful strengthening and calming, an increasing sense of wholeness and creativity giving new meaning to life. You will move into a friendlier relationship with time – *true time*, natural time, fluid time, *real* time.

Mathematical and geometric patterns in many stone circles and ancient sites in Britain and elsewhere show that the ancients set great store by this eightfold subdivision of time. They did so because spiritual participation in manifest form was a vital socio-economic process for them – and society, economics and religion were not as separate from one another as we Westerners now experience. Alignments at many ancient megalithic remains also suggest a sixteenfold subdivision of the annual cycle, demonstrated by alignments of stones or other features to the rising and setting points of the Sun at sixteen points of the year.

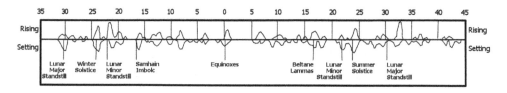

Regularity of incidences in stone alignments to the rising and setting points of the Sun and Moon, as found by Prof Alexander Thom amongst 300 ancient sites in Scotland.

The twelvefold subdivision of the zodiac now used in astrology arose when cultures developed materially to the level where people first stepped outside nature's bounds into a more man-made world, living in the first towns. Freed to an extent from the rigours of natural and agricultural cycles, they pursued imaginative cultural developments leading them to see things in new ways. This was the beginning of a psychological transition in humanity still going on today, moving from a mindset conditioned by the ecosphere to one conditioned by the *noösphere* – the world of human thought. Part of this was a new perception of archetypal forces and newly transcendent gods. Theirs were gods of wealth, law, wisdom, love, power and communication. Their ideas became more metaphysical and philosophical.

Twelvefold zodiacs are traced back to the Chaldeans of the Tigris valley in today's Iraq, and the basis of the astrology we know today was passed to us through the Greeks, Romans and Arabs of the Baghdad Caliphate and Moorish Spain to medieval and Renaissance scholars in Europe. The idea of a twelvefold zodiac possibly preceded the Chaldeans, but they encapsulated it for posterity.

The twelve signs are rooted in the four quarter points, just like the eightfold system: the solstices mark the beginnings of the zodiac signs Capricorn (♑) and Cancer (♋), and the equinoxes mark the beginnings of the signs Aries (♈) and Libra (♎). The eightfold and the twelvefold systems connect here.

Thereafter, the twelvefold system divides each quarter into three signs, while the eightfold divides it into two halves. Zodiac signs tend not to reflect directly observable natural changes in nature in the same way as the eightfold system does. But there is nevertheless an atmospheric, subtle yet detectable tone change when the Sun moves from one zodiac sign to another, making what's called an *ingress*.

It pays to observe and notice both the twelvefold and eightfold systems when examining time and its passing, especially in the case of the Sun's annual cycle. The exact times of the quarters, cross-quarters and ingresses can be culled from an ephemeris or certain computer programs. One day, you might be able to tell when these phenomena are happening without looking at your ephemeris – you'll recognise the *feeling* of it.

What to Do

Moving into an inward harmony with the cycle of the year has several effects. It allows us to live our lives more productively – not only from the standpoint of getting things done but also in following our path of awakening. It's not so much to do with nature-worship as to do with living in accord with nature and with all levels of our being. There's a creeping global emergency afoot, and the heart and soul of the world needs all the help it can get.

If you are moved to mark the quarter and cross-quarter days, then here are some suggestions about what to do. It is auspicious to visit an ancient site that you like in order to do this. The reason is that these are deliberately located at special places where earth energies are strong. These locations are good for consciousness growth and magical-spiritual work – you can shift levels more easily at such places. But if an ancient site is not available, then an inspiring natural location is fine too – use your intuitions to find a good place or ask someone for a recommendation.

It's not necessary to do this at every quarter and cross-quarter day: it's better to sustain your efforts by keeping to modest commitments than to be ambitious and then stop soon afterwards. At minimum, the two solstices are most worth focusing on.

When you visit such a place at one of the eight ancient festivals, you will be able to connect with, utilise and contribute to the value of a power place during a power point in time. If you do dowsing or muscle-testing, you can test for this by getting a friend to dowse or test your aura, before you enter the power place, when you enter it and after you have done your business there – you will find that your aura grows, sometimes quite considerably. Your feelings about life will change too.

Spend some time there and, before you enter, try to set aside your concerns and put yourself into a receptive, listening mode. If you don't find this easy, don't worry – it will probably happen anyway. Then, before entering the place, ask whether it's okay to do so, and listen to see if any thoughts come up inside you to give you a starting clue about the place, its guardians and its atmosphere. Then enter. It depends then on your style of working – do what's best for you. If you like to meditate, find a good place to sit. If you prefer ceremony, you will have your routines to follow, or you can base your actions on the following suggestions.

When I visit a stone circle, I frequently circumambulate (walk around) it thoughtfully, three times. Then I make an offering, light a lamp or offer food or gifts (though please respect the site and other visitors). Then sit or lie down and do what you're here to do. This might include calming yourself, doing some breathing, some chanting or singing, some movement, dance, prostration, music-making, or whatever else you like to do – even just painting or writing. Then, when you're ready, orientate on the particular time you are in.

Winter solstice. This is a time of reflection on the year past and the year to come. Try to wrap up and release any residual feelings or regrets you might have from the past, noting lessons learned or issues to commute to the future for further attention. Let yourself *be*, in the relative quietness of the solstice. Ask yourself what you need to achieve during the coming year – note both big and little things. What contributory factors or circumstantial details need attention? Visualise the eventual fulfilment of your aims for the coming year and then look at the stages along the way toward that. Look at your highest hopes and your bottom-line needs. Look at your fears. Look at what benefits you might bring to the wider world. Then finalise it with a prayer for support and a recommitment to your path, and sit with it for a while. Give thanks and wrap things up well. If you're with friends and it's not too cold, hang out a bit – I sometimes take a flask of tea! The spirits of ancient places like witnessing people having fun – it all gets too serious. True decisions are made when you chuckle about them.

Candlemas or Imbolc. Things are in progress, so it's good to review your intents and where they have reached thus far. Are course adjustments needed? Are there wider considerations or extra factors to reckon into the equation? It's not time to really make a statement or perform major acts yet, in terms of the cycle of the year, but what groundwork and preparation is needed before spring equinox? Coddle and nurture the embryonic seed of potential that sits with you now, and give thanks for the blessing of being able to engage with the life process – you're alive, and this is amazing. Light a candle when back home.

Spring Equinox. It's now time to really do it – sign on the bottom line and get on with it. Have you completed the groundwork and laid the foundations? Are you ready? Is there anything you need to review? How is your energy? What do you need to have achieved by summer solstice? Are there obstacles to overcome? Is anyone or anything else affected? Make a prayer that you can see clearly the difference between what you can and cannot change. Go forward from here with courage and vigour: it's time to make things move.

Beltane or May Day. Be glad: now is the time for the flowering of your life-direction. Review all that is unfolding: are things genuinely progressing? What needs adjusting? Are you applying sufficient energy – or might you be driving too hard? Where's the fun and creativity? By the time you have reached Samhain or Hallowe'en in six months' time, do you feel your objectives will be more or less realised – and, if not, what will help things on their way? Enjoy the stillness amidst the action and give thanks for being alive.

Summer Solstice. You now have a chance to make tactical changes in the light of what has unfolded thus far. Where have you got to? Look back to winter solstice and what you then visualised: how does your reality now differ from that? Is there anything to learn, anything to release? What actual contribution are you making to the world and the people affected, and is there any improvement you're making? If not, what can be improved? Make prayers or intents for the benefit you can bring, to self, others and the overall scheme of things. Look toward winter solstice: what needs to be completed by then? Enjoy the break now at solstice – step out of time. Breathe deeply. This is the time. What needs doing to help ripen the fruits of your labours?

Lammas or Lughnasa. Here comes the harvest – take a deep breath before gathering in all that has grown and ripened. Things should be coming to fruition: if not, review your situation. What is retrievable and what is not? What has been brought into being? Give thanks. And there's more to go: all this has been for a reason, so clarify what that is – not just your viewpoint, but a wider perspective on life. How will this help? Sing songs of praise and gratitude, and dance your dance of life. Life is a gift, and that's why we need to live in the present. So what are the true gifts in your situation – including its apparent problems? How is your current situation an answer to a prayer? It's time to help something or someone in need. Time to make offerings.

Autumn Equinox. What are the compensating factors in your situation? What is in everyone's best interest? Identify what you need to help you make your contribution to the wider situation you're in. If anything went wrong earlier, make it right now, in terms of attitude or real factors. Who are your people? How much do you *belong*? Who are the 'outsiders' in your life and how can you build a bridge to them? Is there anything you're covering over? Be good and nice – though this requires honesty and forthrightness too.

Samhain or Hallowe'en. What's ending and completing here? What can you wrap up, and what is to be carried forward to another time? What's under the carpet or lurking in dark corners? What's the final secret behind all that has happened throughout the year? What has been your part in the great cosmic chessgame of life? Acknowledge the mystery, the unfathomable wonder of it all, the unknowns and the bits you sense but don't see or understand. Life has its tough aspects, things come and go, but something endures too. Talk to your ancestors and appreciate what has now gone. Clear the space and, even if you're wet, lost and cold, take it with good grace. There's something wonderful amidst all this, so light a candle to celebrate it. And tomorrow is another day.

We can no longer impose upon our bodies, on nature or on the world, in the way we have imposed on them up to now. This lands up in disaster, and we see it all around us today. I refer not only to wars, destruction and crises but also to the manner of our civilisation in all its details: your car and the streets you walk down are symptoms of that disaster. The fact that we have prisons, waste dumps, dying species, poor people, cleared land and erratic weather is a disaster. 'Disaster' means 'going against the stars' – considering ourselves far more important than we actually are.

If we want the future world to be worth living in, it involves building a new balance between what we want, what's there and what's wise – and giving something back. Moving into conscious participation with natural time-cycles is part of this, and it has immense and deep implications. The starting place is to become aware of the way that time and change move.

Next, we'll examine the zodiac and the way it works.

5

The Round of the Zodiac

Within the zodiac lies a cycle of archetypal energy-patterns or time-imprints with a very dynamic effect. Familiarising ourselves with the pattern and sequence of the zodiac allows us to perceive the holofrequencies of inner time, hidden within and behind all life and form, deeply imprinted in our depth-psychology. The signs reveal the stages and order of archetypes inherent in any cycle. Understanding these can help us act more skilfully within the realm of time, also to see beyond time and circumstance toward what is perennial or timeless. This chapter introduces the zodiac and chapter 9 gives more details.

To Everything there is a Season

Evolution and *integration*: these are two key undercurrents behind the zodiacal year. Between the solstices we progress from one state to another: through evolution in winter and spring, and through integration in summer and autumn. Neither evolution nor integration, nor any of their varying shades, is the ultimate experience: they exist in relation to each other like the swings of a pendulum. The story of life explores the paradoxes that this creates – it's the in-breathing and out-breathing of existence.

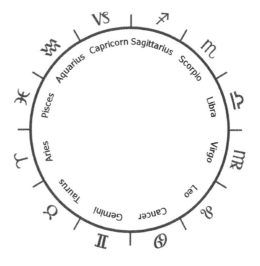

We need to *belong,* to be part of something larger, and we need to *do our own thing* too, to be ourselves. We learn from the outcomes of both. We came to this planet to experience paradox and extremes – the noble feeling of repeatedly getting stuck between a rock and a hard place – to learn how to find a middle way through it all and make the best of a tricky situation. We're charged with the task of materialising the spirit and spiritualising the material. And no one came here by accident.

Within everything lies its opposite. If we have had a fulsome summer, we appreciate the merits of winter, and we also need summer to give us relief from winter's gruelling nature. Spring implies autumn, and autumn is a prerequisite for spring. Oddly, we humans often appreciate things most when they are not there. We also tend habitually to behave as if things are permanent when they are transitory. If at times they seem unchanging, it means that a big head of steam is being built up for major change later on. It's sometimes difficult seeing the larger scheme of things, and it's our challenge to do so.

One fundamental popular illusion astrology labours under is that some signs are better than others. Not so. Scorpio and Pisces have had particularly bad press, and this exemplifies the unhelpful side of groupthink. Each sign invaluably and necessarily contributes to the whole. Without it, something important would be missing. Of course the world would be better organised if it were ruled by Virgos like me, but it would be dead boring too. The signs are equally valuable components of the cycle of time and facets of the fullness of experience.

In *winter* we learn commitment, focusing, involvement and fulfilment of the roles we have cut out for ourselves. In *spring* we learn how to take life in our hands, follow our aspirations and chosen paths, opening up new variants of ourselves, wherever that leads. In *summer* we learn how to extract the maximum from being alive, by being creative, harvesting life's benefits and carving out a personal niche in the grand scheme of things. In *autumn*, we forge our place in the world through contributing, sharing, involvement, togetherness and rising to whatever is needed of us. We also face facts we might previously have overlooked.

Backward and forward, round and round: when looking back retrospectively over the years, we forget this seasonal time-quality oscillation, but it's nevertheless there. Within the short-term perspective of one year, seasonal changes are very meaningful, yet seen over a period of years we remember the overall, net movement, not the ins and outs of how we got there. But the zodiac isn't just about the cycle of the year – Jupiter takes twelve years to move around it and Pluto takes 250. It concerns many timecycles. But for now we'll look at it in terms of the solar year, and we'll come to longer timecycles later in the book.

Modes

Each quarter of the year contains three signs.

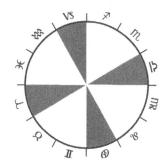

The first sign, starting at a solstice or an equinox point, is a *cardinal* or starting sign. Cardinal signs initiate the mode of operation of that season, investing energy and making things move, in whatever direction that season demands. The four cardinal signs are Capricorn, an earth sign, starting at winter solstice, Aries, a fire sign, starting at spring equinox, Cancer, a water sign, starting at summer solstice, and Libra, an air sign, starting at autumn equinox. Their astrological shorthand symbols are ♑, ♈, ♋ and ♎ respectively.

The second sign, with a cross-quarter point sitting in the middle of it, is a *fixed* or implementing sign. Here the purpose of each season must be effected and we carry out whatever we're now on track to do, wrestling with its realities. The four fixed signs are Aquarius, an air sign, implementing winter, with Imbolc or Candlemas taking place in the middle of it; Taurus, an earth sign, implementing spring, with Beltane in the middle of it; Leo, a fire sign, implementing summer, with Lughnasad or Lammas; and Scorpio, a water sign, implementing autumn, with Samhain or Hallowe'en. Their symbols are ♒, ♉, ♌ and ♏.

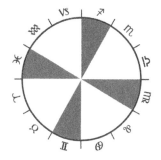

The third sign is a *mutable* or assimilating sign, preceding a solstice or equinox point. Here we complete, digest, make sense of and wrap up whatever has been done, preparing for the next step. We improve, polish, correct and finish things, laying the groundwork for the next season. The four mutable signs are Pisces, a water sign, assimilating winter and ending at spring equinox; Gemini, an air sign, assimilating spring and ending at summer solstice; Virgo, an earth sign, assimilating summer and ending at autumn equinox; and Sagittarius, a fire sign, assimilating autumn and ending at winter solstice. Their symbols are ♓, ♊, ♍ and ♐.

These are called the three *modes*, also called *qualities*. Signs opposite each other, such as Aries and Libra (cardinals) or Gemini and Sagittarius (mutables), and signs at right-angles or squares to each other, such as Aries and Cancer (cardinals) and Gemini and Virgo (mutables), always have the same mode.

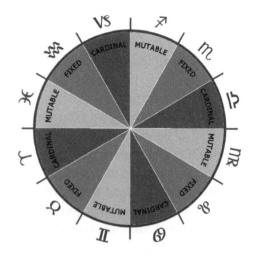

You'll have noticed I've brought in the four elements above too. While there are four signs of each of the three modes, there are three signs of each of the four elements. The interlocking pattern of modes and elements means each sign is unique: there's only one earth cardinal sign (Capricorn) or one fire mutable sign (Sagittarius). This demonstrates the neat divisibility of the number twelve – it can be divided by two, three, four and six.

Since the zodiac is a wheel it has no start or ending, despite what traditional astrology says about Aries being the first sign and Pisces being the last. For some reason, astrologers have replicated this rather counterproductive idea for a long time. A wheel has no end or beginning. However, we have a dilemma, and perhaps this is the reason why.

Since in a book we have to string out ideas along a sequential line, we must start *somewhere*. In order to give a timely boost to the sign Pisces, commonly the last and thus least understood sign (because everyone is tired by the time we get there), we shall start with Capricorn. Since Capricorn marks the darkest and most dormant time of the year this makes some sense – as long as we don't get stuck in the idea that there is an immutable start and end to the zodiac.

The Cycle of the Signs

Winter

♑ **Capricorn.** Capricorn is an earth or grounding sign, and winter is tough – survival stuff. Capricorn faces us with the fact that we live in a situation we just have to accept and deal with, because if we don't we'll suffer cold and hunger. We must carry out our role, fulfil our niche, keep the fires burning, do the accounts and grind through all the other necessaries that we *simply must do*. It's also a time for lying low and beavering away at small, quiet things, systematically and realistically.

Winter solstice or Yule (Christmas) is a time for family reunion and the following of tradition as a socially stabilising factor. We strive for recognition within the social framework, seeking to fulfil what is reasonably expected of us and anticipating exclusion or disadvantage if we don't. We're all in the same boat and we sink or swim together, so we all have to do our bit. Social mores and institutions give continuity to collective life, for in them we find a certain collective protection while the light is low and farms and gardens are unproductive.

Capricorn is the soil in which the seed of a future plant lies dormant, waiting. It focuses on all that is lasting, perennial and relatively unchanging, on routines, established procedures, mores and maintaining regularity. So when the Sun or another planet moves through Capricorn, the issues concern governance, structures, constitutions, laws, accountancy and taxes, history, posterity, wood, metal and rock, engineering and all forms of attempted perpetuity. This sounds uninteresting, but Capricorn contributes stability, organisation and consistency to the world, and that's its gift. At the end of the sign, things can get rather stuck in a groove though, and things become ready for a change. But note that every sign manifests in diverse ways: Capricorn can also be a sign of rebellion, comedy, unreliability and inconsistency – yet these are obverse sides of the same bunch of issues.

♒ **Aquarius,** an air or comparative sign, gets bored with things as they have been. It sees things differently, perceiving the flipside of whatever is customarily accepted and wanting things to move on. There's a spark of promise and hope in the air, yet it's too early yet and winter is still here – so there's a rather contradictory dialogue here between convention and change, and in Aquarius we tend to resolve it by staying detached and pursuing diversions. Our eyes wistfully look to further horizons and we hope for better times, yet another part of us tends to prefer the devil we know to the devil we don't – dualism is a characteristic of all three air signs. Aquarius seeks to enliven conventions with new ideas, shaking up the present and trying to influence collective beliefs with personal insights, wanting everyone to do what it suggests without necessarily wanting itself to take the lead.

Aquarius is a bit restless – it's that cabin-fever feeling. Plans and schemes are made, all fully explained and justified, backed up with principles and ideology. There's a collectivism to it with an individualistic twist, yet heady collective values can also override individual needs and rights, so there is a dialogue here between personal rights and freedoms on the one hand and group interests or the rules of membership on the other. The big question is how to reach a consensus and how decisions are implemented. It can also involve infinite discussions about how to achieve agreement! Majoritarian or populist ideas or values can hold sway, displeasing detractors, making minorities feel overruled and dividing people even when unity was the intention.

Aquarius has some difficulty accepting the current facts of life, which ought, after all, to be different. Things could be better. Come on everyone, let's do it. Yet, in the seasonal round, while the light is increasing at this time, this can also be the toughest part of winter, precisely because the thought of things being different makes pragmatic realism imperative. Aquarius doesn't indulge greatly in feelings or sensitivities, yet there's hope in the air and the future must be better than this. The crisp, frosty present has its virtues too – winter wonderland.

♓ **Pisces**, a water or sensitive sign, knows from long experience that new possibilities need to await their proper time. Big plans survive by excluding all sorts of mysterious factors which, sooner or later, will scupper Aquarian calculations since there's much more to life than meets the eye – and who are we to try to push the river and mould things to our own preferences?

Complicating and delaying factors necessitate a quest to uncover the heart of the matter. We're all small specks in the vastness of creation, and who am I *really*, and what's really what? Wintertime habits and society's mores do indeed restrict individual movement and personal initiative, yet while the thaw is here and balmy days are dawning, the season is still chilly and frosts can pounce, so it's not yet safe to sprout, grow and start afresh. But in this dilemma lies an unseen, up-welling power, and something is brewing. The bottom drops out of things and the void gulps some of our illusions, so deeper preparation is needed if we are to succeed. We need to understand the hidden secrets of how things work.

We must prepare the ground, search our souls, await our time and get on with whatever is within arm's length. Circumstances have a constraining effect but something inside also asks *what about me?* In the mists of unknowing can come times of understanding, for Pisces is tuned to the underlying tides and threads beneath the surface. Answers aren't quite as simple as we first thought, but insights and revelations hold the key.

Pisces teaches us to accommodate conflicting paradoxes, to attend to things others don't consider and to bridge life's yawning gaps – gaps between potential and actuality, between the spiritual and the mundane. Without such perspective we're faced with frustration and confusion, helplessness and incapacity. Pisces is one big prequel, laying the ground for intent (Aries) to meet reality (Taurus). It's all about making the impossible possible – just as springtime, when seen from winter's perspective, seems unlikely and very far away. But now it's coming closer.

Spring

♈ **Aries**, a fire or energy sign, follows spring equinox. The sun is out and seeds are sprouting: the power of creation is unleashed, sometimes with a bang, sometimes creeping up from behind. We throw off inertia, shrug our shoulders and quit waiting. We follow big ideas or new trajectories and don't take no for an answer – after all, *it's important*. Doubt and

hesitation have lost their opportunity: it's timely and right to head for what we want or must do. If in Pisces we didn't uncover a vision and roadmap, life propels things forward *anyway* and we're ripped from our comfortable past. But with a sense of direction, it's mainly a matter of pursuing it.

Aries is rampant, spilling out, proactive and it steps forward, crossing the line. Aries knows what's best and does what it wants – forethought and caution are restrictive. Seize the day or lose your chance: this is the time. Yet there's an uncompromising insecurity to this too, an urge to build facts on the ground before anyone can stop it.

Everything is progressing, competing for space, pushing above ground. Spring is advancing and a prolific new reality is breaking loose. Aries is either sure, firm and resolute, or fitful, precipitate and forceful. Things are now in progress and a momentum is building. At present there is little thought of outcomes and consequences – there's simply an urge to grow and advance. But then, there can be a creeping doubt hidden behind the certainty – am I doing the right thing? – but it's quickly packed away. Too late to worry.

♉ **Taurus**, an earth or grounding sign, works on the basis that the decisions have been made and the course has been set, so we'd better just get it done. Springtime growth, fertility and development are now in full swing and Taurus gets on with the task at hand, sometimes with a magic touch. It can be creative, industrious and gifted, yet there's a lazy, playful

and indulgent, even excessive streak too – after all, spring is rather nice, isn't it? Flowers are coming out, nature is prolific and humming, the past is gone and progress is being made. It's wonderful, delicious, fertile, what Aries wanted, Pisces dreamed of, Aquarius planned for and Capricorn never even thought possible.

This is *living*, *doing*, *moving*, the very stuff of life, and nothing will stop it. Let's build things, fix things, move a mountain – and have a good time too. Practicality and creativity are spliced together in the arts and crafts, or in cooking and gardening. It's too late to change course or back down – this is it. Enjoy it while the going is good: follow your desires, go for it, dance like there's no tomorrow.

Taurus has a steady, rolling power, yet it can be inflexible, disregarding anyone or anything that gets in the way. If you're in the way, you'd better move because I'm coming. Purposeful, sustained and even dogged motion are what Taurus brings – hanging in there. If challenged, it digs in its heels and budges not an inch. Either that, or a lazy or indulgent streak comes out – after all, delighting in the sound of the bumblebees in the bluebells is far nicer than exerting oneself, isn't it? Enjoy the good things of life – the fun, the music and cream buns – after all, you only live once (and if you believe otherwise, you should examine yourself, because my way is the only way). A lot gets done, or enjoyed, and the past is now gone. The days are growing longer and, in temperate climes, this is one of the best times of year. Let's have a slap-up feast.

♊ **Gemini**, an air or comparative sign, with notebook or iPad in hand, is too interested in all that is going on – look at what you're missing! There's a world of variety, fun, colour, alternatives, experiences and ten thousand things to play around with. Gemini can go anywhere and do anything, try things out and enact every possibility that presents itself. Gemini is like a bee in a field of flowers or a swallow in an open sky. Anyone who tries to constrain it will find Gemini gone in a flash. Why get stuck? Gemini maximises on stimulus, situationality, flutter and buzz, and everything is just fascinating, really interesting. Sure, it's complex, and we can talk about it, but hey, shall we have a coffee first? Or we could go on a jaunt.

Gemini isn't quite as captivated by beauty as Taurus is: it looks for patterns, rhythms, formulae and expressions, and it posts them all, with digressive commentaries, on the internet. Life is a fact-finding mission, a movie and a storyline. Everything is relative and nothing is final or fixed, and when challenged to be consistent, Gemini simply replies that that was then and this is now.

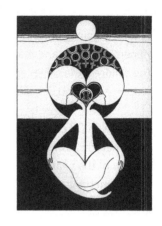

Gemini plays dice with the world and relishes intricacy. There's competition for attention and airtime. Things can pull in many directions at once, so it's best just to do what's next and the rest will work out somehow. Sometimes the pursuit of tangents works quite well because everything still gets done in roundabout ways and it all comes good in the end. Yet often the extent of life's choices and contradictions can present a hurdle that only the clear-thinking can cross. Stuff can get in a tangle, or it can form elaborate patterns. But it's lovely, colourful, the sun is high and the birds are singing. Summer solstice at the close of Gemini is a celebration of being alive, so it's time for some fun! Evolutionary progression has reached its peak, and here I stand. Now where's my mobile phone gone?

Summer

♋ **Cancer**. Hold on, says this sensitive water sign, there's too much happening – it's getting at me. I need to hunker down, put the kettle on and close the door. Amidst all this panegyration I need a safe space of my own, a perch, a standpoint, and to be with my own folk. All these markets and gatherings, these ideas and babble, they're fine, but it's all too big and I'm getting lost – and where is it all going? And when are we going home? I'll nurture what's best, take the safe option and cut the rest – all these people aren't my concern unless they're part of my circle. Though some are welcome at my door, as long as they don't trample on my beautiful rugs.

Things stabilise and reach fulfilment in Cancer, for summertime is now a fact – this is the opposite sign to Capricorn. Possibilities have been explored and we now have actualities. Let's spend summer with our family and network, on our own patch, and make something of it. We need to pull together and look after our own interests – charity begins at home.

Cancer teaches us to cherish what is valuable and look after ourselves in the midst of all the summery goings-on. Mother Earth has given birth and it's a matter of carefully nurturing vulnerable things and making sure they come to fruition. This is how we feed our people. The children, the calves and the chicks are our future – and we must grow what we need to support them and, if necessary, defend them against all the threats out there in the world.

♌ **Leo**, a fire or energy sign, wants us to express ourselves and show the world who we are – and nature shows itself too, in full form. Here the growth, exploration and evolutionary process of the year come to fruition, particularly around Lammas or Lughnasa. It's time to make something of it, act out our truths and show the rest of the world how to do it too. Leo stands at the centre of the universe and everything revolves around it – well, that's how it feels at the time.

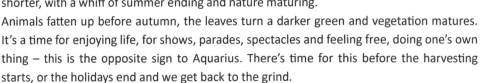

It's a time of year that is special and unique, but at the time it feels as if it ought to be like this all the time. The chicks are fledged, the apples are ripening and the corn is turning gold, the season is as hot as it will ever be... and those damn flies keep getting splattered on my windscreen. Leo acts out the drama and the game of life, dances the dance, believes in itself and enjoys people noticing.

Yet there is a hint of concern: the days are starting to grow shorter, with a whiff of summer ending and nature maturing. Animals fatten up before autumn, the leaves turn a darker green and vegetation matures. It's a time for enjoying life, for shows, parades, spectacles and feeling free, doing one's own thing – this is the opposite sign to Aquarius. There's time for this before the harvesting starts, or the holidays end and we get back to the grind.

Leo loves life yet it realises that perhaps there is more. But in a way it dreads it and isn't ready to face it. The sun is high and the summer is benign, and there's little time or need to think about it, but a niggly feeling says something is coming up from behind. This makes Leo want to party more and draw everyone else in too. Sure, the harvest is starting and we must work together to pull it in, but this is all part of the play of life and the booze-up afterwards makes it all worth it. Just as evolutionary trends were rising in Aquarius at Candlemas, yet they were unready to sprout, so integrating trends creep in at Lammas and there's a need to address pending questions but, well, let's leave them till later. Life is short and then you die, so let's make the most of it.

♍ **Virgo**, an earth or grounding sign, then picks up the pieces. It cleans up when everyone has drunk their fill and even vomited up the results. Virgo, in late summer, has forethought, care, meticulousness and consideration – after all, something concrete needs to be achieved with all this matter of summer, otherwise it's rather pointless and leads nowhere. Virgo believes things when it sees them. The harvest must be stored and processed, the practicalities sorted out and everything put in its proper place. Besides, we each have little significance if we cannot make an enduring contribution that is valued and actually achieves something. It's time to make jam and wine, bottle the fruits, collect the nuts and mushrooms and preserve the fruits of summer – and marauding rats need ingenious counter-measures.

Virgo is not very impressed with the drama of self-expression and seeks a more serious role, a way of quietly making its mark, even if backstage – for here the real power truly lies, in the skilful execution of things. It's the power of organising, fixing and arranging – getting back to work after summer. Virgo attends to things others omit to do, for it's here to bring summer things to a conclusion and fill the gaps, competently, reliably and without fuss.

It's all rather practical, thought-out and efficient, sorting through the consequences of what's happened amidst summertime's jangle, and making something out of it for future benefit and security. Virgo sorts out the details, in hope that they will add up to make a completeness so that things reach some sort of perfection or closure. The opposite sign of Pisces, Virgo also awaits and prepares for a change – the change initiated at equinox. Yet late afternoons can be golden, the dewy mornings refreshing and the reflective nature of this time is rewarding. Watching the Sun go down, it's time for a thoughtful break after a good day's work. Autumn equinox arrives at the end of this sign and a tipping point is reached.

Autumn

♎ **Libra**, an air or comparative sign, surveys the scene and answers, *everything's alright, really*. We can have a nice time, become friends and make things good. We just need to accommodate each other's preferences and come to an agreement. Together we stand and divided we fall, and I'm sure we can work it all out – after all, it's not all that bad. Libra is the opposite sign to self-directed Aries.

The tourists have gone home now and the local community can come back together. If you're at work, routines are bedding in and teams of colleagues engage in shared endeavours – or perhaps, if truth be known, shared complicity in accepting a bad situation. There are advantages in mutuality since relationships create more than the sum of their parts. But it's a question of balancing my interests and yours, though it's nice to cooperate and we can work it out, because life is cruel and we can make it good – we're all in this together.

In Libra autumn creeps up, the nights get longer, the birds have migrated and the season is turning. It's not serious yet and there's scope for enjoying life and exploring new or revived relationships, talking and thinking about things. But the paradox is that there is far more to relationship than being nice: it doesn't work unless relationship is genuinely reciprocal and there's a wider social consensus. Deals must be made and important things need talking through, though Libra hopes to avoid the heavy stuff and trust that all will be well.

Through the unsettling experience of imbalance and oscillation between extremities, Libra seeks a comfortable compromise by accommodating whatever seems needed. Others' views are important, and Libra formulates its position once they've been heard – though fence-sitting is common, to avoid upsetting anyone. There's also a question of whether Libra over-accommodates to others. If pushed too hard, Libra can fight back, even if just for the hell of it, and it can be contrarian and argumentative too: behind the niceties lies a gritty opposition to anything perceived to be wrong. Integrative forces are taking over, and a social contract is needed. There can be frosts and high winds at this time. It's a time of contrasts, and while everything has its compensations, the real business is now about to start.

♏ **Scorpio**, a water or sensitive sign, feels the bottom-line truth deep down. Ouch! Life is hard and part of me hates it – but I'll grin and bear it, stick it out and soldier on through. In Scorpio a social contract is truly forged – you don't hurt me and I won't hurt you. But it's a question of whether this bottom-line statement is stated and agreed or kept unspoken, unaddressed, to avoid explosive encounters. This is a crunch with reality and it brings up a lot of naked feelings, though they're only expressed when truly necessary.

There's no alternative, since it's now dark and cold and we must rely on each other since, if we fail, we'll have to grit our teeth and face the music on our own. The wheels are in motion, winter is encroaching, the leaves have fallen, the weather can be grim and there's something unforgiving about this time. But that's not necessarily bad – it's real life. Sometimes one must just place one's bets and do it anyway, to some extent whether we wish to or not. Yet it's scary - and equally I could pretend it's not there, or spend my life fighting it off.

There's a hidden beauty in this inner struggle, and a deeper truth pointing to ultimate truths and the facts we must accept if we are to survive. In the end we're in life's cess-pit together. Scorpio has a keen gut-level sense of what's motivating others, of hidden agendas and the secretive threads pervading everything. Yet even the rawest of realities have their payoffs, and the more we confront the gritty stuff, the more we'll uncover those benefits. This is the joy of carrying a load and grittily making progress. This is a sign of power, drawing on endurance and second strength when under challenge or duress. Whatever is the case, we must get through it, to see what's on the other side. A change is happening, and Scorpio has the power to pull things through – if, that is, it faces the situation and dares to do what's really needed.

♐ **Sagittarius**, a fire or energy sign, loves life and the possibilities life reveals. This is strange, given the wintry circumstances, but there's something warm and wonderful to getting cold and then coming in to sit round the fire with some mulled wine. There's no point being got down by challenging times – they will pass, so let's make the best of it, eat, drink and be merry, for it's not all that bad. Crisp air, evening fires, new wintertime routines: let's get on with it, stop moping around and look at things another way!

There are lots of things to do, stories to recount, perspectives to share, people to meet, places to go. We're all one big family or crowd of friends, so let's give of our best so that it benefits all of us together. Well, it's not quite so easy, being winter, but Sagittarius won't be got down by it. It accentuates the positive – after all, it's all in the power of belief. So what do you believe? If you haven't figured things out, I can teach you a few things. Life will get better sometime but, in the meantime, let's enjoy life for what it is.

Sagittarius explores the bounty in social life and the great wide world: why get locked up in ourselves when there is all this to enjoy? It's a time for looking at the larger scheme of things, in which we play our bit-part. The Sagittarian feast peaks at winter solstice when, since the dawn of time, the clans have customarily come together to meet. It's time to find out what's been going on with everyone else. The work of the year is over and it's time to enjoy and reap the benefits. Society is re-woven at winter solstice. Then, in Capricorn we have to live it out and, in Aquarius, the social contract will be fully forged, just at the time when evolutionary forces are again picking up.

One cycle ends, another begins

Not quite, says *Capricorn*: we actually need to settle down and be practical – otherwise nothing lasts and it's all hot air. Yes, but let's not get bogged down with your boring routines, says *Aquarius*, let's change things around. Not so fast, says *Pisces*, it's not quite as simple as you think, and we need to see the bigger picture. But we mustn't waste time prevaricating, says *Aries*: it's a matter of just doing it. And really carrying it through, to make sure it works beautifully, says *Taurus*. Ah, you're so one-tracked, says *Gemini* – try out more alternatives too! No, says *Cancer*, I'm staying where I am and enjoying what I have. What you lot need, says *Leo*, is a good dose of my magic recipe – look at this, it will solve everything! Perhaps, says *Virgo*, but look what we've landed up with: it won't work unless we get it really right. Why is everyone arguing? We could have such a good time together, says *Libra*. No one sees how raucous and superficial they are, says *Scorpio*: they're all avoiding the brass tacks of the situation. C'mon, says *Sagittarius*, there's a place at the table for everyone and plenty to be had! And the funny thing is that everyone is right and everyone is wrong, and these are all facets of a diamond.

Hangups!

Capricorn can get stuck in mindless drudgery, *Aquarius* in rebelliousness, placing ideas over facts, *Pisces* can get lost in confused, powerless resignation, and *Aries* can go astray in its insistent desire to be on top of things, while *Taurus* can get bogged down in self-indulgence and dogged inflexibility. *Gemini* gets tangled up in hyperactivity and dilettantism, *Cancer* in defensive self-preoccupation, and *Leo*, well, it just expects everything to go its own way, while *Virgo* gets stuck in nitpicking puritanism and over-concern. *Libra* avoids confrontation and prevaricates indecisively, while *Scorpio* uses up its energy in resistance and resentment, and *Sagittarius* indulges in escapism and over-indulgence. It all depends on how we use our opportunities!

Just watching

There are many ways of experiencing the different signs throughout the year, and year to year you will find your responses to them change. The clues given above might be useful stimuli and pointers, but they do not substitute for your own experience: we could write long tomes on the art of bike-riding, but in the end, riding a bike is learned experientially. A direct feel for time and its modulations is what is needed if we are to live in accord with it, if we are to let it move through us and make the best of each time-opportunity. So let a grasp of the cycle of the signs percolate into you through observation and experience.

It is interesting to observe the energy-change when the Sun moves from one sign to another (an *ingress*). This happens between 20th and 23rd of each month, mostly around the 21st – the exact timing of ingresses can be found in an ephemeris. In the 2-3 days at the end of a sign, things can get stuck in the pattern and mode of that sign, and when a new sign comes, a new atmosphere dawns quite markedly. Things then settle into a rhythm such that, in the middle of a sign, it can feel as if the theme of that sign were always the case. Yet, later on, that sign's message becomes habituated or excessive. The atmosphere or energy-weather lifts and changes again when an ingress comes, and the cycle moves on. It's all a question of underlying atmospheres, time-contexts and energy-frameworks.

The cardinal or initiating signs are at their most typical at their beginnings, the fixed or implementing signs in the middle of the sign and the mutable or assimilating signs are best typified at their end. Thus the twelve signs interlock with the eightfold demarcation of the year. The twelve and the eight intersect exactly at the quarter-points. The cross-quarters, representing mid-process manifestation, sit comfortably in the middle of the fixed or implementing signs.

We could go through the signs again and again, revealing different facets of their nature. The wonderful thing is that they truly cannot be contained in simple definitions. Every time we try to do so, they reveal a new quirk. Getting to speak the language of astrology has a transforming effect on our way of seeing things – it's a language and, as with any language, it's best to learn it to the extent that we need no longer to translate back, so that we think in the new language. It's also an efficient language for encapsulating the deep nuances of time, which mere words can only touch and allude to. Astrological symbolism presents us with dimensional onion-layers to peel off as we grow and progress: new meaning in astrology never ceases to reveal itself. It's over 40 years since I started learning astrology, and new revelations regularly appear to this day.

Take at least a year to observe the ins and outs of the zodiac signs. Observing the Moon passing through the signs, a faster process, gives a clue to the undertones and strands of the signs, but they are best comprehended by following the motion of the Sun. The other planets move through the signs each at their own rate, giving backup and depth to these observations. Within a few years of marking the changing times, a new feel for the pattern and elegance of time emerges.

In the next chapter we'll meet the planets, though there's another chapter about the signs in chapter 9.

6

Wandering Stars

So far, we have looked at the two 'lights', Sun and Moon. The time-energies behind these two are basic and central to the living of our lives, and every enquiring human by rights should understand something about them. When we come to the planets we are dealing with more particular and specialised vibrational resonances, covering different areas of life and reality.

Tapestries of Time

The Earth is not just a physical planet made of rock and water. It's an energy-world, a scintillating, threaded, swirling etheric vitality-ball made up of filigree interwoven skeins of light and frequency-waves, perpetually in motion, forever pulsing and changing. The magnetic field of the Earth is just one part of this – a scientifically measurable part. There's far more, working on a spectrum of levels.

On the Earth's surface, these energies course through meridians and energy-lines like rivers and streams of multi-frequency current, large and small scale. They meet, cross and amplify at power points in space, many of which the ancients worked with to enhance and up-step both cosmic and earthly energies. They utilised subtle energy-technologies to get inside matter, aligning matter and consciousness, not only for their own benefit but also to add their input into nature and the universe. We need to do such work today to help correct what has gone wrong in our civilisation and to heal its damaging effect on the world.

Energy pulses through all living forms, entering physicality through crystals in the rocks, water in the soil, in living things and the atmosphere, through fiery phenomena such as volcanoes and through the dynamics of weather. Physical forms give subtle energy manifest shape and pattern. Subtle energy facilitates life, stirring and affecting climate and ocean currents, the migration of animals, the spread of bacteria and viruses and even the reception on your mobile phone.

This multi-level vibrational field pulsates and fluctuates over time. The twanging and thrumming of the planets of our solar system influence this. This is not just a matter of individual planets affecting Earth's subtle fields – it concerns an interactive solar system which is continually in motion and operating as a whole.

The combined interactions of the planets are identified in astrology by their angular relationships or aspects, as we see them from Earth. Earth's energy-field breathes, heaves, sparks, thrums, calms, blips, ticks over and rumbles in ever-changing ways. An astrologer builds a picture of this fluctuation by looking at the aspects, configurations and arrays of planets and also at the way planets work through the filtration process of the zodiac signs.

We live *within* that energy field – it's all around us, above us and below us, pulsing and circulating in and around the resonator and transformer that is this physical planet, and out beyond its atmosphere, tapering off as one moves further into space. Earth reciprocally influences other planets' energy-fields. This is a psychological, emotional, spiritual, not just a physical influence, and nature itself has its own kind of feelings, thoughts, moods and moments of both sadness and inspiration, which can be picked up by anyone with an intuitive, poetic or symbolic awareness.

Time-energy presents us with changing qualitative atmospheres and psychic climates within which we carve out the stories of our lives, and within which the human race as a whole sculpts its history. There is no directly deterministic cause-and-effect relationship between planets and energy here on Earth or between energy and what we do with it – but they and we are part of the same macro-scale integral system. Astrology is a means of deciphering the way in which these elastic energy-strands interweave, and the way in which, at any moment, certain strands are prominent while others work in the background to come forward at another juncture.

Before we go further, a note on the stars. "What's in the stars" is frequently used as a phrase relating to astrology but, apart from the Sun, no stars are involved. A few astrologers use 'fixed stars' in their work, but astrology is all about the planets, the 'wanderers' of old. For those who do include the stars in their understanding of astrology, they look at the movement of the planets in relation to the stars and the orientation of the Earth to the stars, not generally at the movement of stars themselves.

Why focus on planets? Because in the course of our lifetimes and of human history, the stars do not move appreciably in relation to each other, so their influence provides a constant and consistent backdrop to observable changes connected with the planets. There's one stellar-related issue we shall look at later called the *precession of the equinoxes*, but this is very slow – a 26,000 year cycle. What interests us in astrology is change and timeframes that are relevant to our lifespans and to recent history. That's why we track and study planets.

Identifying Change

The planets are all at work continually, yet there are occasions when some planetary influences are stronger than others – particularly when a thrum of energies or a combination of notes or a chord starts up. At these times it's possible to gain more of a feel for specific planetary energies and the way they combine with other factors, and we can build up an experiential picture of how each planet works in isolation – even though none of them actually works alone. The instances where individual planets reveal themselves most markedly are these:

When they change sign (making an ingress). An ingress brings a distinct change of atmosphere and theme within the area of life which that planet tends to affect, and its flavour reflects the nature of the two zodiac signs involved. This represents a shift of context. Though each sign contrasts the one before and the one following it, there is a sequential meaning to this contrast – each sign contrasts yet leads on from the preceding one. An ingress brings a fresh change since, when at the end of the preceding sign, the taste of a planetary energy can sometimes become soured, clogged, worn or stuck in a groove.

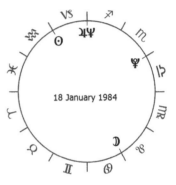

18 January 1984: five planets independently making ingresses. Slow-moving Pluto changed signs six weeks before, and on 19th January both Jupiter and Neptune entered Capricorn on the same day (unusual). It was also a fullmoon, with Sun and Moon both ingressing into new signs opposite each other, simultaneously. This kind of cumulative multi-event doesn't happen very often.

Ingresses, especially in the case of the slower-moving planets, represent times of qualitative choice when we have an option to review and change our mode of operating: these options usually present themselves when the planet is in the last 2-3° of a sign. Then, when the planet changes sign, a fresh contextual pattern emerges and there is a marked change of atmosphere.

When one planet forms an aspect to another planet, or a few aspects to a few planets more or less simultaneously. An aspect is a specific angular relationship between two planets travelling the zodiac – we first met them when we were looking at the lunation cycle of aspects between Moon and Sun. When two planets interact by aspect, they thrum and resonate with each other distinguishably, setting up a third, combined energy-resonance which embodies the 'chemical reaction' they are going through. This is analogous to playing a chord on a piano, where the pressing of a few notes combines to make a new, more complex and tonal sound. More about aspects in chapter 7.

Some aspects are harmonious, some stressful and others mark transitional states of certain identifiable kinds. When exact, they bring forward the influences of the two or more planets involved. There is a grating, crunchy, at times disharmonious energy-buildup to the aspect which then clicks or slots into place when the aspect is exact – rather like a clutch engaging in slow-motion when you're changing gear in a car. Then the outcomes unfold and embed themselves thereafter. While ingresses bring us changes of context, aspects bring actual waves of energy, and they don't just change how things look, they actually pump energy and make a concrete difference.

23rd April 2014: a Grand Cross configuration involving four planets. The Uranus-Pluto square of 2012-15 was upstepped during early 2014 by Jupiter in Cancer and, in April, a retrograde Mars in Libra chugged backwards to make a highly-charged Grand Cross where many wars and peace processes were affected. This configuration was thunderous and edgy in flavour.

When a planet is at a *station* it comes through strongly. It's particularly strong when turning retrograde because, at that time, it is coming as close as it can to the Earth and moving more or less towards us (see chapter 1). This doesn't apply to the Sun and Moon, neither of which turns retrograde, but it applies to all of the planets. A station is a point in time and a place in the zodiac where a planet appears to stop moving, turning from direct (forward) to retrograde (backward) or vice versa. In reality planets move consistently forwards, but we view them from a moving observation platform, the Earth, which creates this effect, analogous to a faster train overtaking a slower train, making the slower train appear to be going backwards when seen from the faster train. A stationary planet usually makes its presence felt for a matter of days around the precise time of the station – an ephemeris will give this time to the nearest minute. More about this later in this chapter.

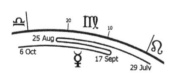

August-September 1990: one of Mercury's retrograde periods of three-ish weeks, with dates of ingresses and stations.

In your perambulations around the pages of your pet ephemeris (it's worth getting one), keep your eye on these and simply *observe* them, without seeking to understand or form quick conclusions. Simply experience, observe and shift your mode of seeing in order to divine imagery, patterns, atmospherics and processes at work in your life and surrounds. By building up a stock of consciously-noted experience, the whole lot will gradually fit into place. This is, of course, a never-ending and ongoing life-process. It's well worth looking at the recent past as well as the present, thinking back to what happened then in relation to planetary motions you can identify in an ephemeris.

Planetary Zodiacal Cycles

These are the cycles of motion of the planets around the zodiac – *sidereal cycles*. They vary greatly in length and behaviour.

The Moon affects us in an hour-to-hour and day-to-day context, although new and full moons, especially eclipses, can raise issues with longer-lasting import – but in this context the Moon usually acts in a triggering fashion for longer-term cycles and processes of change. Things might be brewing or simmering and the Moon can set off specific instances and outbreaks of events, placing these issues before us in definitive terms, even if they last only one day. The shooting of the Archduke Ferdinand in Sarajevo in 1914, sparking the First World War, took place in minutes, but its effect on history lasted years, even generations, killing and impacting on many millions more in the process.

Aspects and ingresses involving the Sun, Mercury and Venus usually affect us within day-to-day and week-to-week timeframes, and Mars on week-to-week timeframes. The time-contexts of these planets depends on their speed at any moment, since all planets except Sun and Moon can accelerate or decelerate, as seen from Earth. Jupiter and Saturn affect us on a month-to-month and year-to-year basis, while Chiron, Uranus, Neptune and Pluto affect us in terms of longer-term issues lasting years, even decades.

Thus we have different levels of time at work and it all depends on what kind of perspective we seek to have – shorter-term or longer-term. It's a bit like looking at an eleven-handed clock where the faster-moving hands highlight the underlying gradual processes unfolding through the slower hands. In other words, a journey might have longterm significance, but you still have to catch the bus or the plane at a particular time, and if you're minutes late, you miss it!

All these levels of time and significance interlace one another. Pluto, moving on a 250-year cycle, can spend 12-35 years in a sign (around 1988 it was moving at its fastest, but as the 21st Century progresses it is gradually slowing, up to 2114). Pluto dredges up deep and slowly-evolving issues of longterm, historic value and significance. Yet the faster planets form aspects to Pluto on their own journeys round the zodiac, pulling longterm Plutonine issues into shorter-term contexts and triggering specific situations and events where Plutonine issues are highlighted.

To give an example of such triggering, in 1989 a Uranus conjunction to Neptune was building up, to become exact in 1993 – this happens once every 170ish years. But in 1989 Saturn conjuncted both of them, while they were still a few degrees apart, while Jupiter and Chiron conjuncted each other in Cancer, opposite them. This was a major five-planet line-up where Jupiter, Saturn and Chiron activated a longer-term process involving Uranus and Neptune. Within days of the Saturn-Neptune conjunction, an historic shift which had been building up for about five years suddenly took shape in the fall of the Berlin Wall, the critical and symbolic point in the transformation of the Soviet Bloc, the reunification of Germany and the wider globalisation process of the time.

The fall of the wall, a local event in Berlin with global significance, marked the manifestation of a bigger, historic, global change. But the conjunction of Uranus and Neptune came 3-4 years later in 1993, itself a quietish year in terms of definite events. It was a year for *trends* more than events – one notable trend being the birth of the worldwide web, leading to enormous consequences unfolding over the decades to follow. So, the fall of the wall and the birth of the web were part of the same historic process, if we stand back and look at things from a distance.

Another example of such an historic shift was the Uranus conjunct Pluto of 1965-66, where longterm changes in awareness, society, geopolitics and technology surfaced as a disruptive and innovative energy-outbreak in those few years and the years that followed. The significance of what took place then will probably take at least 170 years to work through to full cycle, at the next conjunction around year 2130. Do stick around or you'll miss it!

In 2012-15 we reached the first major crunch-point in that cycle starting in 1965-66, the waxing square (a 90° aspect – a quarter of the way through the whole cycle). Even in 2011, the year before it, as the aspect was forming, the Arab revolutions brought stirringly newsworthy events, at times inspiring and at times tragic, yet the overall deeper trends and shifts involved were not limited to that specific time – their causes stretched back at least to the 1920s and their effects will unfold in decades to come. While most of the Arab revolutions were suppressed, except in Tunisia, the full story has not yet unfolded and there is more to come. I can say this because Uranus and Pluto were in a strong aspect at the time, underlining the longterm significance of such events.

There were also significant parallels between the 'cultural revolution' in the West in the 1960s, during the Uranus-Pluto conjunction, and the Arab revolutions breaking out in 2011 during the buildup to the Uranus-Pluto square. In China, the Maoist Cultural Revolution of the 1960s had by 2012 transformed into China's emergence as a world power, and in the period between the nation had transformed from a communist to an authoritarian-capitalist nation.

The next major date to watch in this cycle is 2046-48, the Uranus-Pluto opposition, and a likely defining moment not only in China's history but that of the whole world. How can we say this? Because global trends identified in the 1960s – the 'global village', the 'population bomb', ecological disaster, the space race and many others – and going critical around 2012-15, will reach their climax in 2046-48, by dint of the unfoldment of the Uranus-Pluto cycle. The matters surfacing in 1965-66 will not be fully resolved until 2104, the next Uranus-Pluto conjunction. How that resolution will come, however, is at this stage anyone's guess. Yet these timings are predictable.

The above are big, historic cycles, but we can talk of shorter cycles too, such as the Jupiter-Saturn cycle lasting 20 years, or the Mars-Jupiter cycle lasting on average 2 years and 3 months. Different layers of time are at work, interweaving with one another, and we and the world move through different time-layers at different times, sometimes living through periods of shorter-term significance and occasionally being bombarded with times of deep, longer-term, historic meaning. Only sometimes do we recognise this as we go about life, but these interweavings of duration and significance do take place, and astrology can help us identify and recognise them, using these times to their best advantage.

The Planets' Suite

Here we are looking at the varieties and qualities of energy, atmosphere and situation likely to arise when a planet becomes strongly featured in the energy-weather of any point in time. If you keep a watch on things as you go through life and occasionally refer to this book or to other sources, it will all gradually slot into place. We tend to respond easily to some planets and find it more difficult relating to other ones, though this changes over time.

The planets can be grouped into four main groupings that are worth contemplating. These are:

- the *lights*, Sun and Moon, working with our basic ground of being;

- the *functional* planets, Mercury (average 1 year cycle), Venus (average 1 year) and Mars (around 2 years), working through our mentality, feelings and will respectively, generally affecting periods lasting days and weeks, sometimes months;

- the *organising* planets, Jupiter (12 years) and Saturn (28 years), working through our sense of identity and participation in the world, our sense of involvement and the way we carve out our role. They affect periods of months and years, even a decade;

- the *transformative* planets, Chiron (51 years), Uranus (84 years), Neptune (165 years) and Pluto (250ish years). These work through the group psyche and the soul of nature, affecting historical undertones, socially-shared archetypes and their emergence into consciousness through social figures and cultural imagery. They affect periods lasting years, decades and historical periods.

Each of the planets covers a different area of life – different frequencies, qualities and scopes – in nature, society and on deeper levels. Astrology doesn't really see what is within and what is around us to be fundamentally different things – they are completely interrelated, part of the same wholeness. Things happen around us because they resonate with something inside us, and what happens within us is very much affected by what's happening around us. But what's inside us also conditions the way we experience and respond to events and changes around us: to one person, a shouting, angry person is just a shouting, angry person while, to another, that person can be deeply disturbing, activating responses leading to critical actions and events – and our choice lies in the way we handle these responses.

The Planets in Short

Here's a summary of the planets, which we shall then look at more fully.

☉ **Sun.** Life-force, aliveness, warmth, individuality, our essential way of being alive.

☽ **Moon.** Instincts, life-responses, sensitivities, habits, water, fertility, daily life.

☿ **Mercury.** Thought, connectivity, information, interaction, travel, intelligence.

♀ **Venus.** Feelings, values, love, intimacy, aesthetics, attraction, participation.

♂ **Mars.** Will, assertion, sexuality, energy, progress, effort, desire, competition.

♃ **Jupiter.** Development, involvement, growth, knowledge, beliefs, justice, power, investment.

♄ **Saturn.** Structure, duration, limits, compliance, organisation, pruning, commitment, consequences.

⚷ **Chiron.** Paradox, miracles, dilemmas, blockage, maverick solutions, healing, releasing.

♅ **Uranus.** Shock, reversal, breakthrough, inspiration, contradiction, storms, tangents, shakeups.

♆ **Neptune.** Uplift, faith, doldrums, emergence, collapse, unknowns, illusions, revelation.

♇ **Pluto.** Rumbling, transformation, devastation, harshness, inevitability, finality, might.

We shall now expand on this, starting with the Sun and Moon and working outwards through the solar system.

The Lights

☉ **SUN.** The Sun is a star. It has a completely different status and role to the planets, its children. Sun holds our solar system in orbit and gives it its life. The Sun within us is the 'cubic centimetre of consciousness', the core beingness that holds us together as integral human beings, and all our varying and sometimes contrary facets, our sub-personalities, orbit around it. It represents our potential to shine, to live as if today were the first and last day of our lives, and our capacity to hold to the centre of our being, acting out our truly authentic selves.

Here on Earth the Sun is sometimes obscured by clouds. This is analogous to the way we compromise ourselves by keeping our heads beneath the parapet and staying in line, or getting lost amongst life's pressures and details, forgetting our potential as souls and the reason why we came. We lose track of our spirit and true individuality, going off on sidetracks. This makes life more difficult, complex, humdrum, directionless and depressive. Unveiling the Sun in our hearts, burning the clouds away, we rediscover ourselves, growing up yet growing younger, more enspirited, dedicated and motivated.

Sun is just *there*, being alive. It pulls together the facets of our being and makes us an entity with identity. It isn't about selfishness, since egotism obstructs individuality and inner light. Being authentic, true to our core being, we act within the scheme of things, according to our deepest patterning. When we do this we implicitly sync with others and with life. The universe flows through us and we surf its waves.

When solar energy is strong, life, nature and people move forward, develop, find energy to grow, propagate and create, bloom and bear fruit. All the same, being *yang*, solar energy can also create excess, impose its wishes, prejudices, projections and intentions on people and the world. It can miss out on the need to listen and *hear*, or fail to take in what life is truly offering or signalling to us.

Firm and central, the wise person follows his or her path while also being aware of the world around. We include others and reinforce their own selfhood, tuning into the pulse of whatever is going on at the time. Growing into our fullest selfhood is a lifelong path, and that's one of the things we're here for.

There are twelve zodiac signs, yet just because your Sun sign is Aries or Leo, it doesn't just mean you're 'like this' or 'like that', living according to a dictionary definition. Each sign explores a theme, a hologram. The way we manifest that theme varies according to factors in our charts, as well as our upbringing patterns, previous life experiences, culture, choices and predisposition as a soul. Virgo might be about detail and tidiness, but some Virgos are neurotically tidy, some are systematically methodical, some are easygoing and some downright disorganised – but they're all exploring the same theme, and their relationship with it will change over time too. So you can have meek Leos, Cancers who travel incessantly, reliable Geminis, unreliable Capricorns, impractical Taureans and Pisceans who excel themselves as engineers! Look deeper to see the themes they're working with in their lives.

☽ MOON. Moon is by far the fastest of the moving bodies in Earth's sky. It's our twin planet, co-orbiting the Sun with the Earth in a mutual dance. Lunar energy channels our umbilical, gut-level or womb-based feelings of alrightness or agitation, safety or insecurity in many and subtle ways. Our innate sense of confidence is wrapped around our experience of the situations we encounter in life. These are conditioned by the shadows of past experiences which, if uncleared through awareness, forgiveness and releasing, leave us with vulnerabilities and desensitised bits in our psyches. This renders us subject to psycho-emotional instability, deriving from within or from the world around. The more we open up to life, the more we feel okay and trusting. We are less wobbled by situations, however threatening they might seem.

Our insecurity comes from stored unconscious memories of earlier life experiences, picked up at times when our sensitivities were infringed or we experienced pain, loss or life's rougher aspects. If we had little chance to resolve such issues, or perhaps we blocked resolution, or it was blocked by circumstances or by those around us, then these shadows imprint in us. Later on, when situations arise to reactivate such memories, we can go into a wobble, over-reacting in some way to what's happening, internalising or externalising it.

These memory-programs are drummed in particularly through habituation or trauma. They can be inculcated into us by parents and others, or by social-cultural hand-downs – fear of ghosts, dread of hunger or exclusion, or even fear of hugging or of success – and we tend to act out these programs unconsciously. Thunder means fear, hunger means eat, goodbye means loss, money means happiness or emotion means danger: we all have whole banks of automated emotional programs inside us, activated by promptings from life situations and subjective impressions we acquire on a daily basis. Thus we carry our past around with us – unless we free it up. If we do so, it converts into a strength, a form of resilience.

Lunar energy is *instinctual*. How we relate to instinct depends on how friendly we are with our bodies and with the child inside us, how comfortable we feel being open and vulnerable. Instinct knows things the thinking mind cannot grasp – it is an animal intelligence, and animals know many things without needing education. Every moment of every day we are presented with choices to run old auto-response patterns or to respond to life from a new, open and inherently safe viewpoint, even when we're at death's door. Gurdjieff once called humans 'mad machines', as if automatons at the mercy of our unconscious programming.

Moon energy takes us through ever-morphing moods, changing feelings and angles on life. We're challenged to permit ourselves to be sustained, nourished, cared for and fulfilled, trusting in life as a supportive process. These issues crop up in the smallest of details, in dispositions and situations lasting but moments, on a daily basis. Have you observed the way you eat your food, do your bathroom duties, walk, rise in the morning, respond to the phone ringing, to the wind blowing or to dogs barking?

The Moon influences the movements and the energy-charge of water – not only the sea's tides but also underground water tables and water circulation within plants, in the atmosphere and in our bodies. In gardening, to grow strong leaves, plant and harvest on the waxing moon, and for root crops plant and harvest during the waning moon. Most ancient sites are located above 'blind springs' or 'water domes', (upwelling water flows from deep in the Earth that hits an impervious layer and fans out horizontally, creating an energy-field with both radial and spiral patterns). No one has had the time or resources to do a systematic study of the changes over time of dowsable energy-fields at ancient sites, but it is certainly the case that they are more strongly energised at particular times more than others, not least on fullmoons. Their periodicities seem to vary from site to site.

Often the weather changes on or just before a newmoon or fullmoon. There are no simple rules to this because it concerns large-scale weather systems, but quite often a weather pattern will hold consistently for two or four weeks, then to change around two days before new or full moon, then settling into another weather pattern when the new or full moon pass.

The Functional Planets

☿ MERCURY. Closest of all planets to the Sun, Mercury appears from our perspective to hover around it, always staying within 27° of the Sun – it runs either ahead of it or trailing it as the Sun moves through the zodiac. Mercury orbits the Sun roughly three times in one of our years, seeming from our perspective to swing around it. It turns retrograde three times annually for roughly three weeks each time, when it comes around our side of the Sun.

Mercury is not easily seen in our sky except when rising or setting, and when it is over 20° (40 sun-widths) from the Sun, and on clear evenings or mornings only. The furthest it goes from the Sun is about 54 sun-widths (27°). It's easier seen if you're closer to the equator because dusk and dawn turn from light to dark, or vice versa, more quickly than in temperate or colder climes.

Its only aspect with the Sun is a conjunction, which happens either when Mercury is direct (moving forwards), behind the Sun as seen from Earth, and called a *superior conjunction*, or when it is retrograde, in front of the Sun, and called an *inferior conjunction*.

When Mercury is active, things get zippy and there is much to-ing and fro-ing, chatter, brain-rattling, tickertape, data-transfer and buzzing. Mercury activates our mind, in its capacity to receive, store and process information and ideas, and in its communicative capacity. Lungs, speech organs, hands, ears and eyes are involved, as well as the stomach – all of them organs with which we make contact with our surrounds. Language, writing, rationalisations, travel, information, communications media and wind are all transmitters of Mercurial energy. So is a book such as this, or your computer, or a communicative person.

Our nervous systems and intelligence are activated by Mercury. It separates things out, differentiates people, places and thoughts, then interrelates them by creating linkages and connections. Observe your own mind, the flight of birds, the road traffic, airports and stations, the internet and people's propensity for interchange and communication while Mercury is active.

Even with the weather there are different qualities to wind, rain or sunshine that can be ascribed to the influence of the planets. Mercurial wind can be changeable, breezy and capricious, Venusian wind can be soft, balmy and pleasant, and Mars wind can be cutting and fierce. Mercury is connected with the buzzing of flies and bees, the flight of birds, the creeping of tentacles and the erosive transport of rock and soil. Children of 2-4 years of age are in their mercurial stage, learning to talk, fingers reaching everywhere.

When Mercury is retrograde it's time for a rethink. Connections might not work well, the internet and communications become glitchy and delayed. We're obliged to reconsider things that we took to be given or true, or which are quoted as the norm. Deeper down it can be a time of insight, repairing or reaffirming connections in a different way. It's time to work on the programming code behind a web-page rather than the visible web-page itself.

Mercury is one of the planets connected with that capacity within us to ingest, comprehend and relate to what goes on in our experience. It separates things out and then knits them together in patterns and systems. The explanations we are given by our elders and at school can be crucial in forming our Mercurial mental patterns. It can be grouped with two other planets: while Mercury is a data-processor, Jupiter is a builder of understanding and Uranus is an illuminator and stirrer affecting the way we see things.

♀ **VENUS.** Venus orbits the Sun inside the orbit of Earth and outside that of Mercury. Like Mercury it follows the Sun around the zodiac, except moving further away from it, up to 47° distant from Sun as it travels through the zodiac – so it can form a semisextile (30°) and a semisquare (45°) aspect to the Sun, but no others.

It's often called the Morning Star or Evening Star and, when about 40° from the Sun, at its Great Brilliance, it is bright and slightly bluish, setting after the Sun in the evening (if ahead in the zodiac) or rising before the Sun in the morning (if trailing it in the zodiac). Like Mercury it also moves behind the Sun to make a superior conjunction and then, when retrograde it comes in front of the Sun to make an inferior conjunction. Venus is retrograde for about forty days every twenty or so months.

While Moon energy is umbilical and gut-level, Venus energy moves through our hearts, our likes, love and affections – and our dislikes, alienation and aloneness. Both, together with Neptune, are regarded as feminine planets influencing different levels of feeling and sensitivity. When Venus energy flows well we feel loved, loving, appreciated and included, content, open, creative and emotionally warm. When it's not flowing well we feel separated, sad, distanced, isolated, estranged, closed-up, vulnerable or hurt. It's all to do with the condition of our heart, affecting our feelings about everything. That's why, when you're feeling 'in love', everything around you is rosy and bright. But love is a *choice*, not something that just happens to you if you're lucky. The best way to find a friend is to be one.

Through our hearts we feel goodness, approachability, kindliness and closeness, fondness for people and the world around us, and we're drawn to what we like. We can also feel aversion, dislike or even disgust toward anything we don't feel good about. Imagine yourself lying in a flowery field on a warm summer's day, with butterflies, birdsong and a happy feeling, and that's Venus at work. Children of 4-6 years of age are in their Venusian phase.

Imagine being alone in a strange city where no one makes eye-contact, you're wet and cold and the last train has just left, and that's the other side of Venus. However it's not exactly about circumstances but your *feelings* about it: you might be at a genial gathering of people but not liking it, or you might be standing alone in the rain and delighting in it.

Venus concerns values, evaluations of like or dislike, and the basis by which we make choices based on those likes and dislikes. Choices are essentially emotional decisions, no matter how much you might think about them – Venus either likes things or it doesn't, and it doesn't need rationalised reasons for its preferences. It embodies our aesthetic senses and partialities, our musical and artistic taste, our fancies and romantic tendencies.

Scientists like to think that birds sing for functional reasons such as mating or territoriality. That's true but the bit that science fails to understand is that birds sing because they love it – as do humans – and from a Venusian viewpoint this needs no further explanation.

Venus joins things up, brings people together, fertilises the fields and woods and weaves its magic through music, colour, texture, taste and artistry. To love, one needs to *feel loving*, to give and receive in trust without expectation or requirement. Venus represents the law of attraction and the urge to merge or identify with things we feel good about or drawn to.

When Venus is retrograde we need to re-evaluate our feelings. Relationships can go dry or dysfunctional at times yet, underneath, something more is called for in the way of compassion, empathy, consideration or kindness – a deeper kind of love and support that's needed when loved ones are far away, when affections don't flow normally or when the barren aspect of life shows itself. Nothing is necessarily *wrong* – it's just different. This concerns the kind of love we might have for someone who is ill, failing or struggling – which happens to all of us now and then. In some ways, that's when we need love most.

Astrology identifies three main forms of feeling: the lunar kind, in our capacity to sense what's going on (such as when entering a room) – either it's safe or something's 'not right'; the Venusian kind is our sense of happiness with being alive, our heartfelt feelings of being part of something and bonded with people, places and things; and the Neptunian kind is our capacity to feel deeper, selfless appreciation and empathy, seeing the light in nature or in another person's soul. These are the three planets that work through the feminine in all of us.

♂ MARS. Mars orbits the Sun on a two-year cycle, turning retrograde once in that cycle for about ten weeks. At such a time, Mars can hover in one or two signs for several months – otherwise, when moving forward it spends between a few weeks and two months in each sign, depending on its speed. It lies outside Earth's orbit, so it doesn't follow the Sun as Mercury and Venus do – it does a complete cycle of its own. It's a reddish planet in the sky, best seen at night when around opposition to the Sun – at which time it is closest to Earth, with its illuminated side facing in our direction.

Mars affects energy and assertion: our ability or incapacity to get what we want and to make things work the way we intend. When Mars energy is strong we have a driving urge to make things move, get some action and strengthen our cause. This can bring up feelings of frustration, anger, resentment, restlessness or thwartation too, if we are disposed to feel such things or if things don't go our way. Mars represents action, will and wanting. In the weather, it brings hard rains or fierce winds, or relentless sun or cold, sometimes tense, sometimes exciting.

But there's another, deeper side too, involving patience, fortitude, application, strategy, conflict management and skill – since our ultimate interests are often best served this way. We all need to win, though beating others down, creating losers and spilling blood eventually charges its price and the repercussions of our acts come back at us. Even the greatest of military empires will fall if it just tramples over people and makes people hate it.

Mythologically the god of war, it's also a god of peace since war is a failure to achieve ends by other means. Yes, Mars is about standing up for ourselves, engaging with life, deal-making, exercising muscle and clout, jousting with dragons, making things move and doing the necessary engineering to achieve great things. Yet to achieve truly beneficial results, this must be done dextrously, with strategy and fairness – as the great Chinese general Sun Tzu once said, there's little gain in conquering a country if it is devastated in the process and the inhabitants are driven against you by the force of your own acts.

Mars is a sexual energy, firing up from between the legs and in the solar plexus, moved by desire seeking fulfilment, catharsis and orgasm – whether in lovemaking, running a race or making it in the world. Spiritually it concerns *kundalini*, *tantra*, martial arts and vigorous practices such as prostration, sweat lodge or endurance tests. Things accelerate and are activated when Mars is strong, and an insistent force comes into play. This sometimes clears the air, causing distance to be covered, and sometimes it leads to trouble, hurt or the squashing of finer considerations. It all depends on maturity, skill, technique, gentle firmness and calm certainty.

When Mars is retrograde things can get scrambled, obstructed or they can fall flat, or ongoing projects or plans lose energy. Yet a realignment of the will is possible here: to overcome challenges one must build up one's resources and intent, prepare the ground, act in a timely and appropriate way, hang in there, apply focus and think about ultimate objectives. Sometimes it's necessary to hold back, awaiting one's moment, or perhaps even examine one's motives or plan of attack.

One who knows Mars well also knows how to temper their will by applying firm persistence, diligence, tolerance and focus, applying neither too much nor too little force to overcome obstacles. It's about getting action without creating undue blowback – as Newton stated, to every action there is an equal and opposite reaction.

In nature it's all about rutting, digging and building, competition and survival of the fittest – also gales, floods and erosion. In society it concerns war and peace, competitive games and elections, demonstrations, trials of strength, showdowns, competition, violence and resolution. It gets things done, excels itself and builds masterpieces – but do be aware of unintended consequences.

The Organising Planets

♃ **JUPITER.** The biggest planet in our solar system, bright and colourful in our night sky around the time when it opposes the Sun, Jupiter has a twelve year cycle, staying in each sign for roughly a year and turning retrograde for around 4-5 months each year. As with all of the outer planets from here on outwards, it regularly moves two steps forward and one step back.

Jupiter has an enhancing, furthering, precipitating, extending and enriching influence. It wants to make things bigger, better, more in quantity and more advanced too. Traditionally regarded as benefic, it moves things forward, precipitates and progresses them. Whether or not this is 'good' depends on the time, context, current situations and beliefs. It's the planet of investment and contribution based on hope, faith, confidence, calculated risk and principles, for the reaping of a reward, whether for self or for everyone.

Jupiter seeks a better life, enjoyment, prosperity and increase. It doesn't always work like this, demanding astute choices and enterprise, sound judgement and knowledge to succeed. Without these, Jupiter's ventures can swell into gambling and speculation, inflated hopes, rampant profit-seeking, waste, corruption and ill-considered schemes, leading ultimately to damage and grief. What is it all for, and how much is enough? To answer this, a deeper, wider philosophy, consensus and sense of proportion is required.

Jupiter concerns beliefs and belief-systems, how we widen and deepen our understanding of things and how things add up to a wholeness. Beliefs play a large part in creating realities, and experience also affects our beliefs. Principles, ideologies, myths, received wisdom, memes, cultural biases, worldviews and religious articles of faith are involved, many of them adopted by osmosis, conditioning or the emulation of leaders, intellectuals, high priests or the prevailing drift of society.

Jupiter represents agreements, customs and laws, shared understandings, cosmologies, religious practices and all ways of seeing beyond the immediate, the personal and the parochial. It concerns socially-formed judgements of right, wrong and of shared interest. For us as individuals it concerns our confidence, constructs and mythologies. Jupiter shapes our sense of how we belong and subscribe to society through making a contribution and claiming our rights.

Jupiter cooperates with Mercury, the information-gatherer, sorting Mercury's data into a big picture. It cooperates with Uranus, inasmuch as Uranus can shake and question our beliefs, which then Jupiter sorts into a new worldview.

In nature, Jupiter's roughly one-year stay in each sign indicates areas of renewal and growth in nature, such as pollination in Gemini, fertility in Cancer, fruiting in Leo or seeding in Virgo. When waxing strong, Jupiter urges us to 'cross the great water', make forward steps, reach out and externalise ourselves. It stimulates activity, bravado, publicity and intensified social interchange. Father Christmas is a classic Jupiterian archetype, as is the Hindu Ganesh or the Japanese Fat Buddha. But Jupiter can also provoke invasions, bulldozing, excess and takeovers.

When Jupiter is strong, society throbs with issues, fads, flaps and surges. Beliefs can overshoot realities or they can enhance them. In the end, an accepted belief becomes a reality because it *works*, but sometimes there is first a phase where social persuasion convinces everyone that something is real or true when time proves that it isn't. What tests this is Saturn.

♄ **SATURN.** Saturn is a big planet with a 29.5 year cycle, staying in each sign for around 2.4 years, turning retrograde for 4-5 months each year. It's the outermost planet of our solar system that is visible to the naked eye. When at its brightest, when the Sun is around opposition to it and it is closest to Earth, Saturn is medium-bright, with a dullish pewter-yellow kind of colour.

When Saturn is at work, life can be an uphill struggle. Sometimes this is a positive challenge to grapple with and sometimes it's a big obstacle, wearing you down – depending on the circumstances and your mindset. Overdue matters get forced onto the agenda, consequences stare us in the face and a pruning, focusing, clearing-out and settling up is needed – it *has* to happen. It can be sobering but there's a deeper meaning to this: we must put the number one priority first, get to grips with life's key issues and account for ourselves, to fellow humans and to our souls. Not facing things charges a higher price in the longterm. Saturn makes us aware of consequences – and if we aren't aware, it brings consequences to make us so.

If we omit to get straight our priorities and duties, Saturn teaches by giving us experiences of failure, disability, deprivation, degeneration, guilt, doubt or obstruction. It's a big teacher, giving us three chances. First time around involves the correction of a mistake; second time around involves correction of a pattern; third time around lessons come our way to teach us how to learn. Willingness to learn and to self-correct makes Saturn a friend and guide. Adversity is a gift if we make something of it. There's a big question here: to whom or to what are we truly accountable – to society and its demands, or to our soul? What's most important in the end?

Saturn is about authority, whether we are the authority in our own lives or whether we hand it over to those above us. Since the latter is frequently the case, Saturnine issues often concern obeying the law, paying taxes, conforming to requirements and fitting into the system, setting aside deeper needs or even conscience to do so. But the problem we face today is that the system we live in itself avoids facing big questions, being based on an enormous collective lie, so conforming to such a system makes us complicit in its wrongs and its crimes. For which, ultimately, we all pay.

Who is responsible when things go wrong? Ultimately ourselves. Even if other people made the mistake or did the crime, we somehow were involved, as a result of choices we made. Or if an earthquake strikes or an invading army takes over our town, we have choice as to how to respond in that moment. Recognising this puts into our hands a greater power to master life's challenges. However, we must be careful with this thought when applying it to other people: if you're a child and a bomb falls on you, your sole responsibility is that, for whatever reason, you were standing there at that moment, and it doesn't mean you deserved to be bombed. Also, when applying it to ourselves, we must not use this thought to pump up our sense of guilt. Responsibility and guilt are different things.

Climatic extremes and tough weather events in nature, wet or dry, hot or cold, are Saturnine. Winter and 'Jack Frost' are Saturnine. So are defining events – times when the chop comes down and everything becomes decisively different. The laws of life, nature and society and their sanctions for disobedience are saturnine. It's rather serious.

There are things we can change and things we can't change, and we do need to know the difference. This is quite a profound question. Sometimes acceptance reveals other possibilities or it hones our spirit. Sometimes getting to grips with tough stuff opens possibilities unavailable until we took that step. Saturn is a teacher, helper and supporter, but to make friends with it we must be willing to tread our path alone if necessary, to walk our talk and do what's needed. None of the world's great people got there by taking the comfortable path through life.

Human ways and laws are a mixed bag, some worthy and others favouring a privileged and powerful few. This illustrates two aspects of Saturn – natural and social law. Ultimately natural law (hard facts) overpowers social law, but social law has an enormous impact on everyone's lives. Under a cruel dictator or an oppressive system, people have few options but to lie low, stay out of trouble, to make a sacrifice of themselves or to go into exile. Yet it's also true that such situations arise because most people failed to make a brave choice and stop things developing when they had a chance to do so. This doesn't help a child who is raped. But it does put before us our responsibility to do something, if not for ourselves, then for others, and if not for now, then for the future.

Saturn forces us to improve the conduct of our lives and the construction of our worldview. Key to this is the facing of three big self-limiters: fear, guilt and shame. The defining moment comes when, deep within us, a voice says "I've had enough". A line gets drawn and something turns in our deepest seat of consciousness, causing us to stand up and be counted, or to take up the baton.

Sometimes we must serve time, working long and hard. A work of art or a satisfying achievement is created not by luck or chance but by hard work, skill, focus and commitment. Saturn obliges us to manifest our truth, organise our lives, prioritise what is most important and do what we must. For this, at root we must acknowledge who we truly are, where we're going and what we're really here for. It often involves postponement of gratification until another day, for longterm benefit – but that path has its joys too. If we avoid such acknowledgement we often find ourselves aligning to something that eventually charges a price and stains our soul.

Saturn represents a contract we signed before birth that we came here to carry out – we each have a mission, and holding back means we not only omit to fulfil our potential but also withhold necessary benefits we could bring to the world. Saturnine missions can be the most gratifying worldly actions we can carry out, even if they take a whole lifetime. Saturn brings favourable consequences when we're getting things right, though it keeps us within our confines until we do what it takes to get there. This can involve a crisis that wears us down until we get the message. Saturn's is a planetary influence we need to give attention to in our time.

Saturn works through institutions, laws, procedures, traditions, hierarchies and power structures. Obey the rules and you will gain recognition and rewards, but disobey and you will be punished and cast out. In such a way we are kept, and we keep ourselves, under control, with the agency of carrots or sticks.

In nature, Saturn brings about hard conditions, challenging the strength of tree-trunks, river-banks and rocks – it weeds and prunes the weakest species to prosper the stronger ones and help nature maintain itself. Hardship is a test but it furthers life and new growth – if we treat it that way. This is our free will. Ultimately, everything that befalls us is a gift, even when disguised as the opposite.

⚷ **CHIRON.** This planetoid, discovered in 1977, orbits between Saturn and Uranus on a 51 year cycle, eccentrically crossing the orbits of both – Uranus' when Chiron is in Aries, where it stays for eight years (because it's further from the Sun), and Saturn's when in Libra, which it rushes through in one year (because it's closer, and there's a certain twanging pattern to its orbit). Astronomers reckon it was captured by our solar system and, with its erratic orbit, it will one day ping itself out again – though not tomorrow. Many astrologers have found Chiron to be quite a powerful planet, even though it's small and quite distant.

Chiron is all about our place in the great chess game of life – and from its viewpoint the game is more important than we are as individuals. It highlights and engages our personal gifts, knacks, genius and intuitions in resolving quite concrete yet paradoxical questions, often with both personal and transpersonal significance. Like Uranus, Chiron works through the *knower* within us, challenging us to unclamp our preconceptions and rationality from their anchors. It encourages us to follow that spark of enlightened insight and action that somehow knows what's best and does what's right. To do this, we need to see things another way, a-rationally, perhaps magically, perceiving the conundrums in things.

Chiron tests our capacity to solve riddles with no precedents or immediate answers. Either we stay within our knowns, fears and conditioning, or we step beyond them, following our noses and doing what feels appropriate in the circumstances. If we stay within our knowns, things can get very complicated, and if we step beyond, magic happens. This doesn't require education or training: it's more to do with getting the message life might be telling us. If you're on a journey and all the traffic lights turn to red, there's meaning in it: set aside your worries and listen for that meaning. The situation might mean your journey is fruitless, or it might be testing your resolve, or you might find that the person you were going to meet is late too – so *everything is*, in truth, *perfectly alright*.

Chiron is the maverick. It helps us defy expectations, change the game, create miracles or find a previously untrodden path through life's maze. Even if you didn't know what to do, you found out anyway. When you thought you were doing one thing, it turns out you've achieved many other outcomes as well. A key was turned. When Chiron is strong, we are presented with aggregated and aggravated problems and dilemmas, gridlocked and seemingly irresolvable. Yet with some focus and a shift in the way we do things, a solution is found and often it's dead simple. It's like losing your keys – a small issue with big effects. You find them just when you've given up, taken a break and, lo behold, your hand fell on them. Even if you'd searched everywhere.

Strange paradoxes take place, yet they have their meaning in the bigger picture, even if understood only retrospectively. Having tried all the logical, saturnine solutions we can think of, we open up to Chiron, to find that the problem we thought we had is something else entirely, and that a solution is right in front of us.

In the problem lies the solution. Sure, you had a puncture in your tyre, but it happens to cause you to meet someone you needed to meet. Sure, you had a problem you couldn't crack, but in the process you made a breakthrough in something else entirely. You didn't need to worry about the loss of your job because that loss prompted a rethink, leading you in a completely new and fruitful direction that you wouldn't even have considered had you not lost your job first.

Everything that happens in connection with Chiron seems *meant* to happen – though sometimes it takes years to see this. Synchronicities, uncanny flips and breakthroughs, inner guidance and deeply-engaging predicaments characterise Chiron at work. Its symbol is a key, a very small item with a very big effect – it allows you to enter new territory.

Part of our work as humans is to facilitate the universal flow. When working in harmony with this elusive yet immanent force, our ability to rescue situations grows immensely, leading to outcomes that might well have no personal rewards but it's still worth doing it. This concerns what you become by doing it, and the wider situations you help. But to grapple with this, we must get friendly with contradictions and paradoxes. Just because it's an obstacle, it doesn't mean it can't be cracked. The more difficult it gets, the closer you might be to a solution. But it's a shift of perspective that uncovers it. Drop logic and method: Chiron just *knows*.

The Transformative Outer Planets

♅ URANUS. One of the outer planets of the solar system, first discovered by William Herschel in 1781, Uranus spends seven years in each sign, following a reasonably regular orbit. It's a big planet, as are Jupiter, Saturn and Neptune. Its orbital period, 84 years, is roughly one half Neptune's (165ish years) and one-third of Pluto's (248ish years) – they are loosely synchronised. It's also not far from three Saturn cycles and seven cycles of Jupiter.

Uranus works under the surface by stirring things up, disrupting, activating, sparking and rattling things. It demands improvisation and adaptation by creating acute, extreme or polarised conditions for us to deal with. It creates spikes and surges of energy, ripping up whatever is old and inappropriate, creating edgy situations that force mutation and innovation. Like Jupiter, Uranus precipitates things, but while Jupiter furthers and increases things, Uranus shakes them out. It has a way of forcing about-turns and radical changes of direction.

It tests the validity and flexibility of forms and structures, ways of seeing things, social mores or staid institutions. Suddenly one day things are different, manifesting in strikingly factual ways such as storms, earthquakes, market crashes or political crises. Either that, or Uranus changes the way things *look* – the emperor suddenly has no clothes, the bishop has lost his trousers or floods suddenly make people realise how vulnerable they are. Sometimes it's shocking or confounding at first but, later, if truth be known, things are going more in the right direction than they were before.

Uranus awakens the knower within. This is a necessity, because existing knowledge and solutions become invalid. Uranus takes us out of our depth, obliging us to sink or swim. While Jupiter is a believer, Saturn a rationalist and Chiron a maverick, Uranus is an inspirational prodder, a crazy stirrer, the wildcard or firecracker. It operates para-logically, prompting us to intuit and envision our way through the rubble. It's a game-changer and, from here on in, everything is different. It's already too late to complain.

This still leaves a choice: whether to go along with change or to resist and oppose it. Frequently human societies do both, polarising into conflicting sides. Uranus drives things off their previous course but, even if resisted, there's no return to the former situation – a new direction of travel has already started. Things can get better and worse at the same time. But there's eventual net progression, even when initially things seem to turn backwards. We humans are creatures of habit and Uranus shakes things around, upping the tempo, electrifying situations and giving us a kick.

In the Arab revolutions of 2011, the revolutionary wildfire was triggered by the suicide of one young person in Tunisia – not an exceptional event, since there had been several similar instances before, but it held disproportionately strong symbolism, igniting stored-up energy waiting to overflow. People knew change was needed without expecting it actually to happen. Later on there was a counter-revolutionary fightback – in Egypt a Saudi-funded authoritarian dictatorship in new guise, and in Syria, violent jihadi movements that hijacked the revolution, plus a dogged regime. Whatever their weaknesses, history is on the side of the revolutions, and Uranus' role (in Aries at the time) was to set the Arab world on fire.

In the end, things change because young people, who are often the change-agents, grow up, while older people, often the resisters, die off. Sometimes reformers appear after the conservatives have exhausted themselves or grown old. Change comes eventually. If only it could be easier, less damaging – revolutions, after all, arise only because normal Jupiterian change and progression are blocked for too long.

Sudden, impish, abnormal, differing, dissenting, extremist energy abounds. Things heat up and erupt, whether in the form of mass movements, minority activist groups or reforming leaders. Sometimes events seem accidentally to precipitate change. Sometimes shadowy aspects of the past are revealed, collapsing people's trust in the old order. This wrenching can be difficult and painful, but Uranian moments are often inspired, electric, futuristic, clear, edgy and sharp.

When meeting resistance, Uranian surges twist in strange and perverse ways. A revolution can be hijacked at its moment of vulnerability. Complicating factors can emerge or the movement for change can fragment, often because what has been set in motion proves less simple than first thought. But the longer-term clocks of Uranus' influence bring further waves later on, and evolving history moves on through phases of both change and resistance, pushing forward and pushing back.

Inventors, innovators, rebels or disrupters embody Uranian impulses, with a catalytic effect on public awareness and change – though many also go unheard, living on the margins of society. Artists, musicians, writers, communicators and young people play a catalysing role too. Defining events can quite suddenly change public perceptions and sentiments, tipping the scales by thrusting iconic symbols and images before us, raising issues not confronted before. The consequences of a Uranian outburst can reverberate down the line – a climatic event can lead to economic or social reverberations in distant places, or to consequences in completely different arenas, or shake-ups in mindsets, the puncturing of charades or the loosening of stuck situations.

But sometimes nothing happens except for the piling up of an intense need for change. Conservatism becomes energised to oppose change, pushing back in a counter-revolutionary way, finding innovative ways of keeping things the same. Sometimes the heat rises, but events come to little. Or the king is beheaded and a dictatorship takes his place (as in the French Revolution, giving rise to Napoleon). Or the course of change is hijacked by military adventures, or by inquisitions or suppression. This stores up historical charge for a future time when conservatism has relaxed, lost vitality or undermined itself – followed perhaps by overdue reform rather than revolution.

In nature, Uranus can bring weather extremes, earthquakes, tidal waves, outbreaks of disrupting influences such as viruses and pests, or searing climatic challenges such as droughts or storms. Though humanity frequently fails to learn its fundamental lessons, there's a message and a lesson in such circumstances, requiring a radical change of direction.

It's not easy when Uranus sparks a blowout, yet it accelerates things and draws a line on the past, opening new avenues into the future.

♆ NEPTUNE. Neptune, discovered in 1846 by two different people at the same time, moves through one sign every 14ish years, completing a cycle in 165 years – so in a long life, a person or a generation experiences half a cycle. It represents a higher octave of feeling in the form of compassion and communion. Boundaries soften or melt and structures collapse, yet the insight, uplift and growth that results can heal the pain or loss that such dissolution and vulnerability can bring.

When Neptune is strong, our props surreptitiously disintegrate, the ground dropping away, and we are left with open space and a perplexed disorientation. This arouses fear or relief, depending on one's disposition. Inappropriate notions, obsolete reality-bubbles, outdated identities, inappropriate edifices and bad arrangements are invalidated, rendered irrelevant. This leaves a wide-open situation for which acceptance is usually the best remedy. Neptune is an awakener by literally dis-illusioning us, moving us into a new space of possibility.

A Neptunian atmosphere has a weird, becalmed, stranded, dreamy quality to it, in which it's difficult to know exactly what's what. This can be liberating and reprieving or confusing and confounding. Things just come apart. Neptune removes obsolescence and dumps us in the present, updated and re-booted. It feeds the imagination – though whether this is fantasy, delusion or revelation sometimes comes clear only gradually. Myths, tropes and waves of belief can have both an enriching or a troublesome effect, depending on how real we count them to be.

This imaginal quality can be valuable in the arts and media, or damaging and wasteful in the case of fads, collective delusions and rashes of complicit dishonesty, or corruptions that eat away at a society. But also vain hopes and imaginings (such as property bubbles or social crazes) can be nullified, leaving us facing naked facts and hard consequences, or otherwise relieving us of an insidious, irresolvable problem.

Misunderstanding and incomprehension arise, though on a deeper level things are clearer if we shift perspective or step outside conventional dogmata. Things go out of gear and derail. Yet within this situation a new reality subtly reveals itself. Neptune conveys its insights through visions, poesy, music, art, fiction, bloopers, accidents, between-the-lines messages or unconscious body-language. It feeds our inner life if we give it attention, but without psycho-spiritual growth it can play tricks on our grasp of reality, feeding us with superstition, urban myths, viral beliefs and major misperceptions. We become unhinged.

Mystically, Neptune calls into question *any* fixed sense of reality. It is non-doctrinal, unformulaic, random and mysterious. It can attune us to the Ultimate or nullify our known universe – depending on which way we choose to receive it. Neptunian times can be strange and disorienting, but a new sense of space and openness emerge from them, preparing the ground for something entirely different. Without that cleared space, the new cannot develop and the ills of the past will often transpose into the future.

In nature the rotting process, through moulds and fungi, microbes, insects and damp, is Neptunian. Neptune can becalm the sea, still the weather, make for captivating sunsets and misty days. It can bring out the enchanting aspect of landscapes and atmospheres, though it can also produce anomalies such as smog and strange quirks of pollution.

♇ **PLUTO.** Pluto, discovered in 1930, is an eccentrically-moving planet like Chiron, briefly moving inside Neptune's orbit when in Scorpio (for 12 years), and moving far away from Neptune's orbit when in Taurus (for 36 years) – when it is close it moves fast and when far away it moves slowly. It has a cycle of 248 years – four cycles each millennium. It is small, only the size of Earth's Moon, but it is very dense and heavy, and it has a co-orbiting double planet called Charon (not to be confused with Chiron), and astrologically it packs a strong punch.

Pluto precipitates the surfacing of the deepest inconvenient truths. In an underhand way it manipulates things to bring about the inevitable. Whatever has built up or is building up, it forces it forward insistently, whether anyone likes it or not. There's a cruel aspect to it, but it does make things change. In military terms it would be a sapper, a spy or a special forces operative – it gets behind the lines or underneath the foundations, blowing things up, bulldozing them down or undermining them.

Pluto digs out stored-up blocked energy and held-back situations accrued from periods of prolonged stability or conservatism. It exposes cover-ups, delivers the tough consequences of ill-considered acts and misdeeds, spotlights evasions and dishonesties, then pushes things forward from there. Sometimes the advance signs of this go unnoticed until there's an enormous rumbling quake which could have been foreseen yet wasn't, because everyone was too busy shoring up the status quo, pretending everything was perfectly normal.

Pluto brings out the darkness, ugliness and violence lurking in the unconscious part of the group psyche, but this isn't Pluto's violence, it's humanity's. Or it precipitates an overdue tectonic shift, a demolition job or an avalanche of events. Pluto merely reveals what's there, underneath, and it does so uncompromisingly. When operating negatively it's the planet of totalitarianism, fascism and serious oppression, brought on by the Stalins and Hitlers of this world. Such oppressors exist only because there has been space for them to step into, made possible by the omissions and errors of previous times. Yet, like Lucifer, they are ultimately bringers of light inasmuch as they create situations so bad (such as the Holocaust or the gulags) that we reach a history-changing 'never again' point. This doesn't justify such tragedies, but it gives them meaning in retrospect.

Pluto obliges a truth process leading eventually to enlightening breakthroughs. It makes possible the germination and flowering of a new state of being. But it is harrowing and relentless. In terms of human negativity, outright dictatorships might nowadays be in decline, but they can be replaced by subtler forms, such as democracies where people are fooled into believing they have an influence when, in fact, background powers still hold sway. "Government makes a 10% difference", said Churchill.

To quote the 18th Century philosopher Edmund Burke, "For the triumph of evil it is necessary only that good people do nothing". It is frequently not human badness but laxity that allows negativity to creep in and take over.

Pluto has an uncivilised, libidinous energy, rampant, uncomfortable, urgent, obsessive and cathartic. It rips, tears and bulldozes all available sacred cows, shaky edifices, outdated ideas and outmoded traditions. It reveals hidden agendas, concealed motives, taboos and secrets, often by a hardly perceptible shift of seeing, or through a faux-pas or a simple event which brings with it explosive implications. Whatever has been stoppered, buried, unmentioned or suppressed comes up and out like a bursting of gloop. Pluto promotes unintended consequences, sometimes with historic significance.

An example is the use of nuclear weapons by the world's powers, which later proliferated in rogue formats in places like Israel and North Korea, or which can be obtained by terrorists. This was not planned but it was perhaps inevitable because nuclear arms were not scrapped at the time they should have been in the 1960s-80s. Or they should never have been invented, as many of their early inventors knew.

But again there's choice here, to yield to change or to resist it, to break down or to break through. When there's an urge to grow and evolve, Pluto brings a feeling of liberation, cleansing and relief, unburdening of a load, and when there's resistance, there's pain and horror.

When Pluto is strong, life-and-death issues arise, or perhaps they threaten ominously. But really, there's something here that is somehow supposed to happen, inescapable and an inevitable consequence of earlier bad decisions, avoidances or omissions. So Pluto can be corrective. Its primal, no-bullshit character scrapes at our capacity to survive, to maintain decorum or normality, placing the cards squarely on the table and demanding tough measures. What is worst is that public complicity and mass delusion can drive a difficult situation into a full-on crisis. Hitler's rise was facilitated by an uncompromising polarisation in German society, where opposing social-political influences refused to form a consensus, leading many Germans to crave order and progress by any means. Into this stepped Hitler and the Nazis, using democratic populism as a way of gaining power by trickery.

Pluto is associated with sex and death, both of which are totally engaging experiences demanding full-on presence and attention, both of them scary and wondrous at the same time. Yet Pluto has its beauty too, a naked, tempting, sexual, deep attractiveness that emerges once fear, guilt and shame have melted away, or following a loosening of social standards or taboos. Thus prostitution or crime, themselves not tasteful elements in society, can break down social denial and dishonesty by embodying the darker side of a society. In truth, a society is judged by its refuse dumps, sewage outlets, prisons, psychiatric hospitals, slums and dark alleyways, not by its palaces and cathedrals. Pluto brings changes that perhaps are necessary in the longterm but which use sordid, painful, degenerative or cruel means to get there.

Pluto invokes the deepest kinds of power and, while its apparent uncontrollability can be fearsome, there's a truth within it that can move mountains, remove barriers and grind down resistances. War is completely avoidable, yet it often arises through a perverse collective unconscious death wish, a need to breach normal rules and force big changes. Said Bertrand Russell: "War is not about who is right, it's about who is left" – it's a failure to deal with conflicts of interest by other means. It's a means by which humanity gives itself horror.

Pluto's rumbling force generates resistance and fear, but inevitably this is but a prelude to breakthrough. Pluto drives the onward-moving force of history, toward the fulfilment of human potential. Pluto blows it for us, cracking open and demolishing our weak spots, punching us in the stomach. Yet it precipitates the new. It is the last word on change: when Pluto is at work, *this is it*.

Other bodies

There are other bodies in the solar system which some astrologers use. To avoid overcomplicating things in this book we shall only mention them here. There are four asteroids worth noting (amongst many): Ceres (sometimes called a dwarf planet), Pallas, Vesta and Juno, which are not of equal scale or effect as planets, but some astrologers use them to provide extra detail. Then there are two remote, newly-discovered dwarf planets worth noting, Eris and Sedna. Sedna, discovered in 2003, is about 31 times the distance of Neptune from the Sun, with a roughly 12,050 year cycle, and Eris, discovered in 2005, is closer in, with a 557 year cycle. Astrologers are only gradually gleaning what their influence can be.

There are more newly-discovered planets too, but they are small, and so many of them have been discovered recently that astrologers have not deciphered them yet, except by bandying round ideas or interpreting the mythologies of the names they have been given. Usually, the astronomer who discovers a new heavenly body is permitted to name it, often using the name of a mythological character, and then astrologers tend to take that image and extrapolate meaning from the symbolism of that image. This has its value but it can also obscure an observational understanding of the influence a planet brings to bear.

Planetary modulations

The planets are forever modulating in their expression. We never get them in their pure, unadulterated form, since they are always filtered and modified by three main factors: the zodiac, the aspects and retrogrades.

The zodiac. As the planets move through the signs, their energies are filtered and diffracted over time according to the pattern of the zodiac, drawing out definable issues, ways of operating and a range of assets and challenges, underlying themes and potential outcomes. Even within each sign there is a pattern of unfoldment, a story with a beginning, middle and end. The foundations of this story were explored in the preceding sign, and the results are revealed in the subsequent sign.

Neighbouring zodiacal signs bring out contrasts and shifts, yet they have a distinct sequentiality to them too. Some astrologers use *decans*, ten-degree segments of signs, of which there are three per sign (since each sign is 30° wide). Others use *sabian symbols*, which are assigned characteristics belonging to every single degree of the zodiac – there are 360 sabian symbols.

Decans and sabian symbols are optional details; the main issue is that every sign has its own pattern of internal theme-development as a planet passes through it. Observing the motions of Jupiter and Saturn through the signs can be useful, since their sojourns in each sign (one and two years respectively) are long enough to see the story unfolding, but fast enough to see the differences and distinctions too. The faster planets can be too quick for such a progression to be easily visible or significant unless you spend a lot of time following their antics. The slower outer planets take a long time to follow – the first edition of this book was written in 1985-86 while Pluto was Scorpio, 1984-96, and the second edition in 2014 while it was in Capricorn, between 2008 and 2024, a 28 year gap (a Saturn cycle), while Pluto moved just two signs.

Aspects. The planets interact with each other through the aspects – notable angles of relationship which set up coherent combined energies between two or more planets. Every planet has a cycle of relationship with each other planet, and the art of astrology involves building an understanding of this into a wholeness, to see the whole system at work. Chapters 7 and 8 on aspects and chapter 13 on planetary combinations will help with this. The main aspects between planets are initially the most revealing and distinct to watch – these are the conjunction, sextile, square, trine and opposition. In astro-shorthand, that's ☌, ✶, □, △ and ☍.

Each year, the Sun forms a whole cycle of aspects to the planets (except Mercury and Venus, for reasons explained earlier), and these are well worth observing. Things get really interesting when three or more planets form a mutual configuration, a pattern of aspects, covered in chapter 12. As you can see, we're building up a rather sophisticated picture of evolving patterns of time, as we progress through the book.

Retrogrades and stations. Each planet except the Sun and Moon appears to turn backwards at times. The times of turning are called *stations*. Mercury turns retrograde three times per year for three weeks each time. Venus is retrograde for six weeks every 1½ years (19 months), and Mars turns retrograde for 6-11 weeks once every two years. All the other planets are retrograde for 4-5 months per year – their stations occur roughly when the Sun is in a trine (△, 120°) aspect to the planet, for roughly one-third of the year.

The significance of this is that change is a two-steps-forward, one-step-back process. With the slower-moving planets from Jupiter to Pluto, an aspect between any of them can have three passes – direct, retrograde and direct again. As an example, look at the Uranus-Neptune conjunction of 1993 on the accompanying graph of outer-planet movements, where the conjunction happens three times.

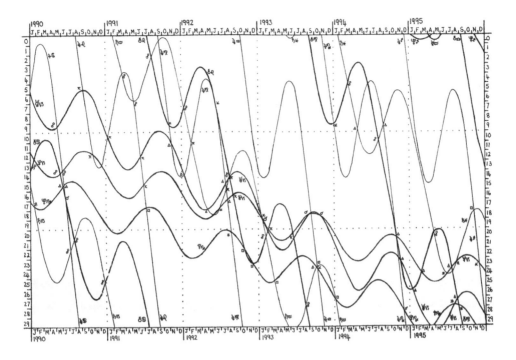

The motions of the outer planets, 1990-95.

It's a journey and a process of making sure we mean it. The Chinese call it *crossing the great water*. In the first stage you leave the shore you're on, stepping forward into the future and its potential, waving goodbye to the past. In the second, retrograde stage, you're mid-crossing and not sure, wavering, wondering if you're doing the right thing but knowing it's also too late and you must continue. In the third stage you reach the other shore and the future now begins – and there's new territory to get used to. With outer-planet changes, this can take one or two, sometimes three years.

A planet is particularly powerful when at its station: you can feel it clearly. When moving direct (forward), its energies move through us in a relatively straightforward way, passing in, through and out of us in evolutionary, expressive ways, 'as per normal'. When a planet slows down, this energy loses impetus, perhaps twisting and getting blocked, or overrunning itself, operating in a somewhat habituated way, losing vivacity, originality and colour. When it is stationary turning retrograde (St.t.R) there can be a slowing of progress, a snarl-up or blocking, out of which a questioning emerges about the way we do things or the point of all our efforts. Our actions are paused and a re-examination of issues arises. This is good and necessary, prompting a reality-check to sort out overlooked issues. Watch this next time Mercury turns retrograde, which particularly affects mercurial sectors such as transport, internet and communications – it does this three times each year.

When a planet moves retrograde there is some relaxation of energy, and out of this dawns a new perspective, an acceptance of emergent facts or a change of approach, peaking when the planet conjuncts the Sun (in the case of Mercury and Venus) or opposes it (in the case of all the other planets). After this transition a new sense of quiet surety gradually develops, bringing a feeling of increased readiness to start over, to move in a clear direction, exploring a new possibility. When the planet slows to stationary, turning direct (St.t.D), all is poised and a surge of energy comes forward, propelling us into intentional and resolved activity. This grows gradually until energy again runs more or less on momentum, more regularised and normalised, until the ensuing retrograde period churns things up again. The universe thus keeps us on our toes.

7

The Cycle of Aspects

The nature of life is such that we circle around the quintessential core of truths of life by experiencing facets of them, strung out over time in a movie-like storyline. Life is a cycle passing through many stages, and if we experienced childhood, youth, maturity and old age at the same time we would miss the main gist of what living in a body on a planet like ours is all about. Thus we have timecycles big and little, major and minor, interfacing spirit with the denser stuff of bodily living, and in gradual doses.

Earlier in the book we met up with aspects, and now we shall look at them properly. This and the next chapter concern synodic or interplanetary cycles of aspects. Here we shall follow the sequence of unfoldment of such cycles, and in the next chapter we'll look at the background structure of cycles and how our understanding of them is built up.

Angles

Aspects are specific angular relationships between any two planets, marking a recognisable phase or stage of development in a cycle. At each stage there is a characteristic flavour and tone to whatever is being rolled out during that cycle.

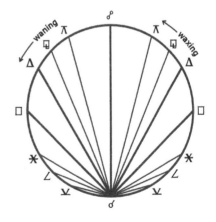

Apart from the conjunction and opposition, there are two instances of every single aspect in any interplanetary cycle, one of them waxing and one waning. When waxing, a faster planet is moving away from a slower planet up to the point where it opposes it, and then it starts waning towards it.

During the waxing hemicycle, things are emerging and developing, becoming visible, and during the waning hemicycle they are completing and being made use of, weaving into the fabric of life.

Imagine the hands of a clock: the conjunction takes place at (say) twelve o'clock, but the opposition doesn't take place at half past the hour – it takes place at 32½ minutes past 12 because the hour hand as well as the minute hand will have moved. The next conjunction takes place at 1.05. Both planets are in motion, one faster, one slower. Now try imagining the 250-year cycle of Pluto, with ten other hands on the clock, each going at different speeds, with some of them moving more consistently and regularly than others – that's what our solar system is like.

Here though, for simplicity, we shall look at just two hands and the significant angles they form in their cycle of relationship with each other. These angles, or *aspects*, are found by subdividing the 360° of the zodiac by factors of 2, 3, 4, 6, 8 and 12. More about this in the next chapter.

Here's an important detail, concerning 'orbs'. An orb is a recognised zone of influence around an aspect, where that aspect can be said to be operating – either *applying* (building up) or *separating* (bedding in). So, if we consider a waxing Moon trine Sun aspect (☽△A) of 120°, you might feel the advance ripples of it around 112°, but more properly around 115°, then it would become exact at 120° and you would feel its effects up to 125° with a hint of it remaining until around 128°. Some astrologers use wider orbs while others use tighter ones – make your choice – though an orb represents a gradual transition, increasing then tapering off, so the boundaries are not sharp. In the sequence of aspects below, both tighter and looser orbs are suggested. The widest orbs belong to the conjunction and opposition, then come the square and the trine. After all, a cycle is an organically-unfolding thing.

The Aspect Sequence

☌ **CONJUNCTION: 0°, orb 6-12°.** *Transition, end/beginning, turning tide, buildup, abiding.*

This is a very powerful aspect, known to the very earliest astrologers since conjunctions are obvious and easily visible in the night sky – two planets together in the heavens. The conjunction is the space between the end of the last cycle and the beginning of a new one. It is a statement of both completion and potential, a condition of beingness, the stirring of something new which doesn't yet exist. There's a reality-override going on where it is possible to an extent to step out of time, even if momentarily, to
see things from a different place and perspective. It's an inwardly quiet place, even if rush-hour is happening. The situation we're in is the situation we're in, and this is where we

stand. It's as if we're starting a journey, except we're standing waiting for the bus – even perhaps searching around for the timetable.

What a conjunction tastes and feels like depends on the two (or more) planets involved: some planets work quite well with each other – Venus with Jupiter or Sun with Mars – though they can still have their flipside. Meanwhile other planets can have some friction and difficulty, since they don't inherently sit together very easily – such as Moon with Mars or Venus with Saturn – though there still are benefits and payoffs. More about this in chapter 13 about planetary combinations.

Conjuncting energies are internally-rooted, inherent and within ourselves, or within the situation we're in, like a bird in its nest. During the waxing hemicycle up to the opposition these energies strive to reach out and express themselves – even if the surroundings are our inner imaginal universe. At the opposition, factors external to us bring to bear upon what's inside us, and during the waning hemicycle our circumstances play a defining role.

At the conjunction we're at a turn of the tide where there's an undertow of potential and usually not much movement unless it involves getting into place for something to happen. It's a kind of prenatal stillness. We might or might not have a notion of where we're heading, and we might have hopes, anticipations or ideas, but we don't know what the journey entails or what the destination will really be like. It's a condition of potential – a bit like when you've just woken up and you're lying in bed simply resting, twiddling your toes or (if you're British) drinking a cup of tea.

Conjunctions imply a larger than normal freedom of choice, an opportunity to reformulate our approach to life, change tracks, shift our mood or vary our responses. We can start over, and it's a new agenda. Qualitative or subtle shifts can occur, and atmospheres around us can change, or the position we are coming from can flip.

Conjunctions sometimes have a strong feeling of in-betweenness. Sometimes they're a waiting time or a clanking-cogs time where we know something is in progress but we don't quite know what – the roulette wheel is simply spinning. Sometimes it's a busy time, dealing with the consequences of the past, packing bags for the future or simply catching up with things that got omitted in the rush.

Life is up to us, and we feel it at this time. Which way things will really go is anybody's guess, but we can still set our intents, visualise possibilities, clear away anticipations, prepare the ground for planting or simply draw a line between past and future. What's gone is gone, what's coming will come, and here we are, this is it. But this isn't nothing – it's quite an important part of cyclical reality-unfoldment. In the end, it's not so much what we do but how we do it that matters, and this is the time for a fresh start, drawing on what we have learned and thus far become, setting forth to become something else.

⚺ SEMISEXTILE: 30°, one sign apart, orb 2-3°. *Emergence and germination.*

This is a minor aspect in which stillness begins to flow: there's a detectable acceleration toward becomingness. Issues and situations emerge and new elements enter the situation – sometimes randomly but showing their meaning in the end. Or sometimes we make our first move. Or something happens to jog us into action. Things just start happening, sometimes with, sometimes without a clear sense of direction, and new avenues open up that weren't visible before. Either that, or you feel as if things ought to be happening (the bus didn't come). Whatever comes up at this stage might or might not seem to have value or use, but its very existence at this stage means something. We receive hints and omens of coming developments. The semisextile is an opening up but still early in the cycle. It is a germination of seeds, though nothing much is showing. Not a good time for writing a progress report. Carry on, for there's more to come.

∠ SEMISQUARE: 45°, 1½ signs apart, orb 2-4°. *Orientation, initiation, commitment.*

The semisquare is half of a square aspect. If the bus didn't come we must get a taxi, since the cost of not doing so can be higher than the price of the taxi. If the bus did come, we're making progress and getting into gear for the next bit. It's a time for getting on the case and making things move. There's a longterm perspective here: it will take a number of steps to get to where we're going, and all the bits need to fall into place for the whole story to work. So at the semisquare we must place our bets, commit to our path, sign and send off the application, get on with the business, invest energy in the longer term and make a push to get things moving – with eyes on the further horizon. What's needed is a narrowing of potentials to make them doable, a setting out of terms and the making of a sound preliminary agreement. The semisquare can be sharp-edged but it is rewarding if we invest energy wisely and devise a plan or adjust it to whatever seems to be unfolding right now. The semisquare asks for clarity, planning, design and orientation.

⚹ SEXTILE: 60°, two signs apart, 3-6° orb. *Progress, developments, unfoldment, activity.*

The sextile is two semisextiles or half a trine, one-sixth of a circle. The ball is now rolling and things are moving and developing at a rate of knots, sometimes faster than manageable. Options are widening, people are joining in and it seems as if things are progressing. This is a time for doing, not thinking about it. We've already made the push and now it's a matter of keeping up, facilitating and easing things, doing the necessaries for things to work out. We're on top of things, hopefully, and the current is pushing us from behind. If not, extra input and a catch-up is needed, because the square is coming soon.

Skills, abilities, creativity, openings and flexibility are all important here, engaging the ability to carry things through and do them well. We're getting there, there's motion and the future is beckoning.
Avoid negligence and rashness – they charge a price later – and be aware of the likely consequences of your current acts. If at this time things aren't developing and you're faced with obstacles or a feeling you've really missed the bus, perhaps this is the theme of this cycle and it's necessary to make that good, or perhaps something else is being given to you instead, so look for it. That's what life is about. Or perhaps you need to mobilise assistance. Whatever is the case, do your best, for this is the time for making progress and getting some miles behind you.

□ SQUARE: 90°, three signs apart, orb 5-8°. *Encounter, effort, facts, obstacles, point of no return.*

Hold on, not so fast – things aren't quite so simple! We now have to face up to things we might prefer not to encounter. We have to square with the world and make things *really* work – no messing around. If we are avoiding or evading things, or missing the plot, they hit us now as problems we must solve or make progress with. If we're prepared to engage with life, this is the first big hump to cross. If we're doing well, there can still be challenges and unforeseen developments, or simply a need to keep going and

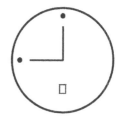

apply further effort – after all, things usually take longer and involve more complexities than first estimated.

The square is a time for work, fixing things, making choices, hard talk, climbing uphill and fulfilling obligations. There's not much choice available: you had choice previously and you'll get it again, but you're already committed at this stage and you've just got to get on with it. Tricky situations come up which perhaps you must wrestle your way through or negotiate skilfully. So you got a flat tyre when already late for an appointment? A rapid recalculation is often needed, to prioritise what's most important or grasp the nettle.

A square requires taking ownership of our own part in things – other people aren't to blame, and I have contributed toward the situation. This is a magic way of solving problems fast, or negotiating complex situations. Here at the waxing square intentions meet evolving facts: you're waiting for that cheque and a bill comes instead, or you get caught speeding, or there's a security-clampdown at the airport and you miss your plane.

There is little clarity or perspective available here: there's simply the task at hand, in your face, demanding attention and resolution. There's scope for an argument with life, so perseverance is called for, because life often wins. Patience is applied timelessness, and application is creation. Nitty-gritties must be sorted out, even if it keeps us up all night.

Squares can face us with our blockages, failings, vulnerabilities and unawarenesses. If we willingly look at these, we can make great progress. If not, we might have a crunch and make a mess of things, with complex results. We have to become more objective, face manifest facts. Delaying is no good, for a clock is ticking. At squares it is usually clear what we need to do, even if the reasons *why* are unclear, and even if we don't feel like doing it. The success of our intentions is at stake and we must work things through, reassess them, drop them or progress them, whichever option is best. But you can cover a lot of mileage on a square, and that's why it's here. A square is half way to an opposition, the zenith of our efforts, and whatever happened at the semisquare is pertinent at the square – and it leads toward the sesquiquadrate too.

△ TRINE: 120°, four signs apart, orb 4-7°. *Free-flow, unfolding, enjoyment, understanding.*

This is a relatively easygoing aspect, a time for going with the current or being on a freewheeling glide, or perhaps a holiday or, if we're working hard, a time of relative relief, synergy and progress. Or it can also become a drift or a slow patch if things aren't working out as expected. Things generally work well though or fall into our lap as a result of previous effort expended at the square. Alternatively we can lose our grip if we have not grappled properly with them.

There is time here to look again at what we are doing, lick our wounds, tinker away at the details, let things be as they are, enjoy coming to a wider understanding of things, lie in bed or have fun. Or perhaps it's simply a matter of carrying on with what we are doing yet *enjoying* it more, adding a creative touch. Things can't be pushed at the trine – they need to unfold as they will. If we push we might waste energy or fall over. It doesn't work to push the river here since, at the moment, it's flowing smoothly and relaxedly, and we're heading toward where we want to go.

It's a time for loosening out, assimilating experience, free exchange and letting be. The trine is a stabiliser – a place for carrying on along lines we've thus far been pursuing. Energy and space might emerge for doing other things, for trying new variations and for seeing different facets of what's been going on. Sometimes things are flat or apathetic, or they drop away if expectations are too high or there's a lack of progress. But if there is accumulated momentum, things move easily and well, progressing of their own accord, and life takes on a more pleasant hue.

Openness, tolerance and space, relaxing old stresses and letting new colour, tone and taste come in: it's time to sing your song just for the singing of it. While this is a time of relative ease, watch out for laziness, for there is a sharp-edged awakening coming up.

⚐ SESQUIQUADRATE: 135°, 4½ signs apart, 2-4° orb. *Choice, readjustment, resolve.*

Here longterm and wider considerations are at stake again, for it is now time to refocus, reaffirm intents and adjust the direction of travel. We need consciously to respond to newly-arisen circumstances and look again at what we are doing, why, and how much our current situation fits in with what was originally intended. If things are to work, we need to let go of some predispositions, patterns that block energy or undermine progress, or examine our tensions, expectations or  rigidities. We ourselves are often the source of the difficulties, or we play a part in creating them, even if the problem seems to be coming from around us. Or perhaps it's both, though we have more influence over our own actions than over the ways of the world.

We are tested in our ability to rearrange plans, adapt and see things from new angles. This facilitates our growth: the universe supports us if we're on track, or if we're correcting ourselves to get back on track, but it can present problems if we're off course without correcting things. The sesquiquadrate encourages clarity and an amount of letting go, since we must accept and work with emergent facts and do our best with them. If we drop unnecessary baggage and re-focus on what really matters, then we open up a pathway to help us through the approaching period of the opposition. So, we've got thus far and some things have been achieved, but what else needs fixing for the process to be complete?

⊼ QUINCUNX: 150°, five signs apart, orb 2-3°. *Tangents, perspectives, letting be*.

The waxing quincunx (called an 'inconjunct' in USA) is intimately tied up with the pre-opposition process. Things are rising toward a crescendo, getting acute. We're on the last lap of the race and quirky things can happen. Here is a likelihood of unforeseens creeping in – things start happening, or inner nuances develop that hadn't been bargained for, and there might be some difficulty getting everything to connect.

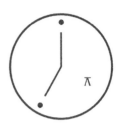

It's not exactly a crisis, more a disjunction. It might or might not be a problem. When in quincunx, two planets have a non-relationship – not even a conflict. One planet might dominate the situation with the other coming in through side-channels, sneakily or unconsciously. Or they simply operate separately, perhaps just heading in different directions. This is one of those situations where we can't really change much. If we move with the drift of things, allowing new factors to enter the situation and trusting that it will be okay, remarkable things can develop. For the disconnect is often caused by our way of seeing things, which needs to be updated and revised right now.

Here the challenge is to do what we can while recognising that many things are out of our hands: we've set up the situation and had the interview, and now we await the results. There's little more we can do. If we have inflexible aims and expectations then subversive factors can come into play, sometimes confounding or compromising us.

This is a case of the great cosmic merry-go-round where, if we're insecure and doubtful, we can lose our way. If we're open to whatever comes, things will work out somehow. Reasons and purposes will reveal themselves in time, perhaps at the opposition or after it. The quincunx brings up questions of perspective and trust. Sometimes larger issues and meanings are invisible or incomprehensible at this time but they are there, implicit in the situation, and we must trust the life-process.

☍ OPPOSITION: 180°, six signs apart, 6-12° orb. *Tension, resolution, climax, transition, turn-around*.

When two planets oppose each other, one is on one side of Earth and the other is diametrically opposite – a powerful configuration. This is the climax of any cycle: whatever has been evolving between these two planets is now at its zenith and established. Our intentions, dreams and schemes have met wider reality and there is a grinding action going on. The result is a validation or an invalidation of our actions, choices and the ways things have gone thus far, or something of each.

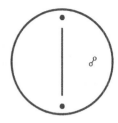

Self meets world, knowables meet unknowables and wishes meet facts – and presented facts matter most at the opposition. Things either join up and connect or they're dissonant. A resolution, resonance or friction is happening, especially during the build-up to the opposition. Sometimes it's intense and sometimes intensely calm: things have reached the high-water mark this time around.

Through conflict or dynamic tension great power is generated: the effects of what has been done are visible, and things previously hidden have surfaced. The news is out and this is a time for standing back and reassessing, learning lessons, releasing the past and realigning to the future. This shift happens on the build-up to the opposition and the outcomes emerge around the opposition and afterwards. Meetings are held and decisions made. Like it or not, what has happened has happened: now it's a matter of what to do with it. Instinct, experience, acceptance and receptivity are called for here.

The extent to which we released or adjusted things at the waxing sesquiquadrate influences the current situation now. Whatever the perceived dilemma is at the opposition, it comes up in full technicolour clarity, demanding solutions. The question is, can we face it? It all depends on our ability and willingness to resolve matters within ourselves and with others and the world.

This is a lesson in using situations to learn from life and then moving on from there. Making a clear decision here can sometimes be difficult, or sometimes it's crystal clear, but something must be done. Issues can be pressing and the best strategy is to quit fretting and do the right thing, whatever that is. Something might have only just emerged during the buildup to the opposition.

There can be a ripping and wrenching, yet there can also be peace and insight. It's a time to rise above the issues and details and see things anew. It's a matter of standing back then re-entering the action from a new standpoint: having got thus far, what now? Sometimes we haven't thought past this point, or perhaps it's now time to start dealing with the outcomes of what we've done, omitted or failed to do.

At an opposition a new context is emerging: we have the chance to become someone or create something quite different from what we first thought was needed or possible. This watershed time marks the beginning of the waning hemicycle, in which our place in the scheme of things and the use we make of our given situation are now the main issues.

Painting a work of art brings personal benefit in the doing thereof, but the picture's full meaning and purpose is fulfilled when others look at it, enjoy and value it. Building a house is fulfilled when the occupiers move into it to make it a home. Transforming clay into a cup finds significance when a drink is poured into it for drinking. The waning hemicycle is a consummation, where we or the world make use of our works: what we have established, developed, accumulated and evolved seeks fulfilment of its purpose, which is now due to become fulfilled. Or not, as the case may be. Or something in between.

This transition, perhaps a showdown, a squeeze or a leap, or perhaps a welcome break, can make life very different in the period after the opposition. The whole time-period around the opposition, before and after, is a crossing-the-hump process. The hottest, most exacting time can often be when the planets are applying to opposition, a few degrees out of aspect. Once this transition has been gone through, the tracks are set for what must be carried out next: it is time to fulfil our contract with life and the world, to bring the business to fruition.

Now for the waning hemicycle…

⚴ Waning QUINCUNX: 150°, 5 signs apart, 2-3° orb. *Contextualising, piecing things together, joining in*.

Having got the job, it's now time to start. Or having built the edifice, it's time to put it to use. Here, we need to find a context into which to fit. Or perhaps a context is opening up and we need to identify it and start doing what's necessary. We must see what the world wants of us, what is required or what is the most obvious thing to do. In this we need to anchor to what we ourselves are seeking out of life, referring back to what we originally sought to achieve.

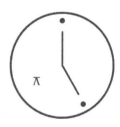

Like its opposite aspect, the waxing semisextile, the waning quincunx is an aspect of emergence, yet the situation is different. The semisextile marked an emergence of new possibilities, while the waning quincunx marks the advent of further possibilities, once the potential has become some sort of actuality. Here we need to avoid moving into a sheepish compliance with others or with circumstances, for things can go adrift. Indeed we need to consider wider circumstances and what others think, but it's still a question of holding true to our starting intentions. Either way, something is emerging, and it's time to get on with it.

♫ Waning SESQUIQUADRATE: 135°, 4½ signs, 2-4° orb. *Getting stuck in, engagement, interaction.*

If the quincunx represented a process of getting used to the new house or job, this is where it gets more serious. Things must be sorted out and the bills paid – the space for action must be mapped out and a strategy clarified. We need commitment to the task and agreement with everyone affected, but our capacity to fulfil our part in the social contract is tested here. As with the waxing sesquiquadrate, an awareness of longterm issues prevails, but we must adjust ourselves to the world we find ourselves in and play its game, or we must do something to change that game, gaining everyone else's agreement or acceptance in the process. To some extent we are pawns in the game of life, and that game can at times become more important than our personal goals.

We must stay true to personal priorities since we need to be mindful of our terms of trade and the limits to our willingness and input. How much should we subscribe to what's on offer? What can we contribute? How much will it affect us? What's the benefit? The world needs us to take on its issues, make them our own and do whatever is necessary, though it needs our personal stamp on it too. In the waning sesquiquadrate we are admitted to the club but, in being admitted, we take on obligations. Soon we must carry them through.

△ Waning TRINE: 120°, 4 signs apart, 4-7° orb. *Going along with things, belonging, harmony.*

Where we have come to by now depends on how we have treated the post-opposition period thus far. If the opposition weakened us and things didn't work out as anticipated, we tend at the trine to go along with life's general flow, doing what seems appropriate or required – willingly or grudgingly. If the opposition strengthened our cause, then we are by now creators and contributors within a larger context, recognised actors and well on our way. The waning trine is a time of productive developments running on established momentum, with things progressing well. This time can be restful, creative, restorative or fun. Here we reap benefits from what has been done, on the basis of reputation gained, results achieved or accumulated experience. We have become something.

People accept us, they are used to us and everything moves along as a matter of course. Normality prevails. Things are as they are. There is space to breathe and appreciate the situation, allowing things to move along as they will. If we are at present unwilling partners in what is unfolding, we're sometimes required by life to comply, awaiting our own time or further developments. All things move along in their channels and the world has its way. It's not a great time for trying to change the course of things, though it is a time for smooth developments. Having climbed a hill, we're in a stretch of free-wheeling progress before the next challenge comes along.

☐ Waning SQUARE: 90°, three signs apart, orb 5-8°. *Effort, dedication, achievement.*

This is a crisis of context: we run the risk of losing ourselves and our objectives amidst the situation that is evolving, or perhaps this is a time to play a major card. Perhaps we just have to comply, conform, work hard or simply do the drudgery required, but sometimes we can change the situation too. There are things to do to make things happen and get them operating well. The momentum and solidity of things can come into question or be disrupted and we're challenged to rise to the occasion and sort out the situation.

This is the time for the big meeting where awkward issues are negotiated, new facts present themselves, or the consequences of what has happened now stand before us. What has been achieved, what's the point of it and what is my place in it? If we overlook tough questions, fail to do the business or take a risk, we're likely to land up having to go along with things we don't actually like, approve of or support. Here we must give meaning to what has happened and do the final, crucial bit.

New elements can trip us over. They oblige us to account for ourselves, make the sale, deal with the knotty question before us and *do something*. It usually presents itself as a concrete challenge, obstacle, breakdown or riddle: perspective is not plenteous, but imperatives are painfully obvious. We must carry out whatever we have said we'd do, or we lose credibility. But this needs to have personal relevance, otherwise something is not quite right.

Our own immediate needs start coming up, yet we must first discharge our obligations and bring things to completion. Otherwise we can be saddled with lasting consequences we don't wish to be encumbered with. Attachment to the fruits of our labours can render us a prisoner of fate, hemmed in by rules, mores and expectations. Having bought and moved into the house, we must pay the mortgage. Having painted the painting we must sell it and say goodbye to it. But the payoff is the benefit we gain from that house, or the money or the kudos we earn for the painting – and hopefully we have worked things out right so that we have no regrets. If not, it's too late.

Yet by generating benefit or recognition, we energise or qualify ourselves for the next move. Here at the waning square the seeds of the next cycle are planted, even while there is still a quarter of the present cycle to get on with. Next, we must complete what we have set up. Through doing this we reclaim our place in the scheme of things, perhaps seeing the true reasons why things have developed as they have – the contribution we have made and the effects this has had. But our assumed roles are not necessarily all there is: who am I, and what's the relationship between my role and my selfhood?

✳ Waning SEXTILE: 90°, two signs, 3-6° orb. *Activity, feedback, completing.*

These are busy times, times of reward. Here we reap a dividend from previous efforts. If we have not done well, this is the backlash, or a discovery that we shall emerge with little - except perhaps a lesson learned. Either way, here we see the results of our actions and a lot is afoot. Inevitable consequences unfold: this can be a source of satisfaction and reward or regret and debt – often a mixture of both. Being a part of everything, recognised and accepted, the world turns around and we turn with it.

This aspect runs on momentum and effect. The past either supports us or weighs us down. We are seen for our role, not specifically for who we ourselves are. I might be a successful bank manager, parent or artist, but what good has it really done me, when all is said and done? The satisfaction or the disquiet experienced here depends on us, what we have done and what we make of it now. Even if things haven't gone right, we can make some good out of a difficult situation. We have an opportunity to graduate towards a new chapter of life, completing the past and gaining satisfaction from it, or we can slide into resignation as a result of what has happened. There is much that's on the move right now: if it was an edifice we built, then it is now being utilised and we can see the results, and if it's a painting we painted and sold, we're now busily being interviewed by journalists, our work is being exhibited by its owners or we're being asked to do more paintings. The consequences and finishing touches of the cycle are happening now, and time waits for no one.

∠ Waning SEMISQUARE: 45°, 1½ signs, 2-4° orb. *Release, voting, sorting out the past.*

What are we going to do with the future, and what have we truly gained from the past? Time to start extricating ourselves from what has been going on, or to move on in some way. Time to separate from what we were identified with until now – otherwise life will someday rip us away from the past, and secretly we know it. Comfort-zones and established habits are no refuge here. Each of us is an individual in need of our own life. Whatever has happened before, the time is coming to move on, learn from the 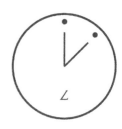 past and commit it to the history file. This semisquare marks a stripping away of the props we've used to hold us up, and it's time to finish things off, clean up, count the profit or loss and move on from here.

By learning lessons, releasing guilt or regrets, sorting out all that was unsaid or undone, forgiving and forgetting, we find a new freedom and clarity, ready to start over with a clean slate, or with lessons learned. Or perhaps we are graduating successfully from the last cycle, having become someone different, and it's time to progress. It's time now to hand in our notice, apply for promotion or drop whatever we might be holding on to. It's time to clear up the mess, sort out misunderstandings or speak unspokens before they go into the repository of memory or forgotten times, to linger there until perhaps they return another day. If things are not now in process of being completed, we shall have to return to them another time: the scenery is beginning to change, time is moving on and history eats the present gluttonously. The door is not closed yet, but it's time to start packing up.

⋎ Waning SEMISEXTILE: 30°, one sign apart, 2-3° orb. *Reminiscence, rounding up, new angles on old themes.*

It's a time for contemplation and comprehension, for quiet recharging, drawing conclusions from experience, integrating, reminiscing and assimilating. Finishing touches are being made, the past exerts a strong shaping influence, and yet within this we can lay the groundwork for something... but what?

Throwing out all that is useless, repairing and updating what is useful, we discover new possibilities or meaning to life. Or we come to understand things retrospectively. We uncover hidden secrets that were invisible when we were in the middle of things. Our personal viewpoint is restoring itself and memories, past connections or tendencies come up here. This is a time for weighing things up, dropping unfulfilled dreams or realising our dreams could have been greater. Doubts or questions might creep in, yet this is part of our preparation for the future. Or perhaps it's time to assess our resources and the benefits we can carry forward into the next cycle – or the lack of them. It is now time to be with the way things have become and live with it. We can't change much right now, though we can accept things and come to peace. This end-of-cycle period is a completion stage in which the past lingers on, but issues and conclusions arising here give us foundations for the future.

♂ CONJUNCTION: 0°, orb 6-12°. *New beginnings, potential, and the here-and-now.*

When all is said and done, being alive is what matters: what's important is what we actually are, not what we tell ourselves we want to be or could have been. What we are is what we carry forward with us into a new cycle, starting at the conjunction. It decides how the new cycle opens up: visions, intents, fears and anticipations are all stuff of the psyche, demonstrating little of who we truly are and can be. The conjunction is a major transition and the scenery of life takes on a different slant, quietly yet fundamentally.

A new vista opens up, perhaps welcome, perhaps daunting. We have a sense of where we're going or we're waiting to see what comes. Both future and past are hypothetical: the present moment and its events and signs are what matters. Like the opposition, the conjunction provides a chance to step out of time, to come to an overview of life's underlying message, hidden in the realm of the timeless.

The final meaning of what we have experienced and achieved in the last cycle fully integrates itself long after that cycle has ended, after we have forgotten the sequence of events, thoughts and issues that went on then. This is a process of digestion, an assimilation of past history in the light of what develops subsequently. What we have truly made of life is what leaves its mark. We now have a clutch of qualities and a quiver of arrows to carry forward as we pass through life's further labyrinthine intricacies. On for the next bit.

We have now reviewed the intervals and sequence of a cycle, but there's more. In the next chapter we'll examine the contributing factors that make a cycle act like it does. We're going to look at cycles as a whole.

8

Planetary Cycles

Each and every planet works with each and every other planet. They interweave energies to affect our experience of time and the possibilities inherent in it. Here we shall look at the inherent nature of cycles and some background on them. If you find this chapter a bit dense, skip through it on first reading to see what it covers and come back to it later.

Cycles

When a planet moves through the zodiac, the zodiac filters its energies to bring out themes, viewpoints, atmospheres, stories, scenarios, feeling-tones and chapters in the saga of its journey. But planetary motions through the signs don't necessarily set in motion events and distinct breakthroughs: aspects do this. A change of sign can sometimes tip situations into events, but it's not exactly in the signs' nature to do so.

Aspects are part of a *synodic cycle* in which two planets move in a cyclic progression of interactive dynamic relationship. While the faster of any two planets might fulfil its zodiacal cycle in a certain time (such as Mars in 1 year and 10 months), it might take some time for it to catch up again with the slower planet, moving along at its own rate (for example conjunctions between Mars and Jupiter take place roughly every 2 years and 2 months). The Mars-Jupiter cycle relates to tides of assertiveness, sexuality, initiative, competitiveness and pushing.

The synodic cycle of Mars to Pluto is shorter in duration because Pluto moves slower than Jupiter, so Mars doesn't have to move so far to catch up with it. The Mars-Pluto cycle relates to a deeper assertive force which can at times precipitate arguments and wars, but it's also about overcoming obstacles and working under pressure or in situations with high blowback-potential. The Jupiter-Pluto synodic cycle, in turn, lasts around 12-13 years, depending on Pluto's speed – this relates to longer-term bursts of progress, breakthrough, growth, forwardness, force and inevitability in social and wider-world matters.

In astrology we have a wide range of synodic cycles, ranging in length from 29 days (Moon-Sun) to around 495 years (Neptune-Pluto). Sun, Mercury and Venus to Mars cycles last around 2.4 years, while Mars cycles to slower planets last just over 2 years. Jupiter-Saturn cycles last 20 years, Jupiter-Uranus cycles 14 years and Jupiter-Pluto cycles 13 years. Saturn-Uranus cycles last 45 years, Saturn-Neptune 36 years, Saturn-Pluto cycles 31-38 years, and so on. Wheels within wheels. Astrology is in a sense a study of the grinding of the gears of our solar system.

Cycles involving Chiron or Pluto can be very variable over time since each of these planets orbits eccentrically – moving sometimes faster, sometimes slower, as they move closer to or further from the Sun. We're thus playing around with a whole range of interlocking and sometimes quirky cycles, which give a lot of scope for ongoing trawling-sessions in your ephemeris and light-bulb moments when you glimpse the beauty of all this.

Average Synodic Cycle durations (in years)

	☿	♀	♂	♃	♄	⚷	♅	♆	♇
☉	0.32 (116d)	1.6 (584d)	2.14 (780d)	1.09 (399d)	1.04 (378d)	1.02 (373d)	1.01 (370d)	1.0 (367d)	1.0 (367d)
☿		♀	Since Mercury and Venus, from Earth's viewpoint, follow the Sun around the zodiac, their cycles of relationship to other planets are all on average more or less as in the column above.						
♂				2.24 (816d)	2.0 (734d)	1.95 (713d)	1.92 (703d)	1.90 (695d)	1.89 (692d)
♃					19.86 (20y)	15.4 (13-20y)	13.8 (13-14y)	12.8 (12-13y)	12.5 (12-14y)
♄						70.2 (64-165y)	45.4 (44-46y)	35.9 (35-37y)	33.4 (31-38y)
⚷							128.2 (103-145y)	73.4 (47-80y)	63.8 (56-70y)
♅								171.3 (170-171y)	127.1 (111 or 143y)
♆									493.4 (492-497y)
♇									

The synodic periods in the table are averages – their actual length at any time depends on the starting-point you're measuring the cycle from. It can be mind-boggling to our thinking left brain and illuminating to our visionary right brain to grasp all this interrelated movement. There's a beauty to it that is not unlike watching ocean waves. Give some time to developing a sense of how it all works, for this is vital.

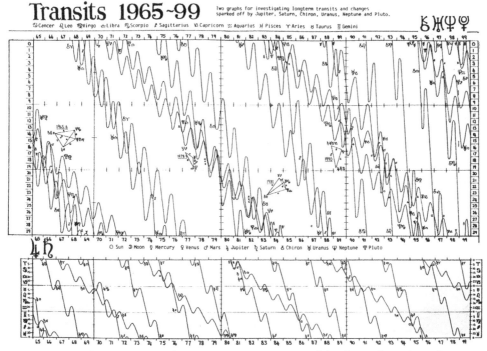

Graph of slower-moving planetary motions 1965-99. Look for the configurations of 1965-66, 1981, 1989-90 and 1993. From a hand-drawn graph of the late 1980s.

You can develop this in several ways on a practical level:

- keep a constant eye on your ephemeris or an astro-clock program, to watch the changing movement and distribution of planets around the zodiac and what they are doing to one another. This takes time but it's well worth it – just get into the habit of checking it while you're having breakfast or sitting on the bus on the way to work;

- the more technically inclined can plot the motions of the planets on graph paper, covering a few months, a year or (say) five years – there are examples in this book. With certain computer programs such graphs can be printed out, though you learn more by hand-drawing the motions and noting each aspect that appears as you do it;

- or you can draw yourself a big zodiac circle on a pin-board (or paint a zodiac mandala) to put on the wall, and then, using mapping pins to represent the planets, move the pins round daily or periodically, reading their positions from your ephemeris. You could even go mad and build a mandala outside on the ground or paint one on your patio, using wood or stones to represent the planets. Then watch what happens;

- there are programs which give a real-time chart or astro-clock of the planets and their aspects at this very moment, which can be very revealing to watch on a daily basis.

Hemicycles

A hemicycle is a half-cycle with a significance of its own. We can look at a complete cycle in terms of two different kinds of interlocking hemicycle.

The **waxing-waning hemicycle** is interesting because it illustrates the developmental and integrating side of cycles. The *waxing* hemicycle starts at the conjunction and ends at the opposition. During this time the faster planet moves away from the slower one, a process in time where new potentials are explored, and dreams and intentions emerge from in-here to out-there in an evolutionary motion. Something is starting up and moving toward its peak.

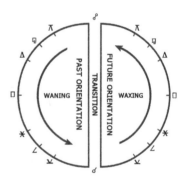

The *waning* hemicycle starts at the opposition and ends at the conjunction. Here, the faster planet is catching up with the slower, a process in which the externalised situation that coalesced at the opposition seeks significance in a wider context. It seeks integration, value and significance, as recognised by people and situations around us. Having become something, so what? It's now a question of making something of it and eventually passing it on to history, preferably in good shape.

Consider the growth of an annual plant: first it grows and takes shape, rising to flowering, then it gives forth its pollen, seeds and fruits to feed the coming generation, and eventually even its leaves or stalk wither to become food for future cycles of growth. Each of the two hemicycles of this kind has its crux point at the square (□) aspect, half way through the hemicycle.

The **subjective-objective hemicycle** crosses and interlocks with the waxing-waning hemicycles above. It illustrates two facets of being. *Subjectivity* is a me-in-here, in-my-own-world standpoint, in which personally-derived aims, plans, ways of interpreting life and defining one's own existence prevail – it's our home ground. This applies to everything, not just humans. The subjective hemicycle starts at the waning square, has its focus at the conjunction and concludes at the waxing square.

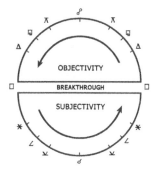

Objectivity is a that-out-there, in-relation-to-the-wider-world standpoint – foreign territory and how we relate to it and stretch beyond ourselves. The objective hemicycle starts at the waxing square, peaks at the opposition and completes at the waning square. Here we adjust to the available conditions in which our lives play themselves out, responding to the demands, expectations and parameters of the wider environment – or dealing with the consequences of its impact on us. Life is thus an interplay of subjective and objective elements. This is even the case in the inner world of dreams, where some dreams highlight our inner feelings about situations while others highlight situations themselves.

Between the waning square and the conjunction we draw sustenance and significance from our role in the world (assimilation), while between the conjunction and the waxing square we explore and state our own terms of reference in life, in relation to the world we live in, which we are coming to grips with (creation). Both processes reveal different aspects of subjective selfhood. In contrast, between the waxing square and the opposition our aspirations and potentials must meet the world as it stands and make their mark on it (manifestation).

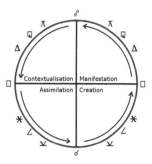

Between the opposition and the waning square we explore our membership in the world and society, seeking subjective value from it and trying to make a contribution to its benefit (contextualisation). In the subjective hemicycle we get what we need out of the world, and in the objective hemicycle the world gets what it needs out of us.

Combining these two pairs of hemicycles, we can thus define four quarters to a cycle. From conjunction we are 'doing our own thing', from the waxing square we are engaging in rapport with the world, from the opposition the world gives us roles and participation, and from the waning square we find personal meaning by drawing on our involvements and roles.

Aspects

Aspects are recognised angles of relationship between any two planets where we can identify certain kinds of energy-interchange between them. They are stages on the journey of relationship around a whole cycle. The general principle behind the aspects is a subdivision of the cycle of 360° by a number such as two (☍), three (△), four (□), six (✳), eight (∠ and ⬠) or twelve (⎘ and ⋏). In advanced astrology, further numbers or 'harmonics' such as five (quintiles, 72°), seven (septiles, 51°25') and nine (noviles, 40°) can be used to subdivide the circle, yielding a weird angle in the case of the septile, but these aspects are not commonly used.

A cycle has within it four main stages: childhood/beginning, youth/development, maturity/application and old age/completion. Gestation of the new takes place within the completion stage, for an ending is the prelude to a new beginning. The transition-points between these four stages (conjunction, two squares and the opposition) are vital humps to cross, and when they involve slower cycles, they represent major points of initiation and historic change affecting periods of decades and centuries.

These initiations can be major when slow-moving planets are involved, since the testing process in these 'hard' aspects can be drawn out over a year or up to three, involving major, fundamental, core questions. For an example, just look at the period 2012-15. Lesser initiations punctuate our lives too, such as when Moon periodically brings up a crunchy situation lasting one day, which can still give us a goodly shake and wobble or demand some effort. It takes seconds to prang your car and weeks to fix it. These small and punchy crunches and scrapes often serve as critical points in larger initiations, even though the whole larger process might unfold over years.

Here's an example. In 2007-08 we had the so-called 'credit crunch' – a critical turning point in the incremental decline of the West and the rebalancing of economies worldwide. This decline started, arguably, in 1993 on the Uranus-Neptune conjunction in Capricorn, though it was staved off by the lift given by new technologies such as the internet, plus financial leveraging mechanisms, both of which started losing their bounce by 2008, particularly on the Uranus-Pluto square of 2012-15, which you can see building up in this chart.

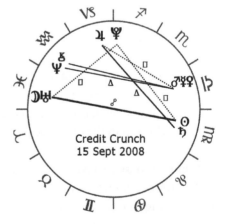

Credit Crunch
15 Sept 2008

On 15th September 2008 came a critical point with the collapse of the Lehman Brothers investment bank – bang on a fullmoon aligned with Uranus. Additional factors were a trine between Jupiter and Saturn in earth signs (concerning money) and a mutual conjunction of Mercury, Venus and Mars in Libra (signifying a tip in the balances of people's thoughts, feelings and evaluations). This was a crisis waiting to happen, but it was visibly triggered by the fullmoon and the three-planet conjunction in Libra – they gave the final push to an already precarious situation. In the end, Lehman Brothers will be forgotten, but this collapse suddenly brought home to people that a big crisis was unfolding.

So here we have a combined action working on several levels. Deep down is the Uranus-Pluto square, and affecting it more temporarily was the Jupiter-Saturn trine, but the triggering mechanisms were the conjunction in Libra and the Uranian fullmoon. Notice also how all of the planets were on one side of the zodiac – an imbalanced situation at the centre of which was Pluto, nearing the end of Sagittarius, a sign of excess. Pluto was approaching its entry into Capricorn, a sign of institutional and financial change.

Challenges and Developments

Aspects are spread throughout a cycle in a regular fashion, at intervals of either 30° or 45°. Each of the aspects has a symbol in astrological shorthand, and when we mention two planets in aspect to one another, we say, for example, 'Moon sextile Jupiter' (☽⚹♃), the faster planet coming first. Note these examples: Sun trine Saturn (☉△♄), Mars quincunx Uranus (♂⚻♅), but *then...* Moon trine Mars (☽△♂), Mars opposition Saturn (♂☍♄), Saturn semisquare Uranus (♄∠♅).

There are two main families of aspects, the *challenging* or *hard* aspects, and the *flowing* or *soft* aspects. The hard aspects concern subdivision of the circle by 2, 4 or 8 – the octile family. They represent something to be climbed over, worked at, confronted, decided upon or wrestled with – particularly with the main hard aspects, the conjunction, square and opposition. The semisquare and sesquiquadrate concern adjustments of direction aimed at fulfilling longterm goals.

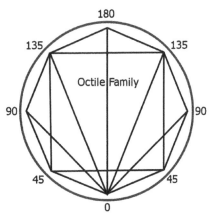

155

The flowing aspects concern subdivision of the circle by 3 or 6 – the sextile family. They represent an opening and widening out, partially an acceleration and partially a relaxation – evolution and making progress. Note that the conjunction and opposition are members of both the sextile and octile families of aspects – they have an element of both to them.

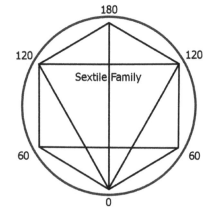

In addition there are what we might call the *incidental* aspects (my term), the semisextile and quincunx. They introduce new elements into the game, incursions from the unknown and questions of perspective, changing our experience of things. The waxing semisextile is a point of emergence of possibility while the waning semisextile is a point of completion and reflection. The waxing quincunx is a point of transition to climax, a state of pre-resolution, while the waning quincunx is a post-climactic transition – a bit like the day after the night before. Each of these aspect types plays its part in the pattern of a cycle, and the sequence of the aspects is significant.

It all very much depends on how we deal with things. Challenging aspects are positive if we are willing and ready to work at things and face them, helping us make definite progress even if under pressure. Flowing aspects, theoretically easier, aren't always so: they can sometimes imply a feeling of stuckness and inability to change or generate motivation. Our experience of each cycle is greatly influenced by the way we make use of our lives and how we're feeling at the time: sometimes it can be beneficial to be ill, and other times it can be catastrophic winning a million in the lottery!

Where it Stops, Nobody Knows

A cycle leads on to the next one, also leading out of the preceding one, and they serve as each other's past and future. But it's not necessarily just linear and sequential. Issues dealt with in one cycle can go underground and reappear in a much later cycle, and issues we encounter today have their roots in cycles going a long way back. Also, cycles exist within larger cycles, playing a part in their unfoldment.

In your astrological musings, it's worth tracking astrological cycles back through life and reflecting on the meaning they throw on events and experiences in your past. For example, examine the 12-year cycles of Jupiter, when you were 12, 24, 36, 48 and so on – these are called Jupiter Returns. Also look at Saturn Returns, which happen around age 28-29, 57-59 and 85-86. While you're at it, look at the seven year stages of these Saturn cycles, around age 7, 14, 21, 35-36, 43-44, 50-51, and so on. You'll find this insightful.

If you watch what happens during a succession of fullmoons, you will notice that they are similar to each other and also extremely different. An underlying fullmoon pattern is there, since all fullmoons are soli-lunar oppositions and they have a definite, recognisable undertow to them. But the precise flavour of each fullmoon is quite variable.

Orbs

Symbol	Angle	Aspect	Tight orb	Loose orb
☌	0°	Conjunction	6°	12°
⚺	30°	Semisextile	2°	3°
∠	45°	Semisquare	2°	4°
✳	60°	Sextile	3°	6°
□	90°	Square	5°	8°
△	120°	Trine	4°	7°
⚼	135°	Sesquiquadrate	2°	4°
⚻	150°	Quincunx	2°	3°
☍	180°	Opposition	6°	12°

While each aspect marks a specific angle (such as 30°, 60°, 90°), it represents a stage, a milepost in the organic unfoldment of a cycle. Like mileposts along a road, they represent markers to show us where we are, when in fact a journey along a road or a cycle is a continuum.

However, there's something to the geometry of it, inasmuch as numbers represent resonances, like musical notes, where the complex cross-rhythms in a vibration come to resonate in a distinguishable frequency which, in turn, elicits a feeling in us. Musicologists say that different musical notes and chords (A flat, C sharp, etc) arouse different emotional responses, and the same is the case with planetary cross-resonances that arise as planets come into aspect with each other.

Each aspect has a field of influence around it where it has a distinguishable effect – an *orb*. Just as any event has a buildup period, a specific time of occurrence and then an aftermath, so it is with aspects. Orbs vary in width, according to the nature of the aspect. There is debate amongst astrologers as to how wide to set orbs – some prefer them wider, some tighter (I'm at the wider end). One discrepancy in this debate is that some astrologers seek a definite orb with edges to it, a degree where the aspect markedly starts or finishes. This is not lifelike, for energy unfolds more gradually and spectrally.

So a range of both tighter and looser orbs are given in this book. The tighter orb denotes the area where a definite effect from an aspect can be detected, while the looser one denotes the area where less distinct rumblings might be felt. An example is the pre-fullmoon period, which can at times be felt quite strongly two days before the exact fullmoon, though sometimes that fullmoon feeling creeps up surreptitiously and the exact fullmoon then shifts something, perhaps by surprise.

Orbs are also widened or narrowed according to the planets involved. Orbs are wide when Sun and Moon are involved, narrower for the visible planets of Mercury-to-Saturn, and narrower still for the outer planets. It's the same with aspects: the conjunction and opposition have the widest orbs (up to 10-12°) and the semisextile and quincunx the narrowest ones (maximum 3°). Suggested orbs for aspects are to be found in the table on the preceding page. When assessing an aspect, therefore, use your judgement as to the width of the orb you use and, if in doubt, start with the narrower orbs suggested here and see how you feel after a while.

Applying and Separating Aspects

These are aspects that are *forming* or *moving apart*. When the faster planet is moving into aspect with the slower, it is *applying*, and when moving out of aspect to the slower it is *separating*.

As an aspect is applying, two planetary energies can judder against one another, seeking to get into gear, meaning some friction, jarring, jangle and tension until the aspect is formed or near to forming – though it can also be a creative, benign and enjoyable tension too. We tend to throw into the bargain our resistances, anxieties and anticipations, heightening the feeling of grating, especially during challenging aspects. A lot of the spadework is done during the buildup to an aspect. But different people respond differently, and we also respond varyingly at different times.

- People who resist growth and change feel they're losing control, trying to block change through denial, blame, avoidance strategies and so on. But then after the transit has passed something in them relaxes or collapses, and a change can then go through, if it is going to. If the lessons are not learned, trouble ensues in the longterm.

- People who accept change when it comes to them might initially go through resistances and questioning until they have figured out what the question truly is. Once they've cracked the question the answers start coming and the situation shifts from a crisis to a manageable or welcome change.

- People who seek to induce change can go through hell some time before an aspect forms, only to land up thriving on it all and making great progress when the aspect is applying toward exactness, integrating the full outcomes afterwards. They will tend to sustain less damage, clear the matter quicker and create positive outcomes more easily, because they're more receptive to getting the message.

In general, aspect energies come into their own around exaction, perhaps starting to resolve themselves 1-2° before, where an alchemical reaction takes place, bringing about transition and movement. Once exact, the aspect starts separating, and a process of digestion and assimilation follows, in which the dust settles and a new *status quo* settles into place, becoming normalised and utilised. Perhaps there is new territory to explore too. As the aspect separates, what once was potential or formative becomes integral and established.

At times the integration process can take its time, especially if concrete life situations need changing (such as selling a house or the completion of a school year or a contract), or if there has been severe shock, confusion or disarray around the time of the aspect, leading to a kind of post-change trauma or numbness, or to material complications that take time to untangle. Usually things become clear and established when the aspect is around 2-3° separating.

Retrograde Waltzes

When slower planets are aspecting one another, two of them can move into aspect, then one or both can turn retrograde, aspecting each other again, and then, when either or both turn forward, they form the same aspect again. It depends where they are in relation to each other in the zodiac, and it applies particularly to the slower-moving planets' respective cycles.

This makes for a three-step process in which changes are strung out over a period, made into a more lengthy process. The *first* formation of the aspect then becomes a news-bringer, in which we become aware that change is needed, pending or desirable. It ends the old situation, inaugurating a transitional period where the matter remains unresolved for now. It is discovered that there's more to sort out than first understood. At the retrograde, *second* aspect, there can be a feeling that things are going backwards, and a struggle or energy-droop can ensue wherein the resolve to make the change comes into question and a fight-back is needed. Life asks, *are you sure?* A lot clarifies and an act of will or insight might be made here, to make that change. The beginning of the future takes place when the third, direct pass of the transit takes place. It's like a journey in which we depart from the past, we travel a journey, arriving later in the

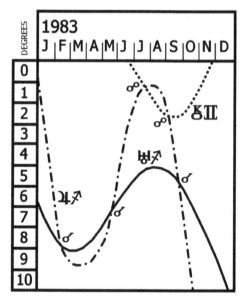

Three passes of a Jupiter conjunct Uranus in Sagittarius in 1983.
Note the Jupiter opposition Chiron also happening – Jupiter got caught up in a gradually-applying Chiron opposition Uranus which became exact in 1986.

future – though, even so, we are then presented with new territory in which to find our feet.

With planets from Jupiter outwards, occasionally there is just one pass of an aspect, even when a retrograde period takes place. This is because the faster planet might come very close to aspect, then turn retrograde before the aspect forms, then to return again, forming only one exact instance or pass of the aspect. Then, when later it retrogrades, it doesn't quite return to form the aspect again. Even so, when planets come close, there's still a rumbling going on underneath. But normally there are three passes, occupying up to a year, sometimes even five with Neptune or Pluto, taking two, occasionally three years. This is not to mention the period of buildup and assimilation of these aspects, which can take at least a few more years each side of the aspect, rendering these into much longer periods of 'processing'.

An exceptional example comes from Neptune and Pluto, which were in an ongoing sextile aspect, passing into and out of aspect many times over a few decades in the 1950s-80s, since eccentric Pluto, at its fastest speed at the time, kept pace with Neptune, and the aspect kept forming and re-forming. This was an important historical aspect, bringing about a steady flow and emergence of new ideas, developments and innovations over a period of a few decades – a fast-moving time of acceleration of the pace of life. Pluto then pulled away from the sextile, which will briefly return in the late 2020s before it finally ends.

Tracking Cycles

Shorter-term cycles are not too difficult to follow – lunations and annual cycles don't involve too much waiting. It is worth observing them as they are happening, and in advance and in retrospect also. This means keeping your ephemeris with you (*Raphael's Ephemeris* is useful, or a program such as *Astroclock*) and keeping a regular watch on the motions of the planets, checking what you see in the ephemeris with what you experience in your life and in the lives of other people around you – also in nature, the weather, the cat's behaviour, the aphids on your roses, your noisy neighbours' behaviour or the antics of a toddler. It's a matter of tuning into the collective psyche and the psyche of nature, to sense the tendencies afoot. It's a life-observational exercise.

Longer-term cycles are different. It starts getting really interesting if you have been studying planetary movements for a decade or more – but it isn't very encouraging to be admonished to wait so long! There are escape routes: if you come across a slower aspect unfolding in the present time, it is possible to look back through your ephemeris at previous dates when earlier aspects in the cycle took place. In this way, the significance of the current aspect can be seen more clearly when compared with past cases and the themes afoot then.

Look back over the past at longer term cycles, when you are feeling reflective, to see what you can make of them by comparing their timing with events and experiences that have happened. If you're interested in history and wish to examine timecycles in history, then visit the *Historical Ephemeris* on the author's website, which is stacked with valuable information.

Cogs in the Cosmic Machinery

Different interplanetary cycles bear different levels of significance and effect. The general rule is: *the slower a planet's motion, the more fundamental, longterm and deep it is in effect.*

Though a fullmoon can sometimes feel like a major soulquake, fullmoons come and go, and in the course of a year you experience 12-13 of them. Sometimes they precipitate significant crux-points and crunches, bringing longterm, deep, earth-shaking issues to the surface.

To give one example, the Chernobyl nuclear reactor blew its top on a fullmoon close to conjunction with Pluto, playing a dramatic role in the story of Pluto's journey through Scorpio between 1984 and 1996. One of the main themes of that period was the ruthless march toward modernisation and globalisation, bringing with it consequences ranging from famines and early signs of climate change to

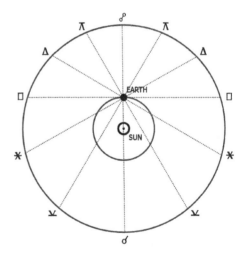

This diagram shows the way that aspects between the Sun and any planet outside Earth's orbit actually look from an astronomical viewpoint. Earth itself is in motion at its own speed, as well as the outer planet, so this simplified diagram doesn't show Earth's own movement.

major social and economic changes. Chernobyl, in Ukraine, had global reach in thoroughly unintended ways.

The Uranus-Pluto aspect cycle is a very different thing from, say, the Venus-Mars cycle – it's different both in duration and depth. It's necessary to sort out therefore what the different levels of cycles are, so that you can form an idea of the significance of a specific aspect or cycle you might be observing:

- **cycles between outer planets** have historical significance crossing the generations and centuries, dredging up new thought-forms, reality-bubbles and possibilities in the collective psyche, in history and the lives of nations and the world. They affect us personally too, and these can be found by studying transits, or aspects formed by the outer planets to the planets in our birth charts – not covered in this book but nonetheless worth watching;

- **cycles between Jupiter or Saturn and the outer planets** have historic significance in terms of years and decades. They affect the way issues surface in society, government, business and economics, law, social movements, even football or theatre. They influence trends and events in nature, technological innovation, emergent ideas, social beliefs and key mileposts in history over the decades. If you wish to track a particular emergent issue, such as the evolution of women's ordination as priests and bishops, styles of pop music or the pattern of conflicts in Israel and Palestine, then check out the key junctures when Jupiter and Saturn contact outer planets. These two planets interlace outer-planet dynamics into real-life terms, affecting society in concrete ways;

- **cycles of Jupiter and Saturn to each other** draw in practicalities, organisational and concrete social issues, with turning-points every 5-6 years, and new cycles starting every 20 years. They affect market fluctuations, political cycles, demographic trends, youth culture, epidemics, global weather patterns, ocean currents, interest rates and the activity-patterns of human generations;

- **Sun-Mercury-Venus-Mars cycles to the outer planets** repeat once every 1-2 years. They feature the surfacing into our personal lives of deeper issues stirred by the outer planets, even if but in fleeting terms – aspects last 1-3 weeks in their effects. They're reflected in news media headlines, labour strikes, the success or failure of public events, sports results and the everyday concerns of people in all walks of life;

- **Sun-Mercury-Venus-Mars aspects to Jupiter and Saturn** act similarly, focused on personality-level and concrete issues and situations. These cycles are somewhat longer than those just above, because Jupiter and Saturn move faster than the outer planets, requiring more chasing by Mercury, Venus or Mars;

- **mutual cycles between Sun, Mercury, Venus and Mars** last only a day to a week yet evoking feeling-tones, motions of energy, shorter-term changes and conditions which feel significant at the time, but which melt into lost detail in a longer-term perspective;

- **aspects between the Moon and any other planet** last only a few hours, yet major aspects between them can still bring about occasionally powerful yet brief atmospheres, situations and occasions, lasting 1-2 days yet well worth noting – especially when they combine with other aspects.

Of course, isolating individual cycles is not really possible, for everything takes place in the context of everything else. Yet an awareness of the different kinds of cycles at work helps sort out what energies are active in any situation as life goes on. All sorts of multiple interactions or sequences can take place, forming interestingly different patterns, and there's a beauty to it all because they never precisely repeat.

Panegyrations

Conjuring up a picture of the living, breathing motion of the solar system can be a boggling enterprise. But it is possible – just give it some time. If you first get a sense of the periodicities of the planets and their motions, you can then build up a picture of the whole system. The solar system is a living, breathing being, with an incredible beauty to its manner of moving.

The planets orbit anti-clockwise when seen from 'above' the solar system. This they do in our sky too (at least, when you're in the northern hemisphere, facing south). Don't confuse this with the diurnal (daily) motion of the heavens as a whole, arising from the rotation of our Earth on its axis. You can watch this anti-clockwise motion on successive nights with the Moon, which moves about 25 Moon-widths daily, leftwards in the heavens, when compared with the stars behind it or with another planet. Give it a try.

In days of old, an astrologer-astronomer would undergo a training of many years, building up a living, moving picture of the motions of the heavenly bodies. Such a trainee would spend years and years observing the stars, planets and Moon, and the rising and setting of the Sun. Of course, they would not then have been aware of Chiron, Uranus, Neptune and Pluto, though there are slivers of flimsy evidence that Uranus and Neptune were known about.

People in those times lived outdoors far more than we, with no electric lights. Their lives were more affected by the daily, lunation and annual cycles. Awareness of what was happening was a natural part of anyone's learning process – from the behaviour of deer to the motions of the Moon. Modern civilisation has insulated us from nature and the cosmos, and we pay a price for this. We're surrounded with ticking clocks, yet we're so much in a hurry that we frequently feel we have no time, even though we're continually striving to be on time.

Next, we're going to take another look at the zodiac and the threads that make up its tapestry.

9

Zodiacal Nuances

The planets manifest their energy-frequencies in many hues, tones and manners of phrase, filtered sequentially according to the order of the zodiac signs. There is an underlying pattern to this sequence: these are the genders, modes, elements and planetary rulerships. Understanding these, we can grasp how and why the zodiac signs behave as they do.

Narratives

The signs process and filter planetary energy. They reveal specific and varied patterns and potentials which, when functioning freely and openly, are balanced and whole in themselves. But they each have characteristic ways of becoming obstructed, corrupted, twisted, aberrated and hampered as well. When you observe the workings of the signs you will see both their distinctive advantages and disadvantages, even at the same time and interwoven. So, Taurus has steadfastness and a capacity to keep on motoring, whatever is happening and whatever anyone thinks, but it can also be inflexible, determinedly pushing against things or refusing to budge. Every characteristic can thus be a strength or a weakness at different times and in different contexts.

These are not just characteristics of signs but also psychological patterns of our own, related to our wishes and anticipations, fear, shame and guilt patterns, and how we respond when life turns out differently to what we believe it ought to be. The signs represent qualities which in themselves are unprejudiced and completely neutral, like sun or rain. Whether this causes us happiness or difficulty rests with us. There's life and there's how to deal with it: in the former we have an amount of control and in the latter we have enormous choice.

It is interesting to pay attention to themes that come up when planets move through the signs or there's a concentration of planets in them. It can be quite uncanny. Jupiter went through Gemini in June 2012-June 2013 and the big concern in the news was 'big data' – data-mining by corporations and intelligence services – and Saturn went through Scorpio in October 2012-December 2014 and we saw horror scenarios acted out in everything from cyclones to a serious Ebola outbreak in West Africa to murderous religious cleansing by jihadis in Syria and Iraq. Going back, when Saturn moved into Sagittarius in late 1985, a worldwide terrorist flap suddenly created a public fear of travelling internationally on

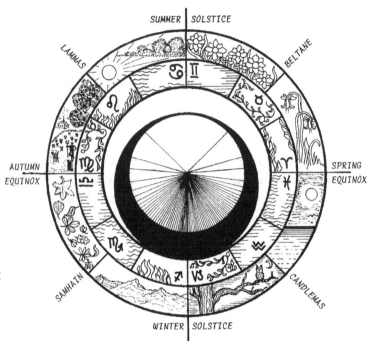

planes. Shortly afterwards, the crashing and destruction of various American and European space shuttles and rockets not only caused setbacks in space programs but also a collapse of society's aspirations to explore space. Terrorism, travel and space exploration are connected with Sagittarius. The events were symbolic, and the response was classic.

Sometimes symbolism-rich events, bringing up deep-seated imagery and implications, can be so literal in their reflection of astrological imagery that it is uncanny to witness them unfolding: one wonders why, after so many instances of this, astrology is not in wider use as a valuable way of understanding things. The Berlin Wall fell on a Saturn-Neptune conjunction in Capricorn, this particular conjunction symbolising the erosion of boundaries and the undermining of state structures. This was a direct hit astrologically, both in terms of timing and symbolism. The line-up should have been front-page news.

It's worth observing your own thoughts and feelings too, for we provide cues and prompts from within ourselves that connect uncannily with astrological patterns at work – we are our own teachers, if we will but hear ourselves. It's a matter of lateral thinking, staying tuned to symbolism and hidden threads within events: if the postman comes late when Moon is in Pisces, he's perfectly in tune with the cosmos and little is amiss! He might well be back in gear when Moon moves into Aries – unless something bigger is going on.

Substrata

The signs are linked with each other in manifold ways. Here we'll look at the contributory factors interlacing the zodiac: the *genders*, *modes* and *elements*, followed by *planetary rulerships*.

Here's how it breaks down. There are two **genders**, *yin* and *yang* (female and male), of which there are six signs each, alternating in sequence. There are three **modes**, *cardinal*, *fixed* and *mutable*, of which there are four signs each, running in sequence. There are four **elements**, *earth*, *air*, *water* and *fire*, of which there are three signs of each, also running in sequence.

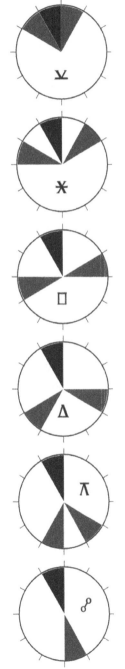

By looking at signs sequentially, as a cyclic series, we see how each sign affects the sign following it, also feeding out of the one preceding it. A sign tends to abreact to the sign before it, acutely aware of the pitfalls it fell into and striving to move on from there. Yet it also stands on the ground that the previous sign laid, working from that sign's experience. It tends to look down on its predecessor, underrating the latter's contribution – probably a self-justificatory ploy. Meanwhile it does not see or acknowledge the possibilities that the following sign can open up, and yet unconsciously it seeks to become like it, to move towards what, to the subsequent sign, is normal reality.

This contrasting of neighbouring signs (30°, ⚺) takes place within certain parameters, for while they contrast one another they are also intimately linked, their themes leading on from one another. Like women and men, they love each other and also have their crucial differences. You can observe this contrast of theme quite easily when a planet makes an ingress into a new sign: the atmosphere changes quite sharply and discernibly, like the turning of a page, while there is also a distinct feeling of sequentiality and follow-on.

Signs at sextile (60°, ⚹) to one another differ in emphasis and approach but they share similarities of energy and viewpoint, supporting each other fruitfully. They share the same gender and a different element and mode. Thus Virgo and Scorpio each internalise their experience and inwardly dwell on it as a matter of habit, Virgo to understand and handle it, Scorpio to get to the bottom of it, and hence they complement and work with one another – as long as they don't encourage each other to navel-gaze too much.

Signs at square (90°, □) either conflict and grate or engage with each other in productive effort. Whether or not they like it, they have to do so anyway. They share the same mode but have a different gender and a contrasting element. Thus, Aries works with courage and willpower, striking out, while Cancer stays in safe territory and can be sensitive and touchy. Yet both need to learn from each other. It's a tricky business: after all, fire and water can create energetic steam, but fire can dry up water or water can extinguish fire – so there's a delicate balance needed. There's something not easy about squares yet ultimately they are crucial.

Signs in trine (120°, △) have a similarity of aims and preferences, a natural confluence which is mutually reinforcing and largely harmonious. They get on well, though they might not create sparks or move mountains – they simply carry on and enjoy the ride. If they don't get on well, it's because they're similar and there's little spice there. They share element and gender but not mode. Thus Capricorn and Taurus both are earthy, grounded in approach and set on their allotted course, yet the former is driven by social obligations while the latter is driven by self-determination – they thus have an innate contrast and collaboration.

Signs at quincunx (150°, ⚼) experience a non-communication and dissimilarity: they have different modes, genders and elements, and they find difficulty forming common ground. They neither conflict nor harmonise – they just have to live with the situation as it stands, and it's not easy to change it. One dominates the other, or they mutually ignore each other, or they come to a manageable coexistence. But there's meaning and insight in it. Thus Pisces tends towards selflessness, sacrificing itself for the general good, while Leo tends toward self-centredness and a sense that the universe revolves around it. Both will at times wonder, each in their own way, why life treats them badly, yet there's an enormous difference of viewpoint. Pisces gets overwhelmed by life while Leo can't understand why life doesn't obey. This dissimilarity doesn't have to be a problem, since the quincunx can bring insights into life's deeper secrets – if not now, then sometime.

Signs in opposition (180°, ☍) work on contrasting sides of the same question. Each has the other sign hidden within it, to some extent complementing it and to some extent contrasting it. Each represents the other's unconscious tendencies or weak spot. Each calls the other into question, yet the meeting is dynamic and charged with potential: they have the same mode and gender but they are of a different element – opposite sides of the same coin. Thus Sagittarius takes a wide, overarching worldview, living according to an idea or philosophy about life, while Gemini takes a relativist and detailed worldview, anchored to whatever is right in front, trying to keep up with multiplex situations, friendly when people are there and forgetting them when they're gone.

Yet together this lot form a family!

Gender

Signs alternate through the zodiac, *yang* and *yin*.

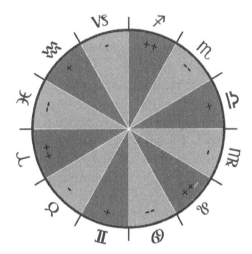

Yin is feminine, working through the water and earth signs, the givers of form and shape. These signs assimilate presented reality and deal with it, making sense of things, grounding and shaping them. They give substance and stability to energy-impulses coming from yang signs.

Yang is masculine, working through the fire and air signs, the movers: these signs create, energise and stimulate movement and change. They operate proactively upon life, enlivening and mobilising the forms embodied by yin, and yin gives yang purpose and structure.

There's an extra level to this too. Water signs are more yin, and earth signs are less yin, while fire signs are more yang and air signs less yang. So, put fire and water together and they kill each other or generate great energy. Put earth and water together and they become clay or mud, but shape them well and you can make them into pottery. Yang and yin point to the gender-energies *within each of us*.

The yin signs make the best of what presents itself, while the yang signs do their best to make things happen. The cardinal signs, starting each quarter of the year, endow that season with a gender according to the zodiac sign that starts the quarter. Summer and winter, begun at the solstices, are yin seasons started by Cancer and Capricorn, living with a given situation that has already come to pass and is there to be enjoyed or survived. Spring and autumn, beginning at the equinoxes, are yang seasons started by Libra and Aries. They seek to change things into something other than they once were, creating a new situation.

The Three Modes

There are four quarters of the zodiac, each with three different modes, *cardinal*, *fixed* and *mutable* – or perhaps initiating, implementing and completing. The modes form crosses, made up of signs at opposition and square to one another. They represent styles of operating. Each modal cross has a sign of each of the four elements – so the cardinal cross includes Libra (air), Capricorn (earth), Aries (fire) and Cancer (water). Each modal cross has two yin signs opposing one another, and two yang signs at square to them, also opposing each other.

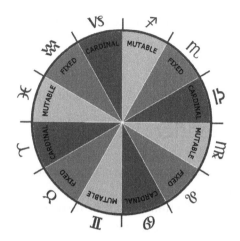

The *cardinal* signs summon and concentrate energy, setting a season in motion. The nature of the season is suggested by the element of the cardinal sign starting it – for example, autumn is characterised by the air element, through Libra. Cardinals are good at starting things and poor at completing them. They try to make facts catch up with potentials, and they get involved with life and its processes. At the beginning of each cardinal sign, an urge arises to make things move, even if, in Capricorn's case, things aren't necessarily going far in the depths of winter but instead are being consolidated. By the end of a cardinal sign a feeling develops that things are by now making progress – but there's more, since the purpose of the season must be truly carried through by the fixed sign that follows. Thus winter, an earth season, initiated by Capricorn, is pulled through by Aquarius, an air sign, and completed by Pisces, a water sign.

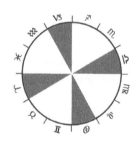

The purpose of the season is tackled by the *fixed* signs: they must hammer down whatever is in motion, ensuring that it actually does something. They work with what is already happening and on the move. Taurus and Scorpio mark the crux of the springtime or autumnal change, while Aquarius represents the depths of winter and Leo represents the fruition of summer. The potential of the season is now becoming fulfilled, something to live with and make something of. At the beginning of a fixed sign there is a sense of engagement of the gears. In the middle, at the cross-quarter point, the activity is really

happening and potentials are by now manifest facts. At the end the implications are grasped and things must be stabilised and nailed tight. Thus, Aquarius gets on with winter, with hope and plans for the future yet also a gritty urge to survive the present – it continues what Capricorn set in motion but it's also seeking something different.

The *mutable* signs adjust, regulate and perfect what has by now come to pass. They put things into their proper place and context – cars are important in themselves, but it's the travelling that matters, and that's what the car is for. The fixed signs are too involved in things to see clearly what has come about, while the mutable signs stand back to gain perspective and give it significance. They  put things into context, finishing things off, dealing with consequences, adding finer touches and ensuring that lasting benefit is accrued from what the cardinals started and the fixed signs made happen. They also learn from mistakes, ask questions and seek answers. At the beginning there is a relaxing of the determination of the fixed signs, leading to a change of possibilities. At the middle there are corrections, perfections and reflections to be made, and at the end there is preparation, thinking about what is yet to arise in the cardinal signs that follow. Mutables prepare the future and identify its potentials.

The different modes or qualities encounter different kinds of challenges. Cardinal signs, while fine at starting things, are addicted to proactivity, staying in start-up or stirring mode, habitually moving on to the next thing and the next after that. At times they impose intentions and imperatives on life without seeing where life as it presents itself is actually heading.

Fixed signs can get stuck in doing things and living things out, omitting to stand back to ask why they are doing it or to what end. Things *must* be done because they're there to be done, say the fixed signs – though sometimes they could be done another way, or without pushing, fixing and moulding all the time. Fixed signs have a job to do, so changes of course are uncharacteristic.

Mutable signs can build up complex rationales for everything, sometimes making an intricate knotwork out of straightforward issues. They can develop a habit of yielding or shrugging shoulders where greater tenacity might be in order. It's all relative and changeability can be an attachment, an excuse for not facing things. However, mutable flexibility gives space for new energy, fresh positions and brilliant ideas.

The Four Elements

The modes, elements and genders represent a warp and weft making up the zodiacal tapestry. They constitute a set of interlinked contributory threads giving character to the pattern of the signs. Thus, Scorpio is fixed, water and yin, and no other sign has that combination. The two, the three and the four interweave to make the twelve. While the modes represent stages in the buildup, breaking and backwash of the waves comprising each season, the elements represent fundamental principles giving character to those waves.

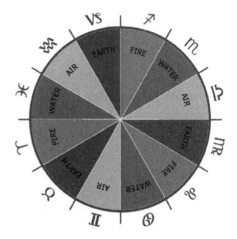

The *fire* signs represent the principle of energy or light, enlivening whatever is around, colouring and amplifying it – they can of course do the opposite too, withholding their gifts, like a wet summer. The *earth* signs represent the principle of solidification and organisation, the structuring and gelling of energy into form – which is fine as long as structure has meaning and doesn't over-clamp things or become boring routine. The *air* signs represent the principle of movement, interconnecting and networking – wonderful if things need shifting around and widening out, but also lacking in substance and not always getting things done. The *water* signs represent fluidity, melting and soaking, sensitising, joining and merging – lovely as long as too much fuss isn't made about things that really are quite transitory.

The four elements symbolise the four states of matter: plasma (fire), solids (earth), gases (air) and liquids (water), each with its own way of embodying energy and form in life.

Earth. What about real, down-to-earth issues that need sorting out? Without realism, practicality and proportion, nothing would function. This applies to metaphysics as much as to money and blocks of stone. Does it *do* anything? *I'll believe it when I see it.* Life gets complicated if things are not organised, sorted and maintained

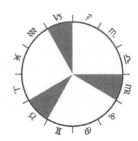

properly: steadiness and regularity get things done over time. We need houses to live in, crops need growing and bills need paying.

Even in relaxation and enjoyment the earth signs are diligent and practical – commonsensically they set it up, get people there, run the barbecue and clear up afterwards. Earth signs find out how things work, mould them, build them, alter them, knock them down, sort out the rubble, make piles and do the necessaries. They keep on going regardless of mood, getting the business done. They also suffer habituation, stuckness or indulgence.

Yin like water signs, earth signs feel they are affected by things, though without the same sensitivity as water signs – the innate stability of earth helps it stand its ground. Underneath there is a sensibleness which, when under pressure, patiently outlasts everyone else. Earth keeps on chipping away at things – changing course is valid only when it's clear and sensible. Earth signs make things last and do things properly. Perseverance makes results but also charges a price in terms of lost freedom, joy or love. Safe bets have their value and help us hedge against loss, but they generate profit slowly.

Air. The air signs contribute mobility and interrelationship. They are movable, detached, making connections, seeing things from contrasting angles, weaving things together in patterns or separating them out in bits. They oscillate between alternatives or extremes, widening life's possibilities and also its complexity. Perceiving contrasts and dilemmas, they're not so good at making choices or reliably standing firm, but at least everything is considered. Yet they shift things around, contribute ideas and inject adaptability into life.

There is a tendency either to go along with the prevailing wind or to take a contrary position, sometimes for the hell of it or just to explore alternatives. In sailing, the tiller and the sails must be continually adjusted to catch the best of the wind and, though air signs might take sideways diversions, they also keep things on course by tacking responsively to get round things another way. Air signs can be opportunist or dilettantist, often avoiding the nub of the matter, yet they contribute useful asides and have a way of being there just at the right time. They seek a middle course even though they oscillate between extremes.

Following ideas, air signs sometimes make ideas overtake reality, but at other times they responsively adjust to the way reality presents itself. Lying in between earth and water signs, they are placed at points in the zodiacal sequence where sideways corrections are needed, moving the chess-pieces around and bringing a fresh approach to bear on situations.

Water. Out of the detachment of the air signs arises the feelingful involvement of the water signs. To water, the full experiencing of life and its pathos is what life is about. We humans have a need to be affected, permeated and washed over by life's experiences so that they move us and permeate us, injecting tone, depth, richness and feeling. We need passion, immersion and dedication if we are to derive real benefit from it – otherwise, life gets boring and colourless.

Water signs uncover sensitivities and vulnerabilities, yet a measure of protection from the cruel onslaught of life is also sought since the fear is that we might be overwhelmed, drowned in it all. Water brings out finer sensitivities: simple, small things matter, and nuance and feeling make human life more *human*. The water signs are subjective, personal, intimate and fragile, yet each has its defence strategies – Cancer's shell, Scorpio's knife or Pisces' magic wand.

When the world loses its harshness and jagged edges, the water signs flow more openly, with warmth and trust. But when the icy blast blows, the water signs hold on tight to whatever is safe, with a tenacity that strengthens as the pressure grows. When the tears roll, people wake up, yet when pretences are maintained, cringing normality prevails. All beings need closeness, belonging, community, family and care.

Fire. Fire quickly converts form into energy, completely and indiscriminately. It doesn't hang around waiting for permission, the right conditions or support, since it just burns and it isn't easily stopped until it runs out of fuel. Fire signs make things move, transform, emerge, blossom, explode and flourish. Fire wants progress now: resistance and obstacles are there to be overcome. It brings up issues, expresses creativity and initiative, sets things simmering and gives them impetus.

Fire does not pause to take in the situation. There must be action, and the trail of destruction left behind can sometimes outweigh what is being created. Anything moving too slowly is overlooked, pushed forward or by-passed. Fire can be enthusiastic, inspired or, at times, volatile and troublesome. But things do happen and the direction is upwards and onwards. The fire signs get us out of the doldrums. They change things.

A sense of rightness, confidence and power drives the fire signs, though they can also be so busy enacting impassioned dramas that they fail to notice the subtler nuances of a situation. Which is why the subsequent earth signs follow them, to stabilise things.

The four elements give very useful ways of looking at the zodiac. All three fire signs have similar energising effects, but they each have a different mode, handling three aspects of energisation. Aries (cardinal) draws a line on the past by asserting itself and pushing things forward, while Leo (fixed) does what it believes in with unceasing energy, creativity and drama, moulding the world to its playscript, and Sagittarius supports people and society, giving a lot and stimulating progress – all of them with a secret control agenda thrown in.

This interwoven system of genders, modes and elements thus makes for a fascinating pattern where all the signs have their own uniqueness. Next we shall look at a further dimension, the planetary connections with the signs.

Planetary Rulerships

Each planet operates differently in different signs: in some they are 'home' (in home territory), in others they are 'exalted' (at their best), while in other signs they're 'in detriment' (in foreign territory) or 'in fall' (showing their rough edge). Detriments are opposite signs to home signs, and falls are opposite to exaltations.

Astrological tradition, handed down to us through Ptolemy in Alexandria, Egypt, during Greek times, and passing through Arabic and European medieval channels to the present day, has given us a symbol language and a set of astrological rules which has not found the need to be altered in more recent times, except for the addition of a few more recently-discovered planets and mathematical techniques, plus the use of computers.

Some astrologers use rulerships a lot while others rate them less highly, emphasising aspects or other factors instead. Every planet has importance and validity in every sign of the zodiac, but rulerships give an inroad into the otherwise complex field of understanding planets in signs.

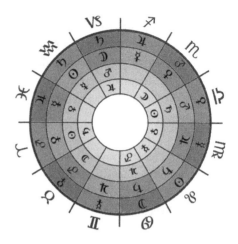

Amongst the personality-building planets (those visible to the naked eye in our sky), Sun and Moon each rule one sign, and Mercury-to-Saturn rule two signs each (see the outer ring of the planetary rulerships diagram). This ancient pattern of rulerships is not only interesting but also revealing. When Sun, Moon or any planet are *at home*, they sit in a sign embodying their particular kind of contribution to the energy-tapestry of time. Thus, we can call Pisces a Jupiterian sign, implying that the energy of Jupiter is highly compatible with that of Pisces (which is also co-ruled by Neptune). When Jupiter is in Pisces once every twelve years, it *becomes itself*, naturally.

Planetary rulerships. Moving from outer to inner circles: traditional rulerships; detriments; exaltations and falls.

Each of the planets except Sun and Moon has a home in a yang sign and a yin sign. This reveals a yang or a yin side to that planet's action. Jupiter is at home in Sagittarius (yang), relating to social and material beneficence and prosperity ('treasures on earth'), and in Pisces (yin), relating to inner wealth, vision and content of character ('treasures in heaven'). We could say that Cancer and Leo, the signs ruled by Moon and Sun respectively, are similar, creating a soli-lunar pair of signs involved with existential, beingness-related issues. Interestingly they are opposite the signs ruled by Saturn.

In astrology, the discovery of Uranus, Neptune and Pluto caused astrologers to assign them rulerships too. (Other planetoids such as Chiron and Sedna have not been given rulerships – or at least, suggested rulerships have not passed the filter of peer review to become widely accepted.) Uranus is at home in Aquarius, Neptune in Pisces and Pluto in Scorpio. Some astrologers have forgotten the old rulerships of Aquarius (Saturn), Pisces (Jupiter) and Scorpio (Mars), rating the outer planets equally to the personality-building planets. This is not entirely astute because the newer-discovered outer planets operate at a rather different level to the traditional, visible planets.

It is valid to use both the old sign rulerships and the newer outer-planet ones together, for these three signs. The outer planets don't generally express themselves clearly at the level of human personality and earthly events except through the agency of the visible inner planets (Sun to Saturn), since they work through the unconscious, the 'back story'. The inner and outer planets work on different energy-octaves, and thus they complement but don't necessarily replace one another in terms of rulerships.

Opposite to the home signs are the *detriment* signs. This unfortunate traditional term (like 'fall', later on) suggests a value judgement which is not really there. Astrology has no 'good' or 'bad' judgements attached to it. When a planet is 'in detriment' (such as Jupiter in Gemini or Virgo) it expresses itself strongly but shows some of its excesses, insufficiencies and rough edges. These need working on if the planet is to express itself well, and this is what happens when planets are in detriment. So, Jupiter in Gemini takes Sagittarius' lust for experience and understanding, turning it into intellectuality and informational knowledge which can sometimes be geeky, abstract and rather disconnected from the reality most of us experience.

Jupiter in Virgo can attach itself diligently to practicalities, which do indeed lead to efficiency, competence and deliverable results, but this also can obscure the vision, perspective and faith that Pisces works with – Virgo plays safe and tries to be realistic, which in some cases makes it miss the point.

When a planet is at home or in detriment it is strong, demonstrative and typified in its expression, and any issues arising here are strong ones. When a planet is in its *exaltation* or *fall*, it concerns quality, nuance or subtlety of expression. When a planet is exalted, its energy expresses itself in a fine, progressive and subtly skilled way – or at least it has the potential to do so.

Fall signs lie opposite the exaltation signs and, when a planet is in its fall, it can express itself in subtly inappropriate ways, insensitively, convoluted or reserved. The goodness of that position struggles to get through: yet a fall, like a detriment, gives material for us to work on, and it can be moved into conscious operation as we develop, becoming a strong point. Jupiter is exalted in Cancer, expressing itself in a munificent, caring, protective and sheltering manner (wonderful for caterers and nurturers). Jupiter in fall in Capricorn can be workaholic, account-bookish, unbelieving or authoritarian (a father archetype paying attention to the usefulness and feasibility of things and proffering 'tough love'), though it can be sensible and judicious too.

Sun is exalted in Aries and in fall in Libra: the magnetic, expressive energy of the Sun works well in Aries, though it sometimes pushes hard and forces things, but in Libra it all depends very much on what others are doing and thinking and on wider considerateness – which is amenable and diplomatic, but being nice isn't always the best strategy. Moon is exalted in Taurus, endowing care, instinctual sensuality and enjoyment of, even attachment to, comforts and the good life, while it is in fall in Scorpio, where it can withhold its feelings for fear of letting out a wild dragon of wants or dependency.

Mercury is exalted in Aquarius, where abstract thought, analysis and enquiry work well, and it is in fall in Leo, where it can become a motormouth know-it-all with listening difficulties. Venus is exalted in Pisces, where it has compassion, hope and a capacity to heal and comfort, and it is in fall in Virgo, where there can be trust issues and reticence, holding back for fear of hurting or being hurt.

Mars is exalted in Capricorn, where it works long, systematically and hard, and it is in fall in Cancer, which can be impulsive, restive or impatient, though impassioned. Saturn is exalted in Libra, where it is prudently detached, fair and judicious, and it is in fall in Aries, where it can be shy, hiding its light, holding back for fear of making mistakes, applying force or being found inadequate – reluctant leader syndrome.

A planet in a home or exalted sign can have difficulties if there are blockages attached to that planet, or excesses or unawarenesses. Home signs in particular harbour a natural energy-expression which doesn't objectively see what it is doing, or its effects. Exalted planets can behave as if their way of doing things is the *only* way, and sometimes they cannot see beyond this. On the other hand, a planet in detriment or fall is faced with the outcomes of its acts, facing challenges that foster awareness and self-correction in a willing, seeking person, thus becoming a positive influence once learned and addressed.

Planets and Elements

Each planet sits more comfortably in signs connected by element to its home signs. They will be in harmonising trine angles to each other. Signs of the same element reflect three different facets of the same kind of energy expression.

Thus Jupiter, at home in Sagittarius and Pisces, fire and water signs, tends to find power in other fire signs (Aries and Leo) and depth in water signs (Cancer and Scorpio). Jupiter in fire signs demonstrates its stimulating, encouraging, even driving nature, while in water signs it demonstrates empathy, care and understanding. Similarly, Mercury (at home in Gemini) is mental, theoretical and intellectual in air signs, while in earth signs (at home in Virgo) it is dextrous, skilled, informed and factual.

On the other hand, when in signs unconnected by element to their home signs, planets find less power, naturalness or originality. Thus, Jupiter in the earth signs embeds itself in a realism which can restrain Jupiterian zest. In air signs Jupiter creates sophisticated ideas and beliefs, yet they might be pie-in-the-sky, hypothetical or difficult to implement.

Or Mercury in water signs gets its ideas mixed up with feelings, becoming more responsive while also losing impartiality. In fire signs it can form strong conclusions and spout them out, often lacking tact, thoughtfulness or willingness to learn anew.

A reminder: *no planet is better or worse in any sign*, and preconceived notions of how they are going to work, or whether they will produce pleasant or intolerable results, will often miss the mark. When a planet passes through a sign it expresses a facet of its complete repertoire, that's all, and that facet is a necessary part of the whole scheme of things. Hard times make good times good, and good times give meaning to hard times – and it's all relative. Perceptions of ease and difficulty depend on our attitude to life, and perhaps our authenticity. Pain and difficulty are directly related to the degree of resistance and obstruction we put up – it has little to do with astrological signs.

The Zodiacal Tapestry

The signs represent *themes*. When a slower-moving planet changes signs, themes in the collective psyche change. Thus, Pluto dredging through Capricorn (2009-2024) creates a collective obsession with the idea that everything boils down to money, business, resource use and 'the rule of law'. This will shift in emphasis into a preoccupation with people,

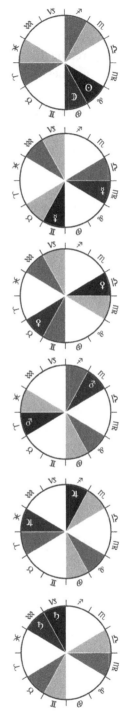

Rulerships and the elements.

181

social subgroups, collective issues and values when it passes into Aquarius (2024-44). Events come along to reflect and precipitate these theme-changes – often triggered by the swinging of faster-moving planets into relationship with slower-moving ones.

Thus, while themes brought up by slow-moving planets usually progress gradually over a period of years, they are sparked and squeezed into specific situations when a faster planet, or several of them, pump up the pace and intensity. Government leaks and atomic leaks had been happening for a long time before the 1980s, but the presence of Pluto in Scorpio (raising issues around secrecy and control) and Neptune in Capricorn (involving shaky structures) from 1984 to 1997 made the matter of leaks into *charged* issues. Pluto was in Scorpio for 12 years, but it took a fullmoon conjuncting Pluto, plus all of the right circumstances, to make Chernobyl melt down one day in late April 1986.

Once the cork has popped, the process continues – that awareness lurks around waiting for reactivation. This happened with the 2011 Fukushima nuclear disaster, reactivating issues first brought up by Chernobyl. Interestingly, when Chernobyl took place, Neptune was at 5° Capricorn and Pluto at 5° Scorpio when, for Fukushima, Pluto was at 7° Capricorn (having been at 5° two months before), and also both Uranus and Neptune were about to change signs into Aries and Pisces respectively. So we could say that one of the triggers for the Fukushima crisis was a sextile of Pluto to its Chernobyl position, and a conjunction to Neptune's position at that time. Of course there were other triggers, mainly geological and connected with nuclear policy and corporate practice in Japan, but all things operate as a wholeness, the identification of which is astrology's strength as an analytical and diagnostic tool. In other words, with astrology we can see the underlying currents afoot, connecting two separate events, which otherwise would seem to be a random connection with no inherent meaning.

However, the underlying issue in both cases, Chernobyl and Fukushima, was not primarily that of nuclear power but of vested interests and sclerotic structures – Capricorn. The problem with both disasters involved operational and organisational issues. The collective unconscious has timings and makes connections of its own, and the question of nuclear disasters involves larger, connected issues about the nature of technology and civilisation, governance, power, boundaries and laws, economics and public feelings.

A theme might lurk invisibly until an ingress or aspect sparks off an event to give it energy in public consciousness, bringing it out as an issue everyone has to face. What has been latent, unconscious or suppressed rises into public consciousness, sometimes shockingly or sometimes surreptitiously. It does so through a set of associations, connections or images that suddenly slot together to convey a powerful message.

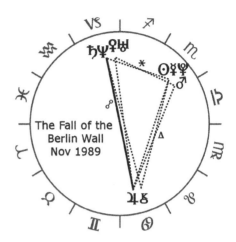

We've had a lot of Capricorn-Cancer themes in recent decades, from 1984 onwards into the 1990s, and then from 2009 when Pluto entered Capricorn. To get a perspective on our current time, let's look back at 1989-90, when Uranus, Neptune and Saturn were in Capricorn and Jupiter and Chiron were in Cancer. In the next chapter there's a chart where you'll see Jupiter in Cancer again, this time in 2014. Jupiter has a 12 year cycle, and 2014 is 24 years after 1990.

The Fall of the Berlin Wall Nov 1989

A concentration of outer planets in Capricorn-Cancer in 1989-90, ramped up when faster planets swung into this alignment, gave much excellent experiential data on what these two signs are about. Capricorn concerns issues around institutions, structures and traditions, money and law, order, stability, agreements, constitutions and social purpose. This vied with the Cancerian sensitivities of crowds of people in the streets expressing their feelings, played out in Tiananmen Square in Beijing, at the Berlin Wall and in the city squares of central Europe. The crowds came out and the soldiers were faced with the choice to shoot, or not to shoot. In China they shot. In East Europe they generally didn't: they saw members of their own families and neighbourhoods in the crowds, realised that they too, as soldiers and police, were human victims of an oppressive system. So they didn't shoot, and many deserted.

The Cancerian issues involved the security and integrity of people and nations, of welfare and food, of resources, fuel and sustenance. In the West this brought the rapid growth of environmental and human rights movements. It concerned ordinary people and their vulnerabilities and needs. The stern father (Capricorn) and the protective mother (Cancer) clashed – with some serious truth coming in from the side, from Pluto in Scorpio. God and Babylon suffered wobbles and weaknesses (Uranus, Neptune and Saturn in Capricorn) while Goddess and small people offered openings and solutions (Jupiter and Chiron in Cancer).

The question of the time was: *do people serve the system* or *does the system serve the people?* This is a big, perennial question, and some progress was made on it at that time. The question was also commuted to another day, coming up again in the

Arab revolutions of 2011. It will probably come up again when Pluto passes through Aquarius (2023-43).

We all have all of the signs working through us, for each of us according to our own patterning. The archetypal issues of all signs come up sooner or later and affect us all individually, in differing ways: selfhood-relatedness issues (Aries-Libra), self-determination or involvement (Taurus-Scorpio), knowledge and belief (Gemini-Sagittarius), security and organisation (Cancer-Capricorn), me and us-together (Leo-Aquarius), competence and insight (Virgo-Pisces).

A grasp of this cycle of archetypes can help us understand and function better. We can then start seeing things from a larger perspective, learning when to persevere, when to enjoy the sheer variety of human experience and how to choose our timings. *To everything there is a season and a time for every purpose under heaven.* Thus we move into closer accord with the flow of time. It connects us with a deeper level of time which has little to do with clocks and calendars – this is *evolutionary time*, a time-dimension that concerns our deeper growth and development. After all, we came here to learn.

The next chapter starts bringing everything together. We're going to look into power points and power periods in time.

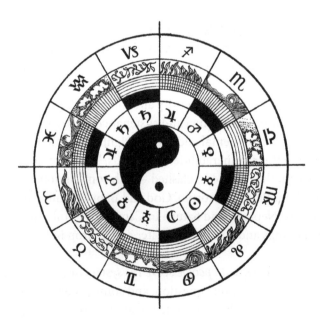

10

Power Points in Time

A power point is a period ranging from hours to years when a special and uncommon form of energy-weather is going on. These are important events and periods. Power points have differing magnitudes, depending on their duration, on how many planets and other factors are involved, and what is happening as a whole. They are definitive, intense, rich in nuance, pregnant with possibility and they make a splash in time and the stream of events.

A power point is identified by looking at the various factors going on together at any time. This includes aspects, ingresses, stations and multiple configurations. They are time-locations when energy is available for bigger than normal changes, re-alignments and breakthroughs, on a quantum scale. They come only now and then but, when they do, they are important – and if we don't make use of them, they make use of us.

Power Pointers

How do we identify power points in time? This question forms the nub of this book, and there's a classic example of such a power point on the next page. Think back to that moment in time and the way it manifested in your life.

Here we'll examine examples of power points and, in the next chapter, we'll look into more details about recognising them astrologically and ranking them in terms of magnitude.

There are greater and lesser power points in time and, if you have a receptive inner ear, you'll probably be intuitively 'online' to catch them and make the most of them, whether or not you use astrology to help. Some power points are astrologically visible in advance and sometimes they come upon us when we're not looking, bubbling up from the collective unconscious and surprising even astrologers. Astrologers might be aware of the potential for *something*, but remarkable events don't happen mechanically – they depend on a coming together of many factors, and often they become newsworthy precisely because they are unpredicted.

Those that come upon us unexpectedly often arrive in the initial form of problems or obstacles, only to transform into assets or opportunities if we accept what's happening, shift our viewpoint and make constructive use of whatever has presented itself. We get stuck in a traffic jam only to find that it gives us thinking time – or perhaps, more magically, a heron flies overhead, bringing a glimmer of light to lift us out of our concerns and tedium.

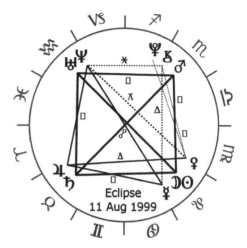

A classic power point in time: the solar eclipse of 11 August 1999 – perhaps a chart for the new millennium. A solar eclipse involved in a Grand Cross with Uranus, Saturn and Mars, plus a T-square configuration with Mercury, Jupiter and Neptune, and with other aspects tying all of the planets into the situation. This kind of multiple involvement of planets in configurations makes for a textbook example of a power point in time.

Those power points that we can foresee, such as fullmoons or solstices, are worth doing something with. Go and meditate under a tree or climb a hill, or share the moment with someone special. Or inwardly take note of what's happening and be quietly mindful of your thoughts and the underlying threads of meaning that you experience. Watch for 'day signs' – omens and symbolic indicators in nature, the weather or the world around. These are keys, portals, openings, opportunities.

A Beltane Fullmoon

Here's an example of a pretty major power point, though short in duration. During the 1980s I organised camps for people interested in earth mysteries, astrology and other metaphysical subjects, and a camp was planned for Beltane in early May 1985. A look in the ephemeris yielded definite signals that this would be an auspicious time. Such occasions often have several different astrological phenomena taking place synchronously, and this was no exception, so I calculated the timing of the camp on this basis.

On 4th May 1985 around the middle of the camp came a fullmoon, and fullmoons are generally good for consciousness-raising activities. This one, however, was upgraded by several other factors:

first, the fullmoon took place when the Sun was at 14♉ and the Moon at 14♏ – this therefore roughly combined the timing of the cross-quarter with a fullmoon, a marrying of solar and lunar cycles;

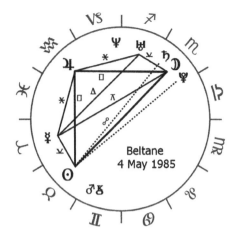

Beltane
4 May 1985

second, the fullmoon was a lunar eclipse that happened to be rising over the eastern horizon just as it was coming into effect. It was stirring to watch. A lunar eclipse is an extra-strong, exact fullmoon when everything goes still and a strong sense of the timeless takes over;

third, this fullmoon formed an exact square to Jupiter at 15♒, creating a T-square configuration (a right-angled triangle containing an opposition with two square aspects). This gave a powerful injection of hearty Jupiter energy, hope and forwardness, coming from Aquarius, the sign of social groups. One interesting quirk illustrating this was that a NATO exercise drawing together different countries' air forces was going on at a neighbouring air base, and they buzzed our camp as if it were a terrorist encampment. This of course was not popular, though we emerged unscathed by holding together and not letting it upset us too much;

fourth, the fullmoon fell at a strong *midpoint* between Saturn and Pluto on either side of the Moon, bringing their combined truth/breakthrough influence to bear – that is, Pluto was at 3♏ and Saturn at 25♏, the middle point between which was, lo behold, at 14♏, *exactly* at the position of the eclipsing fullmoon. A midpoint is a location between two planets that can be regarded as a place where their combined energies meet – useful astrologically when two planets are not too far from each other while not in aspect;

fifth, a separate Mars-Chiron conjunction in Gemini occurred the following day, adding a flavour of activity and an opportunity for healing differences between people – which indeed is what happened at the camp. In the case of NATO we forgave them, praying that their flying machines never be used for offensive action. As it happens, the Cold War ended about five years later: we cannot claim we did that, but we might have contributed an ounce of assistance! This conjunction was not linked by aspect to other parts of the chart, yet it was still there, in operation;

sixth, Mercury in Aries formed a sextile to Jupiter in Aquarius and a trine to Uranus in Sagittarius, and there was also an interesting 'Trapezium' configuration present, adding a taste of open-mindedness, rumination and insight – there's more on configurations in chapter 12.

You don't need to understand all the above – I'm just spelling out the components of this power point in time, to illustrate a classic example. Power points vary greatly, but the principles of how they work are demonstrated in this chart. Any seasoned astrologer can see that a combination like this is well worth using for *something* – and we did. It worked.

At the time of the eclipse 200 people, tuned up after three days of preparation and buildup, stood under the eclipsing Moon watching and feeling it, awe-inspired. We had made plans for what we would do at that moment but, actually, we were overawed and transfixed, forgetting most of them! Everyone went through a deeply stirring reaffirmation of the meaning of their lives and their hope for the world, making deep resolutions and experiencing a quality of shared love which dawns *only sometimes*. For some it was a major life-changing experience. The eclipse, lasting but an hour, though it seemed an eternity, went down in memory as one of those one remembers all one's life. Thoughts and experiences at times like this can be pattern-setting, definitive and highly significant. It's a time of omens. Watch what you think at such times.

As it happens, at the time President Ronald Reagan was visiting Germany, making a few political bloopers in the process, and this weekend turned out to be the turning point of his career as president – it all started going downhill from there. These configurations affect *everyone*, irrespective of whether they are aware of what's happening astrologically.

Chernobyl

Such an energy-situation was not available for the Beltane camp the following year, so I had to choose a *good enough* time, in the knowledge that such power points are only occasionally available. A fullmoon power point was available just before the camp but it was not a convenient date for the event – and this is a typical problem when planning events astrologically.

What actually happened was interesting: during the days before the camp, as we were setting it up, the fullmoon closely conjuncted Pluto in Scorpio on 24th April. Just after that fullmoon, the nuclear reactor at Chernobyl in Ukraine, USSR, melted down on 26th April, causing a shiver of fear to run through the world, not least through the hearts of the people attending that camp!

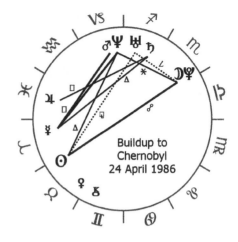

Buildup to
Chernobyl
24 April 1986

This demonstrates how events don't necessarily come at exactly the same time as astrological phenomena, since the energies must filter through the human psyche and the mechanics of real-life situations, often producing a time delay. But when there are forward-thinking people involved who lead the way, social dynamics can arise *before* an astrological phenomenon too. In our case, the whole camp following that Plutonine fullmoon became a resounding process of working with fear and feelings of powerlessness, together with the eruption of our rather chaotic and confused spontaneous reactions to the unfolding situation. Not only this, but we also had to handle the detectable feeling of radiation falling on us. We had a distinctly plutonine experience at this camp.

The result was a feeling of breakthrough. One small thing happened at the camp which, to me, summed it all up. A participant came to say that he could not have his kids out here in the radiation, and that he was taking his family home. I wished them well. But when I was standing in the dinner queue that evening, there they were, queuing for their dinner! The man explained that, as they drove home, they had realised that if they were going to die, they'd prefer to die with us, not alone at home. So they returned! And we all lived to see another day. Now the engineers in Chernobyl, causing the event, were not to know that they would, amongst other things, set in motion a big change in this family's life, but this kind of thing happens at such power points – knock-on effects spreading far and wide.

By the end of the event, participants had resolved their responses to the disaster, and the experience had become a major turning-point for all of us. We had each reviewed our commitment to our life's work and, at the time sincerely wondering whether the world was now entering the End Times, we had assessed and discussed our willingness to work with whatever challenges might arise in future. A power point had precipitated an event, the Chernobyl meltdown, through a series of engineers' mistakes, which in turn awakened deep dynamics in the world's collective psyche – and these collective feelings seemed focused and magnified at the camp. The world had worriedly wondered for a few rather long days whether This Was It, the beginning of the Apocalypse. But this 'irrational' fear was soon packed away again and normality was duly restored.

During this camp group activities were carried out, seeking to work with the nuclear crisis and its effect on us. At one stage, participants did a meditation in which, in our imaginations, we joined hands and flew together over Chernobyl, covering it to stop the nuclear leakages. That was a powerful, moving meditation. Then, next day, someone listened to the news on the radio and, lo behold, it was announced that engineers had at last gained control of the meltdown and – this is the remarkable bit – it had occurred at *exactly the same time* as we did the meditation.

This and other experiences led me, nine years later, to start a new series of camps dedicated to doing such inner work intentionally. So the experience in 1986 marked the seed-point of events that happened much later – and this seed-point phenomenon is a characteristic of power points. I tell these stories at length to illustrate the characteristics of the times in question. The 1985 camp was Jupiterian and the 1986 camp was Plutonine.

To me these experiences validated the notion that careful timing of planned events creates outcomes far beyond what otherwise might be expected to happen. This represents an alignment of human activity with cosmic energy, both feeding one another. One of the funny things about these stretchings of time is that they are difficult to remember when we are back in ordinary daily life. Yet, when we revisit similar modes of consciousness later on, even if years later, the memory can return as if it were only yesterday, as if part of a continuity of its own, existent in another layer of time. This shows the peculiar multilevel relationship between evolutionary time and ticktock time.

Cyclone Haiyan

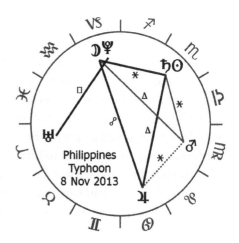

Here's an example of a power point that was both tragic and yet a good sign of progress. On 8th November 2013 hurricane Yolanda or Haiyan devastated the central Philippines, killing, injuring and destroying the lives of large numbers of people, devastating nature, farms and towns. The chart shows the underlying historic issue, the 2012-15 Uranus-Pluto square, and also the triggers, Jupiter and Saturn. The Sun was conjuncting Saturn in Scorpio, and Jupiter, hovering in a rough opposition to Pluto and wide square to Uranus, cranked up by the Moon swinging past Pluto, raised the stakes an extra notch. The Furies were let loose, people crouched in hiding and worldwide media-watchers shook their heads in dismay.

This was classically Saturn in Scorpio stuff – an overwhelming wipe-out with a grim and harsh character to it, safely sitting in the 'worst nightmare' category. Yet look, there is a trine to that Sun-Saturn conjunction from Jupiter in Cancer: Jupiter here represents a nurturing, protecting mother principle. Apart from the general influence of Jupiter, which tends to pump things up and escalate them, we need to look here not just at the typhoon but also at the social and international response to it. We need to see this disaster not only in isolation but also in the context of disasters in general.

A key issue here was the global provision of disaster response systems. Typhoon Haiyan proved that such systems had developed and did indeed work quite well, following from lessons learned in the enormous 2004 Indonesian earthquake and tsunami. Disaster response after the typhoon was quite efficient, and the collective psychological response of Filipino victims was brave and collaborative, avoiding many consequential problems such as large-scale looting, panic, hunger and destitution that could have made this disaster much worse.

So while this was an awful tragedy, it also brought good news. It served as a read-out showing how far modern disaster-relief operations had come, and also how much the disaster victims' own appropriate response to their shocking situation mattered. It was a reminder to the world that we must accustom ourselves to such disasters – this is one of the many threads lying behind the Uranus-Pluto square as a whole. However, the primary lesson has not yet been learned: if we sincerely wish to avoid this escalation of disasters, we must make fundamental changes to our way of life, since our consumptive and destructive habits are a major cause of the problem. And domestic political problems in the Philippines still obstruct fund disbursement and reconstruction.

Evolutionary Time

The examples above show how power points work. Power points are there to be *used* – either with forethought and advance planning or through rapid, appropriate response when they arise. They never return in the same way again. Power points offer special inroads into the mystery of life, special lessons and opportunities.

Meanwhile, we could do better. Our tendency as humans is to divert our attention off the time's main message and lesson, resisting and delaying fundamental solutions, thereby creating consequences and complications which subsequently create more problems as time passes. When these happen we often fail to see the connections between causes – previous bad decisions – and effects. Wars sometimes break out at power points in time, often at times when there are big opportunities for fundamental change, as if wars are a terrible evasion of the real point – and there are vested interests who also like to keep things that way. We *choose* how to use time. The big question is whether our choices have integrity and honesty built into them, and whether we're willing to take brave steps.

The relationship of ticktock and evolutionary time is more important than we usually think. It concerns not just fluffy esoteric issues but very real questions. Ticktock time involves organisational matters, worldly calculations and also the neuroses that exist within the ticktock framework. Evolutionary time involves intuitive, right-brained perceptions which, at times, we ignore at our peril. In ticktock time we try to make things go according to plan, expending a lot of energy trying to make them fit that plan. Evolutionary time on the other hand can disrupt normal plans and lead to inconvenient situations and hard truths. But all that it is doing is trying to move us along easier tracks, which requires the confounding of our plans. It can also put wind into our sails, create miracles and work magic, even in the most practical of situations. Deep down, we usually *know* something about the deeper reasons behind life's unfolding situations, and we badly need to give more attention to that knowing.

Astrology cannot always give answers, though it gives important clues. What's important here is *intuition*, keeping a listening ear open to our feelings and sensings, for here we receive signals indicating that, deep down, we *know* certain things that our conscious mind does not. This applies to relationships, business decisions, politics, car driving and other important issues big and small. For intuition to work successfully, we must sometimes be courageous, giving weight to intuition without obstructing it with the neurotic need for explanations, reasons and rationales. Discernment is needed too, distinguishing between hopes, fears, predilections and preferences on the one hand, and true insights on the other, many of which at the time seem not to make sense. But they do make sense, from a deeper and wider viewpoint. Intuition sees things with an uncanny objectivity. Like making music, the more we do it, the more it works.

Prognosis

Understanding power points in time has two main uses. One is the selection in advance and utilisation of appropriate times to carry out certain objectives. The other concerns encountering events and developments and then using astrology to understand them more quickly, deeply and accurately. The camping events mentioned above demonstrate the former kind and hurricane Haiyan in the Philippines in late 2013 demonstrates the latter kind.

As soon as the unexpected hurricane happened, we could use astrology to see the hidden influences and themes behind the event. This revealed new levels of significance. If astrology were publicly accepted and respected, it would be of immense use in planning, policymaking and decision-making. President Reagan had an astrologer for a few years, who advised on the timing of various treaties made at the time with the Soviet Union (such as the SALT nuclear arms treaty) and, lo behold, those treaties *worked* longterm – the signing of them was timed right. Once Reagan's astrologer was despatched in disgrace after awkward and disdainful media coverage, things went back to normal and the signing of treaties and agreements became a hit-and-miss affair – more of them failed.

Yet even in the area of prognosis and forecasting, when the date for a planned event is being chosen or when a potential outbreak of events can be foreseen, there are many unknowns to deal with. Just because a chart shows that certain astrological conditions will be present at a certain time, and it's reasonable to expect that certain things might happen, it doesn't mean that they *will* happen as foreseen. This is not a problem with astrology in itself – it's a problem with our *interpretation* of the astrological factors that are being seen. Doctors have this problem too, with diagnosing ailments. Politicians have a particularly bad case of it.

We tend to base forecasts on what we *want* to see, even if only unconsciously, or alternatively on the basis of what we have thus far experienced. Contrary to popular belief, astrology is not primarily a forecasting tool except inasmuch as it can suggest possibilities or probabilities. It is mainly a tool for understanding the present and the past. The need to forecast the future is by degrees phobic, rooted in fear of loss. If you ever hear an astrologer making exact, firm, definite predictions of the future, take those forecasts with a pinch of salt – there might be gems in what they say but, regarding the future, it is safest to expect the unexpected. Here's an example.

The Urania Trust Conference

There was an interesting power point on the weekend of 8th-10th February 1986, when Halley's Comet reached its closest point to the Sun in its 76-year trajectory, conjuncting the Sun and Moon in Aquarius, on a newmoon – a good time for the start of something new. There was also a strong conjunction of Mercury, Venus and Jupiter close by in Aquarius. Clearly this was an ideal time for a get-together. In addition there was a wide conjunction of Mars and Saturn in Sagittarius with Uranus close by, and the Mars-Saturn conjunction was opposed by Chiron and part of a configuration called a Yod, linking up with Neptune and Pluto.

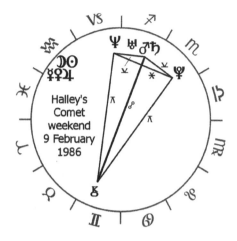

I went to an astrologers' conference that weekend, which happened to start off a new trend in cooperation between astrologers in Britain, after a period of bickering and dissension. The organisers knew it could be an auspicious weekend, but they didn't know how things would actually pan out.

The late Charles Harvey, a leading figure in the British astrological community at the time, wrote to me describing the way the conference fell together. "When in December 1985 I noticed this newmoon I realised it would be an ideal opportunity to launch the Urania Trust's fundraising campaign with a suitable press conference. We decided to put on some lectures too. Overnight a full-blown conference materialised! In the event, in less than six weeks we got over 500 people to that weekend conference, in the middle of winter. It was a great success, but the press conference and the fund-raising aspects were almost non-existent!".

This is a classic example of the way that something which *seems meant to happen* can come about, often using pretexts which later land up being irrelevant – almost a trick of fate. As John Lennon once sang, *life is what happens when you're busy making other plans*. In situations such as this, where we are unwittingly picking up on something the universe seems to want to happen, we need to be flexible and intuitive in the way we see and arrange things. In this case the organisers were sufficiently open to the intuitive thread of what was developing, and magic happened.

In Britain alone, some fifteen conferences and major meetings were reported for that weekend in the media. Organisers in many different places had chosen this time for all sorts of individual reasons but, nevertheless, they were all obeying something. Such congruence ranged from Margaret Thatcher's Conservative party to a major dog show to the Urania Trust for astrologers, and a variety of outcomes were generated. It was a heady, whizzy weekend: a conference just one week later would have missed the available energy.

By the way, comets are not customarily used in astrology, but at that weekend the astrologers couldn't help but notice it, and the conference did have a special flavour to it. It was agreed that comets, by dint of their short-lived visitations, are bringers of a new seed to be planted at the time – an insert into the collective psyche. At least, this was the case that weekend.

Power Periods

If you observe temporal power points you will find all sorts of variations of power point taking place in different instances. We're in a period of history when major energy-surges are taking place with growing intensity. This is not exactly an astrological issue since planetary motions and configurations are not themselves rising in intensity or frequency – they chug along through history as they always have.

What's different today is the intensifying planet-wide situation, involving humanity and all that humanity affects. Never before have so many people been alive and experiencing life and its issues, and never has our planet been engineered, affected and wrecked by us to the degree that is the case now. In addition, the habitat destruction, pollution, climate change, urbanisation and so on have grown by a daunting degree in very recent times – the world's population has doubled since the 1960s. So today we are prone to all manner of shocks, crises and potential great-leaps-forward. The curve of change is rising toward some sort of critical point in human evolution.

What might in the past have been a medium-scale power point in time can thus become major in significance because the stakes are so high and the impact of a crisis today can be so much greater than before – more people die, more issues are raised, there is more to lose, and repercussions can be bigger and more complex. A major earthquake in former times might have affected some hundreds or thousands of people, but nowadays it can affect millions and have wide repercussions in terms of migration, welfare, insurance, economics, commodity supplies, trade and general disruption.

Longterm historical changes such as the Uranus-Pluto square of 2012-15, which is the waxing square in a 143-year cycle starting in 1965-66, are more like power-*periods* than power points. Over the three years, the square goes in and out of aspect, turning it into a process with peaks and intermissions. Within these power-periods, lesser power points accentuate the themes and dynamics that are rumbling on, acting as smaller waves sitting atop a bigger wave and highlighting different facets of the overall issue at hand. In the context of centuries, three or ten years are peanuts, and such a period plays a part in the larger historical context – it's a moment in history, a significant paragraph in the annals of time.

In the case of disasters, in the period 2012 to 2015, and the 2-3 years' buildup too, we have had wars, revolutions, earthquakes, hurricanes, a nuclear accident, ethnic cleansing, economic and consequent social issues, refugees and migrants, all testing our capacities and causing a lot of difficulty for the many people involved. It's an ongoing multi-faceted disaster. It is not the first time such things have happened, yet they are reaching a critical intensity, raising many questions about the nature of life, civilisation and the future. Things are unlikely to quieten down and return to normal anytime soon. The new normal is an ongoing crisis.

These events are manifestations of an underlying mass soul-educational process, highlighted at spike-moments, that registers in the world's psyche, activating evolutionary responses from us as nations and societies. Events and human preoccupations take on symbolically-charged formats – a never-ending movie of murders, riots, court-cases, politicians' pronouncements, storms, droughts, breakdowns and breakups with an intensity never seen before, amplified globally by incessant media-coverage. Sea-level rise, an issue anticipated in connection with climate change, more deeply symbolises event-level rise.

The courageous man with a briefcase, single-handedly facing down a line of tanks in the Tiananmen Square protests in Beijing, China, in 1989, symbolising 'people against the machine', said more than any great politician's speech could say, and he didn't utter a word. He just pointed his umbrella at the tanks and they stopped! That's a manifestation of the working of true power, by a little, faceless guy who nobody knew. He was manifesting particularly the Chiron in Cancer which took part in the line-up of the time – a small, vulnerable person nevertheless capable of stalling the megamachine.

Love was All We Needed

The mid-1960s marked a juncture in history, a turn-around and a mega-shift. The chart opposite is for May 1965, showing the 1965-66 Uranus-Pluto conjunction. It

marked the beginning of a period lasting
some years, as the outcomes of the
mid-60s soulquake worked themselves
through. The after-effects still unfold
today.

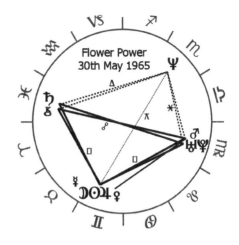

The Uranus-Pluto conjunction in Virgo
was opposed by Saturn and Chiron in
Pisces, and there was also a trine and
sextile to this opposition from Neptune
in Scorpio. In May 1965 further planets
swung into this configuration – Jupiter,
together with an eclipse newmoon,
squared the opposition, and Mars swung in to conjunct Uranus and Pluto. When
multiple configurations like this take shape, the incremental increase in energy is
enormous – it sparks off a major thrum.

One key theme was 'cultural revolution', reaching a zenith in 1967 but brewing and
gathering impetus from around 1961, both in the West and in China. In China
it was top-down, sparked by Chairman Mao, and in the West it was bottom-up,
challenging authorities and established social norms. It shook everything up and
created a great divide between the past and the future. The world moved twenty
years in three years.

This was a time of free-thinking in science, public ideas and technological
innovation (microchips, biotechnology, space and air travel); a social breakthrough
point (civil rights, 'the permissive society', individualism and the dawn of
increasingly diverse and fractured social conditions); it was a spiritual turning-
point leaning toward independent spirituality; it was a corporate, governmental and
financial system transformation too. It marked the dawning and breakthrough of
new ideas that now are commonly accepted – feminism, environmentalism, human
rights, anti-racism, alternative health and technology, liberation movements, rock
and pop music, and a new globalising world view.

The previous conjunction of Uranus and Pluto in Aries happened in 1850 at the
peak of the industrial revolution, as the modern world was being noisily hammered
into place. The 1965-66 conjunction came at a time when the world was ready for
a major leap, at a stage of world change representing a significant break from the
past. The 'generation gap' of the time was not just an inter-generational schism
but the crossing of a major historic jump in time. It marked the beginning of a
process which is still unfolding as the Uranus-Pluto cycle unfolds, lasting until

2104 (the next conjunction) and reaching its peak in 2046-48 (the opposition). But the opening crunch-point, the waxing square, has taken place in 2012-15, the crunchiest point of this period being probably April 2014.

The 1960s show how the historic events accompanying a power point often follow after the astrological power point itself. Things had been building up for about five years before the Uranus-Pluto conjunction happened in 1965-66. Yet the wave peaked in 1967, hitting resistance and becoming revolutionary and confrontational by 1968-69. The issues this coagulated around were such things as the Six Day War (Israel's takeover of the remainder of Palestine), the Ulster Troubles, student protests across the West, the Maoist cultural revolution in China and the escalation of the Vietnam War. Even then, this fermentation continued rolling through the 1970s – it didn't just die down a few years after the conjunction. Once Pandora's Box is opened, it doesn't shut again.

But this period represented a lost opportunity too. Flower Power and the student revolutions suggested a far greater change to Western civilisation than what has subsequently happened in the fifty years since. Vested interests and social conservatism resisted and hijacked change in the decades that followed. It was blatantly visible in the 1980s during the Reagan-Thatcher period, a time of right-wing ideological revival, self-interest, corporate capitalism, renewed consumerism and new forms of soft-power imperialism. A major historic choice was made, far larger than most people of the time were aware.

The Crunch

Yet the fundamentals driving that change haven't gone away. By 2012, the fundamentals started reasserting themselves in ways that could no longer be ignored, owing to the pressures of environmental degradation, population pressure, resource exhaustion, social-cultural conflict, technological complexity, exposed secrecy and climate change.

The 2012-15 change-point reared its head in 2007-08 in the form of the 'credit crunch' in the West. It was not solely an economic crisis exposing structural weaknesses in the Western system: it represented a tipping point in the decline of the West and the rise of the Majority World. A deeper change was emerging, requiring global restructuring and an addressing of the harmful effects of rampant global modernisation. The materialism and denial characterising the period from the 1970s to the Millennium tipped into a tumult of change. This suggests that 2012-15 forms a turning point in global questions starting in 1965-66 which need to be resolved by the late 2040s, when the Uranus-Pluto opposition comes along. The Uranus-

Pluto square has been gnawing away at root-and-branch issues on a multiplicity of fronts, and the risk is that the world lapses, unprepared, into a situation where control is lost, even by governments, as a result of excessive issue-proliferation.

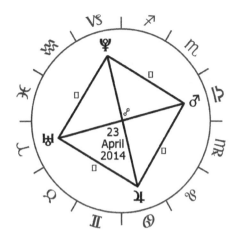

The chart here shows the Grand Cross configuration of April 2014. This is the Uranus-Pluto waxing square, upstepped for nine months or so by Jupiter in Cancer and for two months by a retrograde Mars in Libra. A Grand Cross, an uncommon configuration, sets a major challenge: two oppositions present sharp conflicts and contradictions and four squares demand hard work and forced adaptation – one of the many issues of the time was literally modern slavery, worker exploitation and the 'working poor'.

Pluto in Capricorn focuses attention on institutions, financial and legal systems, nations and their heritages and futures, material resources, a re-evaluation of history and a change in our established ways. Uranus in Aries signifies wildfire phenomena such as riots and revolutions, conflict, spontaneous eruptions of overdue issues, volatility, competitiveness and also creativity. Jupiter in Cancer suggests caring, particularly toward vulnerabilities in society and the ecosystem, and Mars in Libra, retrograde, highlighted disagreements, barriers to cooperation, misunderstandings and projection ramping up conflict. It came to a head in Syria and Iraq, Crimea and Ukraine, also being rampant in Brazil, Mexico, Thailand, Congo, central Africa and many other localities. During this time the Ebola outbreak in West Africa and the Islamic State in Iraq and Syria gained their respective holds too - both of them raising a Plutonine spectre of dark, threatening horror impacting heavily on the global psyche. All these issues rubbed up against one another, creating much friction and an ominous tone of crisis – the world was at risk of catching fire.

Underlying trends are worth looking at here. These include climate change and extreme weather events; growth of mega-cities and urban dominance; the ascendancy of the former Third World and decline of the developed world; social dissatisfaction; ethnic and cultural tribalism and nationalism; incremental transformation of sovereign nations into global cantons; the need for worldwide cooperation, integration, law and governance; extinction of species and habitats; social, corporate and financial-market instability, technological impacts and a host more issues. The underlying longterm trend, visible from the 1960s onwards, is the integration of our planet into one world – by necessity, and arising from pressure of circumstances. But it is an uncomfortable process, sadly dominated and influenced by oligarchs, corporations and faceless organisations, whose interests differ from the needs of the majority.

So, following the logic of what's happened thus far, the coming decades up to the late 2040s are likely to be confronting, tumultuous and rich in change. Mikhail Gorbachev, when identifying *perestroika* (restructuring) and *glasnost* (transparency and accountability) as key problems affecting the Soviet Union in the 1980s, was actually prophetic for the world as a whole. Yet there is an element of brilliance, genius, humanism, spirituality and momentum in these times too. Hardship is high and intense, yet tremendous advances are being made, and the world is working very hard – it's mainly a question of whether it is working on the right things. We live in interesting times.

Doorways

So a power period, characterised by one or more major aspects between outer planets taking place over 2-3-4 years, ramped up by the influence of faster-moving planets, can bring forth historic-scale and root-level processes. Specific events can then be seen within this context. This affects people individually too – some but not all people will experience major pressure on planets in their own birth charts. This is often the case for the game-changers appearing in the public domain, acting out the psychodynamics of the collective unconscious, catalysing social processes by doing so.

Such people might be musicians, thinkers, charismatic leaders, random figures who impact strongly on public consciousness, and people who emerge from nowhere to embody imagery lurking in the social psyche – like the Chinese man mentioned above. They can be portrayed as stars or demons. They enact our own dramas in public, helping us sort out collective problems through the symbolism of what they stand for or the actions they take. This proxy experience, lived out on the public stage, acts as a surrogate for personal experience, but it collectivises imagery, increasingly globally in scope.

Power points in time represent portals through which deeper levels of reality and evolving potential reveal themselves. They allow new elements into our perceived reality. They produce disjunctions, gear-changes, breakdowns, breakthroughs or bursts of acceleration. This isn't easy, though the general rule is that the pain experienced relates directly to resistance to change. Change nevertheless has a wrenching, forceful and scrunching effect.

As portals and gateways, major power points demonstrate that we have less control over our realities than we prefer to believe. The grasp that we have on things, individually and collectively, is undermined by stored-up material in the unconscious, containing the shadow-effects of social pain and frustration. It's also affected by the collective superconscious, containing our highest hopes and aspirations, and a sense of our spiritual, cultural, social and human potential. Power points raise the stakes, increasing the friction in our psyches and unearthing deep transpersonal currents that pervade life and the world. We need to give them more attention.

The rising energy at power points resets the rules of the game, assaulting and eroding anything that gets in the way. There's a rule in geology saying that the erosive power of a river increases as the square of its volume. That is, if the volume increases by three times, erosion increases by nine times. This is a useful analogy. When two planets such as Uranus and Pluto grind and scrape against each other in a square aspect, their mutual effect is more than the sum of their contributing energies. But when more planets engage in such a mutual thrum or din, their power increases vastly, bringing not just a spike in the current but a blowing of many fuses, demanding repair and renewal of the circuitry as a whole.

It's interesting also how, when looking back at a power point in time, it is possible to see how events led up to the situation that unfolded, as if such a power point spreads out in time not only into the future but also into the past. Already, today, the preconditions for the Uranus-Pluto opposition of 2046-48 and the Neptune-Pluto square of 2061-65 – both major power periods of the future – are gradually slotting into place, unbeknownst to us.

This is why the focus of this book is on power points in time and the factors that make them happen. This is why this and the next chapters are crucial to one of the key points this book seeks to make: *that these power points exist and are important, and that the world needs to make more proactive use of them than it does.*

11

Identifying Power Points

Power points have differing qualities, magnitudes and durations. They can call into play significances, threads and storylines originating from long before, and these threads surface and go underground again over time. They reveal issues from the future that are yet to become important, as if pulling us toward them. They also reveal issues from the further past that we thought were forgotten. Their effects have repercussions in all the little and big departments of life and in every sphere.

About Prediction

Sometimes, people get worked up about impending power points, advocating dramatic prophetic scenarios and making claims that don't necessarily hold up when the event actually comes. Such claims fit a scriptural statement, a cosmological possibility, an item of channelling or an eventuality that they foresee, and definite statements are made, then to be lapped up by some sectors of the public. In the 1990s there were significant anticipations around the Millennium, for example – even American foreign policy was affected by this.

In 2012 there were big expectations concerning the Maya Prophecies and, most troublingly, specific dire predictions about what was to happen, made mainly by Westerners, not by Mayans. This obscured a more contextualised understanding of the historic watershed that the year 2012 marked, in the Maya way of seeing things – it concerned the end and beginning of 5,000 year cycles, and it was unwise to predict specific, dramatic events taking place at winter solstice 2012 (except perhaps for boosting short-term book-sales and YouTube ratings).

Once the prediction is made, the event doesn't happen, at least in the way predicted. Worse, the prophets and forecasters don't own up to such inaccuracies once the moment has passed, and even might repeat the process later on. This indicates a problem with the human need to predict the future or have it forecast for us. World War Three has been threatened multiple times, and various kinds of Apocalypse still today affect property prices in Montana, USA.

A common claim is that a forthcoming configuration hasn't happened for thousands of years, therefore it is extra-special and in some way ultimate and final, leading to the Big One. Well, it might well be a unique configuration, but this is simply a symptom of the beauty and intricacy of the motions of the heavenly bodies – they are all unique. All we can predict is that a configuration is coming and that certain kinds of possibility are likely, or that we should keep an eye open for certain kinds of issues and themes. In this book I make a few such prognoses for the future, suggesting the timings of future power periods and what to look for when the time comes. But I do not know or say what will happen.

Life goes on, things come and go, and it's not necessarily the end of the world if Mars, Saturn and Pluto form hard aspects to each other – it's evolutionary time moving on, and it does this in jumps and stages. Not only that, but the expectation, in this case, that a Mars-Saturn-Pluto configuration will inevitably lead to war, is erroneous – it can equally lead to some sort of resolution or progression. It's just that the default human tendency is toward war, and also non-events aren't noticed as much as dramatic events. At the time of writing, the Israeli bombardment of Gaza in July 2014 calmed when Mars entered martial Scorpio after a long sojourn in apparently peace-loving Libra, where the bombardment broke out. People who make big prophetic claims often lack longer-term experience in prognostication and perspective in history, or they have an agenda, or they simply need to put things into proportion.

There can indeed be something in the symbolism offered by some prophets' and pundits' pronouncements, but this can be taken too literally. Perhaps 144,000 rainbow dancers will indeed be preparing the way for the coming of the archangels. But don't let such anticipations, however impressive, benign or threatening, and however great the perceived authority of the person advocating them, override your frank and open experiential perception of emergent reality. *Listen more closely to things than to people.* This is how we develop true resilience in the face of intense change.

What Makes a Power Point Happen?

Now to the main business. Different levels of power point come into operation over time, working in the context of varying time-spans. There are no hard and fast rules to this – there is a magical, outside-the-norm, reality-bending element to power points. Here are some generalised observations.

- **If it involves two or more outer planets, there's a game-changing or reality-shifting situation going on**, hinted at by the planets, signs and other factors involved. It concerns longer-term and historic-scale issues. New influences, viewpoints or side-swipes come into the equation from offstage or under the floorboards, sparking developments quite often unforeseen. Perceptive truth-speakers, not always believed, might see them coming. We're talking here of revolutions, landslide elections, collapses, disasters, breakthroughs and world-shattering events in more extreme cases, though in most cases it concerns shifts of context and scenery, humps crossed, peaks and troughs or changes in the way life is configured. In 2012-15 an enormous, earth-shattering event has not happened, yet a torrent of localised, particular events have all added together to make one big multi-faceted overflow of events – and together, this is pretty earth-shattering.

- **If it involves Jupiter and Saturn, something needs fixing in an organisational, economic, ecological, social and structural sense** – it's time for developments and for the testing of forms and arrangements by the pressure of emergent events or shifting trends. This might lead to steps forward or back but it's probably within the realm of the predictable, not so much a major game-changer. When involved with outer-planet activities, Jupiter and Saturn anchor deeper incremental game-changing issues in the form of real-life situations, concretely manifesting deeper fundamentals to give us facts to grapple with, but the main engine of change will be the outer planets. In terms of media coverage, here we're talking of elections, economic upticks and downswings, legal precedents, political issues and socially-important decisions and developments.

- **The Sun, Moon and inner planets trigger issues within the scope of hours, days or weeks, but they still can be critical.** These events are usually quite transitory, but then the falling of an avalanche or the firing of a gun can indeed have longterm repercussions. When tied into larger configurations with slower-moving planets, deeper issues hiding behind specific events are placed before us. Here we are talking about the speeches of politicians, market spikes, technology issues, streams of headlines and changes in nature which, in the end, usually pass and are forgotten. Such events can lead to crunch situations, sharp transitions, about-turns, swerves or flowerings, or to changes of perception and decision, though in a shorter timeframe.

- **If it involves a configuration of multiple planets, a major thrum is going on.** The planets' individual tunes are up-stepped into a quantum combination with a far greater effect. This is a 'more than the sum of its parts' phenomenon. Configurations can lead to such things as bombshell news, social-economic peaks and downswings, intense situations and issue-proliferation, or sometimes quiet yet surreptitious tectonic shifts. The funny thing is that, though these might at times induce shock or surprise, they are quickly incorporated into our mental map, making them look normalised, yet they aren't.

- **It all depends on the aspects and patterns involved.** If there is coherence to them, such as a Grand Cross, or where there might be a number of quincunx aspects, or six planets in air signs, or an array of planets showing any kind of visible coherence, then it gets interesting. You can also have two or more entirely separate, unconnected phenomena taking place at more or less the same time, and this can be powerful, and part of the amazing beauty of it all.

- As a rule of thumb we could say that, **to be a significant power point, an astrological situation must have three or more significant contributing factors**. Two of the slower-moving planets can aspect one another for a period, but what matters is the times when other planets swing past, amplifying the volume and voltage. Anything less than three factors (such as a fullmoon) will have some import but it doesn't really represent the kind of quantum shift or intensity that a true multi-factor power point displays. However, when two outer planets are forming a major aspect, we can look on this as a power period in which there will be significant specific power points – powerful smaller waves that add critically to a big wave.

The main issue with power points is the sumtotal of all the contributing factors thrown together, and what they do. Their beauty lies in their uniqueness and unrepeatability – though of course there are similarities. Some kinds of power points are very rare – for example, a Grand Sextile (six sextiles, nine trines and three oppositions, all in one configuration).

When slower-moving planets form a configuration, lasting perhaps a year, then it is easier for faster-moving planets to swing into such a pattern, temporarily raising the stakes, creating a voltage spike and making things go critical. For example, in 2025-28, Uranus in Gemini will sextile Neptune in Aries, itself sextiling Pluto in Aquarius, so if there's a fullmoon in the Aries-Libra axis, perhaps with Mercury, Venus or Mars thrown in, we have an energetic situation going on.

Magnitudes

Here are some guidelines by which to assess the strength and significance of power points. We'll start with the most common kinds of 'power blips' and move toward the rarer longterm power points and periods. That is, we're moving from the timescale of daily life to that of human history. Power points are arranged according to seven different magnitudes – these are my own invention, and I am not aware of any alternative way of categorising power points.

Magnitude 7: minor power blips

Simple and single 'power blips' last but hours or days. Yet, within their own domain of life they can be significant as short-term energy-peaks, challenges or turning-points. There are several different kinds, most of which we have touched on before.

Quarters and Cross-Quarters. Times when the Sun moves over one of the solstice or equinox points, or a cross-quarter point, mark shifts of energy, time and theme within the context of the cycle of the year. Solstices are good times for standing back from life and looking at what we really seek to make of the coming period. Equinoxes are better for moving forward, making steps or changing tactics. Cross-quarters are good times to check our alignment and see whether we're on-track and able to carry things through in real terms.

Ingresses. Sign ingresses liberate energy by changing life's subtle atmospheric taste, laying open new possibilities, standpoints, facets and twists of life that previously were not there or not prominent. These lesser power points can augment the energy of any other phenomenon taking place at the time, giving a shade of extra meaning connected with the contrast in theme between one sign and another – especially on those occasions when two or three ingresses happen around the same time.

Faster-planet aspects. When the Sun is in a strong aspect to another planet or to a few of them, there is energy around and take note of it. Similarly, when Mercury, Venus or Mars do a major aspect to another planet or two, something is going on. A Mercury-Neptune aspect can make the internet go weird or produce pointless traffic jams on busy roads, or it makes discussions derail or new understandings arise. A Mars-Uranus aspect can explode a bomb, bring down the chop or cause thunderstorms, and a Venus-Jupiter aspect can be a great time for a party or for get-togethers.

When Venus and Mars make a hard aspect it's time to sort out your feelings, and when Mercury scrapes against Mars an argument can ensue. A Mars square Saturn is excellent for hard work. During a hard Venus aspect to Saturn we might have to accept that sometimes we're all alone, and it's alright. When there's a Mercury conjunct Pluto, truths and unspoken messages need to be voiced. When there is a Mercury-Uranus conjunction, mental energy can fly around, making sleep, logic or simplicity hard to come by.

But we each have choice about what to do in such situations – a Mars-Pluto aspect can bring peace if antagonists calculate that a fight could blow back badly on them, and a Venus-Neptune aspect can bring either romance or emotional entanglement, or a bit of both. It can be good to observe these phenomena. Look back at what happened at earlier times in your life when similar astrological phenomena took place – this can give clues about what's really going on now.

Solar aspects. The Sun activates the life-energy within any issues being explored in connection with another contacted planet – if Jupiter is cooking up a situation, the Sun can give it an extra shove if it moves into aspect with Jupiter. Solar aspects are noticeable for around 2-3 days before and after they take place. These can be strengthened when the Moon swings into it – often the energy is fully released only when the Moon's aspects to the planets in question become exact.

Other contributing factors creating power points in time are:

- **stations** of the planets (when they stop and turn either retrograde or direct);

- **arrangements of planets** that do not shout loudly from an astrological point of view, but still form concentrations in certain signs or types of signs. Perhaps there's a lot of action in mutable signs, or in three consecutive signs, or featuring signs of the same element. Or perhaps there are several separate aspects taking place around the same time, unrelated to each other.

- **arrays** without major aspects, but possessing a balance or visual pattern which stands out and means something. They might all be at one end of the zodiac or forming two or three distinct groups, or evenly spread. Arrays are covered in chapter 14.

- **ongoing periods** of, say, a few weeks, when there is a lot of activity in general. Sometimes astrological phenomena can coagulate into a particular period, making for a busy time – and then it goes quieter after that. Sometimes it's very busy – other times it's quieter.

All sorts of variants can occur over time. The interesting thing is their uniqueness and their sometimes uncanny synchronicities of theme or atmosphere – as if dear old God was up there, flipping through his ephemeris and cooking up configurations to spice up life's movie for the folks downstairs.

Magnitude 6: powerful newmoons and fullmoons

These can be extra powerful when there are one or more other planets involved (not uncommon, 2-3 times per year), or when it is an eclipse, or because the new or full moon fall on a critical zodiacal point such as a cusp or solstice point. Energy-peaks such as these last for days only, but they can be highly energetic and significant in a shorter-term perspective. We've seen a few examples already.

Such times can unlock a situation that then develops further as time progresses. An example was the Scorpio new moon of 2nd November 1986, which unlocked a chemicals spill in the Rhine, an outburst of AIDS paranoia and awareness, the exposure of the British MI5 secret service in an Australian court and of the US government over the Iran-Contra affair. Busy times! These were not isolated incidents – they played their parts in unfolding sagas that continue today. So a full or new moon can push an escalating or pending situation over the hump to make it a full-scale issue. This can be reflected in nature too.

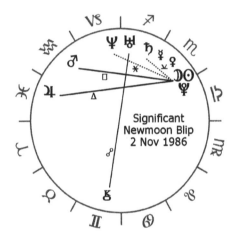

Significant Newmoon Blip 2 Nov 1986

Eclipses. The moon wobbles five degrees north and south of the ecliptic during its monthly journey, but if a new or full moon takes place exactly when the Moon is crossing the ecliptic and one of its nodes, it will be lined up so precisely with the Sun that it either passes in front of Sun at newmoon, a solar eclipse, or into the shadow of Earth at fullmoon, a lunar eclipse. Eclipses and the periods around them can be meaningful turning-points.

What you choose to do during an eclipse is secondary: the important thing is the awareness with which you do it. It is well worth observing and consciously participating in eclipses: the ancients saw their potency and went to great lengths to be ready for them. In my experience, they are key times for setting intents in one's life, and the rather odd thoughts and experiences one can have around eclipses can be oracular and pattern-setting.

Magnitude 5: configurations of faster-moving planets

When there is a configuration of faster-moving planets, perhaps bringing in the odd slower one too, this can make it a peaky time. The quality of energy in a multiple configuration varies according to the planets and aspects involved.

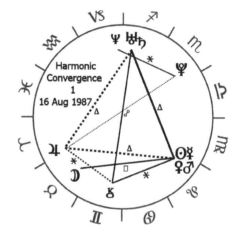

In August 1987 I ran a special camping event to mark the Harmonic Convergence, a strong power point in time. The Convergence was so named in connection with the Hopi and Mayan prophecies then being talked up, though it was significant in astrological terms too.

I learned a lesson at this event. On the big day at the climax of the camp, 400 of us were standing in the middle of the campsite in a big circle, remaining there for hours, swaying and chanting a long, resonant chant. The words included, "I am a circle... You are a circle... We are a circle...", and people were deeply moved, transported to another realm. At one point I opened my eyes and looked around, noticing that we had slowly, unconsciously moved into a perfect *hexagon*. Nobody had noticed. It's hard enough getting a crowd of people to form a circle, but unconsciously to form an exact hexagon, straight-edged and well-proportioned... well, that sits in the miracle category. What's also interesting is that the camp had been designed in the shape of a six-pointed star.

The lesson? Don't miss a miracle by busily projecting an expectation of something else. Better still, don't project *anything*. Just watch and experience. Be aware that a power point is coming, let it be, follow your intuitions and sensibilities, keep plans flexible, keep your antennae up and stay in the moment.

The Harmonic Convergence chart here shows a Kite configuration (covered in chapter 12). The dotted lines show inaccurate aspects but, when so many planets connect together by aspect, inaccurate aspects become more valid – you can widen the orbs of the aspects involved. The main feature was a mutual conjunction of the Sun, Mercury, Venus and Mars in Leo, together with a Grand Trine to Uranus in Sagittarius and Jupiter in Aries – six planets in fire signs. The 1988 Saturn-Uranus conjunction was coming close. Chiron in late Gemini, opposing Uranus, added an extra frisson, making up the Kite. Although this power point contained only one major outer planet, Uranus, this was a strong configuration and a very memorable occasion, a good example of what happens when the inner planets stage a major meeting.

Before we move on, look at this second chart. The Convergence configuration moved on within a week to create a new variant. This time, five planets, now including the Moon, were together crossing the cusp from Leo into Virgo – a multiple ingress which said "so much for all the drama, now for some realism". The trine to Jupiter had grown stronger and more exact, and a trine to Neptune had appeared. Uranus was at 22♐, Neptune at 5♑, and the midpoint between them was at 28♐. The multiple conjunction at the cusp of Leo and Virgo thus formed a strong mutual trine to both. Jupiter was at 29♈, completing the Grand Trine. On 19th August, between these two peaks, Saturn turned direct and Jupiter turned retrograde – an example of the extra contributory details that can often appear at such times.

The main feature is the multiple conjunction, or Stellium, of the Sun, Moon, Mercury, Venus and Mars at 0-4° Virgo. Look also at the overall pattern of loose multiple sextiles, drawing in Jupiter, Chiron, the inner planets in Leo, Pluto and Neptune – this is pretty strong, a Grand Sextile with one missing point. The gap highlights the sign Aquarius, giving a clue – it says *people in crowds*. A gap such as this signifies an area of life where attention is needed to balance things up. As the events of 1989-93 subsequently demonstrated, 'the mass of the people' was in sore need of attention – they were being scrunched by the megamachine.

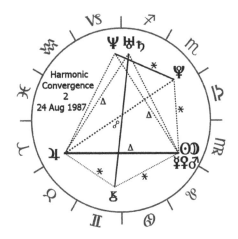

While this isn't a perfect power point in terms of accuracy, the size of the multiple conjunction at the cusp of Virgo and the involvement of all planets but one (Saturn) make it momentous. Within two years revolutions were brewing in Eastern Europe, with a near-revolution in China, and the movements born in the West in the 1960s – the environmental, peace and women's movements for example – reached a peak of their expression at this time. This was also a breakthrough time for the then-new practice of internationally coordinated mass meditations. During the Convergence the bubbly financial markets peaked and then collapsed within months. In Britain in October a hurricane headed straight for London, destroying large swathes of forest and uncannily bringing a message to one of the world's great financial capitals, saying "Don't be too sure of yourself".

Before we move on, in 1989 people in the Soviet bloc realised how much the system they lived in was oppressing them, but people in the West, believing they were free, took until around 2010 to realise the same thing, following the 'credit crunch' and what it exposed. By then, apart from Jupiter passing through Cancer in 2013-4, there was no 'people' energy around – instead there was a rebellious and restless Uranus in Aries, which certainly tore at the shackles and threw rocks at the riot police, but it lacked a sense of direction or guiding principle. However, just wait.

In 2024-2043 Pluto moves through Aquarius. The issues to be worked with will vary from 'extraordinary popular delusions and the madness of crowds' (to quote the title of a notable 19th Century book) through to 'deep democracy'. One catchphrase arising in the Arab revolutions was *democracy is not just about elections*. It concerns deeper and more complete public participation, sharing and cooperation – which happens to be the essence of what communism sought. The world is unlikely to turn communist in coming times, but the cooperative model of human society needs to make strides in relation to the competitive model that forms the basis of capitalism today. Freedom takes on many guises, and the weakness of capitalism is that it endows freedom to the privileged and slavery to the majority.

Get a load of this one. Here's a chart for 2048 where an assemblage of inner planets highlights an opposition of Uranus and Pluto. This is the opposition marking a climax to the cycle started by the Uranus-Pluto conjunction of the mid-1960s. The previous opposition was in 1902, when humanity took to flight and started switching on the electric lights. This is certainly the chart of something major, not least a momentous fullmoon. The Uranus-Pluto opposition

is vastly up-stepped by the incursion of many inner planets, and it's safe to say that people will definitely feel it at the time.

It will be 'cards on the table' for ideas, perspectives and worldviews – this much is predictable. All of the issues uncovered in the 1960s will be climaxing here. According to many forecasts, 2050 is the time when human population reaches a peak around 9-10 billion, beginning then to decline, and the time when the effects of climate change are likely impact most decisively on us. So non-astrological forecasters are pointing toward this date, and this chart shows an astrological reason why this is so.

Some readers won't be alive then. Nevertheless, this is the time we're semi-consciously aiming at in the underlying agendas of our lives today, particularly during the Uranus-Pluto square of 2012-15 – you could say that this is a case where the future is exerting a causative influence on the present. In a sense, during major power points, past, present and future come to meet, with an amount of bleed-through between them. Also, though there are intervening periods between the conjunction, square and opposition, these three cyclic points, around 1965, 2012 and 2048, mark mileposts in an evolutionary continuum.

The involvement of all planets apart from Saturn and Neptune, and their location in mutable signs, suggests travel, communication in all its forms, and new ideas, information and understanding, ranging from the details (Gemini and Virgo) to the generalities (Sagittarius and Pisces). Notice how the opposition is in Virgo-Pisces, while the 1965-66 conjunction was in Virgo. Here, prediction of this future time is speculative, yet we can certainly say this configuration is likely to mark a significant turning-point. The reason it is included here is to give an example of a Stellium and also a multiple opposition. Next, let's look at another Stellium.

In January 1994 came a seven-planet Stellium in Capricorn lasting a week, during which time nightmarish forest fires threatened Australia and torrents and deluges threatened Europe. I use the word 'nightmarish' decidedly – there was a Saturn square Pluto happening at the time, and these two planets working together do bring up such scenarios (9/11 being another example) – the stuff of our worst dreams. This contrast

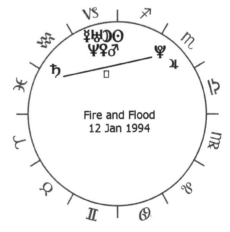

Fire and Flood
12 Jan 1994

of fire and flood made everyone very aware of the globally integrated nature of weather systems.

This magnitude of multi-planet configuration occurs only once in a while, uniquely and differently each time. Such periods bring times of great intensity and imbalance – everything is weighted on one side of the zodiac in what's called a Bundle array. But it's also the beginning of something, a mega-multiple conjunction. With seven planets involved, there are actually 21 individual synodic cycles starting, simultaneously! The Uranus-Neptune conjunction of the year before was one degree separated by now, but the incursion of so many inner planets caused an energy-surge, reactivating it and dramatically affecting the world's weather systems.

Magnitude 4: aspects between Jupiter, Saturn and Chiron

The inter-aspects of Jupiter, Saturn and Chiron are worth watching, especially when up-stepped by other planets or phenomena. Here we are dealing with power points usually lasting up to a few weeks, though it's wise to remember that aspects mark stages in a cyclic process involving the buildup of issues and unravelling of consequences lasting longer.

Jupiter and Saturn conjoin one another once every 20 years, while they interact with Chiron variably since Chiron moves eccentrically. Jupiter to Chiron cycles last between 13 and 20 years and Saturn to Chiron cycles last 64 to 165 years – a big variation.

An interesting configuration came up during the writing of the first edition of this book in March 1986, when Jupiter formed a square from Pisces to a Saturn opposition Chiron between Sagittarius and Gemini. There was also a sextile from Jupiter to Neptune and Neptune to Pluto. Temporarily, the Moon swung into the formation to form a Grand Cross with Jupiter, Saturn and Chiron – otherwise they were forming a T-square (a right-angled triangle). It was near spring

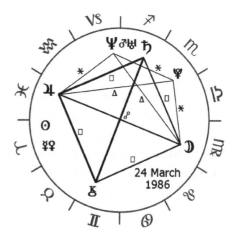

24 March 1986

equinox too. Lots of contributory ingredients of a power point in time. The main issue was the facing of dilemmas and sorting them out.

During this period, many people around me underwent major dilemmas over money, local politics, committee decisions, organisational questions and practical issues. In the wider world the Euro-American alliance of the time went through some stress, showing cracks in what until then had been regarded as an everlasting partnership, and early developments were taking place in USSR with *perestroika*. Perhaps you might remember pictures of lovers walking in Gorky Park, making Westerners aware that Soviet people were *real humans* – Sting sang 'The Russians love their children too'. So there was an attitudinal healing and re-humanisation phenomenon going on here. It was a crunchy configuration with something benign to it. And while we're here, see in the chart how Saturn is approaching Uranus and Neptune, which it would meet in 1988 and 1989.

Magnitude 3: Jupiter, Saturn and Chiron aspects to outer planets

When Jupiter, Saturn or Chiron form a strong aspect to one of the outer planets, it's time for deeper issues to become manifest, and for the world to get to grips with what's happening underneath. Concrete yet symbolically-charged and implication-rich situations arise, often in unusual, unforeseen ways. So a weather disaster in Central America might not only kill people directly but also set off diseases, affect insurance industries in London and Tokyo, influence resource supplies in China and jolt the political situation in Madrid. Seeing media-footage of a village overcome by a mudslide feeds suggestive imagery into the collective unconscious. This said, the key issue here might well have been deforestation, about which little is likely to be done, and here the problem really lies.

There's another matter too: important events can look different from a longer-term perspective. Taking the 9/11 attacks in New York City as an example, while the precise chart for the event is interesting, there was only one significant longterm astrological phenomenon happening at the time. It was a Saturn opposition Pluto, which had occurred exactly on 5th August, more than a month before 11th September 2001. Saturn was in Gemini and Pluto in Sagittarius, two travel-oriented signs, and this concerned airplanes (Sagittarius) crashing into the Twin Towers (Gemini).

There was a much less publicised event a month earlier on 12th August, just a week after the exact Saturn-Pluto opposition. This was the sudden appearance of the Milk

Hill crop formation near Avebury in England, the largest and most intricate crop formation ever. Most ordinary people would consider this at best interesting but not very important. But there is a chance that, from a century-long perspective, this might have been a more significant and historic event than 9/11 – I hope I don't upset Americans by saying this. To put 9/11 into perspective, 3,000 people died in 9/11 but, worldwide, 1.2 million people die worldwide in car accidents every year – now that is a *really big* ongoing disaster, bigger than a world war, and 500 years in the future we might wonder what kind of civilisation could do such a thing. When 3,000 people die in Bangladesh in a cyclone, there is a shaking of heads but it is quickly forgotten.

Meanwhile, historically the Milk Hill crop formation could be significant. It could be that, looking back from the future, we come to acknowledge Milk Hill as a key portent of future times – perhaps a meeting of different worlds, sometime in the future. You might think I've just dipped into fantasyland, but you might not think so in 100 years' time. Just as, in 1902 when the Wright Brothers first took to flight, the Apollo mission of seventy years later would be something only H G Wells could advocate, so is the case today with the prospect of cultural interaction with beings from other worlds. However, the main point here is that it's all a question of how we judge the meaning and import of events, and this can change as we gain more distance from them. Power points can bring quantum shifts that stretch further than we currently can see. In 1950, even Alan Turing would have been surprised that a book like this could be written on a little netbook computer only 50-60 years later.

The relationship between events and astrological phenomena is not direct and mechanical. Major events can happen before or after an astrological power point for a number of reasons. One is that the physical, social, political or natural conditions for an event to happen might not be in place at the time. The energy-conditions are there, but manifesting actual events is more complex. An engineer's shoddy work during a difficult astrological aspect might lead to a plane crash three months later. Or someone might take an initiative before an exact aspect happens, driven by forward-thinking ideas. Birds might migrate on a fullmoon, but it still might take them a week to get to where they're going.

There's also the question of what kinds of events are really significant – those that hit the headlines might not be the most important. Astrological phenomena influence the psychodynamics of humanity and the subtle energy-fields of the Earth more than they directly affect actual concrete events, and the bleed-though can take time.

An astrological aspect can show the time when a defining decision has been made, or an important idea or impulse has arisen – perhaps quietly and privately in the mind of a person or in a backroom or discreet meeting somewhere. The final decision to execute 9/11 could have been taken on the Saturn-Pluto opposition five weeks before it. The impetus to develop powered flight was peaking on the Neptune-Pluto conjunction of 1892 but it took until the Uranus-Pluto opposition of 1902 for the first successful flight to take place – not least because many of the best aircraft pioneers were killed in failed experiments.

Here's an illustration of an event starting before a major aspect happens. The spark for the Arab Spring revolutions occurred on 18th December 2010 in Tunisia. Riots followed the death of Mohamed Bouazizi, a young vegetable seller who set fire to himself in despair and protest at the heavy-handedness of the Tunisian authorities. But the first exact square aspect of Uranus and Pluto took place 18 months later on 26th June 2012. In other words, the growing tension and juddering that precedes a major aspect –

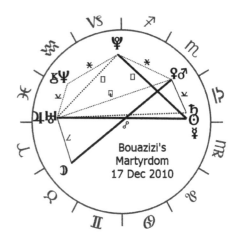

Bouazizi's
Martyrdom
17 Dec 2010

symptomatic of a rising tide – can spark events, especially when there is pressure for change, or a person or a catalytic event opens up the situation ahead of time. The events of the early Arab revolutions, though dramatic, paved the way for weighty events to follow.

By June 2012, the first exact square aspect, the Muslim Brotherhood government in Egypt had been elected to power (to fall one year later), the Syrian regime was attacking its own people in Homs, Hama and Houla, Gaddafi in Libya had already fallen and clashes in Bahrein and Yemen had already happened – though Tunisia came off reasonably well. The revolutions hit complexity during the unfolding of the exact aspect, and a proxy war ensued, fuelled by outside powers, together with significant social splintering and a mushrooming of violence and atrocity. The aspect went exact seven times between 2012 and 2015, owing to the direct and retrograde motions of Uranus-Pluto.

Looking at the Bouazizi chart, few astrologers would predict from this in advance that a major significant event would take place in the provinces of a minor country, sparking a phenomenon fanning flames not only in the Arab world but also secondarily in Ukraine, Thailand, Brazil and the streets of the developed world's capitals (the Occupy Movement). But the chart nevertheless has its spark-points.

Bouazizi is represented by the Moon, and his hurt feelings by Venus and Mars opposite it in Scorpio. What lit up the Arab Spring in this chart was the Uranus-Pluto square, upstepped by Jupiter, Sun and Saturn, with some crowd phenomena added by Chiron and Neptune in late Aquarius. This is an example of a chart drawn after the event to derive meaning from it.

Some events are pretty precise in their timing. A typical example is the fall of the Berlin Wall in 1989. Sorry, but in this book we're returning to this chart repeatedly since it's such a classic. The key aspect here was a Saturn-Neptune conjunction in Capricorn on 13th November, the wall having been breached on 9th November. It was not just the Saturn-Neptune conjunction that did it: Jupiter and Chiron opposed the conjunction, Uranus was close to it, Pluto eased it and faster-moving planets fed into it. Saturn and Neptune in Capricorn represented the monolithic state falling over itself, and Jupiter and Chiron in Cancer represented the crowds in their cloth caps and headscarves. This

was part of a larger shift brought about by the Uranus-Neptune conjunction of 1993 but it took the involvement of Saturn and Jupiter in 1989 to bring about such dramatic effects as the fall of the wall. It might actually have been Pluto in Scorpio that made the critical difference, by oiling the gears and easing the conflicted aspect in this situation. People worldwide joined in the chant for *freiheit und demokrati* and were deeply moved by the sincere striving of East Germans to free themselves.

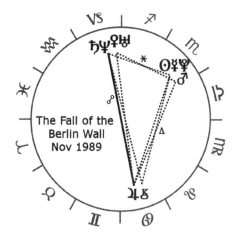

The Fall of the Berlin Wall Nov 1989

There were several high-points to this historic wave. One was the Pluto perihelion of 5th September 1989 – the time when Pluto was closest to the Sun in its 250ish year cycle. This had a precipitative effect, turning down the screws on a bundle of budding issues.

Another was a Saturn-Uranus conjunction on 17th February 1988, mentioned earlier. Such a conjunction has a scissors action, cutting away the past and drawing a line, as if to mark a psychological divide. Here the heat was rising for 1989, the first protests in East Europe breaking out in March 1988. These rumblings had their roots in the Solidarity movement in Poland, emerging on the 1980 configuration that will be mentioned below, and while that movement had subsided its effects and its example had not gone away.

The Saturn-Uranus conjunction came with an ingress of both planets from Sagittarius into Capricorn – representing a shift of theme underlying the events of the time. There was a newmoon on that day, and Mars swung across Saturn and Uranus a few days later. What was happening at the time was momentous, though no one was yet to know that the Berlin Wall and the Soviet system would fall in 1989-90. In 1988 that still seemed impossible.

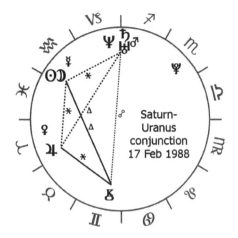

Saturn-Uranus conjunction 17 Feb 1988

The Saturn-Uranus conjunction encouraged a rising tide of doubt in authority in the Communist bloc, giving rise to public acceptance of new ideas of freedom and democracy that, up to that time, had been subversive or just plain fantasy. Established structures were severely threatened and cracks were showing. But at that time we all still believed that the Soviet edifice was a permanent fixture.

Revolutions won't always happen on such aspects as these. It's just that, in 1988-89, historic tides were massing, driven from the future by the forthcoming Uranus-Neptune conjunction of 1993, and the Saturn-Uranus and Saturn-Neptune conjunctions contributed mightily to the overall historic change. Saturn turned a latently simmering tendency into a series of sharp-edged events. On the actual Uranus-Neptune conjunction in 1993, blatant events were not so marked. Things were happening in Somalia, Bosnia, Abkhazia and Palestine and brewing in Chechnya, Rwanda and Mexico – the world indeed was simmering – but 1993 itself wasn't earth-shattering. Trends-wise it was major.

Magnitude 2: lesser outer planet aspects with other factors added

In the previous chapter we mentioned a Grand Cross in which the ongoing Uranus-Pluto square of 2012-15 was amplified in April 2014 by Jupiter and Mars – a classic magnitude two power point. Here's another.

Around June-August 1980 a Yod configuration of slow-moving planets formed, comprising a Chiron opposition Uranus at 18♉ and 19♏, with two semisextile aspects from Uranus to Neptune at 20♐ and Pluto at 19♎, also forming two quincunx aspects to Chiron (see the heavier lines in the chart on the next page).

All of these were aspected by Saturn and Jupiter over the months as they moved through similar degrees of Virgo. They themselves were approaching a mutual conjunction. Throw in a few extras such as an eclipse newmoon at 18♌ on 10th August 1980, latched in with a simultaneous Mars conjunct Pluto, and we had a *very interesting situation!* Needless to say, we all survived.

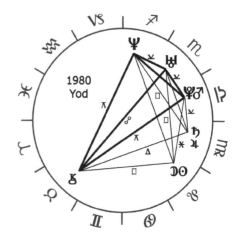

1980 Yod

During this complex configuration and transitional time the impulses of the 1960s, mentioned in chapter 12, percolated into greater public visibility. For many people it was a time of choosing life-paths and taking steps, with underlying issues and new insights sharply informing these deep choices. Many 'alternative' worldviews, activities and lifestyles appeared: healthfood shops, anti-nuclear protests, environmental actions and complementary medicine entered the mainstream, with further awarenesses lurking in the background. This period marked a climax of the Cold War. Political shifts were rumbling in USSR, leading to Gorbachev's rise; in the West Reagan and Thatcher brought forward their deregulated capitalist ideology; and in China Deng Xiao Ping brought his post-Maoist liberalising reforms following Mao's death.

This was not as dramatic as a magnitude one configuration. It was nevertheless a critical transition time in which a surreptitious buildup of potential tipped the world into a new phase. This was typified in the rise of the Solidarity movement in Poland – a precursor of the changes that were to arise in 1989. The Chiron-Uranus opposition brought up many contradictory issues, the semisextiles brought a combination of emergence and closure, and the quincunxes added an atmosphere of questioning. While semisextiles and quincunxes are not major aspects, they can be powerful when working together in a Yod configuration. So while this wasn't a blitzingly dramatic time, it was nevertheless definitive, and its results would show within a decade.

This demonstrates the value of astrology in understanding the underlying dynamics of time. Events are influenced and driven by ideas, urges and undercurrents in the collective psyche and it is these which, in the end, move history onward.

Magnitude 1: major outer planet aspects

When two or three of the transformative planets Uranus, Neptune and Pluto form a strong aspect to each other or they make a simultaneous ingress, we have a significant historical power point or period in which fundamental new strains of possibility emerge – not merely a development of what was going on before but something quite new, jumping the rails. If this is up-stepped by Saturn, Chiron or Jupiter, plus Sun, Moon and the faster planets, we have a full-blown energy-wave on our hands. But the main thing here is Uranus, Neptune and Pluto.

If astro-historical research interests you, *The Historical Ephemeris* on my website provides a lot of useful data, including a 2,600 year timeline showing historical events and astrological movements alongside them. Chapters 15 and 16 in this book also cover astro-historical changes.

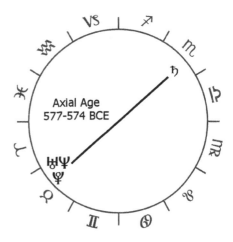

The classic baseline configuration, crowning them all, happened in the 570s BCE. There was a multiple conjunction of all three outer planets in the sign Taurus within just *three years*, with Saturn in opposition from Scorpio for part of the time, adding an extra edge. The next such mutual conjunction takes place in 3370 CE – you'll have to wait a while for that one. It so happens that the 570s BCE approximately mark the beginning of recorded history – before that, we're talking about archaeology.

It was a time of transition of consciousness worldwide, as if humanity was beginning to think seriously about its situation – and new cultures emerged in the succeeding centuries to prove the point. It was a key time in the early formulation of today's traditional belief systems – even though Christianity appeared 600 years and Islam 1,000 years later, both of them being reform faiths arising out of the faiths and mystery schools rooted in this time. In the century or two that followed 570 BCE, Lao Tzu was active, as were Confucius, the Buddha, Zoroaster, Mahavira, the first Greek philosophers and reformers, the Jewish Old Testament writers, the Druids, and things were happening in the Americas too, with the beginnings of the pre-classical Mexican and Peruvian high civilisations. This marked the beginning of the world's doctrinal, scriptural faiths – and I would include secular rationalism with that too, the foundations of which were laid by Greek philosophers.

Humanity was becoming more objective, more individualised, tearing itself away from its roots. The ancient civilisations of Egypt and Mesopotamia were on their way out, to be overtaken by modernising influences such as the Greeks and Romans. Humanity was beginning to look afresh at statecraft, psychology, technology, science, society, economics and thought itself. Across the world, within 400 years, new civilisations developed, of a newly-materialistic bent: Greece and Rome, Han China, Mauryan India, Persia, Olmec Mexico and Chavin Bolivia. Humanity was becoming ambitious, imperialist and assertive, working less *with* nature and more against it, or despite it. You could call this period the rise of the *noösphere* – the human-defined world of thought and belief (a term coined by the philosopher Teilhard de Chardin) – and the beginning of the decline of the *ecosphere* – a worldview where beliefs and activities were influenced by the workings of nature.

Of a similar magnitude was a remarkable line-up in the 1390s, marking the beginning of the rise of the West and the globalisation process it sparked. Every 495ish years Neptune and Pluto conjunct each other – this happened again in 1892 – but in 1391-96 Uranus also did an opposition to them, and Saturn and Jupiter swung through too. This all happened within five years, marking a major watershed in human history. The decks had been cleared for this by the disastrous Black Death of the 1340s,

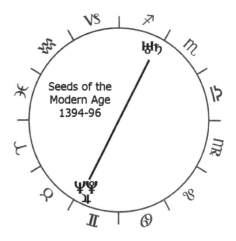

Seeds of the Modern Age 1394-96

wiping out so much of the past across the Old World, from China to Europe. A century after the 1390s capitalism was taking root in Amsterdam and London and ambitious explorers were sailing from Europe to far-flung parts, starting the process we now call globalisation.

What events happened at this time? Well, mega-events didn't happen, though some things were major for those affected by them: this was the time of Timurlenk (Tamerlane) who devastated much of the Middle East, the early days of the Ming Dynasty in China, the ascendancy of the Ottomans, the zenith of the Hanseatic trading league in Europe (a precursor of capitalism), the elimination of paganism in Europe through conversion and witch-burnings and the beginning of the Aztec and Inca ascendancies in the Americas. These were all very significant but not grade-one earth-shattering in impact.

But two very symptomatic localised developments did occur, small in scale though big in eventual impact. One was the sponsorship of early European Renaissance thinkers and cultural creatives by the Medicis in Florence, and the other was the sponsoring of marine exploration in Portugal by Henry the Navigator. These two developments would eventually affect the whole world, their outcomes impacting fully by the time of the following Neptune-Pluto conjunction in 1892, at the peak of the European imperialist period and the ascendancy of USA and Russia as world-dominating powers. This 1390s line-up took place in the signs Gemini and Sagittarius, signs of exploration, ideas, beliefs, expansion and even excess.

Most outer planet configurations aren't as big as these two. In the last chapter we mentioned the Uranus-Pluto conjunction of the 1960s and the Uranus-Neptune conjunction of 1993, both being within living memory. These are more typical, and we get three or four of these each century. The 1993 conjunction saw the birth of internet and 'big data', genome manipulation and the global techno-economic systems-integration which has, amongst other things, given rise to the recent relative subsidence of the West and growth of the former Third World. It saw the end of the Soviet Bloc and apartheid in South Africa, together with the abortive Oslo Accords attempting to bring peace to Israel and Palestine – which failed because the wider world did not have the guts to face the 'threat of peace' and its full implications.

With such major astrological phenomena, we shouldn't look only at their specific dates but also at the ten years preceding and following them. For example, Mikhael Gorbachev in the USSR identified restructuring (*perestroika*) and transparency (*glasnost*) as keys to the future, some 7-8 years *before* the Uranus-Neptune conjunction in Capricorn, yet these terms summed up that conjunction. Visionary reformers can accelerate world change by naming the game and providing catalytic, door-opening guidelines and initiatives for humanity's use. At this time, another such man was Nelson Mandela, who made racism look like a thing of the past.

Major outer planet configurations work to re-stock the group psyche with impulses, thought-forms, innovations and imagery, planting seeds in the collective unconscious, waiting for individuals and groups to cotton on to them and embody them in living form. These seeds grow over the years and the generations until what was once a possibility becomes an everyday normality – quite often following pretty perverse and roundabout routes. In this way, deep impulses filter into cultural and material form, turning the pages of history.

Thus, a power-period between 1890 and 1910, involving a staggered line-up of Uranus, Neptune and Pluto on the Gemini-Sagittarius and then the

Cancer-Capricorn axis, brought forward most of the basic ideas and forms that characterised the 20th Century: flight, internal combustion engines, telecommunications, electricity, film, tin-cans, plastics, democracy, women's and minority rights, atomic physics, medical advances, socialism, psychology, new forms of spirituality and global cultural interchange.

The Big Secret

It is good to be flexible and open to possibilities when looking for power points, since planetary motions are organic and unique. Don't set out to predict what is likely to happen: it is more valid to try to see the kinds of openings it might offer, or to make ourselves receptive to whatever might arise, with whatever clues we have to guide our way. There is a crucial difference between using astrology to stave off whatever we fear, and using it as a way of opening up to life.

Power points don't even need to be identified in advance – though, obviously, peering ahead in the ephemeris is always worthwhile. If you are intuitively receptive, you'll find yourself using energy-peaks and dips to advantage, whether or not you know of them at the time. However, understanding something of their astrological qualities and details really helps.

Noting power points retrospectively helps us learn from what happened, giving new insight into its significance, and also giving memorable living data by which to learn about astrology and time. Looking into the future needs to be done without prejudice, but the main question is understanding and grasping the present. In Britain, a sign placed at railway level crossings tells pedestrians: *stop*, *look* and *listen*. This speaks volumes.

Power points are not just places and times for us to appreciate and mark. We owe it to life to care for our world and our fellow travellers. The world is a being with an existence of its own, on whose skin we live and crawl around, sucking her blood, scraping her skin and depositing crap all over her. Time is not merely a ticking continuum through which we carve our personal histories – it is a medium of psycho-evolution, an ongoing, undulating flow of change within which we play a part in human history and the evolution of consciousness. Every thought, word and deed has meaning.

Especially at energy peaks. Generating wholesome thoughts and feelings at these times has greater than normal power. The stillness and timelessness hidden within time is an access point to life's fundamental secrets. Power points in time and space are places where such access is amplified. Through living *in time*, we can more easily experience what lies *beyond* time. This has the power to heal many ills.

The ancients used power points to gain enhanced access to the inner planes, to long-distance psychic communication, seership, healing, magical work and active participation in the deeper currents of nature and the universe. Many power places in space exist to gather or transmit energy, and temporal power points help with this.

Some spatial power points such as henges, hilltop settlements, ancient temples and sacred chambers were specifically built to insulate spiritual practitioners from the complex energies of time and the landscape, to help foster psychic ability, magical power or spiritual illumination. These places were utilised particularly at power points in time so that there was a double lift. This involved and affected the soul and personality, the local environment and tribe, the wider world and the far beyond, multidimensionally.

On a very short-term basis, every dawn and sunset is a power point in time. The Sun's rising and setting is a common thing, yet sometimes the experience is deeply stirring. A simple attitude of reverence for time, nature and life does amazing things: oneness is more than just a nice idea.

Next, we're going to examine configurations.

12

Configurations

Occasionally, three or more planets form a configuration, all of them forming aspects to one another. These set in motion a surge of energy with an emphatic twang, flavour and intensity, some of them being major historic power points or periods in time. Here we shall look through the different kinds of aspect configurations.

Waves

When three or more planets mutually aspect one another they form a configuration, of which there are several different types. These are often three-sided triangles or, less often, four-pointed structures, and even less often, more complex ones. Any configurations forming in the heavens at any time indicate a temporal power-point, where a dominant chord sounds out with a very strong signal, whether it lasts just hours or up to a year or two. Then there is usually a buildup and aftermath too, extending the duration of the configuration's effects.

There are very definite, clear and interlocked issues at work at such times, raising life's stakes. A configuration gives the energy-wherewithal for quantum leaps, for new things arising that could not have been foreseen. This is a definite case of 'more than the sum of its parts'. When the Moon or another faster-moving planet swings into an already-strong configuration, specific incidents and situations are sparked off, highlighting and nailing down the story displayed in the whole configuration.

Understanding a configuration depends on the aspects making it up. If there is a prevalence of challenging or flowing aspects, then this will define the configuration as a whole. In some structures there is a mixture of both, in which case challenging aspects create action, dilemma, effort and work, while flowing aspects release the pressure and add talent, flow or naturalness. They combine into an algorithm with a particular action and flavour. While a prevalence of flowing aspects can make gifts and assets available, they can also be taken for granted or under-activated, so one or two challenging aspects thrown in can activate the structure and create a measure of acuteness to goad these abilities or resources into action. In this scenario, challenging aspects bring opportunities while the flowing aspects can sometimes bring problems.

Our understanding of configurations can be deceptive – this has a lot to do with the way we see and judge events. We have already seen in Chapter 10, in the case of Cyclone Haiyan, how a harmonious aspect such as a trine can be involved in a serious crisis. The event of the cyclone was devastating for its victims but it also proved that there was a positive longterm trend in terms of disaster-relief mechanisms. It's a matter of judgement therefore, and we must step outside the confines of good and bad, easy and difficult, wanted or unwanted, to see the true nature of what's happening – and often it changes according to the decisions made, or as the configuration works its way through.

The Uranus-Pluto conjunction of 1965-66, with Saturn and Chiron opposing it, was historically a breakthrough period and the dawning of a new time, and yet it also sparked increasing societal disintegration and decline in basic social decency – a new form of short-termist self-interest was born that reached its heyday in the 1980s-90s. The conjunction may have led to the 'summer of love' of 1967, though for Vietnamese it was a horrific time of bombings and defoliation of the jungle – and both experiences were effects of the same configuration.

Multiple aspect structures

Stellium

This is a multiple conjunction involving three or more planets within orb of each other – though orbs can be judiciously loosened out in this case. A Stellium significantly amplifies the nature of a conjunction. A lot of energy moves from within outwards and below upwards, as if life were always like that and everything were perfectly normal – except it isn't. This is a super-ending and super-beginning, the turning of a page.

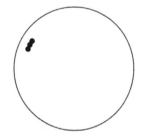

It can be a statement of how things are. Stelliums represent a turning of the tide when, on the surface, nothing much might be happening, but under the surface a lot is moving. Noteworthy events can also happen: it could be that an event was waiting to happen once the space was cleared for it, or that it sets the tone for the cycle that ensues, or that it was a bit like a cocked gun, just waiting to go off with the slightest movement. It can involve new factors entering the storyline, or a significant change of feeling, or simply a relaxation of the foregoing and a sense of a new day.

There can be a difficulty here in objectively seeing the effect or the extent of what is taking place because conjunctions are not objective or relativistic – they are 'in themselves'. There can be a difficulty in perceiving the contrast between sought-after possibilities and manifest realities too. It's comparable to someone living in their own little world and social subgroup, believing that the rest of the world lives like them and agrees with their values.

Quite often a Stellium will involve two slower-moving planets joined by one or two faster-movers – the faster planet(s) will activate specific, noticeable situations or issues to give shape to the messages that the slower-moving planets are bringing up. Stelliums are not always exact – the individual conjunctions might be somewhat spread out, yet they are there and significant, and the sequence of conjunctions is worth watching – especially if the Moon or another planet passes over them, sparking them off one by one.

In chapter 11 we saw examples of Stelliums, including the 'Fire and Flood' Stellium of 24th January 1994 and the Harmonic Convergence – though the latter case demonstrates how a Stellium can be tied into a larger configuration.

Another good example is the newmoon Stellium of 28th December 1989. Following the fall of the Berlin Wall in November, a few symptomatic events took place within days of 28th December which significantly sealed the larger change taking place: the assassination of the Romanian dictator Nicolae Caeusescu and his wife, the inauguration of the respected philosopher Vaclav Havel as president of Czechoslovakia, and the signing in Poland of an edict ending the socialist system to make Poland a capitalist economy. All of these were part of the overall process yet significant steps in themselves, for each of those countries.

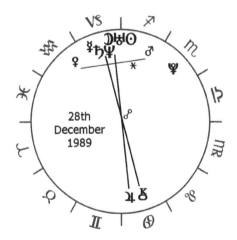

There were six planets in Capricorn on that day: the Sun and Moon conjuncted Uranus (also opposing Jupiter) and Saturn and Neptune were conjuncting each other a little further on in Capricorn (also opposing Chiron). Mercury hung close by. When so many planets are gathered in one sign, the main five can be considered a Stellium while Mercury can be considered a qualifying footnote adding a mercurial twist.

Multiple Opposition

Here, three or more planets form a mutual opposition, upping the stakes tremendously. If there is a weighting to one side (such as three planets on one side and one on the other), then the predominant side will act usually as the side that is 'on top' or in control, while the weaker side will act as a stirrer or irritator, shining a light on the predominant conjunction on the other side and bringing it into starker relief.

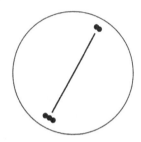

It depends what planets are involved, and also it depends on people's predispositions and responses to the situation. There can be a tendency toward polarisation and tension on the build-up to the opposition, which might be resolved at the exact forming of the aspects, or it might erupt into further trouble. An opposition can lead to a new understanding of things or it can lead to blame, recrimination and damage – and in this lies a lot of choice. You could say that a conflict is caused by a failure to resolve issues at an opposition – though the conflict might not break out immediately.

Sometimes there is a dynamic tension or crisis on the build-up to the opposition which then leads to a dawning of good sense, resolution, or to a feeling of breakthrough or even of stepping outside time to another level which, in itself, creates a new situation. There can also be a switching or oscillation of roles or predominance between the contrasting sides in a multi-opposition, or the emergence of a new reality out of the ashes of the old. In any situation, there are events and perceptions, and either or both can change at oppositions.

This is a peak time, good for breakthroughs, realignments and transitions, opening up the next stage. It isn't a new start – it's analogous to a house that has been built, which is then made into a home. It is a new offshoot reality that wasn't there before, arising out of the former situation. Yet it's often the real reason why the whole story happened, whether intended or not.

It's often a time of accentuated objectivity and factuality: whether we like it or not, this is the situation that has emerged – it's too late to change anything and we must make the best of what has taken shape. But this can be a learning experience, bearing future fruit, and it can also be a refinement and improvement of what went before. Many aspects of the new situation will not have been visible or anticipated until the new situation actually arrived. It can also be a time of fulfilment.

This is a strong, climactic configuration and a moment that is loaded with energy, sometimes tense, at times potentially explosive, or sometimes a time of release: deep choices are enacted here. A multi-opposition isn't common, and sometimes it is tied into a larger configuration, but it is momentous, sometimes jagged and grating, or intensely still, it can lead to breakthrough or breakdown, and it draws a decisive line between what happened before and what comes next.

An example here is (again), the fall of the Berlin Wall, where the dominant side of the opposition was in Capricorn, representing Soviet bloc governments struggling to retain control and retain their relevance. The *nomenklatura* or ruling hierarchy had created problems over time that its privileged members didn't have the mindset, tools or willingness to deconstruct – frankly, they just didn't know what to do.

Meanwhile, Jupiter and Chiron in Cancer represented the crowds of people in the city squares, ordinary working people with a legitimate complaint – and in this lay their power. The Communist system was nominally built for the people, and there they were in the squares, chanting "We are the people!". However, while the crowds highlighted the issues, it was the governments themselves that made the change.

Two key things happened to bring this about: under pressure, the Hungarian government created a precedent, opening its borders to the West to allow a stream of emigrants across the previously-impenetrable Iron Curtain, causing normal systems, particularly in East Germany, to break down through absenteeism; and the soldiers guarding the interests of the state started putting down their guns, taking off uniforms and switching sides. These two key factors (Chiron) tilted the balance, governments lost credibility and operational effectiveness, and soon they fell.

The dilemma of this opposition was eased by Pluto in Scorpio, forming a sextile and trine to the main line-up, adding a 'cards on the table, your time is up' element to the equation. The real action happened in Capricorn, but Cancerian and Scorpionic influences made the critical difference. Powerful stuff: it's a life-changing experience being in crowds like that. It gives us pause for thought: if we personally were faced with such a situation, would we personally take a stand or would we shrink back hiding? Would we risk everything to stand up for our beliefs or would we obey our fear?

T-Square

This is an opposition with a third planet forming squares to both ends of the opposition – a very challenging triangle. The opposition injects sharp focus and dilemma into a situation and the squares inject effort, urgency and imperative. Something is trying to move forward, to overcome inertia or challenges. The choice is to work hard toward progress and breakthrough, or to avoid the issues, leading sooner or later to complexity, breakdown or painful decline. It's a situation where taking the brave or hard path actually lands up being easier in the longterm.

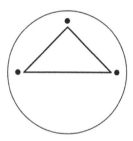

It is an imbalanced structure, yet here lies its power and advantage: the squaring planet acts as an irritator, yet also it carries the solution. The empty point opposite this squaring planet offers clues, balancing the tension and suggesting possibilities. The stress and apparent difficulty in a T-square makes for action prompted by threat, challenge or pain.

At times knotty circumstances arise where we unconsciously undermine our own best interests, encounter obstructions or make things far more laborious than they need to be. Or simply this is a time of effort where we just have to run the race or climb the mountain, to get the matter done once and for all. A lot can be achieved, things can be pushed over the hump and necessary stuff does happen. Challenge focuses minds, provides tough decision-points and demands determined action.

Here's an example of a slow and a fast T-square taking place at the same time. On 6th February 2014 a waxing halfmoon angled up with Saturn to make a short-term T-square lasting but hours, as the Moon swung through a days-long square of the Sun to Saturn. But there was also a longer-lasting T-square in which Jupiter entered into business with Uranus and Pluto to create a veritable stream of events – dangerous conflicts in Syria, Libya, Ukraine, Central Africa and South Sudan, with one simmering in

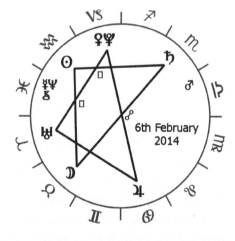

the South China Sea – together with cyclones, electoral earthquakes and a general historic tilting of world geopolitical power. It was quite a tipping-point. Reality bore down hard, yielding far greater consequences than most were aware of at the time. It was a crunch-point with significant longterm implications. Within months Mars would move into the T-square, creating a Grand Cross (mentioned in chapter 9), further upstepping the intensity.

Going back in time, a T-square in 1986 had Saturn in Sagittarius opposition Chiron in Gemini – this suggests hard but valuable learning experiences. This time, in my own circles, posed complex dilemmas and we had lengthy meetings without resolution. With Jupiter in Pisces in square to both, initially there was a struggle for clarity, which was followed by a breakthrough. Suddenly everything started working. It was one of those 'cut the crap and do the right thing' moments. So it was a crunchy time, but worth it in the end.

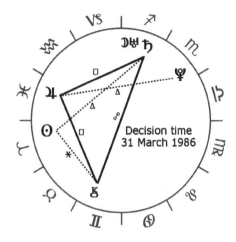

Decision time
31 March 1986

Meanwhile, in geopolitics, Gorbachev and Reagan were working hard to bring the Cold War to an end, but the issues were big and it was taking time – time they didn't have. Saturn opposing Chiron demanded gritty and insightful action, because the costs and dangers of continuing with old Cold War strategies were excessive. Jupiter in Pisces, at the apex of the T-square, introduced a visionary undertone, bringing everything into clearer focus. Big decisions were made quite quickly and, within a few years, world history changed.

Saturn in Sagittarius was obliging the Great Powers to see the big picture, with a little stirring from Uranus in Sagittarius, hovering nearby. Jupiter in Pisces brought inspiration and Chiron in Gemini helped positions to shift. But it involved lots of late nights and hard talking. The failure of these talks could have been catastrophic.

Grand Cross

This is a step further from a T-square, involving at least four planets in mutual square to each other, with two opposition aspects linking them. It is a rare and powerful configuration, not to be taken lightly and to be marked awarely. This is about uphill climbs and the biting of bullets, forced engagement, risk-taking and doing battle with the issues at hand. It means going into overdrive to save the

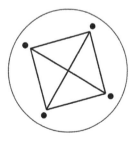

day, getting snowed in with problems, going under, facing catastrophe and heavy lessons, or breaking through to a miracle solution, a courageous step to change the game. The chips are down and something must be done. It concerns root-and-branch questions, all at once.

As with a T-square, the planets concerned will usually be in signs of the same mode, so they will feature the qualities of that mode strongly. If they are not in the same mode, because they are crossing sign-cusps at the time, complications and confusions can befuddle the situation, demanding clarity. A Grand Cross implies that something special, urgent and important is happening, even if its full meaning is not clearly discerned at the time. Usually there is an underlying agenda hidden behind the events taking place, and the historic causes can be deep. The odds seem to be pitted against us, yet this can stimulate getting to grips with the situation.

There is tremendous spiritual power behind a Grand Cross: the challenge to overcome difficulties is sometimes so large that normal solutions are no longer possible, causing a gear-change, or a rising above the normal complications, to resolve things on another level. If the involved parties step back from the brink to find common ground, resolving matters in a sensible, congenial way, the outcomes are very different to a conflicted situation where rhetoric rises and conflict ensues.

When a Grand Cross happens, fundamental choices must be made, bets must be placed and changes accepted. Or at least a threshold is crossed. A potential quantum leap, it provokes accelerated evolution in whatever field the planets and signs allude to. Since many Grand Crosses involve faster-moving planets, they're short and sharp in duration yet their effects reach a long way. But some Grand Crosses are slower.

In chapter 10 we examined the Grand Cross of April 2014, where Mars slowly retrograded back through Libra to form a Grand Cross out of a Jupiter-Uranus-Pluto T-square. There was a risk at the time of conflict-proliferation, especially between Russia and the West, not least because both sides were puffing up their chests and strutting their stuff. Commentators started raising old Cold War ghosts, though this was not an intelligent assessment of the situation.

After 20 years of retreat and compliance with the demands of the West after the fall of the Soviet Union, Russia stood its ground in its own neighbourhood, pushing back at the West, which believed it could bring Ukraine into its sphere of influence. Russia's push-back brought home to USA and Europe that they were not as strong as they wished to believe and they weren't completely in the right. It set in motion a slide into polarisation and rivalry over Ukraine – a clear demonstration of how not to deal with a Grand Cross. The result was weakened Russian relations with the

West and a shift eastwards toward strengthened relations with China and Central Asia. It was a very crunchy time on many fronts worldwide.

An interesting Grand Cross took place in connection with the total solar eclipse of 11 August 1999. Sun and Moon were eclipsing in Leo, Mars was in Scorpio, Uranus in Aquarius and Saturn in Taurus – a tricky combination in a Grand Cross. There had been a series of other Grand Crosses in the two preceding months, as faster planets swung into a wide T-square of Jupiter, Chiron and Neptune, also visible in the chart here. Many regard this eclipse and Grand Cross as the true beginning of the 21st Century. This eclipsing Sun and Moon opposed Uranus in Aquarius, suggesting a stirring in the masses and a jostling of ideas, with Saturn at square to them in Taurus, suggesting rigid standpoints and dogged immovability with Mars in Scorpio showing gritty determination to fight the good fight with all its might – definitely not comfortable and relaxed.

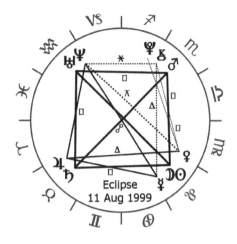

Eclipse
11 Aug 1999

Grand Trine

Here three planets are in mutual trine to one another. This is strong, flowing and stable: it opens up a natural stream of energy, fortunes or events, it broadens horizons, adds abilities and assets, and things seem just to happen, as if they had always been meant to. It is a maturing of the fruits of previous actions. A Grand Trine gives a measure of ease, beauty, grace and fortune, where the energies of each planet mutually back each other up.

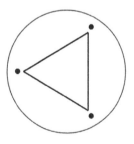

Often things don't happen impressively at such times, but the state of things as they stand at the time is nevertheless significant. Yet there is another side to it: things don't necessarily change with a Grand Trine – they simply unfold and develop. So if the situation is unhappy or unrewarding, we just have to live with it. But if things are going well, it's wonderful – there's little need to push or strive. This configuration is so flowing that we might underutilise its benefits, or there can be a lack of urgency or imperative to fully exploit the opportunity. If change and turnarounds are sought, they're best left until later.

A Grand Trine can set things moving by the sheer erosion of fixities brought about by a quickening of the flow. There is much healing, loosening and relaxing of barriers, but this sometimes has its problematic sides too, since a lot can develop quite quickly, and things can happen that weren't meant to, or they can ease themselves into a funk. Such things as avalanches or volcanic eruptions are caused by a release of tensions. A Grand Trine can lead to the subsidence of financial markets after the buildup of a speculative bubble – though in truth previous profitable gains might have been harmful or delusory, and perhaps the right thing happened.

Often the feeling around a Grand Trine is that the situation is loose or uncontrollable though no cause for panic. Perhaps a necessary adjustment is taking place that might turn out right. It's a time for letting things unfold. It's all a matter of viewpoint, and there's a relaxation of tensions here which can make us step back from the brink or find an easier route. Whatever the situation, what is the best that can be made of it? Often this is a matter of acceptance rather than fixing things. Make it alright, and things will be alright.

An historic example some time back is a Grand Trine in 1771 between Uranus in Taurus, Neptune in Virgo and Pluto in Capricorn. This was a time of growing momentum and buildup of the early industrial revolution in Europe (Priestley, Watt, Lavoisier, Arkwright, Bolta), the voyage of Captain Cook to Australia and New Zealand, the British takeover of India (Warren Hastings) and the accretion of American national feeling that led to the founding of USA in the decade that followed. It was a time of escalating trends rather than stark breakthroughs: something was taking shape, the meaning of which was yet to reveal itself. A Grand Trine of the three outer planets doesn't happen often – the preceding one took place over a millennium earlier in 730-740 (a time of cultural zeniths in Japan, China, India, Kiev and Cordoba and of the rise of the Carolingians in Western Europe).

In the last 200 years there have been no Grand Trines involving the three outer planets because, within a century of a Neptune-Pluto conjunction (the last being in 1892) they do not form a trine aspect in their 500 year cycle – so even if Uranus forms a trine to one of them, it cannot trine both. But when Neptune trines Pluto, the trine often lasts a decade or more. Grand Trines between other planets are shorter in duration and less fundamental, such as when Jupiter and Saturn are in trine to each other and another planet such as the Sun swings around to trine both of them – a Grand Trine lasting a few days.

Here's an interesting Grand Trine involving Jupiter, Saturn and Chiron, lasting for a few weeks around 24th May 2014. Examine the chart closely and you'll notice that the conflict-ridden Grand Cross of April 2014 was still hovering around, though inexact. During the Grand Cross there had been a heated atmosphere of escalating crisis and conflict, but by the time the Grand Trine came along, antagonists stepped back from the brink and a few unexpected solutions started arising – the Grand Trine had Chiron in it, in Pisces, a sign of forgiveness, release and mysterious solutions. Add to this Jupiter in Cancer, a motherly, protective influence, and Saturn in Scorpio, bringing truth and realism, and solutions became available.

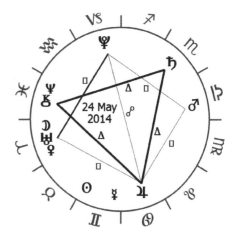

So, in Ukraine, where major conflict was threatened, the heat subsided and protagonists tried seeking ways out of the situation. In Palestine, after the breakdown of peace talks with Israel, a reconciliation took place between Palestine's two main factions (Fatah and Hamas) and the Palestine Authority signed up to a series of international conventions on human rights – not exactly resolving the impasse with Israel but changing the nature of the game somewhat. Neither of these succeeded and trouble ensued, not least because background interests were driving the agenda. In the Central African Republic and South Sudan, where bloody inter-ethnic conflicts were taking place, moves were made to ramp down the friction. Sanity returned – by small, critical degrees, in a rather insane period. Though things were moving fast – during this time the Ebola epidemic in West Africa gained lift-off, made worse by laxity in the public response to it.

Kite

If, between one of the trine aspects in a Grand Trine, there is another planet forming an opposition to one of the planets and sextiles to the other two, then we have a Kite. The opposition injects a sharp edge into the Grand Trine, and the talent, flow and creativity of the Grand Trine is given a specific task to do through the opposition. It is given a poignancy and an element of challenge, requiring clarity of intent and deft handling. It's not an outright crisis, but hands of cards need playing well. The

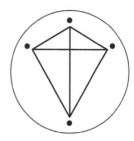

presence of the two sextiles adds dynamic movement and busy application, and the whole configuration, if balanced astrologically and handled well, points to success, progress and a stream of developments.

There is a favourable feeling in the air, but with a twist: the opposition demands a certain factuality and purpose from the Grand Trine, while the three trines release whatever tensions the opposition brings. Issues can be sizable but they are doable, and there's wind in the sails. The planet at the pointy end of the Kite usually holds a focal role, and the nature of the issues at stake is shown by the three planets in sextile.

In the late 2020s we shall see quite a few Kites forming. In 2025-29 Uranus will sextile Neptune, itself sextiling Pluto, which is trining Uranus, so any planet that forms an opposition to Neptune will create a Kite. In the instance shown here, a fullmoon forms the main axis of the Kite, with Mars conjuncting the Moon and, on the other side, Mercury and Venus conjuncting Sun and Neptune.

To add extra flavour, a loose Chiron-Saturn conjunction squares Pluto, with semisextiles to Uranus and the Stellium, plus a quincunx to the Moon – this gives the Kite added deep-drilling action with an extra layer of paradox and choice. When Saturn and Chiron combine, there are important lessons to be learned. This might be a day when you ought to be careful what you have for breakfast and, if the situation you're in confounds you, go and climb a hill or walk along the beach. Change your inner state before

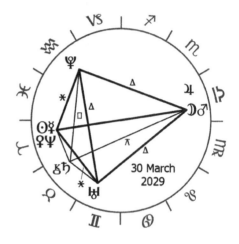

making decisions or doing anything important. This chart highlights the potency of the late 2020s, a time when things are likely to move fast and furiously, with enormous advances in ideas, technologies, 'deep democracy', communications and creativity – a clamour and rush of developments, generally favourable.

While we're on it, a note about Neptune and Pluto. At certain stages of its cycle, Pluto's eccentric orbit makes it move at roughly the same speed as Neptune. These periods happen when they are sextiling or trining one another. This leads to a phenomenon where, in the late 20th Century, they moved through a succession of signs in rough sextile for thirty years from 1950 to 1984. After this, Pluto, moving a little faster than Neptune for a while, pulled ahead while passing through Scorpio in the late 1980s. Neptune catches up from 2026-31 as Pluto slows down, and then as Pluto slows even more, Neptune moves on to form a square to Pluto in 2061-65.

The period from the 1950s-1980s saw a very productive period – everything from pop music, films and TV to jumbo jets, computers and space research – and a rapid unfoldment of global conditions both progressive (modernity and global integration) and regressive (pollution, war and environmental degradation). The sextile in the late 2020s is ramped up by Uranus and by visitations from other planets. You can see in the 2029 chart, for example, that Jupiter had just been through a Kite to Uranus, Neptune and Pluto, before a fullmoon and Mars swept in to create another Kite.

Check back to the Harmonic Convergence charts in chapter 11. This was a tilted Kite, weighted to one side by the inner-planet Stellium in Leo, moving into Virgo in the second chart. In the second chart there was a loose double Kite – a slightly out-of-tune mega-thrum, very loud.

Octile Kite

This is uncommon, sharp-edged and powerful. An Octile Kite lends a strong sense of 'it's meant to be' to situations, as if in some way destined. It demands dedication and a sense of working for eventual results with modest immediate reward, but it promises to be worth it in the end – that's the potential payoff. Necessity draws on skill, realism, proficiency and experience, or highlights the need for them. The planets in opposition highlight the task at hand, with the planet at the end 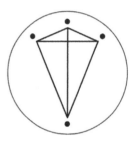 of the 'tail' at the pointy end holding the key to it all, and the three planets in semisquare to one another indicating the resources available or the character of the situation.

This configuration often brings a discovery that there is far more under the surface than was bargained for, or that the time has now come to implement things that have been hidden or set aside and brewing for a long time. Issues can erupt fast, precipitating emergencies, demanding deft handling. There can be fear of failure, since the obstacles seem insurmountable, or at least they require exceptional input. This is part fact and part exaggeration, though the acuteness of the situation does demand more input than just 'the call of duty' and definitely more than 'running on default'.

An example arose on 24th December 2007. Within three days of this date Benazir Bhutto, a charismatic leader in Pakistan, a nuclear nation in a delicate, high-pressure situation, was assassinated, provoking nerves worldwide and a political earthquake in Pakistan. Meanwhile, world food prices were high, leading to threats of social instability and highlighting the fate of the world's poor at a time when others, 'the one percent', were getting exceptionally rich – the problem was caused particularly by financial speculators. The underlying wave building up at this time was the financial crisis of 2008, yet to come – only perceptive people could see this coming.

On this Octile Kite configuration major banks wobbled and scrabbled, and economies were heading for the precipice but there was large-scale denial going on. The Octile Kite was relatively short-lived, the deepest element of it being a Jupiter-Pluto conjunction, but it tested social and economic systems at a time when things were shaky, stressing an issue that reared larger as time went on and didn't go away: a financial bubble in the West and political or poverty-related volatility amongst masses of people across the world.

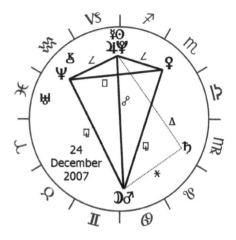

Here we see a similar line-up to that of the Berlin Wall in 1989, with two planets in Cancer (the people) opposing several planets in Capricorn (state and corporations) – though of course the Moon and Mars conjunction in Cancer was but a fleeting presence. But it was sufficient to spark a potentially explosive situation. At this stage Pluto had not entered Capricorn, still being at the end of Sagittarius, but the Jupiter-Pluto conjunction, signifying excess and overkill, underlined the root of the problem. The Cancer-Capricorn axis was again featured in the 2014 Grand Cross, six years later, by which time Jupiter had swing round to Cancer, opposing Pluto.

Yod

This is a quincunx-sextile-quincunx and it crops up from time to time. A Yod involves a crisis of perspective and comprehension in which the energies of the two sextiled planets find difficulty integrating with that of the apex, the double-quincunxed planet, which itself drives an awkward nail into the situation, demanding clear perception. It can lead to refusal to see a situation clearly because old, invalid ideas or even lies or disinformation are resorted to. Or it can lead to the need for acceptance of an unresolvable situation – perhaps the old formulae no longer work and yet there is an incapacity to do anything else. Or it leads to a new revelation where truths bubbling under the surface need acknowledging because they are now more blatantly obvious than they were before. This dichotomy is not exactly a conflict: rather it is a bewilderingly contradictory, seemingly irresolvable and compromising situation. Our capacity for seeing things is tested.

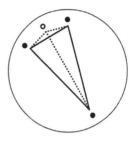

It is a secret to be decoded, an intense dilemma, or a visitation from the unknown. Intentions or people's mental maps refuse to gel with presented realities, yet solutions are available if we accommodate to the situation as it actually stands. This might be uncomfortable: there's a hidden secret lying underneath the situation that needs dredging up. Allowing things to unfold rather than seeking to steer them is what's called for here – it's difficult to change the situation but acceptance really helps.

Yods can show how, sometimes, the wrong thing is actually the right thing – but it can be hard to see this at the time. The Yod used to be called a 'Finger of God' or 'Finger of Fate'.

A Yod can be accentuated when an opposition is thrown into the mix, with two semisextile aspects linking the two sextiling planets. The opposition forces the issue, and the pointy-end planet then becomes critical: whatever it represents needs to be intentionally owned and integrated. Hair-raising situations can lead to remarkable solutions, but a shift of context and perspective is needed to access such solutions. This Super-Yod is a form of Kite, except there is a strong perspective issue here, brought on by the quincunxes. Often new information is emerging too, shifting the situation into something that looks very different.

A Super-Yod formed between Chiron in Taurus, Pluto in Libra, Uranus in Scorpio and Neptune in Sagittarius in 1979 and 1980 – we met it in chapter 11. Around this time many areas of awareness came forward, including the anti-nuclear, green and feminist movements. They gathered strength as part of a deep historic shift of values. At the same time, in the USSR the brakes were hard on – this was the Brezhnev period – resisting change despite the growth of hard facts showing that the Soviet system was seizing up. In the West, the brakes were on too, yet they took the form of an apparently fresh and new, deregulated free-market capitalist philosophy promulgated by Reagan and Thatcher – a wealth-inducing ideology which ran diametrically opposite to emergent ecological, justice-oriented and holistic ideas addressing the longer-term future of the world. So this Super-Yod represented both wishful thinking and longterm idealism which nevertheless was pin-pricked by the sharp-edged opposition of Chiron in Taurus to Uranus in Scorpio.

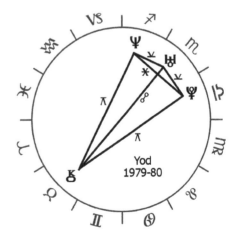

Yod
1979-80

Greater and Lesser Octile Triangles

A greater octile triangle involves two sesquiquadrate aspects and one square. This is a work configuration, giving an acute sense of imperative, with a need for decided purpose and longterm intent. The sesquiquadrate aspects focus attention on using the current presented circumstances as a way of moving toward an eventual end: there is a task cut out to be fulfilled, even if it makes life temporarily difficult – pay now, gain later. Goals should be kept reachable, otherwise the eventual goal

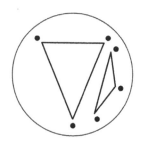

may never be reached – but there can be exceptions to this if a visionary leader is available, making manifest what most people regard as impossible (the work of Nelson Mandela being one example – achieving much of his mission while penned up in jail and incommunicado). In most cases the presented situation should be looked at and learned from, for it contains clues, omens and lessons relevant both to the past and the future. This configuration suggests a deliberate, clearly purposeful time where gritty decisions must be made, facing facts fair-and-square. This can be chosen or enforced by circumstances.

With a lesser octile triangle we have a square with two semisquare aspects. Issues are not dissimilar here: longterm perspectives and wider implications are hauled into everything. The difference is that intentions, dreams, plans and drives are the main issue, while in the greater triangle the issue concerns the way that these meet hard reality or fulfil wider needs. The lesser triangle elicits commitment, while the greater triangle tests it. Strong intent and imperative are implicit in both triangles, imbued with a sharp sense of distinctions and a need to make choices. In a sense there is sharply accentuated free-will here. There's a challenge to develop abilities and momentum capable of meeting a challenge, which might not be present now but it might be sensed or foreseen. There's a challenge to learn from accumulated past experience in order to correct or improve the future – prompted by hints from the present.

An interesting example came up in my own life at the time I was writing the first edition of this book. I was faced with a pressing need to write advertising copy for the educational camps I ran. No inspiration came and I was getting ratty. Around 19th January 1987, a lesser octile triangle came along: Jupiter in Pisces square to Saturn in Sagittarius, with Mercury in Aquarius forming a semisquare to both. Mercury demanded mental clarity of me, seeking a neat encapsulation of the project in words. Meanwhile, I was feeling dull-brained and was getting nowhere. I gave up for the day, feeling pressured, restless and unhappy. By next morning the configuration had become more exact and, lo behold, I awoke with a clear picture of what to write. One hour after getting up, I had written the copy required. I had breakfast, went through it again and tightened it up. Not only was the immediate problem solved, but also, as time went on, the text I had written proved to be a model not only for further use later on but also for other people who started similar ventures based on the events I ran. This shows how immediate pressures force effort with longer-term implications underlying it all. No wonder it was difficult: I was crafting words with greater import than I was aware of at the time.

Rectangle

Often called a 'Mystic Rectangle', there is nothing specifically mystical about it, though perhaps there's an element of 'guidance' involved. Here, two opposition aspects are woven together with two trine and two sextile aspects. This can raise poignant questions yet it also brings solutions and openings, arising naturally or by apparent good fortune. The flowing aspects take much of the tension out of the opposition aspects. There's stuff to work out, but good outcomes are possible.

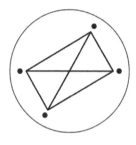

Abilities and assets search for a cause to be engaged in, or situations demand exceptional inputs that happen to be available. Dilemmas might be difficult to resolve in the usual, customary ways, but they seem nevertheless to work out by other means. A paradoxical combination of letting go and focused effort is the main way to break the logjam: our state of mind is often the obstacle, and there could be an open road ahead if we can but allow it to emerge. It's one of those situations where taking a break can reveal the answer. Applied skills or gifts can overcome knotty obstacles, or a burst of insight can shift the context of the situation to make solutions appear. A Rectangle usually brings marked results.

An **Octile Rectangle** is also possible, linking two oppositions with two sesquiquadrate and two semisquare aspects. Hard and sharp-edged work must be carried out here, requiring a concentration of effort: a secret needs cracking and a breakthrough is required, demanding focused energy – perhaps seemingly superhuman input but offering potentially momentous results.

Another Rectangle with two oppositions linked by two semisextiles and two quincunxes is also possible. The dilemma posited here cannot be resolved, but what is learned from the situation can all the same be significant, contributing to eventual success or to a later change of direction. The important thing here is that the oppositions generate the energy while the linking aspects release, entrain or qualify it. The oppositions need focusing and integrating, and the linking aspects demonstrate the talents and assets available.

Trapezium

This is a four-sided figure with two sides parallel. There can be several versions of this, each with their own character. Typical Trapezia involve an opposition with three sextiles (also called a Cradle); or an opposition with a semisquare, square and semisquare; or a quincunx with a sextile, square and sextile. Each of these has its own flavour, but a few norms do apply here: the long aspect (opposition or quincunx) will highlight the main issue at hand, while the perimeter aspects will show the 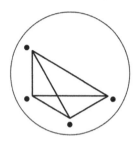 means of release or resolution; of the two parallel sides, the shorter will show the energy source and subjective element in the equation, while the longer side will show the objective situation, the means of expression or the nub of the matter.

No planets focus this configuration, but it is necessary to bring all of them together. The resonance or noise created depends on the planets involved and the use we make of the situation. Any outer planets involved will point to the fundamental issues, while faster planets will indicate the application of these fundamentals in real-life situational format. Trapezia crop up from time to time but they aren't common. When they do arise, conscious attention needs to be given to the opportunities offered by the two planets on the shortest parallel side.

A Cradle, comprising three sextiles and an opposition, has a strong nurturing, brewing, hatching tone in which new situations take shape, or the old situation is given new life and significance. A Cradle is a facilitative formation. Populated by sextiles, it gives birth to a set of skills and gifts or gives them something to apply themselves to – capacities with a potential for stimulating great progress and impetus, naturally rooted and innately 'right'. Cradles act as a receptacle for a strong surge of energy and change.

Grand Aspects

These are rare but they are powerful during their period of operation. The Grand Sextile involves six sextiles and three oppositions integrated together – it includes three Grand Trines and three Rectangles. Even rarer (I've never seen one, though it is theoretically possible) is a Grand Octile involving 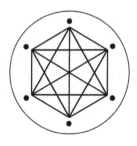 eight semisquares and four oppositions. Though we don't cover quintile aspects in this book, another variant is a Grand Quintile (quintile aspects being one-fifth of the zodiac, or 72°

and multiples thereof, making a five-pointed structure). At these points in time a very strong resonance is set up which, determined by the character of the individual planets concerned, makes for a power point of supreme proportions.

A very special message comes forward at such a time. Many oppositions are involved, creating an intense and sharp atmosphere, but the sextiles in a Grand Sextile will show how the energy is released by all-round integration of all of the energies present in the configuration, in an alchemic fusion. There's a 'facets of the diamond' all-round timbre to it. A Grand Sextile can make so much energy flow that it can become cathartic. Either that or it simply creates a rapidly progressing but comparatively smooth flow of events and developments, though with a sharp edge.

Such a configuration can only be made up of planets and it is not valid to bring in other objects such as the Moon's Nodes to make such a configuration work. This said, if five points on a Grand Sextile are occupied, with one point vacant, this is still a powerful configuration – and the gap signifies an area of life where conscious input is needed to make the configuration whole.

A Grand Sextile is quite often short-lived because one of the planets involved is frequently the Moon. A rare example arose on 29th July 2013, during a short window while the Moon in Taurus swung in to make a Grand Sextile. The aspects were not exact, planetary positions ranging from 4-10° of different signs, but this is an acceptable range in such circumstances. Other aspects weighed in to this configuration (such as Sun squaring a Moon-Saturn opposition and Uranus squaring the Jupiter-Pluto opposition) but they're not shown in this chart to keep it uncluttered.

This configuration took place amidst the heat of the 2012-15 Uranus-Pluto square, the Arab revolutions and many tensions and shifts worldwide. Close to this time came the fall of the Muslim Brotherhood government in Egypt (a return of dictatorship in a smoother format), war in Syria and other events, but the key issue here is to look not so much at specific symptomatic events as at trends. Here we see the exposure of secrets involving American and other nations' secret services, the deterioration of the Arab revolutions, the irreversible bedding in of climate change trends, the downfall of well-known and powerful people in fraud and sex scandals, instability in the world economy, an increasing migration of poor, needy and war-damaged people, and numerous other trends all suggesting a large-scale global historic confrontation with evolving facts. Whether or not people liked it, a torrent of developments were happening. This configuration added to the pile of issues mounting at the time, all of them adding up toward serious change or possible collapse in the years to follow. Events that unfolded in 2014 had their roots here.

Other triangles

Other triangles are not uncommon, bringing three or more planets into a thrum that works as more than the sum of their parts. They can be symmetric triangles, such as two sextiles with a trine, or two semisextiles and a sextile, or they can be asymmetric, such as a square, sextile and quincunx, a square, trine and quincunx, or a semisextile, sextile and square. In all of these, note the planets, signs and aspects involved and watch what happens. It's possible to deduce some of their meaning 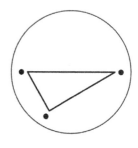 from their constituent parts. To give an example, a square, sextile and semisextile would suggest a situation where effort is needed (square) but there are helping factors (sextile) and either new factors emerging (waxing semisextile) or old factors coming to completion (waning semisextile).

Summing up

With the configurations mentioned here, three or more planets are being hauled into the same basic question, and their individual signals are being up-stepped immensely. They point to times when the signal or message of the time (in distinction to the customary noise of daily life) comes through strongly and clearly. A dominant tone emerges out of what otherwise can be jangled or pent-up energy. The more planets that are involved, the more significant the energy and intensity. Whichever planet is in the focal position must be parlayed with in order to make sense of the time. If there is no clear focal planet, all of them must be engaged together, unless for some reason the configuration is weighted in one direction. Either way, all planets in the configuration must be engaged and worked with – some of them might be more readily accessible, crucial or friendly and others not.

When we are seeking to identify power points in time, configurations are major contributors since so much energy gets caught up with them and they become the biggest show in town. Often these configurations include the Sun and Moon, and the lunar phase is worth examining, especially when a new or full moon is involved, since the short-term issues and implications which arise can be intense, decisive or remarkable in some way.

When slower planets engage in complex configurations they bring with them large scale waves of change affecting the longterm. An example is the Uranus conjunct Pluto in Virgo, opposed by Saturn conjunct Chiron in Pisces, with a trine/sextile from Neptune in Scorpio in 1965-6, which brought a major historical turning-point, a seed-time with longterm effects. It made the mid-1960s into a definitive watershed time by which the social-cultural clocks of the future were subsequently set.

At each major power point we are offered choices. Uncovering the question takes us a long way toward finding the answer. Here's an example: in 2014 the sudden rise of the Islamic State in Iraq and Syria shocked the world and, of course, all blame and responsibility was placed on the Islamist jihadis behind it. But this is an evasion of the true question. The true question is, what is not right with the wider world, to cause such a phenomenon to arise? If this were treated as the main question, the problem would be resolved more fundamentally.

Developing the willingness to make necessary changes is the main point of it all. Change flows naturally when our resistances loosen up. Frequently humanity resists change, clinging to knowns, old agendas and the past, so change then becomes convoluted and complicated, the real message of the time taking sometimes decades to come through, at least in the social mainstream and amongst the powers that be.

Arguably, the configuration of the mid-1960s marked a potential beginning of a new kind of civilisation on Earth – one which would be racially and ethnically tolerant, at peace, ecologically harmonious, socially more sensitive, spiritually more awake and psychologically more open than previously had been known. But society has its vested interests, and each individual and social grouping has resistances and fears, and to many the Unknown is a scary place. In any astrological situation, the outcomes can thus be mixed because fear of change interferes with necessary change.

Configurations are perhaps the strongest power points in time. But the wondrous nature and character of power points is often made up of many contributing factors, some of them integrated into a wholeness such as a configuration, and some separate but happening at the same time. This makes life rather a wonderful affair – if, that is, we remember that one of our key purposes in being alive is to learn from life and to evolve as souls.

Another key purpose of ours is to make a contribution, hopefully to leave the world one percent a better place than it was when we arrived. Here power points are valuable as opportunities for engaging with the time and making something of it. As Thomas Jefferson once said, *it's not what you get for it, it's what you become by doing it.*

13

Planetary Combinations

Like us, the planets are forever having relationships. Planetary energy-fields in relationship set up a third energy, an interwoven, resultant connection specific to that relationship itself. Here we shall look at the ways planetary energies combine, and the new issues they set up, pair by pair. By combining your understanding of the aspects with your gleanings from this chapter, you will get a reasonable idea of what to look for when observing an interplanetary aspect at work in real life. This chapter is one of those you don't need to read through systematically: skip through it and dip into it later for reference.

Planetary Pairs

Planetary combinations represent different kinds and levels of issue, affecting different time-spans, largely according to the speed and behaviour of the planets concerned. Lunar-to-planet combinations will affect time-spans of hours or a day, while Saturn-Pluto ones can hang around for a year, and Uranus, Neptune and Pluto ones for one to three years or more.

Faster-moving combinations bring things to the surface in more tangible, recognisable terms than slower ones, since the issues involved in slower aspects surface over time as an ongoing process which is not always so easy to discern at the time. How things surface depends partially on our openness to receiving and perceiving emergent issues, but they do tend to come up anyway, regardless. It's question of the directness and simplicity or the convolution and complexity by which we respond to change and deal with it. Much of human history could have been done much more simply, and many of humanity's hard times have been avoidable.

A lot could be said about every different planetary combination. They modulate differently when two planets are in different aspects to one another. So take these guidelines as a starter, and watch what happens when different aspects between the planets come up.

☉ Sun

Moving around the zodiac in a year and forming aspects to slower-moving planets, Sun injects life-energy and activation into whatever questions are outlined and thrown up, and they are flavoured by the sign-positions of both the Sun and that planet. Sun brings things alive, lights them up and makes the question important, pressing and actual, or it causes the question to surface into full view, or it commands energy to be put into it, stimulating the need of all things to grow and live out their life-potentials. The Sun infuses life with heat and light, metaphorically and literally.

With the slower planets from Jupiter outwards, the solar cycle of aspects to them is just a little more than one year in duration, digging up and raising questions around the underlying issues these planets are themselves working with at any time. With faster-moving planets, the Sun's cycles of relationship with them are more complex (see Chapter 8). Sun enlivens and pushes other planetary energies into expression in more visible terms than they otherwise would produce. In the body it concerns the heart, circulation and body warmth.

☉☿ **Sun-Mercury**: Sun and Mercury form only one aspect, a conjunction, since Mercury never moves further from Sun than 28°. So they don't even form a semisextile aspect. When Mercury is direct and passing behind the Sun (a superior conjunction) it is facilitative and connective, activating contact and dialogue in manifold ways – it often leads to busy and buzzy times. When Mercury is retrograde, coming between Earth and Sun (an inferior conjunction), there's questioning, deep thinking, reconsideration and a redesign going on. Things don't connect easily and often there are delays, complications and faults in communications and transport systems, or in normal face-to-face contact, forcing such a rethink.

When Sun and Mercury combine, thought-processes, nervous energy, linkages, things slotting into place and hyperactivity prevail. Intelligence and mentality are at work – and if they have problems, there's a disjointed, disconnected feeling, with misunderstandings, misperceptions, delays, lack of response, and travel and telecoms problems. Brains, nervous systems, eyes, ears, hands, lungs, voice and all communications media are influenced here. It's time for journeys, discussions, thinking things through, contacting people, writing, sharing ideas and listening. If Mercury is ahead of the Sun in the zodiac, developments tend to be led by ideas, and if it is trailing the Sun, ideas try to catch up with developments.

☉♀ **Sun-Venus**: Venus moves only 47° from Sun, ahead of or behind it, so that there can be only a conjunction, semisextile or semisquare between them. Around the semisquare Venus is in its 'great brilliance', its brightest period, in the evening or morning sky. Like Mercury, it has a superior (direct) and inferior (retrograde) conjunction: during the superior conjunction the flow of love, appreciation and togetherness flow well and freely, and during the inferior conjunction our feelings about life, about ourselves and other people come into question, prompted to go a level deeper, to become more empathic and profoundly caring.

This is about heart energy, loving, being loved, including and feeling included, appreciating and feeling valued. Conversely, it can mean a sense of poverty, deficiency and isolation, feeling strange, rejected or forgotten. Venus is about enjoying the good things of life, about sensuality, warmth and caring, or their lack or withholding. Issues around closeness, attachment, value, appreciation and roundness prevail here. Time for being with those you like and love and for doing enjoyable things. As with Mercury, if Venus is ahead of the Sun in the zodiac, developments are feelings-led, and if trailing the Sun, feelings are trying to catch up with the general drift of life.

☉♂ **Sun-Mars**: on average 2 years and 3 months, the Sun-Mars cycle drives our assertiveness, action, energy, push-power, wanting, courage, striving and sexual impulses. This can range from steady perseverance to fighting for our lives. To every action there is an equal and opposite reaction, so tact, patience, skill and understanding come into the equation if we are to be effective, together with recognition of others' rights and the world's overall needs. To get results, sometimes we need effort and struggle, sometimes sensitivity, forethought and gentle persistence. Action on the world is like making love with it, so our sexuality is thus connected with our capacity to progress in life. When Sun conjuncts Mars they both push together, and when they oppose, circumstances goad action to overcome inertia or obstacles.

☉♃ **Sun-Jupiter**: just over a year in length (as are the other Sun cycles following this), this cycle is about acts of faith, energy-investment in improvement and doing things in the belief that they will work well and bear fruit. At times we need to make forward steps, putting ourselves on the line, placing our bets and aiming for bigger things – or alternatively we might lack confidence, staying in our shell and comfort zone, hanging back, lacking faith. Issues around self-esteem and mutual value, our power, influence and involvement in society, and social belonging, shared beliefs or differences of belief can arise here, as well as money, resource and rights questions. Combined, Sun's and Jupiter's energies encourage forward steps, expansion and growth, and the precipitation of events and developments. Also they can be excessive or misjudged. Drawing on knowledge, understanding and experience is valuable here. Without Jupiter, things would stay pretty much the same. It's time to step out, make our claim, state our case, market our product, help others and do what we can to bring about whatever is good and right.
☉♄ **Sun-Saturn**: focus, discipline, acceptance of reality and hard work – that's what's required here. We must deal with failure, constraints or hardship, doubt and fear, fulfilling

our obligations and facing the past's consequences. Not easy, but necessary, and Saturn helps us self-correct or overcome barriers of our, others' or society's making. Issues of accountability, responsibility, accepting and working within our limits, organisation and structuring, and getting to grips with hard realities come up here. It's time to be sensible, make decisions, commit to what's needed and do what we must to achieve our goals – or at least, to stay out of trouble! What is most important in your situation, really? Wholehearted resolution is needed, to be *alive* and succeed, even under the most testing of circumstances.

☉⚷ **Sun-Chiron**: knotty dilemmas, and to resolve them it's necessary to take three deep breaths and look at things a different way. Problems can transform into solutions, opening doors and often helping with far greater issues than we thought we were trying to resolve. It is about dichotomies and miracles, using a deft hand, acting intuitively, breaking moulds and expectations, encountering surprise situations and overcoming the feeling of being stumped and stymied by seemingly impossible situations. Magical work and uncanny openings, flips and manoeuvres, knots and balancing acts. Uncannily, it all works out in the end, but sometimes, to get there, we have to let go of things first – the cogs of the universe are clanking and 'spirit has a plan'. Chiron demands that we get the underlying message and act accordingly – that's how magic happens.

☉⛢ **Sun-Uranus**: sudden changes of direction or outcome, with tense, electric, charged or polarised atmospheres. Time for overcoming resistances, making about-turns, taking an independent line, deviating from the norm, distancing ourselves from stuck situations, ripping up the past, changing our viewpoint and embracing new influences. At times we can be stirred or shocked by things suddenly going out of control. Sometimes brilliant, sometimes scatty and disruptive, Uranian influences shake things up, vitalising and refreshing them. At times a systems-check or reboot is needed. Uranus can be a game-changer. Like Mars, Uranus can provoke a reaction, leading to resistance, division, subversion and things turning out not to be as first thought. Then comes a tension between forward-moving and backward-pulling tendencies. Time for a change of tactics and, if you're feeling insecure about life, get used to it.

☉♆ **Sun-Neptune**: things can go weird, flat, empty and nullified, losing their direction and going adrift. Or perhaps things relax and normal concerns evaporate – it's not really clear what's what any more, and who is where. Phantasms, phobias, imaginings, symbolisms, artifices and illusions come up, but so might revelations, inspirations, clarified perceptions, creative outpourings and inspirational solutions. Things can disintegrate, surreptitiously turning inside out, or they can become obsolete or irrelevant. Bubbles pop, tyres deflate and sand gets in the gears, yet through this confusion life's clutter is eventually cleared, past constraints evaporate and an empty space appears for a new start, or a new arrangement of life's many factors. Life is strange and, if you wish to make the gods laugh, tell them your plans. Ultimately all is one and everything works out, but when life hits the sandbanks, going awry, something is going on, so look a level deeper to find what's underneath and behind it.

Time to let things be, get some space and see life more clearly – hidden secrets and insights are available. This isn't just a psychological or metaphysical matter: it concerns the knottiest and most concrete of situations, yet the confusion is often psychological. So, whatever is happening, see it for what it is, not what it should be, and herein lies the solution.

☉♇ **Sun-Pluto**: things can get heavy, ominous and portentous. Something is rumbling and whatever is under the surface is fermenting and wants to get out. Time is up and blowback-potential is high. Stuff comes up, bringing possible confrontations or perhaps a ripening of the inevitable – cruel realities strike. There's a possibility of breakdown or breakthrough and nothing much in between, unless it's avoidance of the key questions at hand. It's time to face ghosts, ghouls and unmentionables. If we avoid acting in integrity by concealing our dirty secrets, cruel and hard outcomes will eventually arise. Unwanted rubbish, sludge and crap threaten to foul things up but there's a purgative, cleansing element here too, undermining or blasting anything that holds back movement. Potent power, charged encounters, revealed secrets, spilt blood, clearing the air and do-or-die transformation. It all depends on whether truth or cover-ups prevail. The issues present involve fear of the dark abyss, powerful urges coming up, a cruel bulldozing force and confrontation with resistance, but there's something liberating and clarifying to it too – cobwebs and rubble are cleared. Sometimes we simply need a new start or to get dreadfully real. Time for getting down on awkward issues, making things work or, alternatively, dropping them.

☽ Moon

Lunar aspects form and then pass rapidly. Cycles of the Moon to the Sun and planets last just 27-30 days. Here our responses to life situations are triggered – we're given the choice to react mechanically or to use daily normalities, moods and events as a gateway to dealing with life in another, more appropriate way, at the moment they happen. Through the Moon we get what we need, also feeding the world with what it needs. It's about the daily round of events and situations, distractions, things arising and the use we make of each hour and day. It's also about conditioned memory, default patterns and the way we let them interfere with our lives. The profundity of this is startling when we become mindful of the many little programmed responses we mix into life. It's all about our sensitivities and security needs, our feeling of okayness or discomfort with life as it is presenting itself, today. In the body the Moon regulates the womb and ovaries, lymphatic system, water circulation and fluids in general. In nature the Moon affects tides, underground water, rainfall, humidity, water-flows in plants, and the behaviour of weather systems.

☽☉ **Moon-Sun**: this concerns the fulfilment we generate by living authentically and doing what we came here to do, according to our true nature, and the ripples and issues we cause when we fail to do so. It's about how we deal with being in the world in all its changing phases. Sun brings conscious intentional action to meet with lunar semi-conscious responses to life as it arises. It's about our instincts and whether we feel okay, safe and in touch with ourselves, or not, in relation to life's many changing situations. The phase of the Moon is connected with our moods, standpoints and feelings about life, and how these affect the way we act and live our lives.

☽☿ **Moon-Mercury**: getting in touch with our needs and articulating them, connecting our thoughts and words with our umbilical feelings and gut responses – how we understand and express what we need. Conditioned habits of thought and word, automated thought-responses to life as it arises, feelings we need to express, unconscious messages behind words and between the lines. Often, to make a decision, we go into our heads, but really decisions are made in our feelings, and this is the question here. This cycle concerns how we connect with what we need or how we grasp what the world needs of us. Time for figuring out the details and how everything relates to everything else. Or it's time for a much-needed sharing.

☽♀ **Moon-Venus**: feelings, sensitivities and vulnerabilities, our capacity for love and caring, warmth and softness. It's about femininity, schmoozing, niceness, pleasure and nurture, receptivity and belonging. It's about nesting and intimacy, issues around needing to be liked, loved or needed, and it also concerns attachment and indulgence. Moon and Venus bring out the child and lover in us and our warmth of heart, though when they're not working well a feeling of neediness, discomfort and emotional coldness can emerge. When Moon and Venus are strong, it's time for quality time with those you like and love, and acts of care and generosity. It's a good time for family, friends and mutual bonding.

☽♂ **Moon-Mars**: assertion to protect self, anticipation of attack or adversity, defensiveness, insensitivity or hyper-sensitivity, stirring up trouble, sore vulnerabilities, close scrapes. Also indulgence and desire for satiation, sexuality, cravings and sensation, argument, rivalry, jealousy, overreaction. It's awkward but it's the stuff of life. Issues here involve fight-or-flight, wanting and aversion. Moon and Mars irritate and are allergic to each other, but through their scrapes and sore points we can still learn a lot. They can also be sensually enticing, indulgent and seductive. Time for setting aside your ratty, tetchy side, getting on with things and clarifying with yourself and others what you really want and how you really feel – with a little patience thrown in for good measure.

☽♃ **Moon-Jupiter**: wellbeing, fun, partying, pleasure and pleasantry, comfort and plenty, social warmth, membership and togetherness. Motherliness, generosity, mutuality and shared understanding. Issues around attachment and rewards, waste and consumptiveness.

Comfort, joy and conviviality, or addiction, over-consumption and dependency. Time for friendliness and helping people out, since whatever is happening brings with it benign opportunities – and the chocolate ice cream is lovely. It's a time of plenty and reprieve, but enjoyment is not the same as overdoing it. It's fine for everything to be alright and good – and give thanks.

☽♄ **Moon-Saturn**: doing without, aloneness and self-sufficiency, foregoing needs and sacrificing for future benefit. Like it or not, when Moon meets Saturn it concerns standing on your own two feet, discipline, work, being reliable, keeping commitments, facing facts, shouldering duties, and applying patience and forbearance. In worst cases it can mean deprivation, confiscation, subdued feelings, sublimation, self-denial and disappointment. Issues around coldness, hardness, depression and loneliness, deprivation, denial and fear of loss. It's not all bad though: the strength of a Moon-Saturn contact is found through prioritising what is most important, persevering, facing the music and doing whatever needs to be done. Time for bearing with your current mood, staying on the case and making do with the situation as it stands – it's all about cultivation of character and doing the necessaries.

☽⚷ **Moon-Chiron**: uncanny problem-solving opportunities, the encountering of paradoxes, riddles, complex and knotty tangles, and the consequent uncovering of maverick solutions and facilitation of genuine needs. Application of knacks and gifts; magical or healing work, godsends; underlying issues hidden within situations; seemingly miraculous fulfilment of hitherto unidentified needs from unexpected quarters. This concerns the mother principle, but it might not be your mother – it might even be the cat, or anyone who expresses care in that moment. It might be you. Issues around feeling used or framed by circumstances, being a pawn in a larger chessgame, or a victim of circumstance; feeling trapped, fated or having one's needs overlooked. Time for giving thanks for what's here because the present is a gift – this is a major clue to the resolution of problems. What's happening is what's happening, and somehow it is meant to be as it is, but can you see this?

☽♅ **Moon-Uranus**: separation, changeability, things moving on, insecurity, vulnerability, stirring and shaking. Course-changes and about-turns and shake-outs, unsettling moments, tense atmospheres; divergence and proliferation, surprises and shocks, release and relief. Issues around reliability, avoidance, trusting change and living with instability. There's a need to be in touch with immediate needs, releasing the tendency to impose strings and requirements on life, and seeing the compensating factors in everything. Gales, thunderstorms, weather extremes. Time for a tidy-up or for trying something different – tomorrow is another day, and it's good right now to shake up ingrained habits.

☽♆ **Moon-Neptune**: things going adrift, derailing and deflating. Subtle nuances and susceptibility to hidden influences. Tendencies toward confusion and disorientation. Stillness and calm, uplift and level-shift, insight and imagination. Undermining and subsidence, strange and unearthly atmospheres. Issues around uncertainty, vagueness, memory, disconnects, unconsciousness. Floods, fog, drizzle and calm weather. Time to relax and enjoy the situation as it is – listen to the birdsong and the sound of the wind. Go a level deeper, or rise above things – it's okay, really. It's just that reality is reconstituting itself.

☽♇ **Moon-Pluto**: encounter, insecurity, hard feelings, underlying stuff, unconscious needs. Loaded and overloaded atmospheres. There's a need here for honesty, to get to the bottom line. Emergence or eruption, storms, clear-outs and purgations. Trust issues and betrayal, clinging or obsession, feeling wounded. Manipulation, oppression and domination. Thunderous, close or harsh weather, or intense stillness. Time for looking under the rug and being honest about shifty feelings – but hang in there, it's not the end of the world, and all things pass.

☿ Mercury

Mercury activates connective nerve cells and synapses, communications media, roads, pathways and interrelationships. In the body it affects eyes, speech, lungs, hands, ears and the digestive system, the organs that connect with the world. When Mercury energy is flying, systems are whirring, contacts being made and ideas are flying around. Mercury moves along life's linking channels, connecting separate components of the chain of creation to get them handshaking and talking. It gathers data, forms ideas and associations, processes experience and converts ideas into words, to be stored in memory or shared through talk, writing and electronic media. In nature it's connected with winds, ocean currents, insects, birds, the migration of everything from seeds to animals and the tributary systems of rivers – all things that are significant for their movement.

☿♀ **Mercury-Venus**: affability, companionship, liking and being liked, appreciation, social interaction, verbalised feelings, poetic expression, sensitised thoughts, mutuality. Evaluation, value-judgement, weighing ideas, assessment. Aesthetic expression, craft, creative design. Chatter, meaningless relating, confusion of thoughts with feelings. Time for sharing feelings and figuring out your appreciation of the good things in life.

☿♂ **Mercury-Mars**: opinionatedness, strong ideas, rhetoric, debate, argument, demands, competition for airspace. Campaigns, elections, negotiations, conflict versus diplomacy, treaties. Shooting, martial arts, technical skill, acuity and accuracy, implementation of ideas, logistics, strategy, racing and speed sports. Issues around competitiveness, interference, incursion, expressions of anger and frustration, motor-mouth syndrome, separative and divisive views. Time for saying some of those things you've not said before and making your point – and hearing others' messages and truths too.

☿♃ **Mercury-Jupiter**: intellectualism, theoretical ideas, learned discourse, beliefs and philosophies, scriptural faiths, knowledge. Considered judgements, opinions and conclusions, legal procedure and jurisprudence, agreements and transactions. Markets, councils and parliaments, meetings, committees, conferences, gregariousness. Established ideas, prevailing memes and conventional wisdom, science as a belief-system. Marketing, advertising and propaganda. Master-plans, petitions, donations, support, generalisations. Issues around intellectuality, exaggeration, ivory-towers, constant movement and activity, mental dominance. Time for a chin-wag, attending a lecture, reading books or making a journey.

☿♄ **Mercury-Saturn**: deliberative, empirical and logical thinking, mathematics and statistics, bureaucracy, authoritative research. Directives, constitutions, sanctions. Scepticism, rationalism, concentration, study, mental spadework. Agendas, procedures, regulations, recipes, orthodoxy, qualifications. Caution, doubt, shyness, quietness, holding own counsel. Accountancy and legal professions. Issues around depressive or negative thought, text-bookish thinking, miseducation, difficulty with speaking out, fear of relying on one's own ideas or of self-authorisation. Time to focus on working things out and thinking through what you know you must do.

☿⚷ **Mercury-Chiron**: knack for problem-solving, conundrums, anagrams, puzzles. Cranky genius and mental gifts, outside-the-box thinking, lateral thought, intuitive connections. Investigation, canny solutions, magical thinking, karmic connections, 'chance' meetings, ideas whose times have come. Issues around bewilderment, mental subservience, attachment to logic or illogicality, difficulty understanding magical realities or trusting associative, symbolic thinking. Time for working out answers to pending issues, but shift your frame of reference and approach.

☿⛢ **Mercury-Uranus**: excitement, quick thinking, sudden changes of mind, intuitive leaps, progressive and inspirational thinking. Genius, dowsing, divination, crazy logic. Humour, about-turns, contradictions, forked tongue, 'Aha' moments and realisations. Suspicion, underhand communication, mind-games, manipulation. Dyslexia, autism spectrum, learning difficulties. Ideology, intuitive reasoning; stress, worry, over-mentality. Issues around scattered or uncontrollable thoughts, stimulants, racing brains, projection, blurting, inconsistency. Fast talk, babbling, charged atmospheres, science fiction. Time for making trips, doing something different, new ideas or brainstorming with friends and associates.

☿♆ **Mercury-Neptune**: visionary and idealistic thought, poesy, music and art, free-association, inspiration. Empathy, channelling, the muse, spiritualism, transcendence, musical and healing gifts. Fantasy, fiction, impersonation, mimicry, photography. Problems in articulation, miscommunication, secrecy. Issues around muddle-headedness, absent-mindedness and attention deficiency, difficulty speaking for oneself and making decisions, unclear agreements. Time for some down-time, letting go of concerns, changing the subject, cultural pursuits and creativity.

☿♇ **Mercury-Pluto**: profound thought, research, investigation and detection. Hidden agendas and concealed meanings, raw honesty, secrecy and secrets breaking out, exposure, subterfuge. Mental breakthroughs, strong ideas and forceful words, persuasion and convictions, shame, taboo ideas. Issues around mental violence or victimhood, con-trickery, scamming, fraud, trusting others, manipulative ideas. Fear of exposure, mental breakdown, flare-ups and cover-ups. Time for some hard talking or facing tough verities.

♀ Venus

Through Venus life softens, melds and becomes more colourful. We draw to ourselves things and people we like and love, and they draw us to them – the principle of attraction. Life becomes more rounded, agreeable, inclusive, satisfying, warm and enjoyable. Venusian rain and cold is nevertheless soft and caressing. Through Venus we evaluate life's situations with our feelings, perceiving music, hue, taste and texture, and we feel for others and those around us, sensing commonality and oneness. It can bring a form of madness too, when we're 'falling in love'. Through Venus we 'have and hold' – hopefully in the best of ways, without possessiveness and attachment. And of course there is the other side of Venus: loneliness, insensitivity, alienation, bitterness and exclusion. Venus works through the kidneys, liver and fleshy, sensual parts. The cycles of Venus are similar in length to those of the Sun, as seen from Earth.

♀♂ **Venus-Mars**: sexuality and sensuality, push-pull issues in relationship, feeling and passion, demonstrative love, wanting and choosing, making love. Upwelling feelings and desires, commonalities and differences, attachment or independence, gender orientation. Keeping feelings in proportion, love and hate, demands, indulgence or, conversely, being out of touch with our bodies, even ascetic, and conflicts between heart and genitals. Time to feel and share feelings, and a good time for making love.

♀♃ **Venus-Jupiter**: socialising, amicability, companionship, gregariousness, partying, dancing and celebration. Faith in people, enjoyment of company and good times. Good taste, caring and wellbeing, generosity, popularity, charisma. Sponsorship, charity, prosperity, benignity and optimism. Family or community warmth. Sweetness. Issues around trust, waste, decadence, confection, attachment to wealth and nicety, obesity, avoidance, falsity and jovial superficiality. Time to have a good time, be with friends and meet new people.

♀♄ **Venus-Saturn**: solitude, self-sufficiency, leanness, commitment in relationship. Love-contracts, marriage, lasting relationships, trust and integrity in relationship. Tradition and antiques. Learning from love and bitter-sweet relationships. Self-denial or being out of touch with feelings, inscrutability. Bearing with adversity. Fear of love and passion, difficulty being close or making relationships last, or a tendency to hold a relationship rigidly. Emotional coolness, isolationism, clinginess, emotional shut-offs, stoicism, poverty-consciousness. Sometimes those we love are far away or unavailable. Time for bearing with relationships or being happy with yourself.

♀⚷ **Venus-Chiron**: a gift for doing the right thing for others – or for inept screwing up. Improbable relationships, maverick lovers, empathy, canny sensitivity. Unusual social skills, 'chance' meetings, soul links. Emotional healing and rescue, long-distance relationships and absent lovers. Turning up at the right moment, knowingness, feminine guile. Issues around fraught relationships and entanglements, emotional victimhood, emotional space and attachment. Learning from relationships deepens feelings and their mystery. Love and friendship come in strange forms and from unforeseen directions, yet magic happens just when you're not looking for it!

♀♅ **Venus-Uranus**: independence, emotional detachment and freedom, love-affairs, flightiness, changeable feelings and unconventional relationships, flirtation, compulsive love, attractiveness and charisma, uncanny beauty. Gender uncertainty, sexual deviancy, bisexuality, serial monogamy, 'cheating', prostitution. Issues around fear of dependency, distrust, emotional inconsistency, getting close, sensuality without feeling, alienation, separativeness, emotional avoidance. Time for some shake-ups in stuck relationships, and freshening up your love for those who matter.

♀♆ **Venus-Neptune**: idealised, perfect love and romance, questing for soul-mates. Compassion and empathy, emotional succour, rose-tinted glasses. Selfless love, creative imagination, music and artistry. Issues around fear of personalised affection, transference and unclear boundaries in relationship, impracticality in love. Forgot the condoms. Impossible or distant relationships, romantic delusions, disappointment in love, seeking to rescue or be rescued, indefinite feelings, emotional confusion. Time for helping someone or showing that you care, or perhaps for hugging, forgiving and ministering to those you love.

♀♇ **Venus-Pluto**: transformation through love, intensity and closeness, emotional obsession or clinginess, sensuality. Bliss-seeking, immersion in relationship, wearing heart on sleeve. Painful loss and separation, manipulative relationships or emotional domination, possessiveness. Issues around loss of selfhood, fear of punishment or laying oneself open to it, fear of abandonment or betrayal, power and control struggles, demandingness, sexual indulgence. Time for forgiveness, getting to the bottom of your feelings and bringing hidden agendas into the open.

♂ Mars

Mars is about making things happen and work, getting what we want, assertiveness, engaging in life's battles, using muscle, clout and willpower, achieving things and acting on the world. Its root lies in sexuality and the search for gratification, though it's also about the effort, push and activity needed to find gratification and get results. Assertion involves tact, skill, patience, upfront and measured dealings, not just force, war or competition, otherwise complications, rebounds and blowbacks will obstruct the desired outcome. With Mars we overcome challenges, build empires, make love, make a difference, and resist pressures and incursions on our space. On one level it's about winning or losing, yet on another level it concerns creating win-win situations or at least 'fair dinkum', bringing about benefit for all concerned. Included in this is humanity's tendency to conquer, exploit and degrade nature, and our current need to cooperate with it.

♂♃ **Mars-Jupiter**: assertion of power and ability, overcoming resistance and inertia, moving mountains, pushiness, strength, ambition. Athletics, rat-racing, deal-making, urge for achievement and impact, making a mark on the world. Issues around bombast, force, rivalry, impatience, insensitivity, excess, creating reactions and causing dissension. High expectations of success, overlooking details and ignoring small things. Time for some effort and making a few things happen. This cycle is 2 years and 3 months long.

♂♄ **Mars-Saturn**: hard work and perseverance, focus of power, discipline and ability. Painstaking diligence, realism, skill, application of technique, patience under duress, deferred gratification, uphill climbs, self-sacrifice. Making life difficult on oneself or others, battling against nay-sayers and obstacles. Issues around suppressed wants, fear of assertion, sexual blockages or puritanism, bottled-up anger, self-punishment, overstrain, self-denial, violence, workaholism, difficulties with father or authority figures. Time for sorting things out and fixing things up. This cycle is 2 years long.

♂⚷ **Mars-Chiron**: second strength and physical gifts, miracle-working, uncanny ability to make things happen. Conflict-resolution and conflict-management, hidden strength, engineering genius, warrior archetypes, ability to do the right thing from many viewpoints.

Getting tangled in knots. Issues around victimisation and force, exclusion, accusation, connivance, sexual complexities. Time for seeing whether a change of strategy is needed and for following what life prompts you to do – what is meant to be is meant to be. On average this cycle is two weeks short of two years (it varies greatly).

♂♅ **Mars-Uranus**: independence, separation and division, rebellion and rioting, impulsiveness, eccentricity. Mutation, sudden shocks, explosions, blowbacks, landslides, storms. Striking out, opposition and contrariness, schism, freedom-fighting. Issues around violence, projection, inconsistency, impatience. Speeding, detachment and exclusion, distrust, not knowing own strength, disrespect for elders and authority. It's a good time for clarifying what you're fed up with, and striking while the iron is hot. This cycle is 1 year 11 months long.

♂♆ **Mars-Neptune**: service, transcendence or sublimation of desire, idealised or licentious sexuality, machoism, hero-worship. Activity-oriented healing or channelling ability, will of the gods, acting for ideals, wider causes or selfless ends. Obfuscation, confounding situations, tyres stuck in the mud, confusion, diversion, energy-dissipation. Directionlessness, disempowerment, indiscipline, chaos. Issues around weakness, susceptibility, helplessness, transference of power onto symbols or strong people. Idealisation of sex, glamour and appearance. Subservience, difficulty fending for self. A good time for accepting what's happening, letting be and seeing what unfolds. This cycle is 1 year 11 months long.

♂♇ **Mars-Pluto**: libido power, primal sexuality, big challenges, hard work, obsessive dedication, resistance of oppression. Drive, relentless activity, ruthless ambition, control, military discipline. Going against the odds, all-out battles, force and violence, overkill, blowback. Issues around power battles, pain in sexual encounters, exploitation, slavery. Brutality, fascism, terrorism, hidden motivations, fear of power, encounters and collisions or lust for power. Self-harming. Time for tackling some uncomfortable tasks and finally sorting out a few important things. This cycle is 1 year 11 months long.

♃ Jupiter

The reality we create in our lives begins with our beliefs, how we construct them and give them shape, substance and form. We pick up many of our beliefs in childhood and adolescence, and throughout life, some of them personal, some cultural, some based in experience and some imposed by or adopted and absorbed from others. Jupiter concerns our involvements in society and the world around, our hopes, investment of energy and resources toward making things better, and the overall contribution we make to life. Through Jupiter we chase success – however we define that. With faith and application, we can build what we believe in and achieve satisfying results, if we play our cards well. Jupiter helps us go out and take on the world, or also to go within and develop an inner world – values, philosophy and cosmology. It brings benefit, growth, extension, creativity, knowledge and conviction. Jupiter works alongside Saturn: without Saturnine constraint, Jupiter loses its way or goes too far, and without Jupiterian stimulus and prompting, Saturn's structuring has a clamping effect, losing its life and purpose.

♃♄ **Jupiter-Saturn**: getting organised, commitment toward making progress, decision-making. Optimism meeting realism. The urge to make a lasting mark on the world and leave a legacy. Business, government and charities, committees and structuring, planned and regulated growth, policy formation and implementation; social institutions, procedures, laws; integrity and moral rightness; architecture, monuments, temples. Social-mindedness, standing, status, authority, public figures. Issues around faith, escapism, depression, risk-taking, abuse of power, regulating freedom, institutional corruption or sclerosis. This combination engages gears. It's time for organising things, starting businesses or projects, making things work, facing challenges and overcoming obstacles. This cycle is 20 years long.

♃⚷ **Jupiter-Chiron**: bridge-building, being of service, resolving schisms and peacebuilding. Consultancy, counsel, finding or giving help, shifting viewpoints. A magical touch, healing situations, manifesting unlikely new initiatives. Issues around being a victim of others' advice, judgements or pressures, lack of understanding of unusual things, unbelief in deeper currents or questions of how to work with them. Intellectual uncertainty or difficulty realising one's beliefs. Sometimes we serve as chess-pieces in a larger chessgame, and it's time to let ourselves be utilised by the universe to help bring about whatever heals and helps the world. This cycle is between 13 and 20 years long, very variable.

♃♅ **Jupiter-Uranus**: freedom, dissidence, dissenting minorities, human rights, challenging authority or conformity, radical leaders. Social reform, humanitarian intervention. Religious sects and reform movements. Crowd scenes, protests, revolutions, rebellions, coups, takeovers. Loss of collective fear, breaking with tradition. Flaps, fads and breaking trends, youth movements. Changing fortunes, high-risk living, adventure, leaps in the dark. Eccentricity, innovation, invention. Issues around freedoms and social control, commitment, perseverance and consistency, difficulty settling into regular patterns. Time to rise to higher principles, strike out and blaze new trails. Taking initiatives or working for what you believe to be right, even when the social consensus goes against it. This cycle is 13 years and 9 months long.

♃♆ **Jupiter-Neptune**: idealism, hopes, visions, spiritual aspirations, mystical and religious experiences, dreams and dispensations. High times, inner freedom, healings and revelations.

Charity and altruism. Imaginative and creative times or cultural upswings. Unconscious social memes and beliefs. Denial and indifference. Issues around groundedness, realism and practicality. Confusing and confounding events. Omitting to look after personal interests, pursuit of unrealisable goals. Nonplussment, flakiness, lack of focus and clear objectives. It's a time of healing, forgiveness and uplift, though be careful not to tilt at windmills. This cycle is 12 years 9 months long.

♃♇ **Jupiter-Pluto**: rampant progress, galloping growth, economic bubbles, cutthroat competition. Invasion, imperialism, subversion, spying, special operations. Deep drives to succeed and overcome limitations. Taking on causes, challenging established ways. Iconoclasm, social projection, victimisation, dehumanisation, ethnic cleansing, dictatorship, terrorism. Bringing wider benefit, seeking posterity, fame-seeking. Corruption, oppression, kidnapping, excesses of government and law-enforcement, Machiavellianism. Issues around conflicts of power, disproportionate force, insensitivity, ruthlessness, overexertion, rebelliousness, inability to let up. Time to make things move, though consider others and longterm outcomes. This cycle is on average 12-14 years long, and variable.

♄ Saturn

Through Saturn things are grounded, structured, implemented and made to fit the rules of the soul, nature or society. It concerns what is obligatory in life – in the end, a choiceless choice. It works through societal awareness and our sense of responsibility – whether that's self-assumed responsibility, freely taken on, or whether it is, at root, driven by guilt, fear, shame or compliance. If we own our actions and the consequences we create, Saturn becomes a creative force, leading to fulfilment, achievement and recognition in whatever sphere of life we operate in. If we don't do this, sooner or later the question comes back at us, leading to difficulty, failure, adversity and deficiency or, failing this, difficulty enjoying the blessings we have.

When Saturn is around, we just have to do what we have to do. But this is special: in the end, it means getting on with our life's work. But it is about the necessary input and labour we must carry out to achieve anything significant, and this, in the end, is one of the more fulfilling things we can do, here on Earth. We need to train, develop and discipline ourselves, and preferably enjoy it. But if we're not following our calling in some way, something is missing.

Life is a predicament and we must make the best of it. Saturn's blockages, fears, no-go areas, guilt-complexes and self-limiting beliefs can be transformed into a sense of substance, purpose, direction, identity and service if we face up to things. Ultimately, this is a collective, not just an individual question: where is our world heading and why? What is more important: short-term benefits or longterm priorities?

♄⚷ **Saturn-Chiron**: profound lessons derived from knotty, insoluble life-situations. Deep learning experiences that define limits and unveil new solutions. High-pressure paradoxes and repeating predicaments. Problem-solving by digging deeper, illness that helps us resolve deep questions, constraints turning out to be blessings. Factual, functional issues with deeper connotations. Questioning of purposes and priorities. Tight scrapes and fine lines, finding needles in haystacks. Scapegoating, blame and misunderstanding. Challenging and difficult, this is the stuff that makes great teachers, leaders, role-models and healers. Time to stop, take stock, change perspective, let go and try again in a different way. This cycle is very variable, between 64 and 165 years.

♄♅ **Saturn-Uranus**: rebelliousness and iconoclasm, changing or breaking rules, questioning norms. Reform or revolution, conformity or dissidence. Conflict between tradition and modernity, past and future. Sudden cut-offs and separations, lines drawn on the past, destruction of the past. Enduring and testing circumstances. Irreconcilable options, divergent realities, social schism, balkanisation. Extremism, repression. Exposure of cover-ups, secret manoeuvrings. Subterranean rumblings, earthquakes, crises, definitive events. Issues around conventionality, dissatisfaction and need for change. Sharp-edged fear, social castigation, guilt over past actions. Running away from realities, dualism or schizoid behaviour. Time for honesty and integrity, getting opposing sides to talk and resolving contradictions. This cycle is 45 years and 5 months long.

♄♆ **Saturn-Neptune**: manifesting ideals and visions in real terms. Discernment between reality and imagination. Disillusionment, disappointment, dreams falling flat, deflation, subsidence. Leaks, subterfuge, boundary infringements. Sculpture, visionary architecture and practical arts, skill in expressing dreams. Blind spots and areas of life needing attention. Sense of service. Unclear arrangements. Paranoia, fear of madness or loss of selfhood, guilt over selfishness. Self-denial, sublimation, transcendentalism, insight. Sense of unworthiness, separation of spirit from body, poor resistance to disease or to confrontation. Transference onto others, unclear boundaries. This cycle is 40 years long.

♄♇ **Saturn-Pluto**: horror and crisis scenarios, real or imagined. Dealing with hardship, shouldering of burdens. Suffering, enforced restriction, facing darkness. Repression, militancy, terror, social control. Making it in the end, survival against the odds. Raw truth, cleansing and purgation. Guilt and pain as transformers, generation of light amidst adversity and darkness. Betrayal, deception and subterfuge. Pruning, digging, clearing, demolition. Self-punishment, withholding of power or truth, violence, hopelessness, resistance to change. Dread of death, the abyss or breakthrough, fear of social chaos. Time to face the music, overcome fear and do the necessaries. This cycle is 31-38 years long and variable.

All the planets below form aspects only occasionally, lasting a year or longer and affecting history and the group psyche. They act impersonally or transpersonally, with longterm developments or 'dispensations' arising from deeper origins. Yet they nevertheless impact very personally on us too, exposing us to new realities and possibilities, exerting a changeful effect on us.

⚷ Chiron

Chiron is like a key, a small object with the power to open doors in big walls. If we're willing to work with paradox (seemingly irreconcilable opposites), irresolvable problems can be turned to solutions, almost magically. Chiron brings forward ridiculous, knotty, clogged situations within which remarkable answers lie – if, that is, we see them by shifting our frame of reference, forgetting what *should* have been happening and looking at what's underneath. It helps us outwit normality and expectation, finding openings that are appropriate from multiple viewpoints, beyond self-interest and personal viewpoint. It gives access to our magic side, our capacity to learn from life's symbolism and its deeper meanings, integrating personal and universal ends. Maverick qualities, skills, knacks and gifts uncovered by learning life's deeper lessons and honing our spirit. Healing, bridging and resolution. Being in the right place at the right time. Or, chronically missing the point of it all and floundering around feeling like a victim of circumstance.

⚷♅ **Chiron-Uranus**: deep unexpected impulses for change and innovation, realisation of visions, inventiveness. Crucial personal initiatives taken in collective situations, inspired maverick leaders, self-sacrificing heroes or martyrs. Unforeseen yet apposite developments, factual situations with magical solutions, idealistic movements offering appropriate answers. Solutions appearing at first as problems. Breaking the mould, sudden obsolescence, breakdown leading to breakthrough. Death of doctrines and roadmaps. Intuitive, lateral reasoning, bursts of genius or inspired streams of consciousness. Fragmented social situations. Issues of faith in the face of difficult issues and situations. Difficulties in adjusting to changing times, polarised rejection or, alternatively, welcoming of anything new. Time to step back, drop past ways, await your moment and do what seems right in that moment. This cycle is 103-145 years long, and variable.

⚷♆ **Chiron-Neptune**: channelling of insight and revelation, accessing spiritual resources. Insights, revelations and exposures. Spiritual healing, sense of service, will of the gods, 'divine intervention', sense of the Beyond. Religious movements, spiritual teachers, crazy wisdom, the healing power of faith. 'Extraordinary popular delusions and the madness of crowds'. Illusory or enlightening memes, groupthink, fashions, cultural and religious illusions and their collapse. Doldrums, things falling flat, things not happening as expected. Over-sensitivity, inner truth, psycho-spiritual discernment, inner objectivity and proportion. Time to have faith and exercise judgement. This cycle is 47-80 years long.

⚷♇ **Chiron-Pluto**: jumping over the abyss, quantum leaps, navigating troubled waters, facing tough lessons of the times. Power battles, decisive moments, fight to the death, encounters, showdowns. The bottom line, extreme exertions, turning points. Deaths, sacrifices and martyrdom. Blowback of consequences from long before. Fear of the Great Unknown and shying away from the power of the moment. Distrust of deeper urges or imperatives, resistance to the inevitable. Time to take brave steps, though be careful about what is destroyed in the process. This cycle is 56-70 years long.

♅ Uranus

Uranus brings radical changes and shifts, new ideas, mutations, innovations and breakouts from the norm. It wrenches us away from the past, prising open old habits, customs and restrictions. This often coagulates around heroes, crowds, places, poignant situations or events imbued with symbolism, catalysing a change in everything, whether by changing attitudes, manifest facts or both. Uranus works impulsively, in flashes and spurts, with the power to shock and surprise and attack from behind, but it can also relieve and release pent-up pressures, ending oppressive situations and changing the agenda. Socially it often brings dissension, alienation, polarisation, protest or revolt. It bypasses existing ways and patterns, pulling us toward the future and causing the long term to override the short term, taking territory by storm.

By causing things to wobble and shake, Uranus loosens up all areas of life, and secondary effects and reverberations are many – though it can lead to unforeseen complications too. It can also stimulate conservatism and new ways of resisting change. Sometimes change is suppressed, yet a process starts where it comes about more gradually, especially through underground movements or cultural developments, or ultimately because younger generations grow up and gain power. Amidst the flurry of change, there's a danger of wheel-reinvention or of changing only appearances, not substance and core issues. Yet however it happens, change often starts with Uranian quickening and energisation, fired up by its urgency, vision and sense of possibility. It unleashes an inspired brilliance and inventiveness, at least among some people, opening up evolutionary possibilities that just weren't there before.

♅♆ **Uranus-Neptune**: Surreptitious, backdoor change and strong undercurrents. Life suddenly looks different, even if initially only imperceptibly. There's a sensing of the far horizon, often explored by visionary, radical political or innovative movements. Deep questioning, illusion-building and illusion-breaking. Revelations and exposure. Level-shift, context-shift, insight, grand designs. Integrity and legitimacy questions. Witch-hunts and collective madnesses, social allergies, aversions and phobias. Exploitation of weaknesses. Boundary and jurisdictional issues or shifts of power. Seduction and persuasion, the arts, fantasy. Events with mixed or inconclusive outcomes. Public dissatisfaction and spiritual discomfort, seeking new horizons or holding on to familiar territory. It's time for new possibilities to emerge and for cultivating faith in the future, letting reality update itself. This cycle is 171 years long.

♅♇ **Uranus-Pluto**: Ripping up the past and conceiving or birthing the new. Visionary, radical or violent outbreaks, social rebirth, deep rumblings in group psyche. Dissident movements, uprisings, revolutions and outrages by them or against them. Changes of direction and mindset, things turning out differently from expected, correction of past history. Rapid obsolescence. Reactionary forces, separation movements, social polarisation or splintering. Schizophrenia, bipolarism and insanity in society. Fear of the unknown and resistance to change. It's time for the world to move on, yet to every action there is an equal and opposite reaction and the clash between the two can dominate the agenda. This cycle is 111 or 143 years long, alternating.

♆ Neptune

With Neptune there is a reality-uplift where the past is surreptitiously invalidated, crumbling and disintegrating, opening up new options and creating empty space. It mysteriously infuses new light into perceived reality, loosening up the old, melting and sifting it and removing all that is obsolete. It reconfigures everything by introducing chaos, disorientation and derailments. Things come unstuck, old fixities dissolve and people see things in a different way – periodically a new reality presents itself, or an open space into which a new reality can move.

Neptune brings a level- and phase-shift, a slippage that the majority becomes aware of some time after it has already started. While Neptune helps the flow move, it can also bring confusion, loss of anchor-points and direction. While it can clarify our seeing, stimulate inner vision or reveal overdue truths – 'the emperor has no clothes' – its imaginal stimulation can also lose us in glamours, glosses or diversions. It opens up the vastness of the unknown – and occasionally dunks us, threatening drowning, to open us up.

♆♇ **Neptune-Pluto**: destruction of past worldviews and realities, rebirth of new perspectives and possibilities. Fundamental historic changes – a feeling of a new world dawning – and the sweeping away of the old. Investigation of the mysterious, psychological and spiritual breakthroughs, opening of new thresholds and horizons. Deep underlying shifts and the birth of new possibilities that might start small, yet they have the power to fundamentally change everything in the course of time. Issues around the dark night of the soul, unsubstantiated fears, sky-high ambition or profound acceptance. It's a time for recognising that a major historic shift is under way, and making fundamental changes. This cycle is 492-497 years long.

♇ Pluto

Pluto drives forward inevitable destruction and renewal, burning, demolishing and crushing all that is no longer useful, yet vivifying all things through freeing up life-energy and unclogging log-jams. It has a soul-quaking, transformative influence, forcing confrontation with truth. If this is not done it brings deeply painful lessons to force transformation in the longterm. It has deep libidinous power, stimulating unconscious urges for new life or bringing death-wishes, thereby breaking through blocks and resistances.

Yet Pluto challenges our fear of being overwhelmed, feeding that fear and causing people to cling on to safe knowns. This can strengthen social repression or self-repression, often reflected in obsessive, self-destructive and fetishistic social behaviours. Through resisting change we ultimately discover the true need for it, or we are overcome by it – thus resistance, fascism and violence are a part of change, tragic though they may be, and not a final obstruction of it. Plutonic power and life-urges always win through and truth prevails, but the damage and pain on the way can be problematic. Generally, the more resistance, the more pain. Pluto offers us an opportunity to choose deeply to welcome transformation and make things easier.

Some Examples

The above interplanetary relationships represent a hierarchy of different cyclical significances, largely related to the speeds of the planets involved. Aspects formed by the Moon to any other planet are short-lived, even if significant or crucial at the time. But major outer-planet aspects can have far-reaching implications: one example was the birth of the Worldwide Web on the Uranus-Neptune conjunction of 1993, the full implications of which have as yet not fully dawned.

Let me tell you a story from the 1980s to give examples of how things work. Once, I ran a series of two week-long groups in a house in the mountains. I planned to drive there on a Thursday, when there happened to be a Mars conjunct Jupiter in Pisces. The fullmoon on the Tuesday, two days before, had been one of those overloaded 'it's-all-too-much' fullmoons, but there was an underlying tone to it of forgiveness and looking at things afresh. On that fullmoon I rang one of the group participants to offer her a lift, for the journey was long.

When we started out, it turned out that giving this lift was a significant quirk of fate – here comes the Mars-Jupiter conjunction in Pisces. We found we had a lot to discuss about releasing and forgiving recent events in our individual lives. Though Mars conjunct Jupiter is usually a strong-willed and assertive kind of aspect, it was classically Piscean in this case: to start on the next phase of our lives we each had to free up shadows from the last phase, and this we did on the journey through sharing our situations.

Another quirk of fate came along. We visited a friend *en route* who, it turned out, seemed meant to meet us at that very moment: we all connected on a deep, wordless level – it was encouraging and strengthening for all of us. The mysterious element of Pisces modified the Mars-Jupiter energy, creating connections 'out of time' which proved significant.

We continued on our journey on the Friday, on the buildup to a Mercury conjunct Saturn in Sagittarius that evening. I was deliberately patient, for all the way along the winding roads we had tractors, slow trucks, wandering sheep and dozy drivers in front of us, making the journey something of a test. Nevertheless we got there. At the exact moment of the Mercury conjunct Saturn, my passenger had me down on the floor while she was manipulating my back and cracking my bones – a very relieving bit of Saturnine therapy!

The next day there was a Mercury square Jupiter at 6.45pm in Sagittarius. All of the group participants arrived within one hour after that! It's amazing how people fit in with astrological realities even if they do not know they are doing so. A wide square of Jupiter in Pisces to Saturn in Sagittarius was hanging around, and this was re-enlivened by Mercury: for me this event was the first step in an entirely new chapter of work. So here we have an example of how a shorter-term cycle involving Mercury interweaves with a longer-term one (Jupiter-Saturn).

Late on the Sunday there was a Mercury square Mars. Some honest truths had to be faced in the group, and one of the participants chose to go home because of difficulties he was encountering. This involved some deft handling, but it worked out. Things brightened up in the evening of the Monday, in connection with a Venus trine Jupiter – everyone started mixing congenially and openly and the group bonded and we all opened up to each other. On the Thursday, there was a Mercury conjunct Uranus in Sagittarius, around which time I was expecting an outburst of excited prattling and hyperactivity amongst the group but, interestingly, this did not happen.

What did happen was that, within themselves, several participants came to conclusions about questions they individually were working with – something clicked for each of them, and the atmosphere in the group picked up. On the Friday a combination of Sun semisquare Venus and Mercury semisquare Pluto forced everyone to face up to the fact that the group was ending, and that we would all soon be parting company. This duly took place the next day. On that day was a Sun-Neptune conjunction: I learned that, in future, I would arrange for groups not to end on such an aspect, for it leaves everyone somewhat unready to leave! Such an aspect, bringing up a generally spacy, indefinite atmosphere, is best for the middle of a group rather than its end. You live and learn!

Another group of people was to arrive that day, to start a new week-long session. In classic Neptunian style, many were delayed and we had a fuzzy, staggered start to the group. The late arrivals came two days later on a Mars square Uranus, which brought enough zap and initiative to get everyone there. Yet, again, all of the people arriving got there within one hour of the aspect at 5pm. The group continued, and I shall spare you the remainder of the story.

However, a footnote. During this time there were more than the usual smattering of aspects going on – this was a contributory factor to my choosing those dates. But the Sun-Neptune conjunction didn't work well. You cannot always have things as you want them, and sometimes you have to go by diary dates, weekends and public holidays when planning events, so this is a 'luck of the draw' issue. But this wee anecdote illustrates how things work, and it's also a reminder that it's best to observe how things actually unfold, without seeking to fit reality into an astrological preconception of how things will be. This said, astrology nevertheless offers good clues.

Experiencing it all

The trouble with giving potted descriptions of astrological concepts is that they can oversimplify things. While the descriptive paragraphs in this chapter will give you ways of tuning into changing tones of energy, their scope is not limited by what is stated. We can all experience the liberating and fulfilling sides of a planet one day, and then the restricting and unwholesome sides the next – part of this is the 'energy weather' and part is our mood, frame of mind and choices made.

Observe time as it moves and you will gain a feel for the workings of the planets. Piece together the jigsaw bit by bit. When you feel it is all getting laborious, try less hard, stay on the case and let your deeper self lead you to whatever you need to find out next. When you feel at a loss, as if you'll never fully understand astrology, you're on the edge of something: *let it come*. You have your own way of seeing things and working with astrology: *let it speak*.

Next we're going to look at planetary arrays – the spread of planets around the zodiac.

14

Planetary Arrays

This is about the general distribution of planets around the zodiac at any time. Arrays give an overview of whole energy-atmospheres and the way that energy-weather knits together astrologically. This chapter is mainly for reference, but it's worth a skip-through.

Spreads

At any moment, the planets as a whole form an array or a spread which at times can take on interesting patterns. The planets do not have to be *in aspect*: what we are looking at here is the way they are splattered around the zodiac. This helps in diagnosing the underlying message of the time. A whole range of different arrays are possible: below we shall run through the main variations.

The general rule is that, the more tightly packed a group of planets, the more focused, specific, concentrated and one-sided is the character of the energy-weather of the time. The more widely-spread they are, the more varied, rounded, multi-tasked and eclectic is the atmosphere.

The question for tighter arrays is whether that issue-focused bias imposes heavily on the world, creating imbalanced situations with difficult longterm effects, or some sort of disjunction or unfortunate drift of events. Things might look good or important within the limited viewpoint of the time, but are they beneficial in the longterm? The question for wider arrays is whether sufficient attention is given to specific issues, or whether they are overridden or obscured by a relative cacophony of disparate issues all competing for attention or getting fudged together.

There are some loose parallels here to the difference between a conjunction and an opposition. With a conjunction we see the world from within our own personal or group viewpoint. With an opposition we are much more affected by the wider situation we find ourselves in and with questions of how to fit in with it.

Hemispheric pattern (Bowl)

Here all planets are arrayed within half of the zodiac, leaving the other half empty. Time-energy and activity is highly focused in one particular part of the full spectrum of life (symbolised by the full half and the signs and sequence of planets there). The other area of life (the empty half) remains either unfulfilled, overlooked or omitted. Tight clusters within this bowl will focus the issues even more.

The question is whether the issues connected with the signs in the empty half can be integrated intentionally by giving them attention, compensating for the imbalance present. This configuration will of course counterbalance itself over time, for while all planets can be in one half of the zodiac for a time, the Moon and faster planets will move out of this array, leaving the slower planets where they are, eventually forming a contrasting Seesaw, Bucket or similar shape.

With this and the following two arrays, the leader and trailer are important. The leader is the first planet in the array, and the trailer is the last, in zodiacal order. The leader gives a clue about the way the world is approaching the issues of the time, or the cutting edge of the issue, and the trailer indicates the wake it is leaving behind or the unintended effects the situation is creating.

Interestingly, the discovery of Chiron in 1977 changed the perception of what was happening at the time because, when it appeared, it was in opposition to a Bowl array of planets, then in the autumnal area of the zodiac, forming a Bucket out of the Bowl. The last Bowl formation of consequence was around the autumns of 1945-48, when all planets lay between Cancer and Sagittarius (except when Moon swung into the empty part of the zodiac to form a Bucket).

This was a time where social welfare and the common good were rather emphasised, sparked off particularly by the Jupiter-Chiron-Neptune conjunction in Libra in autumn 1945 – a configuration bringing peace and the dawn of social welfare systems in Europe, the founding of the United Nations, the seeds of the European Community and the beginning of the post-war social democratic heyday. The Yod of 1980, arising when Chiron was discovered in 1977, is mentioned elsewhere in this book.

Bundle or Cluster pattern

In this formation all planets are tightly arrayed within 120° or just four signs. This concentrates energy further than the Bowl, to the extent that the collective psyche can become single-minded, obsessed or imbalanced, focused so much on particular preoccupations, ways of seeing things and areas of attention that there is little perspective present. This piles all the energy into particular issues to the exclusion of other things, which at the 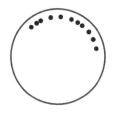 time are regarded as peripheral or trivial, or even non-existent. It certainly makes certain possibilities come into being, converting potentiality into actuality in limited areas, for this is a powerful concentration: but the question is what the purpose is, and whether the means are justified in their intensity. People can get carried away, fixated and monomanic during such times.

Thus, it is wise here to consciously widen awareness to overall issues, to see how the question at hand fits into the bigger picture and the longer term. The signs opposite this array give reflective insights into how this should be counterbalanced – otherwise there is the risk that such a situation will go off at a tangent, creating ripples and effects which later have enduring or regrettable consequences.

An example of the bundle at work was the mid-WW2 period, around autumn 1942, when all planets lay between the signs Gemini and Virgo. At this time WW2 turned around as a result of decisive all-out battles, and the newly winning Allied side, fighting Germany and Japan, became fixated on winning the war at all costs while the other side, of course, was fixated on not losing. The worst and most damaging aspects of WW2 happened during the time when the matter of WW2 was more or less resolved – though at the time no one was sure of this. In history, declining empires can be at their most destructive.

As with the above example of a bowl formation, this array formed, when the faster-moving planets swung into the same zodiacal area as the slower moving ones. It was a time of one-pointed, even fanatical warmongery, with all planets focused in the self-oriented summer signs. As soon as Neptune, Chiron and Jupiter moved over the autumn equinox point into Libra at the end of the war, this narrowness of perspective eased off, and international cooperation generally grew thereafter, leading to the pursuit of the notion of human rights and the founding of the UN.

Locomotive or Open-angle pattern

Here, all planets occupy up to two-thirds of the zodiac or eight signs, leaving a 120° four-sign gap empty. Energy is quite all-round in expression, but there is a hole in the empty one-third of the zodiac, an area of life needing acute attention: the centre of this empty segment and its sign is particularly significant as a key to making the whole array work.

The empty part points to an area of life to be fulfilled to render the array whole, and sometimes frenetic energy must be put into it to plug gaps or deal with important unattended details – especially when the Moon moves through it. This balancing does not happen naturally: it must be *intended*. The gap shows a hidden gift, a vital piece in the jigsaw, a weak link in the chain.

Autumn 1952 provided an example of a Locomotive array: at this time, Jupiter, the leading planet, had crossed to Taurus, and Chiron the trailer was in Capricorn, creating a gap between them. Another example is autumn 1966, when a gap appeared between Saturn-Chiron in late Pisces and Jupiter in late Cancer. The former array focused energy on empty Pisces – indicating a need for deeper vision – and the latter focused on empty Taurus – need for ongoing, steady perseverance, grounding and creativity.

Bucket or Wedge pattern

With the Bucket, all but one planet occupy up to half of the zodiac, but then one planet, a *singleton*, occupies the empty half. Sometimes two planets can act as singletons if close together. The singleton then becomes a focal planet, a key to the whole formation. The handle doesn't hold water, but it does allow the bucket to be borne easily. If this singleton planet is grasped and made use of, it focuses all of the other planets, turning the key to the whole energy-configuration.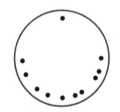

With a Wedge array, all planets apart from the singleton are within two-thirds of the zodiac or eight consecutive signs. This is more energy-balanced than the Bucket but still, the singleton plays a focal role in the array as a whole.

Often there is resistance, fear or hesitation to use the singleton in a Bucket or Wedge, for the stakes can be high, and it represents something in the meaning of the time which is quite radically different from the dominant tone of the array. (The author's own birth chart is a bucket, with Jupiter in Pisces as the singleton).

If or when there is an opposition formed between the singleton and one or more key planets in the full half, then this opposition provides a link to resolving major dilemmas that might be present, and any flowing aspects from the singleton, such as a trine, will ease up tension or conflict. Since there is a good chance the singleton will be retrograde (since it is near opposition to the Sun – unless it is the Moon), initially it becomes a mystery to crack, a factor that requires some grappling and wrestling, but it pays big dividends when mastered. Mercury and Venus cannot be singletons because they are always close to the Sun, and if the Sun is in the empty half it will not be alone, so it can't qualify as a singleton, and the array won't be a Bucket. The leader and trailer of the main body give clues as to how we can move forward (leader) and work with the after-effects of our acts and choices (trailer).

In the early 1980s, especially in autumntime, several bucket formations formed with Chiron in Taurus as the handle, provoking interesting opportunities to wreak miracles and maverick solutions to the problems of that time. Thus we saw the rise of grass-roots single-issue movements, groups of people who began to play a large part in influencing public attitudes, or who seeded new solutions to large-scale world problems: here came the rising public effect of feminism, complementary health, the Green and disarmament movements, Islamic fundamentalism, Polish Solidarity and third world localist movements.

In springtime, after such bucket arrays in the 1980s, when faster planets moved to join Chiron, an approximate Seesaw formed, featured strongly at certain fullmoons. In a Bucket, power is generated by the main body of planets but focused by the singleton, while in a Seesaw, power is generated on both sides, juxtaposed in dynamic tension. Chiron, in this case, made a subtle yet magical contribution to world affairs following its 1977 debut, summoning the strength to become catalytic when in Gemini from 1984 on, bringing about major flips of perspective – such as the quite sudden and historic end of the Cold War, moving the global emphasis from an East-West to a North-South dialogue.

Seesaw pattern

Here there are two definite groups of planets, ideally in opposition to one another, with a minimum of two signs on either side separating their groupings, and no more than one sign empty in either group. This carries an amplified opposition symbolism, just as the Bundle carries an amplified conjunction symbolism. However, if the two groups of planets are not directly opposite one another, being skewed, then look for the prevailing aspects involved to form a judgement on what it implies. In general, life here resolves itself into two quite separate components, tending to pull apart, each attempting dominance or separation.

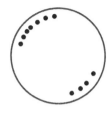

The task at hand is to recognise that this tension is happening. Dualism can have polarising and negative consequences, but there can be wonders and benefits too: it is necessary to connect and integrate the two if significant progress is to be made. Without this, longterm splits and schisms can occur, reflected in social groups or world issues. If there is success in reconciling the dualism, breakthroughs are likely since a healing takes place bringing about relief across society.

If the configuration has more planets on one side than the other, then there will still be two factors at work, but they might not outrightly conflict: instead one side might dominate the other, although the other side might attempt to subvert or weaken the stronger side. The two sides need proper introduction and reconciliation.

The results of this dualism can be varied, depending on the relative weighting of each side, what planets are involved, and what people do. One side can dominate the other but be irked by guilt or subconscious self-sabotage; one side can lead the other but keep it subservient; both can compromise one another, leading to indecision, fudging and non-resolution; one can be consciously held as 'us' while the other is projected outwards and seen as 'them'; or both can be recognised and a balance sought, through oscillating between extremes and taking a middle path. When the Moon swings through this configuration, to one side and then the other, each side will alternately be featured or strengthened. Crucial points come when Moon forms a square to both sides.

One example of a Seesaw was the oft-quoted 1989 line-up of planets, mainly in Capricorn-Cancer. In the Cold War and also in South Africa, a dangerous polarisation was quite miraculously resolved, mainly through relatively enlightened and sensible thinking – the conflict between governments and people was resolved in the Soviet bloc and major conflict and repression was avoided and, in South Africa, the apartheid system was dissembled. However, in China, with the Tiananmen Square democracy movement, suppression ensued and the matter of popular influence or control over governmental power was squashed, to await another day.

Tripod pattern

This pattern is formed when there are three distinct groupings of planets, ideally forming trine links between each other – though often it's more skewed than that. This can make for a time where there is considerable understanding and stability (depending on the symmetry of the pattern), with energy left over for creativity, cultural ascendancy or inventive potential. These times are relaxing, bridge-building times, fostering agreement and synergy: growth and developments are furthered.

Whether this pattern flows well depends on its symmetry, the planets and where they sit, how concentrated in groups they are, and also what humans do. If the pattern forms a roughly T-square configuration, then there are hurdles to cross, pointed out by the empty gap. If there is a preponderance of sesquiquadrate aspects, then longterm aims and projects and historical perspectives become the issue, prompted by immediate circumstances. With a preponderance of trine aspects, life can become easy and decadent, or productive and creative, with an opening up of society and culture.

Splash formation

Here the planets are randomly arrayed with no noticeable patterns. Deducing what this implies depends on looking at any dominant aspect-patterns that are present, which might pull out key themes. This formation suggests an all-round versatility or wide spread of issues, which might either be related but contrasting (if strong aspects are present) or unrelated and diffuse. A single clear message or theme is not present, and life goes on. Times like these have disparate issues going on, leading in different directions. There are various assorted issues to work through rather than one or a few 'biggies'.

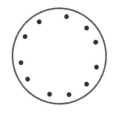

A Splash is often the formation identified when no other formations can be found, making it a general-purpose pattern to answer various calls. Thus it is not clearly a pattern in itself. Look at the empty gaps in the splash, if there are any, for indications of areas of life that need attending to.

Splay

Not unlike a Splash, there is a wide spread of planets, but with distinct clusters of neighbouring planets, giving this array a certain coherence, establishing dominant themes and movements of energy. Certain areas of life will possess special meaning, indicated by the concentrations present. These take on a predominant flavour, providing decisive influences in an otherwise generalised field. Splays should be interpreted case by case.

Star patterns

Very occasionally the planets form into a relatively regular or symmetric Star pattern, highly inter-aspected, with four, five or more points to it. In rare cases it will be symmetrical (such as a Grand Sextile as mentioned in chapter 12). The planets do not have to be aspected to each other: they need simply form a roughly regular pattern which stands out. It can be, for example, that while the planets do not form a coherent pattern of aspects to one another, they do form angles repeating themselves throughout the array: situations such as this indicate a uniqueness to the moment, a special magic that comes once every now and then.

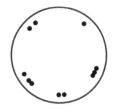

How arrays manifest in real-life terms depends on the planets involved, and the signs and aspects. Often you will find thematic links where different astrological factors, unrelated to each other, point to a particular message that is coming through. This is not uncommon: if there is a distinct message to the time, it will often show itself in a few different ways. Every power point in time and kind of energy-weather is in some way *meant to be*, in the organic logic of universal unfoldment, carrying a special dispensation.

Arrays give us an insight into the overall atmosphere. They can help us integrate a complex diagnosis of the times into some sort of wholeness. They don't tend to activate energy specifically, except through the aspects forming within them. But they do give a period a certain overall flavour, helping us form an overview of the current of the time.

15

The Slower Planets and their Capers

The slower, outer planets move in their own longterm time-spectrum, bringing about energy-periods, historic trends, peaks and troughs that affect decades and centuries. Here we shall examine the deeper background issues of history affected by the outer planets.

World Change

In our civilisation we live a schizoid life, sectioning up our psyches, with two sides operating relatively independently, though regularly interfering or conflicting with each other. One side is the 'front story', the conscious, that programmed, socialised, educated side of us that toes the official line, well stocked with rationalisations, beliefs, obligations, habits, judgements and narratives that we tell ourselves are happening and real. It's official, legal and approved, as long as you behave yourself.

Then there is another side, the 'back story', rooted in our deeper selves, that sees and senses things in another way, perceiving a very different slant on what is underneath and behind what we tell ourselves is happening. It feels moods, hunches, intuitions and knowings that are semiconscious, unconscious or at least privately held. It operates in the context of social subgroups and society as a whole, as well as for nature and time – all entities have thoughts and feelings, and collectively-held feelings can greatly influence personally-held ones.

Usually most people don't intentionally access the back story, though it comes up at moments when normality is suspended, when we are feeling relaxed, ill, shocked, dying, overwhelmed by life or simply 'feeling strange'. It comes up in the public domain when powerfully symbolic or impactful events hit us in the news, and sometimes a collective intuition can go against a publicly-held official truth. This side of us knows things our conscious, socialised, front-story side doesn't.

The 'official line', the collective front story, is maintained largely by Jupiter and Saturn, which in this context are like a carrot and a stick keeping us in line. The outer planets have more to do with the back story, less controllable and a source of gifts and challenges that, in the end, push forward our evolution as souls, wearing down our resistances and at times taking over our lives. They cause involuntary changes in society and nature, raising important, deeper questions with a game-changing effect. They are acted out every day in the public domain in social dramas, news headlines, documentaries and real-life situations, enacting triumphs and traumas, humour, poignancy and inconvenient truths.

To live more in accord with nature and human need, we need to embrace the energy-impulses of the outer planets. This involves loosening our rather neurotic, controlling relationship with the known so that it responds better to the elasticising and reality-bearing input of the unknown. It means opening channels between the worlds of Jupiter-Saturn and Uranus-Neptune-Pluto, with Chiron as a linking agent. The challenge is to make this a wider social phenomenon, taking it beyond the personal into the social and cultural domain. This is a para-political, meta-cultural and pan-spiritual issue.

Fundamental social changes often arise spontaneously or emerge from the back-streets, though occasionally visionary activity at the top of society takes the lead. This is where the back story impinges on the front story through the symbolic power of events, or through people, movements or ideas who communicate or embody potent imagery or messages.

The outer planets move slowly, affecting historic-scale undercurrents lying within and beneath present-day events. A hot summer, a political shift, a disaster, economic fluctuations, social phenomena, wars and celebrations all have their accepted manifest characteristics – denoted mainly by Jupiter, Saturn and the inner planets – yet their deeper significance and impact is what the outer planets bring into the equation. They add extra dimensions of depth to normality, tinkering with the rules of the normality game itself.

Thus, with extreme weather events, Jupiter and Saturn might influence routine variations in weather such as storms or droughts lying within an accepted range of possibility, even if at times extreme. But Uranus, Neptune and Pluto inject wider implications, imagery and significance into such situations, or they turn down the screws to bend normality. They can turn a storm into a nightmare or an inspiration, a phenomenon carrying a message and impacting more profoundly. The outer planets make a deeper impact down in life's cellars and foundations, affecting social values, collective experiences and systemic economic conditions. They contribute toward migrations, wars, technology disasters and other large scale phenomena, influencing collective conclusions drawn from events such as these.

If this subject interests you, refer to *The Historical Ephemeris* on the author's website.

Discoveries

In astrology it is said that a planet is discovered when human consciousness is ready to incorporate what it brings. Uranus was discovered in 1781, Neptune in 1846 and Pluto in 1930. Each of these times marked a turning-point: Uranus came just before the American and French Revolutions, as the early industrial revolution gathered momentum; Neptune came along at the time when urban-industrial culture was embedding itself, with new capital owners, bourgeoisies and working classes, and as the fruits of contact with other cultures through expanding European empires were having an increasing effect; Pluto came at the dawn of totalitarian dictatorships, mass-media and techno-globalism, at the lift-off period of the modern electronic age. Such discoveries do not *cause* events, yet they bring new factors and perceptions into the equation which hadn't been seen before.

In the *Historical Ephemeris* (see the author's website), a 2,600 year timeline of historical events is laid alongside the movements of the outer planets. A few hours spent perusing this timeline will reveal that the outer planets indeed had a marked and visible influence on human affairs long before they were discovered, and without the astrologers of the time knowing it. Jesus was born on an opposition of Uranus in Pisces to Pluto in Virgo. Rome fell to the Visigoths on a Neptune conjunct Pluto in Taurus, squaring Uranus in Aquarius, indicating that, to survive, it would have had to regenerate and rebirth itself, or it would die. It was indeed rebirthed in the founding of the Byzantine empire in Constantinople, as well as in the rise to dominance in Rome of the Pope and the Catholic Church, for the next thousand years – though these were offshoots from a failed civilisation rather than the transformation of an existing one.

In 1977, Chiron was discovered. Though a small planetoid, its orbital position between Saturn and Uranus gives it particular significance. Its symbol, a key, suggests a small item with a big effect, and around 1977-80 something shifted in real terms. Chiron is a link between two worlds – the known and the unknown, the inner and outer planets.

In recent decades a number of new planetoids have been discovered beyond Pluto, all except one of them (Eris) being smaller than Pluto and having longer orbital periods than that of Pluto. Faraway Sedna has a cycle of 10,500 years, though most cycles are measured in centuries. These planetoids act as minor qualifiers to our understanding of life and astrology and it will take time for astrologers to identify their specific contribution and natures, though starting stabs at this have been made.

The planets were always there. Once discovered, a new planet shows us something about reality that we have just become ready to see. Even if this knowledge is limited to astrologers, the identification of new sidereal and synodic cycles involving newly-discovered planets helps us understand the way that the cogs and gears of history work.

Evolution of Consciousness

Here we are in a large-scale realm of astrology: the study of history and its manner of progression. Acts of Parliament, the accessions of monarchs, battles fought or specific events that happened matter less here than overall trends and developments, except when such specific events symbolise something larger, or unless they act as definitive tipping-points.

This introduces a deeper aspect to the study of history – psycho-history. Giving focus to Uranus, Neptune and Pluto highlights the undercurrents and hidden psycho-emotional background to events. When we talk of events, we usually focus on the time when these impacted on the world or on majorities of people, but often they were brewing for some time before – inventors quietly beavering away in workshops, ideas being discussed, plans being hatched and circumstances falling into place – and it is this invisible or formative aspect that constitutes a key part of the historical process. Astrology highlights this.

Thus, while the Russian Revolution took place in 1917 (when no major outer-planet aspects were happening), the first and failed Russian Revolution of 1905 created the social preconditions for 1917. In 1905 a Uranus opposition Neptune was building up (1906-1910). Additionally, a major schism had taken place between reformists and revolutionaries in 1902 during a Uranus opposition Pluto and a major surge of political awareness occurred in Russia in a famine in 1892-3 during a Neptune conjunct Pluto – these were the ground-laying factors. So while the revolution took place in 1917, perhaps even running late, the groundwork and heavy lifting happened previously during a series of earlier outer-planet aspects, brought forward by heroes and pioneers largely forgotten and unsung. The real action often takes place amongst quite small numbers of people, unbeknownst to others until it becomes news. A seed is a small, fragile thing compared to a tree, yet without that seed a tree wouldn't exist.

Our present time, far from being historically boring, is a valuable time to live in, from the evolutionary viewpoint of the soul. Not least because we as individuals each consciously or unconsciously channel the energies of the outer planets ourselves, and there is now more than twice the population on Earth as in the 1960s, so there are far more souls partaking of this than before. We are creators of the future and we need to set a historical precedent by choosing our future more wisely, participating more actively in history-making and in the profound choices involved. Social intent and change-inducing contributions by individuals and movements, as appropriate to their situation, locality and people, are globally crucial issues today.

Manifestation: Jupiter and Saturn

Uranus, Neptune and Pluto move in tune with cycles and waves of motion deep within the collective unconscious. We individuals are micro-cells within the world psyche, and the social sub-groups we play a part in operate as molecules or bundles of micro-cells. But our behaviour as individuals is rather different from our behaviour in a crowd or in the context of social subgroups we belong and subscribe to – a person's character and personal views might be different to their political behaviour; and their groupthink beliefs. There is also a difference between espoused, consciously-held attitudes and unconscious behaviour.

Jupiter and Saturn, within their own sphere, work in the realm of the known and the intended, on a more conscious, social-institutional level, through the agreements, norms, conventions, laws, structures and culturally-agreed behaviour patterns that make society work – the stuff that's routinely reported in the newspapers, taught in schools and usually called 'reality'. When they connect with Uranus, Neptune and Pluto they bring deeper impulses into ordinary life, translating their transformative influences into institutionalised form through their cycles of aspects to the outermost planets.

Jupiter, on a twelve year cycle, regularly conjuncts each of the outer planets every 13-14 years, passing through a cycle of relationship with each of them. Jupiter precipitates events and trends in the social and natural domains, pushing issues forward, bringing them to a head, mediating deep outer-planet tides of change into the realm of the known and the recognised.

For example, the entry of Neptune into Capricorn in January 1984 brought with it an impulse to ground and realise the perspectives which thirteen years of its sojourn in Sagittarius – a cosmic and visionary place for Neptune – had stimulated during the 1970s. Computers had developed since the 1950s but, before 1984, they were used by big organisations only as mainframes, while in the 1980s the PC and the first portable devices appeared, making computers more widely available to ordinary people. This shift laid the ground for further shifts: by the time Neptune entered Aquarius in 1997, this process gathered momentum, leading to such socially-transformative phenomena as online social networking (MySpace, Facebook and Twitter), a major social-cultural development facilitated by technological change. Uranus had also entered Aquarius in 1995 for seven years, also powering up the technological and social-group aspect of Aquarius.

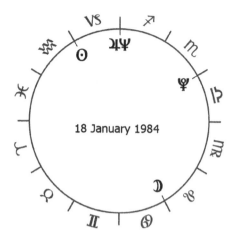

18 January 1984

Hapwise, back in 1984, Jupiter moved into Capricorn *on exactly the same day* as Neptune (that's rare!), boosting Neptune's ingress. Around this time there was a creeping perception that things were potentially falling apart, or materialism was in decline, and that we were making a quantum shift into a new and promising, or scary, world – depending on your viewpoint. It gave new life to corporate oligarchy, capitalism and consumerism during the Reagan-Thatcher period, by giving materialism, property-owning and financial markets almost cult status. Underneath this was an unconscious urge to 'get rich quick before it's too late', staging a clearance sale of the bounties of humanity and planet Earth, in the face of looming ecological threats, social change and a feeling of pending crisis.

Jupiter in this case brought the Neptunian influence into more concrete form, during the mutual ingress. Later, this influence was tested by the Saturn-Neptune conjunction of 1989, when the Soviet system proved unviable, China was transiting into a new state and Western military and consumer capitalism sought new stimuli to keep on growing – this it did by extending into the Soviet system and developing countries, growing its markets and resource base, resorting to new technologies and creating new wars to give it extra lift. The Saturn-Uranus conjunction in 1988 had scissored the future from the past, putting an end to various obsolete ideas, such as that of the Cold War and all that it implied. However, this time was characterised, in classic Neptune in Capricorn fashion, with a feeling that everything was perfectly normal and stable when in fact it wasn't – arguably, people were being fooled, bribed and cajoled into compliance and belief in a renewed cult of materialism, and many of them knew it but went into denial. Denial and illusion-building are classic Neptunian syndromes.

The Uranus conjunct Pluto in Virgo of 1965-66 was grounded in a similar way by an opposition from Saturn conjuncting Chiron in Pisces. The immense technological changes of the time (Virgo) gave birth to the microchip, genetic engineering and a new high-tech age, counterbalanced by Piscean-style large-scale perspectives – the 'global village', consciousness change, the space race and a burst of new ideas both scientific and alternative. (The chart for this time is in chapter 10.) The consciousness revolution of the time was both counterbalanced and fired up by many of the sobering hard realities of the day (such as Vietnam). The seeds of the new dispensation were grounded in definite, available forms – drugs, sex, music, new diets and lifestyles – which acted as a gateway to further things. The headiness of the mid-60s was supplemented by Jupiter in Gemini in 1966 – books, ideas and musical beats and rhythms!

The 20-year cycle of Jupiter's relationship with Saturn is worth watching. Once every sixty years they conjunct at roughly the same place in the zodiac – traditional Chinese astrology is built on this sixty-year cycle, called the *mutation cycle*. In addition, successive twenty year conjunctions occur in signs of one element, the element changing (on a 'great mutation') every so often. Jupiter conjuncted Saturn in Capricorn in 1842, in Virgo in 1862, in Taurus in 1881, in Capricorn in 1901, in Virgo in 1921, in Taurus in 1940, in Capricorn in 1961, then in Libra in 1981, and in late Taurus in 2000. The Libran conjunction in 1981 was a harbinger of future conjunctions in the air signs through the 21st century.

The Jupiter-Saturn cycle affects organisations and institutions, business, social causes and groupings, money markets, technology and engineering, energy and resources, production and consumption, manifest cultural changes and shifts of values, education, diplomatic and trade relations. Since conjunctions mark beginnings and trans-cyclical watersheds, they might not necessarily bring immediate manifest developments except in symbolic form. The action happens throughout the cycle, with crunch-points at the squares and the opposition.

Thus there was a Jupiter-Saturn conjunction in 1961, waxing square in 1965, opposition in 1970, waning square in 1975-76, a conjunction in 1981, waxing square in 1986, opposition in 1989-90, waning square in 1995, a conjunction in 2000, waxing square in 2005, opposition in 2010, and there is a waning square in 2015 and conjunction in 2020. Think about the progression of events in recent decades, and you'll see this cycle at work. As an example, in the case of recent Soviet/ Russian history, we had the Solidarity movement in Poland in 1981, Gorbachev and *perestroika* in 1986, the fall of the Berlin Wall in 1989, Yeltsin and Chechnya in 1995 and the arrival of president Putin in 2000.

Worth noting also are Saturn's seven-year sidereal sub-cycles, dividing its 29ish year cycle into four quarters: it often takes seven years or multiples thereof for an idea or possibility to be grounded into normal reality, to move from plan to actuality. Jupiter's quarter sub-cycles are three years long. The movement of each of these two planets through the signs greatly affects the social realm and our participation in it. It is worth observing changes occurring around the times when Jupiter and Saturn cross the quarter and cross-quarter points in the zodiac too, as well as ingresses.

Jupiter and Saturn handle relatively short-term developments, historically speaking. Twelve and twenty-nine years seem like a long time, but in terms of the life of a big centuries-old tree, or the passage of history, they're small-fry. Yet Jupiter and Saturn do help fix longer-term influences from the outer planets, injecting these influences into manifest reality – the synodic cycles of Jupiter and Saturn to Uranus, Neptune and Pluto indicate and time this process. When occasionally they come together, as they did in 1965 (Saturn opposition Uranus and Pluto, squared by Jupiter) or in 1989 (Saturn conjuncting Uranus and Neptune, opposed by Jupiter), sparks fly. As it happens, Chiron was involved in both line-ups, though this is not automatically the case – it's simply a sign of the beauty of the way things happen.

Deeper Stuff

There is a difference between an ingress and a major aspect involving the outer planets. When there is a sign-change, a change of theme, backdrop and orientation takes place in which old issues and viewpoints lapse and new ones emerge. When, in 2008, Pluto shifted from Sagittarius (where it had been since 1995) into Capricorn, the 'credit crunch' struck. Normally, such an ingress wouldn't necessarily produce clear events such as this but, in this case, it demonstrates how economic confidence rests on the subjective beliefs of investors, lenders and borrowers – their mood changed, and the economy of the developed world plummeted, wiping out trillions very quickly.

Those Sagittarian beliefs (growth, optimism and expansionism) rapidly subsided when Pluto shifted into conservative, sceptical Capricorn, and the economic excesses of previous years were suddenly judged no longer viable. It wasn't Pluto that brought recession to the West: it was a collapse of optimism and confidence, prompted by Pluto. Lessons should have been learned in the 1980s and early 1990s when Uranus and Neptune were in Capricorn, concerning debt-leveraging and the creation of dangerous high-profit financial artifices in the money markets, but they weren't learned, so when Pluto hit Capricorn, reality struck.

To give another example, Pluto in Capricorn concerns national boundaries and nation-states as institutions. Since 2008, many state boundaries have been eroded through migration, smuggling, trade laws, investment, terrorism, civil war and other incremental factors. Separatist movements burst out, particularly when the Uranus-Pluto square started kicking in around 2011. This didn't concern inter-state wars, which are increasingly non-viable: it was an erosion of borders, increasingly by 'non-state actors' or simply by masses of migrating people. It also started a phase of proxy wars, mainly in the Middle East – wealthy powers and reckless billionaires giving money to non-state military groups to fight wars for them.

The hidden underlying theme here is that nation states are gradually yet rapidly becoming obsolete – founded as many are by oligarchies and imperialists of the past, not necessarily shaped by peoples, geographical realities or current needs. The growth of nationalism is a sign of a belated emotional reaction to this incremental erosion. Things are changing: the world has massive global-scale problems and the jostling of nearly 200 sovereign states is not a viable way to solve world issues, so the world has been forming into socio-political continents, particularly since 1993 and the Uranus-Neptune conjunction. The world map will probably look different by the time Pluto leaves Capricorn in 2024. *Impossible*, say most, believing that normality rules. Well, it's happening. The only fixed boundaries on planet Earth are the coastal edges of the land – and even these are rather in doubt if sea levels change.

At these points in history, possibilities seep through into current realities from the future: the future becomes a cause of the present. Poignant events make a headline out of an otherwise surreptitious trend. Humanity has an insidious habit of walking into the future facing backwards, meanwhile ignoring or denying inconvenient chunks of reality – this is a bad formula for creating a better world.

When an important outer planet aspect forms, semi-conscious dynamics are set in motion in the group psyche. This produces transformations and breakthroughs – or breakdowns, breakouts, failures, collapses, disasters and dramas. The latter can be tragic, yet it's what we do with them that matters. If in the sacrifice of lives we learn fundamental lessons helping us to save future lives and more fundamentally address the causes of the world's problems, then there is meaning to people's suffering, even though individuals suffer terribly. People don't have to suffer as much as they do – it's our politics, economics and social psychology that do much of that. Even in natural disasters there is a variation of responses we can make which, even when lives are lost, can assist the survivors and help the future. Cyclone Haiyan was an example of that: affected people responded to it cooperatively, avoiding many potential negative effects – this is an example of social choice in action.

Outer planet aspects bring times when a dispensation is filtered through from deep down, laying the seeds of subsequent changes, even if they take years, decades or centuries to emerge. To go a long way back, when Uranus, Neptune and Pluto did a major mutual conjunction in 578-575 BCE, the Aryan people were in the ascendancy in northern India, the Phoenicians were spreading across the Mediterranean, the Upanishads and parts of the Old Testament were being written, and Lao Tzu and the Buddha were soon to begin their work. But the underlying historic issue was that a new realm of thought, spirituality and civilisation was starting – more patriarchal, hierarchical, impressive, cross-cultural, violent, doctrinal and urbanised – to unfold across the world over the following centuries. This configuration is something that still affects us now.

In 1395-96, Uranus opposed a Neptune conjunction with Pluto, bringing the clear end of the medieval period and the seed point of the European Renaissance. It brought changes across the world too (the Incas, Ottomans, Ming China and Mughal India), but developments in the relatively backward Europe of the time became the seed-point of a story that was to unfold over the following 500 years until Europeans dominated the world. The underlying theme here is the planetarisation of humanity, with its roots in the 1390s, today achieved technically and economically, though we are yet to work out the full and rather painful cultural, religious and human aspects of it.

Orbits

Uranus moves round the zodiac in 84 years, Neptune in 165 years and Pluto in just under 250 years. Neptune's orbit is roughly twice and Pluto's is roughly three times that of Uranus. Also, Uranus' orbit is three Saturn orbits and seven of Jupiter. So all of the outer planets are approximately, though not exactly, in sync with each other.

Uranus conjuncts Pluto either in 111 or 143 years (variable because of Pluto's eccentric orbit), Uranus conjuncts Neptune every 171 years, and Neptune conjuncts Pluto roughly every 495 years.

Chiron is on a cycle of 51 years, eccentric to the extent that reliable figures over a long period are difficult to calculate – the earliest reliable date for Chiron's movements is around 1700. Chiron is closest to the Sun (perihelion) when at 8° Libra (in 1945, 1996 and 2046), and furthest (aphelion) when at 8° Aries (1920, 1970 and 2021). Chiron comes inside the orbit of Saturn at perihelion and outside the orbit of Uranus at aphelion. Note the symbolism – Chiron acts as a link between the conscious and unconscious. It is probable that Chiron is not indigenous to our solar system, instead gravitationally captured, and astronomers theorise that it might swing out of the solar system at some point in future astronomic time (don't worry – you'll have swung out yourself long before then).

Pluto is in perihelion at 12 Scorpio (1989) and at aphelion at 12 Taurus (1865-6 and 2114). Pluto comes inside the orbit of Neptune when at perihelion (1978-2000) – and it moves far away when at aphelion.

Pluto is a bringer of the inevitable, destroying the old and forcing emergence of the new. When it was discovered in 1930, steam power was dying away in favour of oil and electricity, and the extremes of the 20th Century were presenting themselves in the form of economic depression, totalitarianism and major social and technological change. Pluto turns the pages of history, sometimes disastrously through 'creative destruction', ripping us out of the past and thrusting us into a daunting future. Though this is only because the seeds of it have already unconsciously been set up by humanity – Pluto simply delivers the inevitable.

The outer planets through the signs

Chiron

Chiron catalyses paradoxical situations and dilemmas, throwing up sharp-edged issues in concrete formats, seemingly irresolvable yet nevertheless demanding resolution. It brings solutions in disguise, calling for a shift of perception. Old solutions no longer work and customary concealment of the core issues fails: an impasse develops where there seem to be hundreds of questions and no answers. To a few people the solution can be blindingly clear, yet making no sense from a customary logical viewpoint.

Then, appearing seemingly out of the blue, either at a grassroots level or through a stroke of leadership genius or a change of circumstances, a solution emerges, frequently when all other options have been exhausted. It answers definite, often multiple connected questions, with simple, basic yet far-reaching solutions. This can be difficult for society to handle. But there is something uncannily right about Chironic answers, and if they are not adopted immense complications can ensue. Bridges must be built, linkages made, activities initiated and wholenesses recognised, bringing small but critical shifts with big outcomes.

In 1898-1901 Chiron conjuncted Uranus and then opposed Pluto – a Uranus opposition Pluto then formed in 1901-02. Around these years we saw the publication of Freud's *Interpretation of Dreams* and the emergence of Planck's Quantum Theory, the first radio transmission, the first public use of electricity and the first powered flight. This configuration took place on the Gemini-Sagittarius axis, the signs of ideas, communication and travel. But the work done to create these iconic events was done during the Chiron aspects, powering the innovative and game-changing effect these events had. This time also brought the beginning of a transference of world dominance from Britain to USA, also inserting a nail in the coffin of the czarist Russian state (the Russo-Japanese war), and signalling the rise of American big-corporate capital.

Chiron, entering Aquarius a few years later, was instrumental in the near-revolutions of 1905 in Russia and China – popular uprisings against the Romanov and Manchu dynasties. Next time Chiron entered Aquarius, fifty years later in 1955-56, there were uprisings in Poland and Hungary against the Soviet system, which had supplanted the Romanov tsars. At intergovernmental level two further collective actions took place in 1955-56 – the founding of the European Community and the Warsaw Pact.

Chiron was involved in the immediate postwar healing process around 1945, when Neptune, Jupiter and Chiron conjuncted in Libra, bringing peace, the Declaration of Human Rights and the groundwork for the founding of the United Nations. It was involved in the happenings of the mid-1960s (Chiron conjunct Saturn in Pisces, in opposition to Uranus conjunct Pluto in Virgo) – and the key it brought here was LSD, a small thing measured in micrograms, with a big cultural effect. It was in the line-up of 1988-89 (Chiron conjunct Jupiter opposing a conjunction of Saturn, Neptune and Uranus), in effect reuniting Europe and ending the Warsaw Pact – this time it was in Cancer, pointing to the role of women in this transformation. Note also the Yod formed by Chiron to the three outer planets in 1979-82 (see chapter 12 and above), a tipping point in the emergence of awareness-seeds planted in the mid-1960s and also one of the most dangerous periods of the long Cold War.

Owing to the acceleration of Chiron when it swings through Libra, it forms far more aspects when at the Libran side of the zodiac. It takes one year to pass through Libra and 6-7 years to pass through the opposite sign, Aries. Thus it is far more active and precipitative in and around Libra than when around Aries, though arguably it digs deeper in Aries because it is slower.

The motions of Chiron through the signs

As Chiron moves through the signs it leads to quirky and contrary behaviour in the following areas:

Cancer (1938-41, 1988-90, 2038-39): protectionism, public sensitivities, the victimhood of the vulnerable, crowd control, ethnic identity and tribalism, social care and welfare, homes and homelands, nationalism, parochialism, inclusion-exclusion, refugees, mother-figures, maternity, babies, injured or disabled people;

Leo (1941-43, 1991-93, 2041-42): self-interest, national interest, dominion by the powerful, public figures, stars and icons, invasions and showdowns, charismatic oppressors, travesties and excesses, public dramas, eccentric leadership, monarchs, unsung or maverick heroes, performers;

Virgo (1943-44, 1993-95, 2043-44): healing of wounds, resolving of conflict, problem solving, correction and reparation, environmental degeneration, conservation and ecology, making the best of a bad situation, health concerns and healing, reorganisation and rebuilding, protest and civil conflict, technical and medical advances, construction, farming, harvesting of results;

Libra (1945-46, 1996, 2045): international and social-subgroup relations, marriage and contractual relationships, social dialogue, diplomacy, mediation, misunderstandings, agreements or schisms, treaties, conferences, tipping-points and turnarounds, innovative art, arguments leading to solutions, multifaith, multi-ethnic and multicultural situations;

Scorpio (1946-48, 1997-8, 2047-9): resource-use, borrowing, lending and money markets, mining, perceived threats, secrecy or exposure, spies and special operations, investigation, research, hardscrabble pragmatism, survival, relentless change, hard reality, magical forces, underlying dynamics, waste and pollution, harshness, showdowns;

Sagittarius (1898-1900, 1949-50, 1999-2001): travel, ideas, publishing, higher and public education, marketing, prosperity, persuasion, globalism, cosmopolitanism, visionary expression, charismatic leaders, far horizons, international relations, law reform, social welfare, philosophers and philosophical dilemmas;

Capricorn (1901-4, 1951-54, 2002-05): structures, laws, constitutions, civil and infrastructural engineering, stability, authority symbols, vested interests, tradition, land and legal reform, law enforcement, trees, land use, social control structures, institutions, antiques, heritage, monuments, museums, revision of history;

Aquarius (1905-10, 1955-60, 2005-10): social planning, ideas and ideologies, inclusion-exclusion and inequality, humanitarian intervention, social, ethnic and belief movements, inventions, scapegoats, martyrs, minorities, ostracism, cooperatives, mass behaviour, social networks, justice, rights and freedoms;

Pisces (1910-18, 1960-68, 2010-18): social empathy and caring, relativism, insights, visions and perspectives, spiritual-religious issues and impulses, cults, collective madnesses, exposure of secrets, paradoxes and dilemmas, social and health services, boundary issues, chaos and degeneration, peril and disintegration-reintegration;

Aries (1918-26, 1968-76, 2018-2026): self-improvement, self-interest, discrimination, agitation, antipathies, riots and rebellions, acute conflict, militias, skirmishes, lobbying, pioneers, pace-setters, scapegoats, breakthroughs, infringements, competitiveness;

Taurus (1927-33, 1976-83, 2026-33): self-sufficiency, food and resource security, consumption, stability, technology, fertility, husbandry, land-fertility, agriculture, construction, property rights, pleasure, affluenza, creative arts, resistance, endurance, uncompromising polarisation;

Gemini (1933-37, 1983-88, 2033-38): transport and communications, reversals and diversions, instability, ideas and theories, bridging dualisms, shifts of allegiance, changing arrangements, diversity and multiculturalism, insects, meeting-places and marketplaces.

Uranus

Uranus is a bringer of uplift and shake-ups. It opens new avenues into the future and breaks us off from the past. This can sometimes be shocking, yet it takes loads off the world's shoulders by offering new tracks to follow in the group psyche. New, divergent or dissenting ideas and ideologies come forward, bringing radical gales of change. Suddenly things are different from before. Often these outbreaks do

not turn out as their instigators hope – for example, the French revolution blew itself out in a decade, 1960s flower-power wilted and the 2011 Arab revolutions were subverted. But such upwellings do plant seeds of a new order, introducing new perspectives, innovations and situations. They can seed underground movements that exert a longterm effect – feminism and the green movement can be seen this way.

Uranus conjures up new visions and possibilities, the precise forms of which might pass away (like the Beatles) but their effects unfold for decades afterwards and something will have changed permanently. Uranus is a true bringer of revolutionary change, of overthrow or mutation of the old, in whatever manner is needed. It operates so abruptly that established ways often cannot adapt quickly enough and simply have to yield – at least, in the first instance. However, such shocks can also generate innovative resistance to change – for example, aristocratic refugees of the French Revolution became the avid plantation- and slave-owners in the American South in the 19th Century. In the Arab revolutions, new dictatorships and ruling systems evolved in response to the revolutionary challenge, while the Russian revolution spawned a dictatorship in revolutionary guise (Stalin), arguably worse than the regime of the tsars that the revolution had brought down. However, there is still usually a net forward motion because history is often on the side of reformers and change-bringers, even if it takes longer than many might prefer.

Revolutions based upon ideology or regime-change can fundamentally fail because true change must be rooted in genuine transformations of public behaviour and psychology, and this takes time. Marxists saw this and sought to guard against it by creating 'permanent revolution' and a 'dictatorship of the proletariat' to guard the revolution from subversion or loss of momentum. This led to totalitarian social control systems – the regime of Chairman Mao in China, with his cultural revolution of the 1960s on the Uranus-Pluto conjunction, ripped up social bonds, trust, families and communities, leading to tragedy for millions of Chinese.

Revolution and profound change is a more difficult and incremental thing than revolutionaries would like it to be. Nevertheless, the longterm effects of revolutions seep through history, influencing the future and setting new standards – an example being the notions of liberty and political rights from the French Revolution, or the notion of constitutions born in the American Revolution.

Uranus moves around the zodiac at a regular pace, spending seven years in each sign, marking out a regular pulse of collective reorientation with regards to the sequence of varying issues that the zodiac signs symbolise. Uranus in each sign shows how things change and expose areas of focus for change, yet it also shows different manners of resistance and conservatism too.

Revolutions aren't common. Change is more often lived out more incrementally through people, situations, books, films or events symbolising the issues at stake, causing social fermentation and change processes that, failing all else, work through the growing up and maturing of generations. Uranian ripples often come through upstarts and crazies, radicals, eccentrics and deviants, though sometimes also from ordinary individuals who suddenly find themselves in a key position to do something, or the spotlight falls on them uninvited.

Uranus marks out seven-year generations of people stirred up by or seeking change each in their own ways, according to the sign involved. It shows the source and manner of insecurity in a generation, the area where shake-ups happen for them. It also shows their particular kind of inspiration and way of breaking with the past. Uranus opens up questions and doesn't let them rest. Heard of that seven-year period before? Yes, it's a quarter-cycle of Saturn too.

In 1901 Uranus was involved (with Chiron) in an opposition to Pluto, and later a conjunction to Pluto in 1965-66 (opposite Chiron). Both in mutable signs, these periods represented vigorous breakthroughs of consciousness and social change: humanity took to the air on the opposition and reached for the Moon soon after the conjunction. Uranus last opposed Neptune in 1907-08 and conjuncted it in 1993, both times in Capricorn, putting great pressure on rigidities and structures, making life at the top very trying.

Note the rise of Hitler when Uranus entered Aries in 1927, the rise of the modern welfare state when it hit Cancer in 1949 and, when it entered Libra in 1969, the rise of the global village, of Saudi wealth and Islamic radicalism, the ascendancy of Japan and of the decolonialising developing world in general – a sudden re-balancing. Uranus entering Capricorn in 1988 brought loosening of structures, through computerisation and free-marketeering in the West and *perestroika* in USSR.

The motions of Uranus through the signs

As Uranus moves through the signs it leads to shake-ups, inversions, reversals and wrenchings in the following areas:

Cancer (1865-71, 1948-56, 2032-40): security and threats to security, social welfare, shifts in national interest, conservatism, nationalism, territorial issues, preservation or disruption of order, families, children and the vulnerable, social subgroups, people power;

Leo (1872-78, 1956-62, 2039-46): self-determination, liberation movements and independence, power-struggles, civil wars, dominance, monarchs, oligarchies, strong public figures, heroes, steamrolling forces, victims, hedonism, entertainment, performing arts, creative movements;

Virgo (1878-85, 1962-68, 2046-52): technological implementation, financial and organisational change, dissent and protest, public service, extremism and social ostracism, health and self-improvement, ecology, economic disruption, research and development, aid and disaster relief, accountability;

Libra (1885-91, 1968-75, 2052-59): relationships, marriage and inter-group social relations, treaty and alliance changes, détentes or power-swings, unexpected oscillations and reversals, innovative arts, changing values, aesthetic shifts, conventionality against radicalism, stirring of social complicities;

Scorpio (1891-98, 1981-88, 2059-65): crunches, revelations, therapies, disasters and rescue operations, unravelling of secrets, business instability, relentless march of progress, seediness and squalor, underground movements, quests, inquisitions, spying, endurance of suffering, stirring of social pain;

Sagittarius (1898-1904, 1981-88, 2065-72): changes of perspective and the big picture, new theories and worldviews, international relations crises, invasions and boundary incursions, exploration, legal and educational changes, freedom movements, financial market bubbles, transport issues, tolerance-intolerance, extremism, excesses;

Capricorn (1904-12, 1988-95, 2072-79): governmental, structural and institutional instability or change, revolt or reform, nonconformism, iconoclasm, departure from tradition, earthquakes, economic and legal jolts, constitutional change, new nations, infrastructural development, technological implementation, geological shakeups;

Aquarius (1912-19, 1995-2003, 2079-87): inventions, inventors and genius, independence, minority groups, dissenters, social movements, ideological-cultural issues, social exclusion, refugees, sudden social developments, humanitarian initiatives, crowd manias, social mind-control;

Pisces (1919-27, 2002-11, 2087-94): awakening and stirring of awareness under the surface, chaos and derailments, intrusion of unknowns, omens and signs, eruptions from the unconscious, escapism, manic pursuit of illusions, manias, spiritual-visionary impulses, social empathy, charitable movements;

Aries (1927-34, 2011-18, 2094-2102): heroes and villains, demonisation, individualistic initiative-takers, militarism, activism, uprisings, rivalries, antipathy, courage and daring, youth disaffection, futurism, restlessness and volatility, ill feeling toward leaders and oligarchs, impatience;

Taurus (1934-41, 2018-25): building, bulldozing, engineering, agriculture, rampant materialism and consumerism, conventionalism and resistance to change, creative upswings and cultural florescence, xenophobia, power battles and attrition, empire-building, colonisation and takeovers;

Gemini (1858-65, 1941-48, 2025-32): ideas, discoveries, communications, transport and media innovations, new styles, trade disruptions, shifting alliances and markets, reversals and switches, schisms, contradictions, social mobility, changing circumstances, intelligence agencies, social dissonance and diversity.

Neptune

Neptune spends around thirteen years in each sign, marking out distinct periods in which idealised perceptions and imagined fears and phobias manifest in differing social and cultural contexts. Neptune reveals the illusions, cults and delusionary disconnects that each generation can fall into, and also the particular ways each generation generates a vision, uplifts and enlightens itself. At times when Neptune is strong it's often not clear what is truth and what is illusion. Public groupthink can persuade itself that illusions are real and realities imaginary – and it is this collective self-persuasion, consensus-manufacture and creation of reality-bubbles that lies at the heart of the matter.

Neptune is a bringer of light, sanity and awareness, and of glamours and falsities. So it concerns fundamental perceptions – the optic by which we see life overall. It renders old forms irrelevant and invalid, void and outdated, leaving a clean slate or a feeling of disorientation. Or perhaps the clean slate appears once disorientation is accepted. Openness can allow new possibilities to emerge, replacing old ways. Whatever is sure, fixed and definite becomes questionable and hazy – this is potentially revelatory, exposing things as they actually stand. Eventually collective dreams, fantasies and fears show themselves to be the imaginations they truly are, and society gains something from that – this can relieve burdens too. Yet imagination adds flavour to reality, and it's the stuff of human culture, infusing life with normality-busting magic and wonder. But it is harmful when charismatic or diabolical symbolism is transferred onto people or situations, obscuring the reality of what's really going on.

When Neptune was discovered in 1850, new beliefs were emerging (Marxism, Darwinism, Theosophy, Spiritualism), including a new sense of modernism – in the

West the urban-industrial and imperial era of the 1800s was in full swing, with its mission to civilise and its high regard for itself. The historical illusion here was that Western empires would rule and civilise the world, lasting forever – in fact, they lasted just a century more. Little did they then know that these empires were simply a mechanism by which humanity was to move into a position where it could begin to unite itself in the 21st Century.

The mid-1800s saw the advent of the novel and soon film was to appear, giving birth to a new, media-fuelled, surrogate life, with film-stars acting out our fears and fantasies, and news reports, advertising and media coverage telling us all what we need to think – with many people believing it too and even paying for the privilege. Yet also we have been exposed by the same means to distant realities beyond our furthest dreams, and when we saw Earth from the Moon in 1968, at the time of the Apollo missions, something deep clicked for human consciousness, pointing to the future.

Our dreams guide us forward, yet also we overlay dreamstuff on reality, sometimes causing great damage. Socialism, a noble attempt to bring justice and equality, killed millions in the Stalinist pogroms and Mao's Great Leap Forward. Yet capitalism too, as an ideology, has eaten up the world, bombed just as many millions and caused untold suffering, while telling us that it gave us freedom and happiness. Beneath and behind these cruel realities is an evolution of society and collective experience leading toward humanity's planetarisation and transformation into a truly civilised race. Well, we can but hope – it depends on whether you take a Neptunian or Saturnine approach to the future.

Neptune is a builder of cults and a destroyer of illusions. It is a psycho-spiritual patron of the arts, giving us everything from Rembrandt to Dvorak to Disney, and of faiths, giving us spiritual and moral frameworks with which to live our lives and decorate our cosmological bubbles. Yet our prejudicial God-driven religions permit us to kill, rape and pillage too.

Neptune has very real influences. When it was in Capricorn in 1820-34 we saw the rise of steam-powered railways and steamships, and when it was there again in 1984-98 we saw the growth of computers, internet and many fancy technologies. When Neptune was in Scorpio (1956-70) we saw 'the pill' and 'free love', helping catalyse the women's movement which, in turn, marks the beginning of an immense historic change in human and social relations. But it's not railways, 'the pill' or internet that are the main issue here: it is the growth of new human experience, social and global realities and their full implications. They are game-changers, extending into every department of life worldwide.

Neptune's influence is surreptitious and its influence hides behind a disguise. It's both a wolf in sheep's clothing and a sheep in wolf's clothing. It opens us up to new realities by eroding the old and clearing the decks for the new. At times it brings great pain: when Neptune entered Scorpio in 1792 the French Revolutionary wars broke out, unleashing a new militarism at a time when warfare was losing its shine – and Napoleon harnessed it to build an empire. When it entered Aries in 1861 the disastrous American Civil War broke out – the world's first truly modern war – and when it entered Leo in 1914 World War One broke out. At times it brings relief: when it entered Libra in 1942 World War Two turned around, and when it entered Pisces in 2012 major security exposures (Wikileaks and Snowden) revealed the extent of political subterfuge and electronic surveillance in the West – a question concerning the fundaments of civilisation. So Neptune is not just woolly and vague.

The motions of Neptune through the signs

When Neptune passes through the signs, it brings renewal by introducing chaos, eroding what went on before and highlighting areas such as these:

Cancer (1901-15, 2066-79): security, routines, customs and knowns, social vulnerability, care and welfare, hospitals, beleaguered children, women and families, nationalism, homelands, parochialism, xenophobia, conformity, comfort zones, secret groups and mystery schools;

Leo (1914-29, 2079-93): heroic struggles, charismatic leaders, stars and icons, dictators, status symbols, commercialism, totalitarianism and grandiosity, national pride, persuasion and force, showmanship and entertainment, cultural output, glamour, drama, film and fiction, largesse, ambition, victimisation, oppression of the masses;

Virgo (1929-43, 2093-2107): economic downturns, subsidences and changes, technological outcomes, Keynesianism, work and employment, assembly lines, economism, dissenters and deviants, integrity, efficiency, unaccountability, ethnic, religious and racial distancing, bureaucratism and statism, conservation, charitable sector, architecture, academia;

Libra (1942-56): shifting associations and alliances, idealised relationships and communities, coexistence and tolerance, polarisation and clannishness, projection, accommodations, joining or parting of ways, social movements, mutuality, fine arts, music, justice and human rights, war and peace, meetings and conferences;

Scorpio (1792-1806, 1956-70): the abyss, collapses and failures, power and manoeuvring, subterfuge, deception, suspicion, questing, sexuality, morality, cruelty and death, truths, resources, finance and business, scandals, corruption, renewal, turnarounds, rebirth;

Sagittarius (1807-20, 1970-84): new perspectives, religious beliefs, philosophies, internationalism, travel, mass media, marketing, law and civics, belief in progress, knowledge, historical revisionism, learning and higher education, expansion, imperialism, takeovers, excesses and overruns, wealth, gambling, investment, upswings, celebrations;

Capricorn (1820-34, 1984-98): incremental institutional and governmental change, legitimacy, 'in office but not in power', land-ownership, change from beneath, cult of money, heritage and status, organisational change, restructuring, transparency, financial institutions, social obligations, lapsing of traditions, seeking posterity;

Aquarius (1834-48, 1998-2012): social-political issues, crowd phenomena, inclusion-exclusion, 'we, the people', mass manias, democracy, social reform, radicalism and conservatism, socialism, solidarity, revolutionary and community movements, public opinion, social planning, intellectualism, science, ideology, populism, individual freedoms versus social obligations;

Pisces (1847-61, 2011-2025): spiritual-religious awakening, the hidden meaning of things, enhanced understanding, disillusionment, cults and memes, religious extremism, tilting at windmills, service and participation, social and cross-cultural compassion, loosening of fixities, change through chaos, potential for paranoia, indifference and fatalism;

Aries (1861-75, 2025-39): adulation of leaders, stars and heroes, icons, brilliance, triumphalism, infringement, interference and invasion, individualism, social splintering, cult of progress, ripping up the past, ice-breaking, explosions and pollution, impacts and vulnerabilities, initiatives, hybridisation, forwardness, over the top;

Taurus (1874-89, 2038-52): maintaining stability, cult of progress, extension, construction, engineering feats, economic growth or subsidence, property, capital appreciation, landowning, horticulture, industry and crafts, sensuality, posterity-seeking, fixity, resistance;

Gemini (1888-1902, 2051-66): big ideas, theories and master-plans, scientific, technological and communications breakthroughs, new ideas, educational advances, idealistic movements, esoteric systems, geopolitical shifts, collapsing and emergent worldviews, cross-cultural interchange, confusion of ideas.

Pluto

Pluto's eccentric orbit gives it a variable input into history. In the decades around the late 1980s it was strong since it moved at its fastest and closest to the Sun (perihelion), in its home sign Scorpio. Its previous perihelion was in 1741, at the very beginning of the industrial revolution, and the one before that was in 1493, the time of Columbus. Each period following these perihelia has seen significant uprooting of peoples and deep historic shifts.

Neptune-Pluto conjunctions, at nearly 500 year intervals, describe a fundamental longterm cycle of history. The Neptune-Pluto conjunction of 1891-92 marked the watershed not only of the Victorian era into that of the 20th Century – it marked also the end of a bigger era beginning at the start of the Renaissance at the previous Neptune-Pluto conjunction of 1398-99. The year 1891 marks the beginning of a cycle going through to 2386. The opening square of the cycle takes place in 2061-65 – today's children will see it. The 20th Century was but the beginning of something far greater than we can currently see.

While the Uranus opposition Pluto of 1901 laid the tracks for the 20th Century (flight and electricity), its meaning became fulfilled at the Uranus conjunct Pluto of 1965-6, by which time electronics and flight had become commonplace. Something new started in the 1960s: modern civilisation awaits a profound change, and this was mooted at that time. A battle for the hearts and minds of humanity starting then has not been concluded yet.

Since the 1960s world climate has shifted, population has grown, nature has come under increased attack and global integration and interdependence have become a fact. Life on Earth can now be destroyed in a variety of ways, and counterbalancing this is an increased awareness and activism in in ecology, human relations, psychology and spirituality. Concepts, outlooks and realities are transforming faster now than ever before, and we are in the middle of a quantum leap in human evolution, without being fully aware of its full implications.

It is Pluto that drives such changes. It likes to narrow the distance between possibilities and actualities and, if there is a tendency or need for something to happen, Pluto will force the matter. This happens over decades. If we omit to act wisely or take heed of earlier lessons, Pluto forces a learning experience, often by delivering hardship or horror, or by driving things forward until they are irreversible. It pushes us over the brink, exposing hidden agendas, hypocrisies and collective collusions. This is uncomfortable yet there is something relieving and cleansing to it – truths come out, the chips are down and something must be done.

Pluto's movements through the signs show the pet obsessions of each time. Obsessions take over – they're the only important thing and all else is secondary, until the next obsession comes along. They are one-tracked, biased and sometimes dangerous. They are a learning experience too. When Pluto moves to the next sign, the last obsession forms the backdrop for the next one. At the time of writing, with Pluto in Capricorn, the world believes economics and resources are everything, and humanity, seen from this viewpoint to be human resources and consumers, is undervalued. This will change when Pluto enters Aquarius, when the obsession of the time will be peoples and rights. The current obsession with money will sink into the background – other things will prove important. What will drive this shift is a tiredness with economism and corporate-style thinking.

The motions of Pluto through the signs

Pluto's movements signal the preoccupations and imperatives of the time and the areas such as the following where change is urgently needed:

Cancer (1913-39, 25 years): obsession with security, leading to social insecurity, the mother principle, unfulfilled needs, hardship, nutrition issues, homelands and nationalism, mob rule, violation, vulnerabilities, social insensitivity and reactivity, families and communities, care systems, children, dependency, addiction, protection, memory and sentimentalism;

Leo (1938-58, 20 years): leaders, monarchs, dictators, figureheads, idols, power, imperialism, force, self-preoccupation, achievement, self-expression, creativity, dramas, games, patriotism, inequality, expansionism, music, performance, certainties, zeniths, bubbles, takeovers, gambling, chauvinism;

Virgo (1956-72, 16 years): distinctions and divisions, skill and craftsmanship, organisational systems, cleanup, correction, self-examination, analysis, social splintering, protest, reliability, anxieties, environmental issues, health, education, medicine and healing, technology components, conservation, agriculture;

Libra (1971-84, 13 years): equalisation, reversal, extremes and polarisation, contradictions, oscillation, crisis in relationships, legal and social justice, compensation, separation, schism, reprisal, reconciliation, diplomacy, mediation, civil war, pretence, evasion, diversions;

Scorpio (1984-95, 11 years): death of the old, crunch-period, breakthrough, revolution, power manoeuvring, social control, oppression, secrets, cover-ups and exposure, deception, backlash, force, cruelty, criminality, fear, covert operations, truth, retribution, reckoning, purgation, redemption, resolution, finality, rebirth, survivability;

Sagittarius (1995-2008, 13 years): beliefs and worldviews, reason, expansionism, wealth, progressive attitudes, reform, philosophies, religion and faith, fanaticism, internationalism, aid and relief, generalisation, PR, marketing, excess, escapism, celebration, completion;

Capricorn (2008-24, 16 years): restructuring, dying customs, obsession with money, law, government, institutions and corporations, land-ownership, social status, organisations, radicalism and conservatism, insurance, heritage, hierarchies, oligarchies, materialism, rebellion, disruption, perpetuation, father principle, elders;

Aquarius (2024-44, 20 years): crowds, clans, communities, democracy, populism, dissension, alienation, disengagement, exclusion, discrimination, refugees, collectivism, labour unions, solidarity, social change, planning, ideologies, migration, rights abuses;

Pisces (2043-67, 24 years): loosening, restructuring, fundamentals, chaos, disintegration, confusion, madnesses, perspectives, insight, understanding, spirituality, faith, revelations, cosmologies, paranoia, derailment, cultural revival, transparency, social empathy;

Aries (1822-53, 2066-96, 30 years): relentless progress, modernisation, pioneering, demolition of the past, uncompromising behaviour, conflict, engineering, iconoclasm, individualism, separatism, master plans, energy, conviction politics, ascendancy;

Taurus (1851-84, 2095-2129, 33 years): continuation, security, stability, land and resources, horticulture, realism, growth, perpetuity, conformity, construction, comforts, luxuries, enjoyment, beauty, arts and crafts, architecture, infrastructure;

Gemini (1882-1913, 31 years): new ideas, electrical and communications technologies, hyperactivity, travel, innovations, radical theories, literature, news media, intercultural relations, marketplaces, conferences, change of direction or fortunes, dilemmas and contradictions, language, popular music, teenagers.

Options

The outer planets have been grinding away throughout known history, but something has changed in the last 100-200 years. Human population has grown immensely and the effect of this on nature and human life has exploded in scale and magnitude. This would matter less if our civilisation were not so destructive, consumptive, exploitative, warlike and parasitic – if society involved more sharing, enhancement of nature, justice and truly humane behaviour. The world is now in a critical state as a result of burgeoning population and the caustic effect our civilisation has.

This means that a Uranus square Pluto today has a bigger effect than once it did, since more people are affected, it's global and more impactful. Life's intensity is rising. This means that the stirring effect of the planets has an increasing effect. There are more souls here to experience and participate in what's going on – the amount of psycho-emotional activity on Earth is mushrooming.

During the Uranus square Pluto of 2012-15 humanity has become more aware of the effects of fundamentals it has long known about but failed to act upon. These entered wider public awareness from the 1960s onwards. Some are now irreversible, the damage already done, and others can be fixed if there is a will, but this involves root-and-branch, not just cosmetic change. This question is enormous, and the motions of planets won't answer it: planets and the social climates they stimulate give opportunities for correction but it is we who decide.

Meanwhile, the planets grind out their tunes, resonating within the Earth sphere, affecting us all and offering us choices, opportunities and learning experiences. They do not steer us and determine our futures – we have free will. And the ultimate act of free will is to align ourselves intentionally with the deeper laws of nature and the universe, to act in wisdom and to do what we know we need to do.

16

Making History

The historian Eric Hobsbawm used to talk of 'the short 20th Century', lasting from 1914 to 1989, and he had a point. But he wasn't an astrologer, working instead on the basis of major events such as WW1 and the Fall of the Wall. From an astrological viewpoint we could say that the 'long 20th Century' started around 1891 at the Neptune-Pluto conjunction in Gemini, ending perhaps at the Uranus-Pluto square of 2012-15. Similarly, the 19th Century began perhaps on the Uranus opposition Pluto of 1792-93, the French Revolution, ending around 1891.

Let's look at the modern period and its backdrop, starting around the 1740s. What matters most in astrology is understanding the present, but understanding the past helps us see the historical context to our current time.

For a 2,500 year timeline of historic planetary motions and events, consult the Historical Ephemeris on the author's website, and for accurate detailed tables go to the Astrodienst site astro.com. The charts in this chapter are generalised to show overall patterns and configurations – they are not exact and accurate.

The Industrial Revolution

The industrial revolution germinated in Britain when Pluto was in Scorpio in 1736-48, reaching some other parts of the world by the time Pluto revisited Scorpio a long time later in 1984-96. In the 18th Century the towns, canals and coal mines opening up in Britain seemed to some people to be a sign of humanity's degeneration into the Slough of Despond – a symptom of the relentless wrenching of Pluto in Scorpio, ripping us out of the past and propelling us into the future.

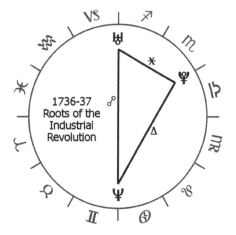

1736-37
Roots of the
Industrial
Revolution

Nowadays we can afford to think of this painful yet changeful chapter of history as an urban-industrialising phase from which we in the developed world now are departing – though in truth we exported it to the so-called developing world. With this hindsight, the 1740s take on a new significance. At the time no one was to know where things would lead, and developments were then small and localised, yet an historic watershed was being crossed and, within 70 years, industrialisation was going full steam ahead – no more horses and sails, this was a clanking mechanical revolution, something utterly new.

Following the Enlightenment of the 1750s-60s, a time of vigorous new humanistic and proto-democratic thinking, the philosophy of the modern West took shape (Hume, Voltaire, Payne, Rousseau and others). Battles were also going on for colonial dominance between European powers in America and Asia – classic symptoms of Pluto in Sagittarius.

The momentum of the industrial revolution grew stronger when Pluto was in Capricorn (1762-77), to which it has returned today. The issue wasn't just about industry: it concerned the drawing of masses of people into an urban-centred employment-consumption system, leaving behind a rural, village-centred, largely self-sufficient subsistence system. Today we see the whole world being drawn into the modern system, even in the wilds of Mongolia, Peru, Kenya and Kazakhstan.

Then came the American and French revolutions while Pluto chugged through Aquarius (1778-98), heralding the end of the old social and monarchical orders and the beginning of the constitutional republic, plus the concept of the modern 'social contract' delineating the rights and duties of citizens and state. At this time we saw many new laws, principles, norms, inventions, precedents and impulses which later were to characterise the culture of the West. Western values have since then been pervading all corners of the world yet also today we see a cultural push-back beginning, which might be more visible when Pluto is again in Aquarius (2024-44), since Western culture has no monopoly over new ideas.

Critical in the late 18th Century was the Uranus-Pluto opposition of 1792-94, a turning point setting a pattern of political revolutions that continues today – Uranus was in Leo and the French king literally lost his head, and Pluto was in Aquarius, applying grass-roots pressure and leading to mob rule.

The longterm outcome was typical of Uranus-Pluto hard aspects: frequently the revolutionary ideal is hijacked by new, updated regimes – in this case the new order and continental system of Napoleon, who attempted and ultimately failed to unite Europe, though in the process revolutionary thinking spread widely across Europe, making Europeans aware that there was an alternative to what they were long accustomed to. Meanwhile in USA the constitutional democracy established there gave birth to new freedoms yet also to the beginnings of a hidden shadow state nowadays commonly known as Big Brother – another case of a revolution making some difference though turning out differently from the way it appeared at the time.

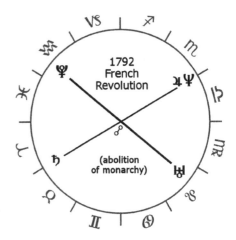

Pluto in Pisces, 1798-1822, was dominated by Napoleon's attempt to build an enlightened authoritarian system across Europe. Had he succeeded, European history would have been very different but, like Hitler later on, he over-extended his ambitious invasions and Europe's extremities in Spain and Russia proved to be his downfall. Europe divided into the liberal West (Britain, France, Netherlands) and authoritarian East (Germany, Austria, Russia). Something deeply visionary failed to happen during this time, which could have united Europe – and this was a root cause of WW1 and WW2 in the 20th Century, which proved to be Europe's downfall.

By the time Pluto entered Aries in 1822, the steam engine had emerged fully, powering new forms of large-scale manufacturing and travel on land and sea, shrinking the world and opening up all manner of new possibilities. By the end of the 1800s worldwide travel was well established and the appurtenances of modern life, from cocoa and tin cans to photography and mass media, plus a new society of capitalists, middle classes and workers were all in place, as if they always had been so. By year 2000 over half of the world's population lived in cities. Two centuries might sound like a long time, but in that time the world went through a millennium's-worth of change.

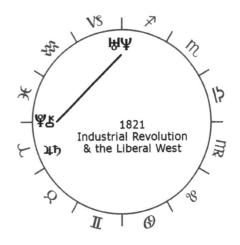

The Uranus conjunction with Neptune in Capricorn, squaring Pluto and Chiron in Aries between 1816 and 1821 was a crucial turning-point defining modernity. This major configuration brought us industrial urbanism, intercontinental trade, big

ideas, widespread European imperialism and a fundamental infrastructural shift –
initially in Britain, Belgium and France, later in Germany, USA and Japan. By the
next Uranus-Neptune conjunction in 1993 this had spread to countries like Mexico,
India, Thailand, Brazil, Taiwan and China.

This 1821 configuration, including a crucial Neptune square Pluto (closing square
of the 1390s-1890s cycle), had major historical significance: amongst other things,
it decided that the English language, and British-style capitalism would dominate
the world economy in times to come. Few were then to know that the young nation
of USA would carry the baton through the 20th Century, or that Russia would be a
major contender for that role too.

In 1850, Uranus conjuncted Pluto in
Aries. This was the time of Marx's
das Kapital, the 1848 revolutions,
the triumphalist Great Exhibition in
London, Queen Victoria, the white-
man's settlement of the American West
and Australia (devastating indigenous
peoples), the colonial invasion of Africa,
and a time of scientific advances and
global interconnection by trains and
steamships. At this time the European-
originated industrial-urban way of
life and its ideology of progress and
modernity was flying high, extending its tentacles worldwide.

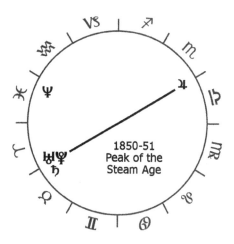

Acceleration

The astrological transitions we've seen
thus far were outclassed by what took
place in the 1890s and up to 1910: this
was an historical turning-point par
excellence, the true beginning of the
global village, with all the pluses and
minuses that it has thus far brought.
It started with a Neptune-Pluto
conjunction in 1891-92 in Gemini – a
truly Geminoid time with the invention

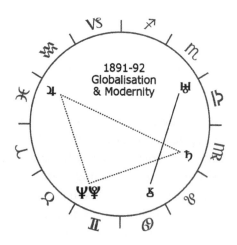

of the petrol engine, telegraphy, cameras and film, radio, electric lamps and motors, rockets, Freudian psychotherapy, socialist ideas, and the rise of American tycoons such as Carnegie, Rockefeller, Morgan, Astor, the music of Tchaikovsky, Gilbert and Sullivan, Sibelius and Mahler, the writings of Kipling, HG Wells, Strindberg, Yeats and Tolstoy and the esoteric ideas of Madame Blavatsky, the Spiritualists and Orientalists. These gave birth to a new cultural wave and to secular ideas of an entirely new kind, defining and characterising the 20th Century.

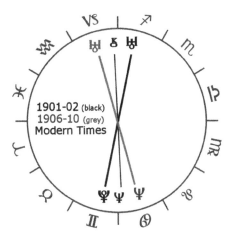

The Neptune-Pluto conjunction was soon followed by two further major aspects which can be considered part of the same process – after all, two decades in history is nothing. We had a Uranus-Pluto opposition in 1901-02, giving us flight, public electrical systems, nuclear physics, oil drilling and workers' parties, and then a Uranus opposition Neptune in 1906-10 giving us mass-production, plastics, suffragettes, revolutions in Russia, Persia and China, national insurance, jazz, skyscrapers, big guns, tanks and many wrenching social and political changes that were to play themselves out in the First World War. Humanity went into future-shock, so rapid and profound were the advances, issues and crises taking place.

Each of these changes represented a change of awareness too. Women's rights, workers' movements, growing belief in science, psychology and evolution, new spiritual and ethical beliefs – these all reflected shifts of perspective brought by these major aspects, taking place in Gemini and Sagittarius. Radio, photography, telegraphy and flight were to exert a tremendous influence on humanity's worldview in coming times. The breakdown of traditions, family and community structures and the growth of individualism were to characterise the world we now live in. The two-decade period from 1890-1910 marked a thorough and fundamental turning-point in history. Today we live in turning-point times too, but arguably they are extensions and extrapolations of what started in the 1890s.

At these turning-points, seeds are planted. They take time to surface into general awareness: often the generation born in such seed-times takes it upon itself to turn possibilities into actualities and mainstream experience, 30-40 years later. Thus the generation born in the 1890s, active adults in the 1920s-40s, were those who, amongst other things, gave us totalitarian systems (Hitler, Stalin and modern capitalism), and who laid the ground for the later 20th Century and the complex, wired-up multicultural societies we now live in.

From 1900 to 1965, history unfolded along on the tracks established around 1891. Neither WW1 nor WW2 took place during major astrological periods – they arose out of earlier causes and an overconsumption of change. This said, worthy of note is the fact that WW1 broke out when Pluto ingressed into Cancer, and WW2 when it entered Leo.

The immediate roots of WW2 lay in the Uranus-Pluto square of 1931-32, which gave us the Wall St Crash, the Depression, Hitler, Stalin and the New Deal – all expressions of the proliferating Orwellian mega-state of modern times, which was fully established during WW2. This was the waning square of the Uranus-Pluto cycle starting in 1850, while the waxing square in the next cycle took place in 2012-15 – see a connection?

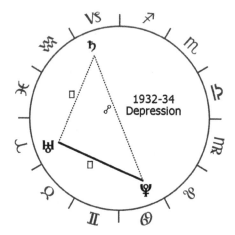

WW2 broke out when Pluto entered Leo, with a little ingressional help from Saturn and Jupiter entering Aries. Neither Leo nor Aries cause wars as such, but their uncompromising pushing can lead to war, as can Sagittarius. Neptune entered Libra in 1942, marking the turning-point of the war and, at the end of it, peace came during a wide Jupiter-Chiron-Neptune conjunction in Libra – a burst of light in a dark time.

Saturn and Pluto are instrumental in the start of many wars, in 1914 (WW1), 1939 (WW2), 1956 (Hungary and Suez) and 1965 (Vietnam), as well as 1992 (Desert Storm in Iraq), and 9/11 in 2001 (leading to wars in Afghanistan and Iraq). However, this doesn't have to be so: Saturn-Pluto demand the facing of hard truths, and many wars represent a tragic failure to do so, a diversion from the real issues – and good business for some.

In 1954-55 came a Uranus-Neptune square. These two planets do bring up concrete issues but primarily they represent shifts of collective worldviews. During this aspect came the dawn of the high-tech age and the birth of rock'n'roll – precursors to the breakthroughs of the 1960s and also connected by theme with the Uranus-Neptune conjunction of 1993. Here came the nuclear age, early

computers, genetic research, advanced
plastics, TV and the folding up of the
British and other European empires,
with the beginning of many more
nuances than meet the eye. A cradle
formation of ingressing planets plus a
T-square changed the tone of the time,
moving things toward what was to
unfold in the 1960s.

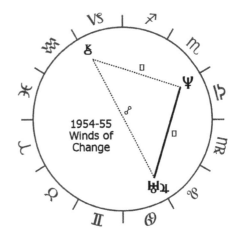

1954-55
Winds of
Change

A Dream Surfaces

Then came the mid-1960s, like an exploding starburst rocket. In recent decades
it has been fashionable to pass off this time as a wild holiday or an eccentric and
foolish deviation, but this need to rationalise away the virtues of the 1960s reflects
the suppression of something very major, which mainstream vested interests didn't
like. The Great Unknown impinged strongly on human awareness and profound
new seeds of change were planted – it was a cultural revolution in the making, and
an opportunity for the dominant West to make a shift in its priorities and direction
of travel. The generation born in the 1960s is historically an important generation,
today holding the reins of office.

The Pluto in Leo 'baby boomer'
generation, born between 1939 and
1956, emerged into adulthood in the
1960s, ready to run with the dispensation
offered: that generation, at the peak of
its power between 1980 and 2010, had
a calling to swing the underlying tide of
world awareness, in the areas of creative
expression, technology, worldviews,
lifestyle and spirituality – the internet
was devised by a strange mixture of
ageing hippies and military men. A

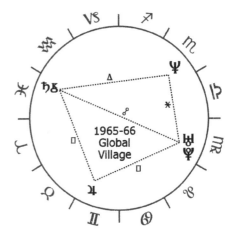

1965-66
Global
Village

dominant minority of this generation
(the Yuppies) went into moneymaking and self-fulfilment, though others held
true to their beliefs, pursuing a low-consumption alternative lifestyle while others
shrugged shoulders and did their best within the system, by degrees raising its
human standards. The generation gap experienced in the 1960s represented an

ideational-visionary watershed in history, a rapid shift of ideas that normally might take decades.

A hard day's night, 1965-66 saw the birth of a dream and cultural leap: spirituality, political and ecological awakening, the microchip, rule-breaking and a cultural revolution East and West. This time planted seeds of a new order yet to come, which is why this deserves a mention here. By 1967-68 Jupiter entered Leo and Saturn entered Aries, and the dream of love and peace got more serious, a fight for power between radicalism and conventionalism.

Those born in the 1960s with Uranus and Pluto in Virgo are builders, regulators and technologists with a degree of corrective rectitude after the moral excesses of the Pluto in Leo generation of 1939-56. Their danger is control-freakery and generational neurosis, tending toward somewhat puritan standards that make life increasingly regulated, complicated and inquisitional, yet their strength lies in a certain visionary pragmatism and competence that suits the time.

Many of the preceding Pluto in Leo generation, losing track of their soul and spirit, indulged in self-fulfilment and affluence, producing gizmos and creative innovations though also creating as much damage as the very parents they revolted against. How the ills of one generation can pass to the next: the hardships encountered by the Pluto in Cancer generation in 1914-39 became an obese consumptiveness for the Pluto in Leos and their offspring. This said, a deeper learning takes place underneath, and although love and peace have led to an excess of indifference and war, a deeper process of historic change is still fermenting in the background, which might or might not win through in the 21st Century.

The configuration of 1965-6 produced three symptomatic elements:

- the development of the microchip, genetic and space engineering and nanotechnology, bringing a material possibility of revolutionising our relations with the material world – small, quiet, intricate bits of technology with immense implications, and very virgoid;

- flower-power, a visionary explosion, induced through use of LSD but also surfacing in new politics, spirituality and cultural waves which, while seemingly impractical and way-out, planted potent seeds for the future;

- the sexual revolution and 'permissive society' born out of Neptune in Scorpio, bringing a weakening of marriage and family – a tendency started by the Pluto in Cancer (1914-39) generation. In the longterm this represents a profound shift from small nuclear families to a larger communitarian tribalism, including a dramatic shift in the social role of women, being brought through by the Pluto in Libra generation of the 1970s and those that follow them.

The germination of this seed took place at the Yod formation of 1979, making a first step toward concrete realism at the Uranus semisquare Pluto in 1986 and coming under test in the Uranus square Pluto of 2012-15. There's more to go on this, and the Uranus-Pluto opposition of 2046-48 promises to be a critical time when some variant of what was foreseen in the 1960s will have succeeded or failed to become mainstream The overall vision concerned transforming society into a less materialistic, more spiritually-driven, ecologically sound, humanistic, deep-democratic and creative society.

Other factors arising at the time included the proliferation of mass travel, medical engineering, large-scale planning, advances in engineering and manufacturing, the rise of the modern guerrilla and terrorist and the dawn of a new questioning of the meaning of life – fundamentalism, found in all traditional faiths as well as in rationalism, is a reaction to the deep uncertainties created by this quandary.

Social polarisation often characterises these major power-periods in history – a rift between forward- and backward-looking social sectors. In 1890-1910 such polarisation involved socialism, early feminism, agnosticism and other reform movements. In the 1960s it concerned education, war, peace, minority rights, gender politics, racism, nuclear, ecological, farming, health and lifestyle issues, music and media, intoxicants and spirituality.

The Post-Industrial Era

This period was brewing from the 1960s onwards, inherent in all that had been building up during the 20th Century. The post-industrial era moved from a futuristic concept toward a dawning reality when three outer planets changed signs in 1984 – Pluto into Scorpio, Neptune into Capricorn and Chiron into Gemini. With this came the decline of rustbelt industries and old social formats in the West (formerly the First World), disintegration of the Soviet system (the Second World), and modernisation in the former Third World.

This process went critical in 1988-89, with Pluto in perihelion, Uranus semisquaring Pluto and the 1989 Capricorn-Cancer line-up. Suddenly, ecological issues, women's and minority rights, sexual abuse issues and freedom and democracy were uppermost in the public domain. Saturn was strong, obliging concrete fact-facing – in Tiananmen Square, Beijing, a democratic movement was quashed, in Russia social changes were hijacked by mafiosi posing as businessmen, and the West rubbed its hands, foolishly believing it had won the Cold War.

One of the predictions I made at the time was that, being in denial, and believing it had won the Cold War, the West would become what it hated, unconsciously taking on the shadow of the USSR that led to its downfall – a top-heavy *nomenklatura* or privileged class of power-holders and managers whose own interests would eclipse those of the people and the countries they ruled. This has indeed happened in the West in the twenty years since: a system dominated by CEOs, lawyers, bankers and experts which, as in the case of the Soviet Union, lack the tools and understanding for reforming the system it controls.

The Capricorn and Scorpio flavour of the time emphasised matters that many would have preferred to skip over. The sclerotic West was increasingly throttled by its top-heavy military and business interests. Meanwhile, the melting of national borders worldwide as a result of globalisation stimulated revived nationalism or ethnicism in many parts, partially as an emotional reaction to the standardising and culturally-insensitive effect of globalisation, and partially because many nations were proving inappropriate to current need. The old order hung on, giving appearances of bringing change when in fact pouring new wine into old bottles. It was to come under test during the Uranus square Pluto of 2012-15.

In the 1987 edition of this book I wrote, "We have all the solutions available to us or close at hand, spiritually, socially, economically and technologically, but we yet have to generate the overall global will and capacity to apply them". Saturn, Uranus and Neptune conjuncting in Capricorn between 1989 and 1993 implied structural change – a global *perestroika* – though one of the biggest such changes, largely unnoticed, was the concealed takeover of governments by corporate interests.

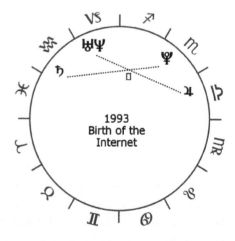

1993
Birth of the
Internet

Sophisticated evasions of the real issues took place during the 1990s: potentially liberating inventions such as internet and mobile telephony emerged around the

1993 Uranus-Neptune conjunction, yet their full social benefits were constrained by the uses people put them to – not least manic money-making and the creation of a virtual world which became to an extent an escape from and surrogate for real life. Early developers and adopters could not then foresee that the information superhighway would be abused by spammers and scammers, and for disinformation, commercial hegemony and surveillance.

O Brave New World

The multiple conjunction of 1989-93 in Capricorn implied a major change in institutions, laws and the economic system, to render them more appropriate to the needs of the time. This happened in the Soviet bloc, across the developing world and to an extent in China, but not significantly in the West, which temporarily prolonged its shelf-life through technological change and an extension of corporate reach worldwide. But what was missed was a global need for economic and institutional reorientation to emergent ecological and climatic facts and social needs. Denial and resistance were strong (the shadow side of Capricorn), creating ever more complex and convoluted outcomes and postponing fundamental change. This later continued when Pluto entered Capricorn from 2008 onwards: faced with a deep 'credit crunch' as the ingress happened, and the threat of more to come, token reforms occurred in the West and the global economic system but fundamental restructuring this was not. Pluto remains in Capricorn until 2024: there is more to go on this story. The key issue here is that organisational systems need to adapt to and fulfil the needs of people and nature, not vice versa.

The world economic system is based on a competitive, not a cooperative, model of operation, yet the cooperative model is where things are heading, by force of necessity – corrective cooperation amongst people and nations and cooperation with nature. The pressure for this is brought by environmental, climatic and resource factors, yet it concerns the way that society is organised and the structures providing the framework for civilisation. It requires a fundamental systems-change, and the cost of making such a change would in the longterm be less than the cost of not doing it. But short-term, narrower interests still prevail, at great cost to the future, and the big question is, when and how will this change?

To survive, a structure and system needs to adapt to energy-changes so that energy can flow through it most efficiently. This is why the West is now tipping into decline: its vested interests, including consumers and property-owners, prevent it from moving where it needs to go, largely out of fear of loss. The new direction of travel was established in the mid-1960s and we have used up a lot of time failing to follow it. Hence that the former Third World now overtakes the developed world on the outside – this is an evolutionary adaptation. The same happened a century ago when the centre of gravity in the West shifted from Britain and Europe to USA.

This is partially a natural historic shift and partially the result of refusal to change at and after a culture reaches its zenith. As the historian Arnold Toynbee once taught, if a civilisation fails to regenerate its indwelling spirit, creativity and guiding ethic when it has reached its zenith (which was reached in the West in the 1960s-80s), while it has the resources and initiative to do so, then it resorts to default behaviour, replicating established successful formulae until, sooner or later, it loses energy and is sidelined and superseded.

The period 1984-2024 has been Capricorn-dominated. While Capricorn's role in the zodiac is to contribute stability in the longterm, its shadow side resists change regardless of need. Thus the developing world is starting afresh, increasingly making its own rules and defining the global future. The dynamism of a culture is quite accurately reflected in the average age of its inhabitants: in Europe it is around 45 while in much of the developing world it is 20-25. Youngsters push for change while older people tend to keep things pegged where things stood when they were young. The proliferation of older people worldwide is both steadying and damaging in these times of much-needed change.

Many astrologers anticipated more dramatic events during the 1993 Uranus-Neptune conjunction than seemed to take place. Yet with a conjunction like that, blitzing headlines aren't necessarily to be expected unless perhaps Jupiter and Saturn are involved (which they weren't significantly). A conjunction such as this generally starts trends and developments that become visible later on as the cycle unfolds. Yet what was happening in the 1990s was an increasing systemic avoidance, by resorting to increasing consumptiveness, entertainment, disinformation and resource exploitation. The developed world lost its sense of direction, opting for 'more of the same', while the initiative was incrementally taken up by the developing world.

Assisting this was an ingress shift in 1995-98: Uranus and Neptune entered Aquarius and Pluto moved into Sagittarius. These ingresses didn't have to mean avoidance – they could have meant a genuine deepening of freedom and democracy and the cultivation of new perspectives. The emphasis shifted from structures to people, to public opinion and belief, with a growing Sagittarian cult of optimism, yet this didn't go deep enough to bring the global *perestroika* and *glasnost* or restructuring and transparency that were needed.

People sought change as long as it didn't affect them, being well informed yet unwilling to be the first to change. Increasingly complicit in collective denial, we busily pursued our lives while knowingly permitting incorrect and unwise trends – everything from over-fishing to the revival of slavery – to continue. The cult of progress peaked, despite increasingly impactful crises in the human and natural worlds, and people shrugged shoulders and carried on with their lives. 'Someone ought to fix it as long as it doesn't affect me'.

Then came a sequence of ingresses and a major configuration. In 2008 Pluto entered Capricorn and the West entered the 'credit crunch'; in 2010-11 Uranus entered Aries, turning a time of Piscean insight and revelation into an Arian burst of kicking and screaming; in 2011-12 Neptune entered its home sign, Pisces, bringing a feast of revelations piquantly drizzled with a garnish of chaos and derailment; in 2012 the Uranus-Pluto square, rumbling ominously since 2008, went exact. In 2014 it was jacked up by Jupiter in Cancer into a T-square and the storms blew, then it was pumped up further by Mars in Libra into a Grand Cross and the bombs flew (the chart for this is in chapter 10).

At the time of writing (2014) the story is not complete. The exact Uranus-Pluto square continues into 2015 but, if you look back at the Uranus-Pluto conjunction of 1965-66, the peak of the action in terms of visible events took place in 1967-70, *after* the exact configuration, with the consequences unfolding thereafter. In other words, a configuration prises things open, often amongst a smallish minority of people who incubate the change and extend it from there. So things don't necessarily 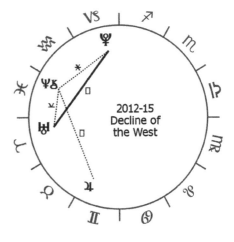 die down and return to normal when a major aspect passes: the cork pops and a lot of fizzing happens, spilling all over the future and setting off chain-reactions.

Fundamental change *is* happening. It could have happened faster or more easily, but it is now coming through the back door and the floorboards. Some have believed that fundamental change would come as an apocalyptic shock or disaster but it is coming more surreptitiously, accentuated by small yet potent, catalytic events. We are well hardened to disasters and threats, with our resistance, indifference and busy distraction duly strengthened, so perhaps we need wearing down in another way, eroding our weak spots. We all know *something is going on*.

So the big question of the Uranus square Pluto period has been: what will cause the world to acknowledge that it has a major problem, that the clock is ticking and that we must throw all our resources at it and do whatever it takes to deal with it? There are no easy answers to this, no simple ideologies or master-plans to follow. This said, we know quite clearly what *not* to do: carrying on as normal, hoping the problem will go away. Things are moving fast and, if you are reading this book some years after its publication, some answers might already have emerged.

What Next?

Predicting the future is a mug's game and a trap many astrologers and pundits regularly fall into, including me. However, we can foresee future power-periods and estimate some possibilities.

The late 2020s. Next up comes a mutual sextile of Uranus in Gemini, Neptune in Aries and Pluto in Aquarius between 2025 and 2028. This is potentially promising. It compares with a grand trine of Uranus in Taurus, Neptune in Virgo and Pluto in Capricorn occurring in 1771 during the build-up to the American and French revolutions, at a time of inventiveness, creativity and exploration, cultural, political and scientific florescence. Old structures lapsed and new possibilities sprouted.

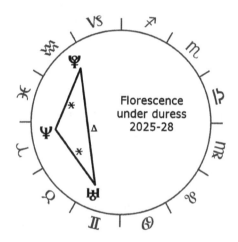

Florescence under duress 2025-28

What actually unfolds in the late 2020s depends very much on the overall outcomes of the Uranus-Pluto square in the 2010s, but there is the potential here for a cultural and scientific upswing, as well as major social changes and political about-turns. The sextiles and trine involved are likely to open up the flow of events and developments, leading to a time of great progress and creativity – probably manifested most amongst the young adults of that time – those born in the first decade of the 2000s.

The early 2040s. Following this is a square of Uranus in Leo to Neptune in Taurus in 2040-41, the opening square following the 1993 Uranus-Neptune conjunction. This could be a significant time of transition – the preceding waning square, another transitional time, was in 1954-55. Since the 1993 conjunction signified a major burst of globalisation (the fall of the Soviet system, the rise of China and India, the dawn of the internet), of proliferating atrocities (Bosnia, Rwanda and terrorism) and technical advances (nanotechnology, the Genome Project, mobile phones and the International Space Station) we might expect a progression of what emerged around 1993. Perhaps the big question here is, *who decides* in this globalised world, especially in the face of likely waves of multiple crises? This question of global

governance, however it is to be done, is perhaps the key question here in the 2040s, since other pressing issues depend on this issue working well. The 2040s will be a busy and intense decade, perhaps a critical turning-point, and there's more to come.

The late 2040s. Next comes an opposition of Uranus in Virgo to Pluto in Pisces in 2046-48, the climax of the Uranus-Pluto cycle begun in the mid-1960s. This period could be crucial. The 1960s represented an enormous leap – so big that the older generation of that time completely failed to understand the younger generation and what it was conceiving. The full consequences of the 1960s will fully face us by the 2040s – they are already facing us today. We have long known that this would happen, and the period between the Uranus-Pluto square in 2012-15 and the opposition in 2046-48 will be critical in defining what we're left with after 2050. We are now closer to the late 2040s than we are to the mid-1960s and the future is exerting an increasing pressure, in a sense fighting with the past for control of the present.

Several issues of the 1960s can be identified here: ecological and climatic questions, interracial and gender issues, matters of health, lifestyle and meaning-of-life, digital technologies, decolonialisation and globalisation, community life, food and resource security, space exploration, genetics and organics, spirituality, sexuality, population demographics, mental health, human behaviour and human rights. It can be assumed that issues such as these,

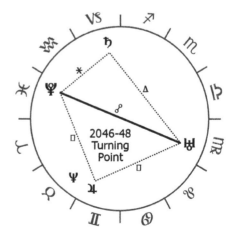

with which the current Uranus-Pluto cycle began, will have climaxed by the late 2040s: it could be a major turning point. By this time we will probably finally know whether Earth and all who sail on her are undergoing rebirth or destruction – or somewhere in between.

A New Time – of some sort

The 2060s. It doesn't stop there. In 2061-65 comes a waxing square of Neptune in Gemini to Pluto in Pisces, with Uranus adding two sesquiquadrates from Scorpio. This Neptune-Pluto waxing square follows on from the conjunction of 1891-2 (the electronic age) and the waning square of 1819-21 (the steam age). My guesstimate is that this could be a post-crisis hump to cross – the main crisis conceivably being in the 2040s. By the 2060s we will be living with the consequences of such a crisis, challenged to make something of the new situation we find ourselves in. Arguably, our current horizon of seeing into the future ends here, since there are so many open questions and unforeseeables ahead that it is impossible at this stage to estimate where we will be standing by the 2060s, or what happens afterwards.

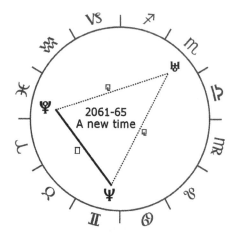

Let's look at the previous five-century Neptune-Pluto cycle, beginning in the 1390s and ending in the 1890s. Although in the 1400s it did not look as if Europeans would come to dominate the world by the 1890s, this cycle, with the urban-industrial, imperial and globalising effect it had, did indeed begin visibly moving that way by the time of the opening square in the 1560s – Europeans were seriously impacting on the Americas, Africa and Asia and the end-product of that cycle was beginning to become visible.

The peak of that cycle, the opposition, was in 1648-49, and Uranus conjuncted Neptune in Sagittarius at the same time as Neptune was opposing Pluto in Gemini. This was the end of the Thirty Years War in Europe, the English civil war and the High Baroque – a time during which Europe was painfully moving toward a new world-dominating future which would be visible by the waning square around 1820 and fully operative by the conjunction of the 1890s. The opposition of the 1640s brought the rise of the Manchu Ch'ing dynasty in China and the zenith of the Mughal empire in India, the development of the Americas, now dominated by Europeans and a growing globalisation of trade.

The waning square of 1820 showed the shape of things to come. USA was founded, South America fully latinised, India, China and the Middle East were seriously influenced by Europe, and Africa was being colonised by Europeans. The steam age had begun and the pace of human history was accelerating. By the conjunction of the 1890s all the pieces were in place for a globalised world – for better and worse – and a new cycle started, in the opening quarter of which we now are.

What is the overall theme of the current Neptune-Pluto cycle? Well, the semisextile took place in 1916-17 in WW1, the semisquare in 1930-32 during the Depression, the long sextile went through the 1950s up to 1984 with a revisitation in the late 2020s, the square is in 2061-65, the opposition in 2137-40 and the next conjunction comes in 2386. Thus far we have moved from the peak of the steam era and the beginning of the electrical era around 1900, where the world's centre of gravity was London but soon to shift to New York City, through to a transition point today where human, economic and cultural activity are widely spread from Dubai, Mumbai and Shanghai to Mexico City and Sao Paulo, and the world is fast becoming a truly global entity – probably by the 2060s, and by necessity since so many of its big issues are global in extent.

Yet the paradox here is that it is unlikely that a global megamachine, however effective, will have what it takes to handle the issues before us. Some of the key issues here are the question of human happiness and of willing mass-participation in human affairs, the dawning of genuine peace and ecological security, and the ample supporting of an enormous planetary population of probably ten billion souls. There is an important local and personal element to these questions, without which a megamachine organised from top down, forcing people to comply with its norms, is likely to go seriously off-course.

This is not just a matter of electoral democracy, public opinion and ethnic and cultural self-determination: it goes far deeper, requiring a transformation of human behaviour that permits practical resource-sharing and resolution of conflicts of interest. Human behaviour cannot simply be regulated, legislated, manufactured and programmed – if this were so, then the socialist systems of the past century would have succeeded more than they did. Such a change as is required needs to come, I continue to believe, from a change in the indwelling spirit in all of us as individuals.

Yet getting through the forthcoming decades is a key crux point in humanity's long history. It involves living through and responding to a state of emergency, with both the tragedies and the blessings this can bring. It concerns dealing with the consequences of the past and the choices we have made, but it does not involve a clear sense of where we are heading – except for salvation from a self-created disaster. If we assume that the world survives the current crisis reasonably intact, what is the aim? What stage will we have reached by 2140, at the opposition of Neptune and Pluto, in 120ish years from now?

Will we be devastated and much reduced, or living in a mega-tech world where we're all Orwellian drones, or living partially off-planet, or dwelling in something approximating an ideal world, a heaven on earth? It seems to me that we're deciding this between now and the 2060s, with the crunch-point in the late 2040s. Yet this is a prognosis, not an existent fact. Today's children will be the ones able to report back.

We can certainly cultivate hopes and fears, and our guiding philosophies and current experience also inform our vision of the future, but the future itself remains in the Neptunian realm of imagination, yet to pass through the Saturnian filter of hard facts. And there we must leave it. I have my hopes and preferences, as you probably have too, and the creation of our future reality is all up to all of us, together.

Yet one thing is true. We live in a crux period of human history, and everything is at stake. These are not boring, routine times. We are all involved – even the few isolated tribes who as yet have not interacted with the modern world. And the onus rests with us, with humans.

The Aquarius-Leo Age

Before we go, we must look at this question. There are many misunderstandings about the Age of Aquarius. First of all, it is not clear when it begins – estimates range from 1550 to 2300. The problem is that there are no clear boundaries to the constellations, so it all depends where you place them and how you measure it. The constellations are not of equal ecliptic length or longitude, just to confuse things. If we were astronomically diligent, according to the best calculations, the beginning of the age is yet to happen in year 2691, when the sidereal spring equinox point enters the constellation Aquarius (as currently defined by astronomers): thus all the excitement about the Aquarian Age is a little premature. At the time of writing in 2014 the spring equinox (or sidereal vernal) point stands at 5° Pisces, moving backwards at one degree every 72 years.

The dawn of the Aquarian Age was popularised in a 1960s musical called *Hair*, and the idea caught on from there. It told of a time when our world would reach a state of spiritualised perfection where everything would be nicely sorted out and we would all be happy and okay. The mechanisms for getting there, put forward in the 1970s-90s, included 'critical mass', the hundredth monkey theory and hopes of a spiritual transformation in humanity or a sudden shift of planetary energy, yet movement in that direction has been faltering and, if anything, the world's ills have got manifestly worse. Though equally this could be understood as 'the darkest hour before dawn' of a global catharsis, since so many interrelated issues need sorting out at once. We return to the question therefore of building, negotiating and thrashing out the details of the future with our bare hands – it looks as if God, the ETs or the archangels aren't going to rescue us from this one.

The astrological ages, approximately 2,148 years long, are part of a 25,772 year cycle of precession of the equinoxes, caused by the gravitational effect of the Sun and Moon on the Earth's equatorial bulge, causing a slow secondary movement of the Earth's poles, over and above its daily rotation on its axis, rather like a spinning top's net motion.

The cycle of orientation of the Earth's equator, which is at at 23° from the plane of our solar system (the ecliptic), is not exactly the same as the cycle of motion of the Earth around the Sun – it shifts by one degree every 72ish years. The point in time where the Sun is exactly at the spring equinox point, with equal days and nights, moves retrograde through the backdrop of the stars behind it, over 25,772 years. The Earth's north pole doesn't always point toward the Pole Star as it does now – it pointed toward Thuban (*Alpha Draconis*) 4,500 years ago, in 8,000 years' time it will point toward Deneb (*Alpha Cygni*), and in 12,000 years Vega (*Alpha Lyrae*).

So the astrological ages represent historic shifts of theme and viewpoint on a global-historic scale. This does not automatically imply a major global consciousness-breakthrough of the kind sought by some new age believers, however. Also, as already mentioned, there is debate over when this happens. If enlightenment were to occur on a planetary scale, there is little inherent reason why it would happen on the cusp of Pisces and Aquarius. It simply implies a change of themes preoccupying humanity on a longterm time-scale.

Meanwhile, humanity's enlightenment remains a mass human choice which certainly can be prompted by celestial circumstances, but whether humanity utilises that opportunity is another matter. Arguably, in and following the 1960s we had a major evolutionary opportunity which some have utilised and most people on Earth have not, or not completely. Yet one thing is true: humanity, once segmented into cultures and localities, is now merging as a global people, growing immensely in numbers, and this in itself represents an enormous evolutionary change.

Many have been the times in history when we have believed we are on the edge of a new age, but the pressure of world population in the 21st Century, peaking around mid-century before slowly declining, makes a big difference to our collective experience. The psychic and vibrational effect of 7-10 billion people, all thinking thoughts, feeling feelings and having experiences on the same small planet, cannot be overlooked. Contrary to the perspective of current scientific ideology, it could, for example, be a major cause of extreme weather events, by dint of the stirring effect on climate of billions of people broadcasting their thoughts, stresses and concerns. And not only this.

Since this cycle of 25,772 years is related to the precession of the equinox points backwards through the stellar constellations, we need to look at *both* equinox points, spring and autumn, not just one. Thus, since around the time of Christ or 221 CE, whichever date you choose, we have been experiencing a Pisces-Virgo age, and now we are moving toward an Aquarius-Leo age. Pisces-Virgo concerns the power of beliefs (Pisces), and their relationship with facts (Virgo). This has been an age of cosmologies (Pisces) and organisational systems (Virgo) – and it is interesting that, hapwise, the mid-1960s and the late-2040s line-ups discussed above occur in these signs.

The age of Aquarius-Leo is about social solidarity, social forms, rationality and collectivism (Aquarius), *and* individualism, personal creativity and significance (Leo). It also concerns leadership (Leo) and 'intelligent followership' (Aquarius) – and perhaps a transformation in what these mean. In the coming age we need to explore the advantages of collective cooperation without losing the significance of the individual: public life needs to serve the individual as much as the individual serves public life.

This was an important principle which Aquarian ideas such as socialism tended to miss out, since they obliged the individual to subsume themselves to the machine, sacrificing individuality for the benefits of solidarity – or cruel dictatorship, depending on your viewpoint. To participate wholeheartedly in a collective social adventure, an individual has to feel *personal significance*, making an autonomous choice to be part of the wider world, to actively *belong* and contribute. This applies to social subgroups, ethnic, religious and national groupings too. Social cohesion cannot be applied through rules, bureaucracies and ideologies since these are riddled with problems. It comes instead from the heart of every individual, as a freely-inspired, conscious impulse engendered without coercion.

A confusion has arisen between the notion of a new age and that of the Aquarius-Leo age. The notion of the new age is derived from an observation that humanity stands at a critical stage in its evolution, never reached before. Everyone and everything is involved. We now have the capacity to devastate everything, or to create something new. So we do stand at a critical stage, yet the coincidence of this with the beginning of an Aquarius-Leo age doesn't necessarily mean that the astrological age will bring an enormous human or spiritual breakthrough. Nevertheless, our passing into the Aquarius-Leo Age, sometime in future, has relevance, but it is unlikely to constitute The Big Solution To Everything. It will simply mean a new unfoldment of reality in new format, and what we do with that is up to us. Sorry if this is disappointing news!

17

Time and Motion Studies

If this book is of any enduring use, I hope it encourages you to develop more of a living feel for the nature of time, with some help from astrology. Having waded through this book and thought things through, what actually can we do with what we have learned?

Bringing it all Together

If you have worked through all of the contributory factors mentioned in this book, you might feel you've jumped into a bottomless pool, with an overload of things to watch and learn, but it's not really like this. This is not a course for a professional qualification for systematic rote-learning: it's a life-improvement strategy to help us understand what's going on underneath life's daily details. Absorbing the amount of astrology you need to augment your overall understanding of life is a lifelong pursuit, with rewards that crop up continually and at unexpected places. So just start with those things you're drawn to, and progress from there.

The key ingredients here are an ephemeris and a computer program, so that you can track the motions of the planets. I recommend both, but one will do. The secret is to keep your eye on them and watch. In astrology the permutations of different patterns and configurations is continually changing, and over time there is a beauty and sequentiality to it all that is wondrous to behold. It is from observation that we need to do most of our learning, because a book can only generalise and share the author's perception of things. Meanwhile, there's the beauty of the actual way that things unfold in real life.

To give an example, a configuration of three or more planets will rarely be exact on one day. If several planets are forming into a configuration, there will be a sequence by which the aspects and factors become exact and, at the time it is happening, this in itself is significant. Let's take the 'Fire and Flood' Stellium of 12th January 1994 as an example. The newmoon late on January 11th, at 23.10 GMT, was at 21 ♑. Meanwhile, at that moment, Mars was at 17 ♑, Venus at 20 ♑, Neptune at 20 ♑, Uranus was at 22 ♑ and Mercury was at 26 ♑ – all of them within orb and part of the same configuration. Also Saturn was at 28♒ and Pluto at 27♏, adding their sub-clauses from the side – they weren't part of the Stellium, but it was significant that they were at work at the same time. So let's look at the sequence of events in this Stellium.

Uranus had last conjuncted Neptune at on 25th October 1993, 3½ months earlier – this was the major outer-planet aspect underlying the time, and they were still only two degrees from each other in January. Mercury conjuncted Venus at 27♐ on 25th December. Sun conjuncted Mars at 5♑ on 27th December. Mercury conjuncted Mars at 9♑ on 1st January. Saturn squared Pluto on 2nd January. Sun conjuncted Mercury at 13♑ on 4th January. Venus conjuncted Mars at 13♑ on 6th January. Mercury conjuncted Neptune at 20♑ on 8th January. Mercury conjuncted Uranus at 22♑ on 9th January. Then the new moon took place at 21♑ on 11th January, highlighting, tying together and triggering the whole configuration. Sun and Moon conjuncted Neptune at 20♑ on 11th January too. Venus conjuncted Neptune at 20♑ and Sun conjuncted Uranus at 22♑ on 12th January. Venus conjuncted Uranus at 22♑ on 13th January. Mars conjuncted Neptune at 21♑ on 16th January. Sun conjuncted Venus at 26♑ on 17th January. Mars conjuncted Uranus at 21♑ on 18th January. Busy and intense times, huh? Lots of stuff happening.

When the Moon swung through on 11th-12th January, the sequence of its conjunctions with other planets was: Mars, Venus, Neptune, Sun, Uranus, Mercury – the critical point being when it hit Neptune, Sun and Uranus. So we could characterise this sequence as being emotional first (Mars and Venus), then transpersonal (Neptune, Sun and Uranus) and then connective or mental (Mercury). The energy-atmosphere changed over time.

But when we look at aspects from each planet to the others, the Stellium cleared its Mars aspects at an earlier stage (27th Dec-6th January), its Mercury aspects between 1st and 9th January (Mercury was moving quite fast), and its Venus, Neptune and Uranus aspects later on, after the watershed newmoon. This says something about the Martian fierceness of the buildup at the beginning, connected up by Mercury, fully highlighted on the Neptune-tinted newmoon and eased out somewhat by the Venus and Neptune aspects that followed. Had we had Venus and Neptune aspects first, followed by Mars and Uranus aspects later, the ruthlessly cruel aspect of the fires in Australia and floods in Europe might have been very different. The deeper meaning of the whole scenario emerged only later in the sequence, when the Neptune and Uranus aspects came through properly, activating the ongoing longterm Uranus-Neptune conjunction that had been exact in 1993.

Now, isn't that interesting? From a distance, we see this configuration as one Stellium but, at the time, there was a sequence of events that did the spadework of the actual event, very much affecting the way it affected nature and people. It was an intense few weeks. The bushfires in Australia lasted from 27th December to 16th January, and the rains in Western Europe began on 19th December, ending around mid-January. We have not considered here the added factors of an ongoing war in Bosnia, the historic Kremlin Accords on nuclear missiles between USA and Russia on 14th January, acute political problems in Pakistan, the build-up to the Rwandan massacres in April-May, troubles in the West Bank of Palestine (the Hebron massacre on 25th February) and the political transition out of apartheid in South Africa (with the inauguration of Nelson Mandela as president on 10th May). All of these were symptomatic of the underlying Uranus-Neptune conjunction of the time.

Astrology allows us to dissect such a juncture as this in detail, seeing the sequence of psycho-historic trends afoot at the time. It helps us understand what's behind it all. In the case of our example, it was a statement saying "Extreme weather events are here to stay, so get used to it – and it has something to do with the way society is organised and governed, so what practical measures in terms of money and legislation will you do about it?". Well, in this case, the answer was "Nothing much – we're in denial, so perhaps you'll have to impact harder on us before we get the message". But the decision to do nothing much is nevertheless a decision, affecting the way things will go in the future.

What to Look For

When watching the flow of time, looking out for power points in time, there are no hard and fast rules about what to do, but here are some guidelines:

- Keep your eyes on newmoons and fullmoons, and particularly eclipses;

- Watch the solstices, equinoxes and cross-quarters (and also times when other planets, particularly slower-moving ones, cross these points);

- Look out for conjunctions, oppositions and squares formed by the Sun to the other planets (if you wish, add sextiles and trines too);

- Watch for conjunctions, squares and oppositions by other planets to each other;

- Keep an eye on the stations of Mercury, Venus and Mars, and also the annual stations of the slower-moving planets;

- Look out for multiple aspects or configurations involving three or more planets – these are important;

- Keep in mind the movements of the slower planets from Jupiter outwards, and their ingresses into new signs;

- Look for general patterns in planetary motions and aspects, such as a preponderance of certain kinds of aspects, or clusters of ingresses;

- Watch in general for odd astrological quirks and developments that crop up from time to time – these might be disconnected from each other astrologically but nevertheless, if they happen around the same time, this is significant.

By doing this, you will accumulate a body of experience and noted memories of events which will add to your experiential observations over time. When something is happening astrologically (such as a Jupiter opposition Saturn, a Grand Cross or a period when various stations happen close together), it's always worth tracking back through your ephemeris to look at previous instances of similar astrological events. This might soak up 10-20 minutes every now and then, but it's worth it.

It helps to make a special zodiac chart for following planetary motions. These motions can indeed be followed using a computer program, but engaging in a manual process helps to memorise and watch more closely whatever is happening at any time. This can be done by making a board or a using a noticeboard with the zodiac signs on it in a circle, and gathering some pins or pieces to represent the planets, which you then can move around on a regular basis, using your ephemeris. Over time, this method helps greatly in tracking and understanding the motions of the Sun, Moon and planets. After a while, you'll be able to visualise such things in your mind.

If you have a studious bent, there are further things you can do. One is to make graphs or an astro-diary of the aspects you want to watch (choose your level of detail). Do this each year – it might take several hours, but it's worth it. Or you can work through the ephemeris, writing in an ordinary diary all of the aspects, stations and other astrological events that you choose to observe. There are a few astrological diaries available on the market that do this (though many come from USA, using American time zones). But the advantage of doing it manually is that it makes you think about and note things that a glance at a pre-printed diary might not reveal. If you are so inclined, it can also be valuable to keep diary notes of your observations of what has happened in connection with astrological energy-weather events, for reference at future times. Choose your level of detail to suit your inclinations and needs.

About Transits

In this book we have been looking at the overall movement of the planets and the astrological events they bring to pass. We have not examined birth charts at all. But related to this kind of work is the study of transits, the motions of the planets in the heavens in comparison to the positions of the planets in your own birth chart. Transits help us to understand what's going on for us personally in relation to the overall picture of motion of the planets at any time.

To give an example, while writing this book, Saturn was hovering around a conjunction to the Mars in Scorpio in my birth chart. This was both a cause of frustration and it was hard work at times – especially when Saturn was retrograding toward my Mars and then stationing on top of it – yet it was also helpful in terms of helping me pursue the necessary discipline of writing a book – long hours, with lots of focus. It also helped greatly to know that this was happening, so that I could distinguish between the astrological phenomenon in question and my responses to it. In other words, I didn't get into grumbly moods for nothing – something was happening to nudge me that way and, by understanding that, I could deal with it more clearly and productively, turning it to good use.

So examining your transits can be very worthwhile, not only as a way of learning about your birth chart and the real-life way that the planets and positions in your chart actually operate, but also as a way of understanding the planets in motion now, and how they work. You can find information about transits in a variety of astrology books. But again, it's mainly a question of observing transits, using them as an awareness and learning exercise in your own life and using this as one further way of familiarising yourself with astrology.

Back to the Roots

One of the important jobs of early astronomer-astrologers was to identify power points in time and to figure out what to do with them when they came. They knew that there were special times available when it was possible to go beyond the normal round of life, to engage with the spirits of place and the powers of nature and the universe. They felt part of everything, as if there were a contract or covenant to fulfil with the universe, and they felt a responsibility to play their part in it. Nowadays, in our morally-compromised societies, we tend not to think much about our responsibility and duty as souls until perhaps we are threatened with death and forced to be honest with ourselves in ways that we tend to avoid during life. But they knew they were lucky to be alive, blessed with Earth's bounties, and they sought to pay their dues and do their bit. It's only natural.

Rites would be staged at power points such as stone circles, mountaintops and holy wells, at specific chosen times when it was possible to access deeper levels of reality, to work with the spirits of place and the causal threads within creation. Power points in time and space are portals, gateways to deeper levels of reality where people could get under the bonnet to engineer the threads of time and creation, not just for their own benefit but also to help Creation itself, since they were an integral part of it. We still are part of Creation, whether or not we clearly understand this, and we and our descendants pay an enormous price for failing to understand it clearly. Ancient people worked within the group psyche, the soul of nature and spirit of place, with ancestors, deities and powers, tapping into infinity. The mathematical and astronomical format of stone circles and other ancient sites represented an attempt to embody the coding and essence of universal design in microcosmic form, here on Earth.

Critical to this was working with power points in time, when the veils between reality-levels became thinner and more pervious. It would allow deep-level problem-solving and help with the new season's crops, it would facilitate distant communication, bring healing or help with enhancing magical intentions, and it would please the gods, however they were then seen. Festivals, ceremonies and gatherings would coincide with these special times and people would migrate sometimes long distances to participate – remember, in those days they walked or travelled by boat, but this was an investment they felt was important. And it brightened up their lives too, enabling them to meet distant friends and relatives or people from other tribes. They were literally going away on their holy days.

In astrology we lend symbols to energy-frequencies and identifiable kinds of experience. This names and defines them, helping us identify them and perceive their relations with each other. Thus we can mention Mercury in Capricorn sextile to Venus in Pisces, and anyone who understands astrologese will get a fix on what we're talking about. In astrology's case, the existence of observable planets means that, despite having different cultural formats, methods and rules, astrologers round the world work with essentially the same variables – planets and their relative positions – and those variables do roughly the same things, even when seen through the optic of cultural interpretations and astrological systems from different parts of the world.

Our depth-consciousness recognises subtle forms and meaning through *symbols*. When we dream we cook up symbols and scenarios that are not only visual-mental but also feelingful-tangible and, in the end, dream experience is as meaningful and real as waking life – the same watching consciousness experiences both. Some symbols in our dreams are spontaneous, creative and transient while others draw on a stock of universal or cultural archetypes in the collective unconscious.

If I say 'Santa Claus', most people will know what I mean, referring to a bundle of qualities that constitute a shared understanding of who this archetype is and how he behaves – though different people will still have differing reactions to that. Santa, an ancient shamanistic archetype from the Baltic region, has inveigled his way into the lives of people worldwide. Even in Bethlehem in Palestine, where I do my humanitarian work, Santa is invoked in Jesus' birthplace at Christmas, bizarrely liked by both Christians and Muslims. Chinese love him too, nowadays – archetypes can be quite infectious, and people will sing of sleighbells without even knowing what they are, and perhaps never even having seen snow. 'O Little Town of Bethlehem' is also a strong archetypal image – even though Bethlehem now has over 100,000 people, many of them refugees, and it is walled in by the oppressive concrete separation walls of a military occupation.

Imaginal work can be used as a way of accessing deeper levels of consciousness and reality. It can help us understand ourselves and the dynamics of the unconscious, and also it has a healing effect, helping us resolve inner contradictions, stepping more fully into ourselves and dealing with the rough edges of our relationship with the world. Even in the case of people new to visualisation or conscious dreaming, and to astrology and its concepts, when they are asked to call up within them an image of Mars or Saturn, they often come up with images that are surprisingly similar, without any prompting, suggestion or advance knowledge.

They might be fresh to astrology and its symbology, yet they gain direct access to the essential archetype, even if it shows itself in a variety of forms reflecting the state each individual is in at the time. That is to say, Venus or Pluto might show themselves in a variety of guises to different people, but they are still recognisably Venus and Pluto, and different people's perceptions will have commonalities to them. The symbol is already *there* – we just need to see it and *get* it. Yet amazingly, though universal, it speaks to each of us individually too.

Awareness

Our connection with awareness rises and falls, taking on differing qualities and facets over time. Yet for each of us there are particular moments when we make significant breakthroughs in awareness, often prompted during crunches and confrontations, illness, moments of truth, 'Aha' revelations or relaxed musings. We experience a time- and reality-distortion within which profound, even life-changing insights can arise. Not just insights but profound changes in our patterning, health or the fortunes of our lives.

When we experience amplified timelessness, clocks might tick and normality grinds on around us yet we ourselves are in a different place: minutes might go by seeming like hours, or a day can pass really quickly. This stretching or compression of time is a natural symptom of being situated in a moment of consciousness growth.

Twenty minutes of meditation can sometimes have the same effect as days or weeks of normal psycho-emotional spadework. Judicious use of psychoactive substances can assist our evolutionary momentum, as can a day in the wilderness, the witnessing of a childbirth or a peaceful death, or experiencing one of those days when normality simply recedes and another reality takes over. Often, when we fall ill or experience a mishap, our soul is performing an override to force us to have 'down time', to prise us open and help us process something deep and necessary that ordinary busy life might not allow.

Thus we live in perhaps three interweaving dimensions of time.

- One, ticktock time, is based on the daily and annual cycles of light and darkness, winter and summer, giving us the clocks and calendars we all know, love and rather slavishly obey. This form of time lies within the realm of the known, connected particularly with Saturn.

- The second is an *evolutionary* kind of time that, relative to clock time, stretches and compresses in an elastic fashion. From our normal daily-life viewpoint it comes and goes but, from its own viewpoint, it has a regularity and continuity of its own, running its own 'back-story'. It is particularly affected by the momentum of our inner growth and progression, and it is connected with the outer planets. The continuity it endows in our lives depends greatly on the extent to which we allow space for the back story to participate in and even occasionally change the story-line in the front story of our lives.

- The third form of time we could call 'quirky time', which forms a bridge or a wormhole between ticktock and evolutionary time, causing them to influence and interfere with each other, with or without our willing participation. This comes in the form of situations such as illness, accidents, shocks or eye-opening moments, even orgasms or occasions of meditative or psychic insight. We could connect it with Chiron. In mythology, Chiron was a ferryman carrying souls over the river separating this world and the other world.

An old friend who died at age 50 told me before her death that her life had divided into two halves, the 48 years of her ordinary life and the two years of the extraordinary life she experienced while slowly dying of cancer. As a Buddhist and a natural optimist, Bryony made her slow death into a positive experience with accelerated inner evolution – though not without experiencing deep pain and tribulations. At the end of her funeral she had prescribed that Satchmo's 'What a Wonderful World' be played out loud – and this was her final statement. Evolutionary time registers duration in terms of intensity of experience and its depth and profundity, and her example demonstrates this. Two years and 48 years can each contain the same quantity of meaning and evolutionary experience.

I used to take groups of people to visit crop formations, which are special energy-spaces par excellence. Most people consider these weird and insignificant, or perhaps fascinating though hardly relevant. I would disagree – but then, ever since the Summer of Love in 1967, I've always been, for better or worse, a detractor from the opinions of the mainstream of society. Yet bathing in their energy fields can have a deeply transformative effect – it is really noticeable, and also a great blessing and honour to experience. Time-stretchings and paranormal experiences were common in the formations – everything from auditory distortions or strange lights in the sky, or amazing meetings with remarkable people, through to camera batteries suddenly going flat or physical ailments suddenly disappearing. The single most common piece of feedback these visitors would give was, "I feel as if I have come home". That is, their perceptual centre of gravity had shifted from ticktock to evolutionary time – to a realm where their souls indeed felt more at home, even when standing in the middle of a wheatfield. In some cases, there was visible reluctance in some people to return to the ticktock world. Understandable, but it is we who choose where to allocate our life energies and attention. And 2-3 hours in a crop formation sometimes felt like an aeon of time.

This time-slippage or time-pulsing isn't just a personal experience – it's also collective, and on occasions millions of people go into a time-warp together. This happens particularly when everyone is focused on the same thing, feeling shared feelings and co-resonating with each other, such as at a big event, in a crisis, revolution, war or disaster, or even at a concert or a football match. It's one of those "Where were you when President Kennedy was shot?" moments, imprinting deeply on all of us together. Such moments build up a group resonance field which takes on a life and reality of its own. They act as a pegging-point in time where people share a common frame of time-reference, thinking of it as an occasion when time momentarily stopped to let something else in, before we all returned to humdrum 'reality' again.

Sometimes society needs its altered states and catharses – there's far too much investment in normality, in hedging bets and taking safe options, and this leads to chronic dullness and spiritual poverty on a vast scale. It is destroying the world, since the collective front story says, "I don't have time to worry about this – someone ought to do something", while the back story says "I love this world and want to leave a good world to my grandchildren, and it matters". Customarily, the front story wins the argument, but the back story swoops in occasionally to completely overwhelm the front story and change history.

The times when the back story impinges on the front story are often crises where powerful archetypes become visible – such as the loss of children's lives in the bombings of Gaza, or when Yazidi refugees are marooned on a mountain in western Iraq, or Ebola disease breaks out in West Africa, or another boatload of refugees attempting to enter Australia is turned away (all of these being the current stories at the time I was writing this chapter in 2014). Meanwhile, crisis permits many issues to be processed together in an intense quantum-shifting manner – a crisis is a heated time-crucible where major issues are hot-housed in an accelerated, intensified way. The improbable becomes actual and the impossible becomes possible. Millions of people become aware of such crises at the same time, especially nowadays in our media-connected world, feeding their concern into a pool of collective concern and inner activity to create a reality-field with considerable power to change things.

When lying on our deathbeds and looking back on our lives, these times of intensity are often remembered more clearly than ordinary times, arousing a feeling that we've been part of something noteworthy in our lives. To an extent this depends on the amount to which we have permitted or sought such intensity by opening up the hatches rather than battening them down. Security-attachment, normality and affluence have a slowing or suppressing effect on evolution – they make time less memorable.

Learning to identify these access-points, or to recognise them when they arise, helps us catch the wave, to make constructive use of it. Otherwise, these streams can use us, like a wave that hits us and bowls us over. It's valuable to catch such temporal power points when they arise. By this I mean *being aware* of them, making ourselves inwardly available to them and their energy-benefits, letting the wave carry us forward. It's mainly a matter of *inner availability* and *presence*, of being conscious and *with it*. Visiting a power point in space at a power point in time or devoting special time to ventilating the soul really helps.

More than just Ancient Remains

Ceremony, when well enacted, raises our awareness, bringing magic into the realm of the humdrum. I find I greatly benefit from visiting ancient sites. While at such places I put myself into a receptive mode, opening myself up to the Unknown and to the Great Mystery, inwardly acting out a dialogue with the place, having a largely wordless chat with its hidden powers and its presence. Others might see me waving my arms around in a peculiar way, while I myself might be acting out the profoundest dynamics of the great universe.

A characteristic quality of a power point in space is that we find, when we leave such a place, that we have moved into a significantly different, more positive, clear and relaxed state than when we came – we've undergone a level-shift. Not all places everywhere have the capacity to affect us in this way. For me, places such as Glastonbury Abbey and Tor, Hippocrates' Asclepeion on the Greek island of Kos, the Ibrahimi Mosque in Hebron in Palestine, the Ring of Brogar in Orkney in Scotland, crop circle ground zero at Alton Barnes in England, or Carn Lês Boel in Cornwall, have all been places where I have experienced major mileposts in my life. These moments have lasted but hours, yet they have had a profound, defining effect on me and life's course.

Dowsers say that the presence of underground water domes or blind springs (underground sources of 'primary water' and subtle energy from deeper in the Earth) and of intersections of sub-surface water-flows create the kind of subtle energy-fields that make for a power place. The ancients sought out, sensed these places and modified them, erecting stones or mounds and doing spiritual work to enhance them. They did this out of a recognition of power points' value in accessing deeper states and shifting reality. Power points are places of magic, uplift and atmosphere, where inner work takes on an increased dimensionality and potency.

When I arrive at a power place I approach it slowly, pausing before entering, asking whether the site's guardians will accept and welcome me. Then, if permitted, I enter respectfully, perhaps planting an offering, and most of all sitting quietly and listening within. Listening is really important. Sometimes I feel an urge to circumambulate the site (mindfully walking around it several times) or to sit in a certain spot, or I sing or chant, or touch my forehead to the ground or carry out all manner of weird, unpremeditated antics, as the spirit moves me. Whatever arises at the time gives life a feeling of enrichment, depth, belonging and clarification. My perspective changes and problems I thought I had tend to resolve themselves. My state is changed, far more than would happen if I simply took a walk in the countryside.

Combining a visit to a power point in space with observance of a power point in time makes these potent moments all the more charged and moving. Time stretches and our spirit surfaces from underneath the incessant garbage of daily concerns. Dowsers testify that the aura expands radically at power points in space. Power points in time also encourage our auras to expand, or to brighten and modulate with the time-potencies available. At major power points and periods in time, the aura and energy-field of humanity as a whole grows stronger, and we as individuals feel carried by it, more *connected*, part of something bigger.

We need to receive these states and energy-conditions more willingly into ourselves. This is natural and easy if we set aside our concerns and preoccupations, permitting it to happen, through such practises as meditation or simply going out walking in the hills. As the Buddha taught 2,500 years ago, there is actually *no self* – it is a conception, a construct – and we are in truth the eyes, ears and hands of the universe experiencing itself. It's difficult to reconcile this with the pressures of modern life, where we are urged to assert our self-interest, but it's true: the division between ourselves and our world is largely a construct of our own making.

Levels of Time

Astrology is a language. It is not a belief system. It is a set of tools for application in any domain. It's always "Astrology and... (something else)", be this horticulture, psychotherapy, current events or health and healing. Whatever is your area of focus, astrology offers insights. Though it involves our brains, it's something that grows into our cells and bones, and it is something that is *felt* – you can sense and detect Neptunian weather, Saturnine situations and Marsy news headlines without recourse to ephemerides or mental deduction processes. It's a matter of paying attention to experience and gathering astrological gleanings through it, over a period of time. It does take time, but the investment is well worth it. Gradually you get a feel for astrology and, rather like learning to balance on a bicycle, while it's hard at first, before long it comes easily and naturally.

Throughout this book we have looked at a variety of levels of time, as highlighted by the different sidereal and synodic cycles of the planets as they move through the signs. We have looked closely at the faster cycles of the Moon, and at the Sun and inner planets, regulating cycles lasting around one or two years. We've examined Jupiter and Saturn and the way they affect the more momentous and weighty issues in our lives over the decades, at Chiron and its quirks and at the outer planets and the effect they have on the unfoldment of history and our part in it.

This way of seeing things helps us see the underlying threads and themes permeating life, not only enriching our understanding of things but serving quite functionally too. It can help us to plan out our lives, taking advantage of the quieter times and the times for action. It helps us become intuitively more efficient, moving more in harmony with the drift and undulation of life's energy-streams. It can save many frustrations too.

The breakthroughs, the despair, the contentment and the hunger, the togetherness and aloneness – these are ingredients in the magical brew we call life, and our experience of them draws attention to what is more abiding, timeless and perennial. The planets perpetually go their ways, and time and circumstance come and go, but there is something else, the witness, our 'cubic centimetre of awareness', which simply sees and experiences all. We learn most when it hurts most, when it shakes, quakes and rumbles, when there's nothing left to hang on to – this is what deepens our connection between the life-process and deeper consciousness.

What About Me?

We each are part of the collective, in our localities, social subgroups, regions, nations and cultures, and we are personally affected. We play a personal part in this collective unfoldment. The ultimate expression of this is to stand up and be counted, to add our personal energies to some kind of collective movement, in whatever sphere we're called to serve in. If we find ourselves in an escalating public situation such as an uprising, times of protest or celebration, then we're faced with a deep choice to come out and show our colours or to hang back and stay in our hole. There have been moments when people come out on the streets, in which many individuals have reported a feeling of compulsion to *be there*, to be part of it.

This involves losing our fear and playing our part. This does make a difference, even when such up-wellings of public opinion and collective power seem to fail. Taking the 2011 Arab revolutions as an example, though they were mostly suppressed or hijacked, they set an historic benchmark which eventually will work through into people's reality. Had people not stood up, sometimes making great sacrifices, such a benchmark would not have been set. The bit that's not reported in the media is the personal awakenings and growth-processes that started as a result of the revolutions, setting in motion processes of development that will unfold over the years. I can testify to this, having been part of the near-revolutions we had in the West in the late 1960s: the revolutions didn't work, yet they changed me, and many other people, and we've all been beavering away since then in keeping the light alive and reminding the world that love and peace indeed are all that we need. This message is still laughed at by some, but the story is not yet finished – there's more to come.

These big events are localised, and we cannot wait around for such opportunities, or also they might not be to our liking. The other key action we can take is to *pursue our life-purpose*, whatever that might be. God doesn't come down to tell you what it is, but you definitely feel it when you're on it: you feel as if you're in the right place at the right time, doing the right thing. The sign of not being 'on purpose' is a creeping feeling of depression, being stuck in a blind alley in a situation that goes on forever, where your true nature seems unnoticed and you're not even sure what your true nature actually is.

Here come power points in time again. These times of heightened intensity are occasions when choices are offered to us. At times we need to stir ourselves and rise to the occasion, when the issues seem most acute, sharp and uncomfortable. Problems can arise – mishaps, illness, adversity – and our challenge is to make the best of a bad situation, to make it good.

Pursuing our life-purpose is not always dramatic. Many people look at me and the work I do as a humanitarian in the Middle East, believing it must be romantic and exciting, but actually it involves long hours sitting at computers, lots of drudge, waiting, hearing people's sad stories, moments of risk, and even the disapproval of loved ones. For many people it's less dramatic. It can mean quietly growing vegetables, whittling wood, editing video footage, tending to the sick or working to protect badgers, with few accolades and lots of sweat and personal input. But if it's your life-purpose it will nevertheless feel good and right – and yes, you will at times wonder why on earth you're doing it and whether it really makes a difference. But it does.

Once upon a time I met a burned-out teacher who had reached the end of the road with her job. I recommended her to take the plunge and be brave, leave her job, take a break somewhere entirely different, give the process a few years and do her best. She did so and took a cheap holiday in Tunisia, choosing to stay in a Bedouin village instead of a hotel. While sitting there doing her knitting, the ladies of the village started watching her. One came over to ask about her knitting (theirs was a weaving culture). Soon all the ladies were there.

At the end of her stay they asked her to leave her knitting needles, and when she came back, would she bring more? Within three years she had started a movement spanning many villages in Tunisia and Algeria. This concerns not just knitting, but women sitting together, talking, empowering each other. Unwittingly, this ex-teacher had started a women's movement by giving the Bedouin ladies a portable craft. She now has a second home in Tunisia where she is honoured and welcomed back. This would not have happened had she not taken the plunge. Magic happens.

So when life treats you roughly and you've had enough, go out to a power place under the fullmoon. Lie down and let yourself drift off. Make yourself available to the currents of change. Address your fears. Stop withholding. Say your prayers. Note what comes up within you. Get clear on what engages and motivates you. Go home and come out with it. If the word "can't" comes up, change it to "won't", examine the statement again and ask yourself "Is this me?". Or if you can't do it now, when will you do it? Yes, you will experience fear, guilt and shame – that's okay. You'll want to run the other way. Others might discourage you. But actually, your ultimate responsibility is to your soul, to the contract you made with your angels before you even were conceived.

Turning the Wheel of Time

This leads to another point. It's what the Tibetans call 'Turning the Wheel of Time'. Time has qualities and potentialities attached to it, and once a time is passed, it's gone, never to be repeated. The main point of this book has been to share tools with which these nuances can be identified and worked with – not only as a coping strategy, but proactively. We have a possibility, even a responsibility, to identify and invoke these special qualities, working to strengthen their influence in our world. How do we do this? There are several ways.

In the more esoteric area it can be through meditation, innerwork, prayer and affirmation. In a more mundane sense, the challenge is upon us to find and develop our life's work, and through this to develop our contribution to the world, using the knowledge, wisdom and skills available to us. Astrologically, this means that, when approaching a fullmoon, we may act in ways to harmonise with lunar energy and make use of it as it climaxes at fullmoon. At any moment the Moon lays open potentialities we can make use of to further what we believe to be right and appropriate. Not only this, but it helps the Moon itself, as an energy-frequency.

We can apply this in relation to playing our part in history. When Uranus is passing through Aries, certain possibilities are available which will change when it enters Taurus. We can act to accentuate and bring forth those possibilities not only in our own life-domains, but also in the wider world, whether by innerwork, writing letters and e-mails, carrying out activities to further a cause we believe in or dedicating our lives to a certain set of goals. We can bring forth the meaning of our time, and thereby more consciously and intentionally play a proactive part in history.

To the ancients, this was vital. It was one of the driving forces causing ancient sages to devise the system of astrology: if you did not act to invoke springtime and fertile conditions, the coming season could not be counted on to fill our food-stocks sufficiently, and if the tribe did not move in accord with the powers and forces of nature and the universe, its fortunes would suffer. This was very logical – and it didn't take things for granted.

When President Clinton had Uranus in Aquarius opposing his Sun in Leo, he was exposed by the Monica Lewinsky debacle. At this point he was offered a soul-choice: to try to cover his tracks and persuade the public (Uranus in Aquarius) that he wasn't a 'bad boy', or to stand to face the public and take a big risk – to face down his opponents and rise to his fullest stature. After all, one of his greatest critics was caught with his pants down not long after – so it would have been legitimate for Clinton to say "Yes, I did it, and I made a mistake and perhaps I'm an asshole, but now, in all honesty, hands up all you politicians who have *not* done the same yourselves". In doing so he could have fundamentally changed the American political culture, exposing many of its hypocrisies and evils. He might conceivably have even shifted much of the world agenda. His successor as president, George Bush, might not have come to power. The Iraq war of 2003 might not have happened. All sorts of things might perhaps have been different. This would have involved staking his life on it. He had an opportunity to expose some hidden truths by owning up to his own hidden truths, painful though it might have been. Thereby he would have *turned the wheel of time*, moving things on further and faster. Unfortunately, he didn't do it. Sorry, Bill, if you feel I'm picking on you – it's just that becoming a president makes you the subject of astrologers' perceptive gazes.

At different points of our lives we are given opportunities such as these – awkward moments of truth when the chips are down and we're given a chance to own up and change something. The default response to such possibilities is to run in the other direction, or to keep one's head down, withholding one's truth and shying away from the opportunity. As a result, opportunities are lost. Human history is littered with such non-events.

Turning the Wheel of Time does not mean trying to make the world go the way we want – this is part of the problem, not the solution. It means helping forth *what truly needs to arise* – which, in many cases, we cannot even see. But the same process is involved in childbirth, making love, gambling, saving lives and exploring new frontiers. It means *allowing* things to come forth, proactively standing up for the best options and often for the greatest challenges. There are few rules to this and, in the end, we must follow our instincts, our guidance or our commonsense. Yet this constitutes one of the great challenges of our day. Astrology gives a tool to identify those points in time when opportunities are available, and suggestions about what to do with them.

Future generations will look back at this phase of history in the way we look back at the past – fascinated, but wondering how on earth we got ourselves into this mess. Today we have the capacity to *create history* more than we ever have done, and the future is ours. When the creative potential in humanity is truly unleashed, all (or most) things will be possible – after all, there are billions of able-bodied souls here, available for the task. The tide can be turned in our lifetimes and that of our children. The future is an open door.

When a major power period or point in time is approaching, it is often impossible to see beyond it, for so many unknowns come into the equation. So we just have to work with what we've got. But there are astrological grounds for hope in the future. Let's stay alive and grow to see it.

With this thought I leave you, with thanks for wading through this book. The rest is up to you. I'll do my bit in my corner of the universe, and I hereby humbly request that you do your bit in your corner. Good luck! Oh, and by the way, 'luck' isn't about accidental good fortune – it's about skilfully surfing that wave. The German word 'glück', which shares the same root as 'luck', means 'happiness'. So, again, good luck!

To quote the late Maya Angelou: *The thing to do, it seems to me, is to prepare yourself so you can be a rainbow in somebody else's cloud. Somebody who may not look like you. They may not call God the same name you call God – if they call it God at all. I may not dance your dance or speak your language. But be a blessing to somebody. That's what I think.*

Appendix One
Glossary

Angles, the Four: four points in an astrological chart marked by the ascendant, descendant, midheaven (zenith) and nadir. See *horizon* and *meridian*.

Aphelion: the time and point where a planet is furthest from the sun; see also *perihelion*.

Apogee: the point or time when Moon is furthest from the Earth; see also *perigee*.

Applying aspects: aspects approaching exact, into aspect; see also *separating aspects*.

Aquarian Age: one of the twelve great ages, each lasting 2,148 years, brought about by the precession of the equinoxes; properly known as the Aquarius-Leo Age; we are entering this age sometime around now or in the future – the date is debatable, though the astronomically-correct date is around the year 2691.

Array: a general spread of planets in the heavens which forms an overall shape, without having to involve aspects or configurations; examples are the hemispheric/ bowl array, bundle/cluster, locomotive/open-angle, bucket/wedge, seesaw, tripod, splash, splay and star.

Ascendant: the point on the eastern horizon, on the left of a birth chart, where the zodiac, Sun, Moon and planets rise; the opening cusp of the first house, the place of persona and personal aspiration.

Aspects: angles of relationship between two moving planets; stages in a synodic cycle at which recognisable developments, transitions or crises can occur, found by subdividing the zodiac by divisors such as 2, 3, 4, 6, 8, 12. The *main aspects* are the conjunction, sextile, square, trine and opposition. *Minor aspects* are the semisextile, semisquare, sesquiquadrate and quincunx. There are also finer angles found by dividing the zodiac by 5 (quintiles), 7 (septiles) or 9 (noviles or nonagens). The *challenging aspects* are the semisquare, square, sesquiquadrate and opposition. The *flowing aspects* are the sextile and trine.

Astrology: the study of the motions of the planets and rotation of Earth in relation to them and the zodiac, for the purpose of eliciting meaning and significance, as indicators of fundamental energy-permutations on Earth; the study of subjective time; the mother of all sciences; a path to awareness and a brilliant way of whiling away the hours!

Astronomy: the objective study of the heavens and their physical mechanics through observation, using the eyes (instead of the inner senses).

Birth, moment of: the valid moment of birth of a person or animal is its first breath, while for a venture or event it is the first moment it can definitely be said to have started as a real event, usually physically (such as moving into a house, convening a meeting, getting into the car for a journey).

Cardinal signs: see *modes*.

Chiron: a small planetoid orbiting eccentrically between the orbits of Saturn and Uranus, on a cycle of 51 years, discovered in 1977; it works through the knower within us, through lessons learned, and with a miraculous touch, if we are open to it.

Configuration: a structure of aspects between three or more planets, linking them together into a distinguishable shape as a whole circuit.

Constellations: star patterns to which symbolisms and identities have been given; those on the ecliptic own the same names as the signs, but are moving apart from the signs at the rate of one sign every 2148 years (see *precession*); the constellations are not used in astrology generally – the confusion of names for constellations and signs is regrettable.

Cradle: usually, three consecutive sextile aspects plus one opposition in a bowl-like structure; can be a string of 3-4 consecutive aspects of the same type, plus a wide aspect such as opposition, sesquiquadrate or trine.

Crisis: an intense situation where things come to a climax or crunch, characterised by a slowing of time, feelings of extreme difficulty and obstruction, irresolvable problems and an inevitable giving up of previous expectations or ways of seeing things – a possibility for a breakthrough or a new start.

Cross-quarters: the four midpoints between the quarter points of the year (solstices and equinoxes), at or around 15° of the four fixed signs; Beltane in early May, 15 Taurus, Lammas or Lughnasa in early August, 15 Leo, Samhain or Hallowe'en, early November, 15 Scorpio, and Candlemas or Imbolc, early February; at these points the seasons go through definite cyclical changes; these are points of energy-manifestation, and were marked by the ancient British and others as fire festivals, to mark stages in the annual cycle of life-force.

Cusp: the boundary of a zodiac sign.

Cycles: *diurnal*: the cycle of day/night; *sidereal*: the motion of the Moon or any planet around the zodiac; *synodic*: the cycle of aspects between any two moving planets; *lunation*: the synodic cycle between Sun and Moon, creating the Moon's phases; *metonic*: the 18.6 year retrograde cycle of the Moon's nodes around the zodiac.

Descendant: the point on the western horizon, on the right of a chart, where zodiac, Sun, Moon and planets set; opening cusp of the seventh house, the place of relationship.

Detriment: a planet is in detriment in a sign opposite its home sign(s), and its energy is in some way hampered by the quality of that sign, while still being strong; see also *rulership, exaltation, fall*.

Direct motion: forward motion of a planet through the zodiac; see *retrograde* and *station*.

Eccentric planetary orbits: the orbits of Mercury, Chiron and Pluto, which are elliptical and inclined to the ecliptic, while all other planets orbit on roughly circular, regular orbits.

Eclipses: a partial or total cutting off of the light of the Sun (at newmoon) by the Moon passing in front of it, or of the Moon (at fullmoon) by Earth's shadow passing over the Moon; these are mega-transitions; they can occur only when a newmoon or fullmoon is close to the lunar nodes; they tend to happen in twos or sometimes threes around the time of this closeness to the nodes at opposite times of the year, varying through the *metonic cycle*; the ancients paid great heed to these and to their symbolism and stillness.

Ecliptic: the plane of the solar system; as seen from Earth, it's the path of the Sun through the heavens – most of the planets orbit within a few degrees of the ecliptic.

Electional charts: charts cast in order to help in the making of choices and the selection of auspicious times for planned activities.

Elements, the Four: fire, earth, air and water, characterising different energies which work through the zodiac signs; there are three signs of each element, in trine formation, each sign representing one of the *modes*.

Energy-weather: subjective atmospheres, nuances, energy-conditions, which can be sensed in life, and described astrologically.

Ephemeris: a book of tables showing the motions of the planets, plus other useful data, usually for either noon or midnight GMT each day; the sourcebook of the modern astrologer.

Ephemeris, noon or midnight: as long as you are clear as to which you are using, neither is better; if you are better using the 24-hour clock, use a midnight, and if better using am/pm, use a noon ephemeris; estimates of timings must be adjusted when using either.

Equator: 1. *terrestrial*: 0° latitude, an imaginary great circle around the planet which is perpendicular to the poles of Earth's rotation; 2. *celestial*: Earth's equator projected out into space, used largely by astronomers, inclined at 23° from the ecliptic.

Equinoxes: spring (0° Aries) and autumn (0° Libra), the midpoints between the solstices; the days when day and night are equal through; times of energy-transition.

Event charts: charts drawn up for events, to examine them closely, timed for their moment of occurrence or beginning.

Exaltation: each planet is exalted in one sign, where its energy is refined and elevated to a qualitatively perfected level; see also *rulerships, fall, detriment*.

Fall: a planet is in fall in the sign opposite its exaltation – here its energy is qualitatively obstructed and comes over problematically; see also *rulerships, detriment, exaltation*.

Fixed signs: see *modes*.

Focal planet: a planet which, by dint of its position, sometimes also rulership patterns, tends to focus the energy of a chart or array.

Genders, yang **and** yin: the male and female forces, respectively; these alternate sign to sign through the sequence of the zodiac (fire and air signs are yang, Earth and water signs yin), and hemicyclically (summer is yang, winter yin).

Grand aspects: major and rare *configurations* where a string of planets encircles the zodiac with the same aspect between them – for example, the grand trine, grand cross, grand sextile or grand octile.

Grand Cross: at least four planets in mutual square aspect to one another, with two oppositions and four squares; a very powerful and challenging configuration.

Grand Trine: three planets forming a triangle of trine aspects; a powerful and harmonious configuration.

Group psyche: collective consciousness, and its various states at any moment or time; the transpersonal.

Halley's Comet: a prominent regular comet, well known, which lives mostly out beyond Pluto, but plummets into the solar system to swing closely to the Sun once every 76 years (last in 1910 and 1985-6); it introduces new, unforeseen energy and issues and turns of events into the concrete sphere of life, usually of small form but big significance.

Hemicycles: half-cycles of lunar or planetary motion; these can be waxing/waning, beginning and ending at conjunction and opposition, or objective/subjective, beginning and ending at the two square aspects.

Home signs: see *rulerships*.

Horary charts: charts cast oracularly in order to answer questions; the time of the asking of the question is used, and special rules apply.

Horizon: the ascendant-descendant line, horizontally drawn across a chart, above which is the visible sky, below which is the area of the sky hidden by Earth; see *meridian*.

Houses, the Twelve: a twelvefold subdivision of the Earth's sky (six houses above and six below the horizon), found by subdividing the quadrants between the four angles into three. There are different systems of calculation of houses: the three main ones are the Equal House, Placidus and Koch systems (the author uses Koch).

Indigestion, astrological: what happens when you study too much astrology – the best remedy is to talk to trees, climb mountains, shower in cold water or drop the lot for a while.

Individualisation: a process whereby people explore their own individuality and define their own realities; the process at work in the zodiacal hemicycle beginning at Capricorn and ending at Gemini, and in the waxing hemicycle of any planetary relationship.

Ingress: the entry of a planet into a new sign, crossing over their cusps; usually these indicate a change of themes, a fresh breeze and a choice.

Intercepted signs: signs which can crop up in a chart which do not cross any house cusp, always in pairs, opposite one another; more common in temperate and polar latitudes, or when one of the solsticial signs is rising.

Issues: charged ideas, feeling-tones, associations, around which we preoccupy ourselves, restricting openness of responses to life, triggering trains of reactions when certain questions or associations come up.

Kite: a grand trine with an opposition from one of the planets to another, which forms two sextile aspects to the remaining planets.

Latitude: *terrestrial*: N-S coordinates of position on the Earth's surface; *ecliptic*: position above or below the ecliptic – for most planets only a few degrees.

Lights, the: generic term for the Sun and Moon, to distinguish them from the planets.

Longitude: *terrestrial*: E-W coordinates of position on the Earth's surface; *ecliptic*: position along the ecliptic, measured in degrees and minutes of signs; see *latitude*.

Lunar Maximum: times every 18.6 years when the Moon's North Node is at 0° Aries; at these times the Moon moves 5° north of the ecliptic when in the summer solstice signs (Gemini and Cancer) and 5° south of the ecliptic when in winter solstice signs (Sagittarius and Capricorn); the ancients marked these with alignments in stone circles, considering them very significant; at these times the variation of the Moon in its height in the sky is at a maximum.

Lunar Minimum: times every 18.6 years when the Moon's North Node is at 0° Libra; at these times the variation of height in the sky of the Moon, during its lunation cycle, is at a minimum.

Meridian: the zenith-nadir line, roughly vertical in a chart, running through the centre of Earth from the point where the zodiac culminates in the sky to a point beneath the Earth; see *midheaven* and *nadir*.

Midheaven: the point the Sun reaches in the sky at midday; a point where a line moving up from due south meets the ecliptic; the top of the meridian; opening cusp of the tenth house, the point of social identity.

Modes, the three: the three phases of each season; modes of operation of the zodiac signs; the cardinal signs initiate and set the tone for the season (Aries, Cancer, Libra and Capricorn), the fixed signs carry through the purpose of the season (Taurus, Leo, Scorpio and Aquarius), and the mutable signs conclude and assimilate the season (Gemini, Virgo, Sagittarius and Pisces).

Mutable signs: see *modes*.

Midpoint: the degree half way between any two planets, where it can be said that the combined energy of those planets is strongest, regardless of whether they are in aspect; some astrologers use midpoints, but others do not; they can be useful when two planets are 15-45° apart, for sometimes their midpoint forms a strong aspect to another planet, where neither would individually be in aspect – this gives extra underlying meaning to a chart or situation.

Mutational cycles: a mutation is a conjunction of Jupiter and Saturn; successive conjunctions tend to fall in signs of the same element, but when there is a change of element, there is a Great Mutation.

Nadir: the bottom end of the *Meridian*, a line projected downwards through the centre of the Earth from the Midheaven; the point Sun reaches at midnight; opening cusp of the fourth house, the place of personal identity.

Nodes, lunar: the points where the Moon's plane of orbit round Earth intersect Earth's plane of orbit round the Sun (the ecliptic); these are at opposite sides of the zodiac; at the north node, Moon is climbing above the ecliptic, at the south it is falling below it; the nodes move retrograde through the zodiac in 18.6 years (a generation); also called Dragon's Head (N) and Tail (S); when a new or full moon occurs close to the nodes, there will be an eclipse.

Occultation: an eclipse by the Moon of a planet or star.

Octile: one of the aspects of the 45° family, mainly sesquiquadrate and semisquare , but also including conjunction, square and opposition.

Octile Triangle: *greater*: sesquiquadrate-square-sesquiquadrate; *lesser*: semisquare-square-semisquare; *octile kite*: semisquare-semisquare-semisquare-sesquiquadrate, with an opposition on the long axis and a square on the short axis; *octile rectangle*: semisquare-sesquiquadrate-semisquare-sesquiquadrate, with two oppositions crossing it.

Orb: an area around a planet or aspect wherein it may be said that the aspect is operative; orbs can be defined closely or widely, and do not have fixed or definite cut-off points.

Perigee: the point or time when Moon is nearest Earth; see also *apogee*.

Perihelion: the time and point where a planet is closest to the Sun; see also *aphelion*.

Precession of Equinoxes: a 25,772 year cycle of motion in the Earth's axis of rotation, caused by gravitational pulls from Sun and Moon, causing the equinox points to move westwards through the constellations at the rate of one degree every 72 years, one sign every 2148 years – at present, they are 25° from the start of the cycle. See *Ages*.

Planets: *functional*: Mercury, Venus and Mars; *social*: Jupiter and Saturn; *transformative*: Chiron, Uranus, Neptune and Pluto.

Power points in time: exceptional times when there is a more intense or poignant energy-configuration at work than usual, where it is possible to make greater than usual leaps of consciousness or to attain subtle states; when slower-moving planets are involved, we can have power periods which can last several years and affect history on a longterm basis.

Psyche: the whole of our consciousness, including awareness, thoughts, feelings, all modes of consciousness, imagination, perception and sense of self.

Quarter phases of the Moon: newmoon, waxing halfmoon (first quarter), fullmoon and waning halfmoon (third quarter).

Quarter-points: the opening cusps of the cardinal signs; the solstice and equinox points.

Raphael's Ephemeris: a somewhat archaic but very useful noon GMT ephemeris, packed with data, easily portable, covering each year in a separate volume.

Rectangle or mystic rectangle: A trine, sextile, trine, sextile configuration, with two oppositions crossing it; can be formed by *octiles* too.

Retrograde motion of planets: the apparent temporary backward movement of the planets (not Sun or Moon) through the zodiac, caused by our being on a moving observation platform; the planet itself does not truly change direction.

Rising and setting points of mainly Sun and Moon, but also planets and stars, on the local horizon were used by the ancients both for observation of their motions, and for ceremonial and energy-working purposes; in the northern hemisphere, when Sun or any planet on the ecliptic is in a summer sign it rises NE, when in a winter sign it rises SE, and when in an equinoctial sign it rises E; Moon can oscillate up to 5° N or S in latitude of the ecliptic; the ancients built alignments of stones or markers to various rising and setting points.

Rulerships of signs: Each planet is at home in, or rules, two signs, and Sun and Moon each are at home in one, while the outer planets each co-rule a sign with other planets; rulerships qualify the character of each sign, and show which signs best embody different planetary energies; in its home sign, a planet is strong and typified. See *detriment, fall, exaltation*.

Separating aspects: aspects going out of aspect, after the aspect has happened; see also *applying aspects*.

Singleton: the sole planet in the empty hemisphere of the zodiac in a bucket configuration, also called the 'handle' – this becomes a strongly focal planet.

Solstices: winter (0° Capricorn) and summer (0° Cancer), in which the Sun is lowest or highest in the northern hemisphere sky; the shortest and longest days of the year; gateways to the timeless or to the power of life.

Stations: times and zodiac places where any of the planets is stationary, turning either from direct to retrograde (St.t.R), or from retrograde to direct (St.t.D); these are times when it is possible to feel a planet's energy strongly and clearly.

Stellium: a multiple conjunction with at least three planets involved.

Summer Times/Daylight Saving Times: many countries change their clocks by ordinance for parts of the year, usually by one hour, ostensibly to lengthen the evenings for recreation; each country has its own dates, although there is now standardisation in all states of USA and in the countries of the EU. Details are found in V. D. Chase's Timezones books, or in the ACS World Atlas or American Atlas; dates of the current British Summer Time are found on the opening page of Raphael's Ephemeris; astrological computer programs usually have them programmed in.

Time: 1. *Clock or 'ticktock' time*: accurately measurable objective time, based on the diurnal cycle of 24 hours; 2. *evolutionary* or *subjective time*: inner experiential time, which can stretch and contract with changing energy-weather or states of consciousness.

Time zones: each country is in a time zone, which is measured in hours east or west of Greenwich, so that all clocks in that zone are coordinated; in astrological calculations and ephemeris consultations, account should be made if you are in another zone than Greenwich (GMT or UT), since almost all ephemerides are calculated for GMT (also called UT or Universal Time). See also *Summer Times*.

Transits: motions of the planets in the heavens in relation to planets, cusps or points in an astrological chart; a useful technique for understanding personal changes.

Trapezium: a four-sided aspect structure with two sides parallel and the other two sides the same aspect.

T-square: a square-opposition-square configuration.

Unconscious: that part of our psyche which talks in urges, imaginal symbols, knowings, irrational fears, of which we are unaware or partially aware; distinguished in this book from the conscious (what we tell ourselves is going on), the subconscious (what we could be aware of quite easily, were we more awake) and the superconscious (our sense of spirit); the unconscious can also be seen as personal and/or transpersonal/collective.

Void-of-course: when the Moon has gone through its last major aspect (conjunction, sextile, square, trine, opposition) to other planets before leaving a sign it is *void*; it is best not to start new activities until it has ingressed into the next sign.

Yang: see *genders*.

Yin: see *genders*.

Yod: a quincunx-sextile-quincunx aspect triangle; this can be up-stepped with an opposition from its apex to the midpoint on the sextile, bringing in two added semisextile aspects.

Zenith: see *midheaven*.

Zodiac: the twelvefold subdivision of the ecliptic, anchored in the quarter-points which mark the extremes (solstices) and midpoints (equinoxes) of Earth's cycle of polar axial tilting to the Sun, or seasonal cycle.

Appendix Two

Planetary Positions

There is a variety of ways you can track the movements of the planets:

1   Astroclocks;

2   Printed ephemerides;

3   Astrological programs, and

4   Online ephemerides.

With a few exceptions, free and shareware programs are often not very accurate or useful.

Astroclocks

The best I have found is Astroclock, by Rod Suskin in South Africa, available from www.vega.co.za. There is a free version but the Pro version is worth getting, for just 12 USD. It's a lightweight program in a small window in the corner of your screen that shows the planetary positions for the current moment. Useful for void moons. It has a few other useful functions too.

Astroclk from AstroWin at www.astrowin.org is reliable and free but not well designed visually.

Otherwise, Google 'astroclock'. Some programs are astronomical, not astrological (don't get one). Apps for smartphones are available too.

Printed Ephemerides

- *Raphael's Ephemeris* is a small booklet ephemeris for each year. Accurate, useful for carrying round and quick reference. Must be bought each year.

- *The American Ephemeris* is a full ephemeris for a century, computed by the late Neil Michelson. Accurate, useful, perhaps the classic. There is a cross-century edition for 1950-2050 as well as one for each century. It is computed for midnight and midday – get the one that suits you (I prefer midnight).

- *The Astrolabe World Ephemeris, 2001-2050 at Midnight* is accurate and valuable, by Rob Hand, a respected leading astrologer.

- *Llewellyn Astrological Calendar.* Includes lots of data in a calendar format, including void moons, times for planting and fishing, etc. American timezones used.

Programs

Most programs have an astroclock function within them. Useful if you're using the program for other astrological uses, but not lightweight if you just want a quick look at planetary positions for the current moment.

- *Solar Fire v9* is by far the most popular program, with all of the astrological functions any astrologer would need. Not cheap though.

- *Nova Chartwheels.* A full astrology program by Rob Hand. Accurate and useful.

- *Win*Star* is another popular and recommended program, and commonly used.

- Other programs include *Startrax for Windows* and *Janus*.

Free astrological programs include *ZET Lite* (accurate and well and thoughtfully built, though poor graphics – Russian, from www.zaytsev.com), *Astrolog* (accurate, a little fiddly but useful, from www.astrolog.org) and *Astrowin* (a bit complex but accurate, from www.astrowin.org/astrology_software.php).

Recommendation: don't get a program that includes 'reports'. These are interpretations of astrological charts, of limited use and extra expense, for use in commercial astrology.

There are apps available for use on smartphones – they change too much to list here.

Online Ephemerides

- *The Swiss Ephemeris* is technically accurate, goes back a long way, and is very reliable. www.astro.com/swisseph/ - click on 'Ephemeris' on the lefthand side. It includes Chiron. Comes up as a PDF file which can be printed out.

- *Khaldea.* www.khaldea.com/ephemcenter.shtml. Online ephemeris, easily accessed. Does not include Chiron.

- *Cafe Astrology.* www.cafeastrology.com/2014ephemeris.html (or alter the year in the address). Good ephemeris for each year. Chiron not included.

About the Author

Palden Jenkins is a Virgo with Gemini Moon and Sagittarius rising, born near Forest Row, Sussex, UK, on 5th September 1950 at 15.45 (14.45 GMT), growing up in 1950s Cardiff and 1960s Liverpool, attending university at the LSE. He has had a long track record since 1970 of involvement in astrology, ancient mysteries, Buddhism, alternative education, book publishing, politics, esoterics, peacemaking and humanitarian work in the Middle East. He works as a book editor, webmaster, photographer, writer, speaker and researcher, living in Cornwall, UK. He has written several books, including The Only Planet of Choice (1993), The Historical Ephemeris (1993), Living in Time (1987), Healing the Hurts of Nations (2003) and Pictures of Palestine (2012), and he has contributed to many other books such as the Kingfisher Encyclopedia of World History (1999) as well as being active on the Internet since 1996.

Lightning Source UK Ltd.
Milton Keynes UK
UKOW06f0345191214

243372UK00001B/1/P